SOCIAL RESEARCH FOR CONSUMERS

EARL R. BABBIE

WADSWORTH PUBLISHING COMPANY
BELMONT, CALIFORNIA
A DIVISION OF WADSWORTH, INC.

Cover image © Raymond G. Lauzzana/The Penrose Agency
Production Editor: Hal Lockwood, Bookman Productions
Designer: Nancy Benedict
Manuscript Editor: Susan Weisberg
Technical Illustrator: John Foster

Printed in the United State of America

8 9 10 — 97 9 95 94 93 92

Library of Congress Cataloging in Public   Data
Babbie,
    Social   rch for consumers.
    Bibliogra
    Includes in p.
    1. Social scie es—Research.   I. Title.
H62.B225   30 72   81-19807
                                  AACR2

ISBN: 0-534-01125-X

ISBN 0-534-01125-X

To my mother, Marion Babbie.
We go back a long way together.

CONTENTS IN BRIEF

CONTENTS

PREFACE

The book in your hands, in my unbiased opinion, is very special. It is, first of all, a textbook, and since you have this book, presumably you have enrolled in a course on social science research methods. This book will teach you everything you need to know to be literate in social research methods. If you master the materials in this book, your instructor can certify that you have learned research methods at the introductory level, and your university will know that the social research methods requirement for your degree, if any, has been fulfilled.

Having taken care of business, let's get down to what makes this book special. This is the second general textbook on social science research methods I've written. The other one—*The Practice of Social Research*—has been the standard in its field since it was first published. The purpose of the earlier book has been to train students in the logic and skills of social research, and it has done that by teaching students how to *do* research. I have grown increasingly aware in recent years, however, that many of the students who take the course you are taking never actually undertake research projects of their own after college. Perhaps you will never conduct a research project.

At the same time, whether you ever do a research project, I know that you will be reading and hearing about social science research throughout your life. In a great many ways, social science research findings are going to have an impact on your life. It is important, therefore, for you to be able to understand research, regardless of whether you actually conduct studies of your own. As a consequence, this book is written from the point of view of the *consumer* of social research.

While this book covers all the materials normally expected in an introductory course in social science research methods, I have presented each topic and example in such a way that you will be able to evaluate something you read or hear. In accordance with this theme, I've concluded each chapter with a "consumer's checklist" to remind you of the things to look for in reading research reports. Also, Appendix B presents an example of how to read a journal article from a methodological point of view.

By the way, if you do plan to conduct research projects on your own, you can learn what you need to know from this book. I think you're going to enjoy the book regardless of whether you plan to be a researcher or a consumer of research.

A great many people contributed to the production of this book, and I want to acknowledge them here. First, Curt Peoples was the sociology editor at Wadsworth responsible for the book, and the final product should be regarded as the result of a partnership. Some of the people working with Curt were Lauren Foodim, editorial assistant, Jerry Holloway, production services manager, Marlene Veach, marketing specialist, and Hal Lockwood, of Bookman Productions.

In writing this book, I have had the good fortune to have the advice and guidance of numerous colleagues across the country. Some of those who made invaluable contributions were:

R. G. Amonker, Southwest Missouri State University
Leland J. Axelson, Virginia Polytechnic Institute and State University
Rosalind Dworkin, University of Houston
Morris A. Forslund, University of Wyoming
William M. King, University of Colorado
Larry M. Landis, Drake University
Ron Lustig, San Diego State University
Charles Maxson, Friends University
Elizabeth A. Rooney, San Francisco State University
Art St. George, University of New Mexico
Eric Soares, University of California, Santa Barbara
Kristen Wenzel, College of New Rochelle

Finally, I want to thank Bonnie Memeo for her support and dedication to the success of the project. Her willingness to commit herself totally to my spending my time writing is truly inspiring.

I have dedicated this book to my mother, Marion Babbie, to acknowledge her loving support over the past forty-four years (we go back a long way together). I have not always turned out the way she expected, yet she has trusted and supported me in being who I am. Moreover, watching her over the years has taken the sting out of growing old.

SOCIAL RESEARCH FOR CONSUMERS

INTRODUCTION

The 1980 presidential election campaign in the United States had a great deal in common with previous political campaigns. Then-President Jimmy Carter and challenger Ronald Reagan differed in many ways: party, ideology, programs, promises, and partners. All that was understandable and reasonable—the nature of democracy centers on the people choosing between competing orientations. Less reasonably, and more frustratingly, the two candidates disagreed on the *facts*.

On October 28, 1980, Carter and Reagan met before an international television audience of tens of millions to debate their different points of view. They differed in almost every regard. Carter argued that his administration had been good for the working people of America; Reagan said it had been disastrous. To substantiate his contention, Carter said 9 million new jobs had been created during the course of his administration. In bold contrast, Reagan charged that 8 million Americans were unemployed; 2 million, he said, had lost their jobs during 1980. Who was right? The *Washington Post* news service reconciled the apparent contradiction succintly:

Both things are true. There were about 87.5 million jobs in this country in 1976, the year of the past presidential election. There are nearly 97 million now. But the number of jobs has not increased as fast as the number of people wanting them. There were 6.1 million people unemployed last December, 5.9 percent of the work force. There were 8.2 million out of work in July, 7.8 percent. (*San Francisco Chronicle*, October 29, 1980)

The competing presidential candidates apparently disagreed on the facts of inflation as well. Carter said that, in the third quarter of 1980, the inflation rate had been 7 percent. More gloomily, Reagan said inflation was 12.7 percent. Who was right? Again, the *Washington Post* resolved the puzzle:

Both are right. Consumer prices have risen 12.7 percent in the last year, and rose at an annual rate of 12.7 last month. But in the last three months the annual rate was 7 percent.

National defense was also an issue of contention during the 1980 presidential campaign: Reagan argued for more defense expenditures, Carter for relatively less. As with unemployment and inflation, however, the two men seemed to have examined two radically different realities. Reagan challenged Carter's commitment to defense by alleging the president had sharply reduced the five-year defense budget projected by Republican President Gerald Ford. Carter countered by contending that defense spending had actually declined during seven of the eight Republican years of the Nixon-Ford administrations that preceded his own. Who was right? You guessed it.

Defense spending did fall in seven of those eight years, not in dollars — the defense budget rose from $75.8 billion to $105.2 billion — but in so-called "real" terms, after allowing for inflation. In 1972 dollars, defense outlays fell from $81.2 billion in fiscal 1971 to $66.5 billion in fiscal 1977. It rose the next year to $66.6 billion. But Carter did chop back the Ford defense budget to which he fell heir. . . .

PURPOSE OF THE BOOK

My purpose in presenting these figures on the 1980 presidential debate is to make the point that you and I cannot be responsible citizens without some degree of literacy in research methods. Nor is the importance of research literacy limited to responsible citizenship. It also affects the extent to which you can look out for yourself and your family. Consider advertising, for example. Milt Moskowitz (1980) offers a powerful example:

Continental [Baking Co.] was back to its old tricks this fall when it introduced a new campaign for Wonder, which reigns as the best-selling loaf of bread in

America. Continental has long been pumping vitamins into this spongy white bread—and this time it came up with the cry that Wonder has the "nutrition that even whole wheat can't beat."

As this rhythmic claim was being dinned into our ears, figures darted across the television tube, citing U.S. Department of Agriculture sources to show that Wonder bread has more vitamin B1, vitamin B2, niacin, and calcium than the average whole-wheat bread. Hence the proud boast: "Nutrition that even whole wheat can't beat."

I don't know about you, but I was persuaded when I first heard that. I was turned off by the fact that the nutrients in Wonder were added artificially, whereas they were natural in whole wheat bread, but I didn't question the truth of the claim. After all, the Department of Agriculture said it was true. Nonetheless, the company withdrew the ads shortly after a complaint was lodged by the Center for Science in the Public Interest (CSPI). In case you don't know this story, take a minute to think what the objection might have been.

While granting that the specific claims made by the company were accurate, CSPI researchers pointed out that the comparison was incomplete; Wonder bread compared poorly with whole wheat bread in terms of vitamin B6 (22% as much), vitamin E (4%), protein (80%), pantothenic acid (56%), magnesium (28%), iron (82%), zinc (38%), and other nutrients (Center for Science in the Public Interest, 1980:4). In response, the company canceled the ads comparing Wonder to whole wheat.

The point, again, is that you are living in a world filled with research findings that affect your life and that you are often expected to act on. Since some of the claims made on the basis of research are misleading or simply false, it is important to be able to sort out what is valid and what isn't.

The same point can be made in connection with any field of endeavor you have chosen to enter. This is particularly the case with regard to social science research. If you've chosen a career in the social sciences— sociology, anthropology, political science, psychology, economics, and so on—you'll be dealing with research findings continuously. Even if you don't engage in original research, you'll be teaching research findings to students, putting the findings to work in practical situations, or using them in some other fashion. Much of the research done on deviance, for example, is directly relevant to professionals in social work and law enforcement. Physicians and nurses have learned the significance of social variables in connection with health and illness, so they, too, must learn to evaluate social research. Public-health programs may succeed or fail because of social variables.

In recent years, social science findings have become increasingly important for professionals in a great many other fields as well. Architects now pay special attention to social research on the human use of space in order to create physical structures that will support and enable people rather than constrict them. Drama professionals conduct surveys of theater-goers to learn more about their reactions to various offerings. In advertising, social research is used not only to persuade consumers but also to prove to agencies and their clients that an ad campaign is effective. The list could go on and on. Virtually every field of endeavor today has some traffic with social science research, so people need some familiarity with it. My intention in this book is to satisfy that need.

Whereas most social science research textbooks are oriented to the *doing* of research, this one is specifically oriented to *consuming* it. To be an effective consumer of research, you will need to learn many of the same fundamentals you would need to master in doing research, but there are many things you don't need to know. And though learning to do research will sharpen your abilities as a consumer, there are certain techniques and skills specifically related to being a good consumer that you might not get in training to do research. Those techniques and skills will be highlighted here.

In offering this view of research to you, I have two orientations. On the one hand, as I've already indicated, I want to teach you to protect yourself from bad research and misleading research conclusions. At the same time, I'd like this book to empower you in the *use* of valid social science research. As I've written elsewhere, I am convinced that the major problems facing the world today—hunger, poverty, war, prejudice, ecosystem ills—all depend on *social* solutions, rather than on new technological breakthroughs. Hence, social science research has never been more important than today. We need to improve the quality of social science research and to make better use of what is learned. So, I've aimed this book at enabling you to make use of what is discovered about how we operate as social animals.

RESEARCH IS EVERYWHERE

A theme running throughout this book has to do with the veritable ocean of statistics that each of us sinks or swims in. You have been bombarded with social research findings all your life, and this is not going to change in the future. In your professional life, you will often make decisions that ought to be informed by those research findings, and the same goes for your private life.

In preparing the book, I was struck one day by the large number of research measurements that I had heard about all my life—but which I actually knew very little about. Specifically, I was driving in my car one day when the news broadcast carried a story about the Dow Jones industrial average passing the 1000 mark. The announcer indicated that the business community welcomed the passing of that milestone, and I noticed I had a general feeling of well-being. That's good news, I told myself. Then I realized that I didn't really know what the Dow Jones industrial average was. I knew it had something to do with the price of selected stocks on Wall Street, but I didn't know which ones, how it was computed, or why passing the 1000 mark would be of any value to me.

In this section of the book, I want to present a number of social research measures that are probably familiar to you as names. I'm betting that you don't actually understand how some or all of them are calculated and what they really stand for. Let's start by finding out why Wall Street was so happy when the Dow passed 1000.

DOW JONES INDUSTRIAL AVERAGE

Charles H. Dow is generally credited with first publishing an index of American stocks. On July 3, 1884, the *Customer's Afternoon Letter*, a two-page newsletter that would become the *Wall Street Journal*, carried a list of average closing (end-of-day) prices of 11 stocks which Dow felt would give readers a reasonable picture of the state of the stock market generally. The list included nine railroads plus the Pacific Mail Steamship Company and Western Union. Since computerization was nearly a century away, it wasn't easy tracking down the relevant sales figures among the quarter-million shares traded in an average day, but Dow located them. For his "average," he merely added up the 11 closing prices and divided by 11. Dow suggested that his readers follow the trend in prices of the 11 stocks as an indication of trends in the market as a whole (Farrell, 1972).

Dow experimented with his index for 12 years, adding some stocks and deleting others. The general pattern he developed was to list certain industrial stocks that could be taken as representative of the market. The Dow Jones industrial average began its continuous publication in 1896, Dow having teamed up with Edward Jones in founding the *Wall Street Journal*. The list from which the average was calculated contained 12 stocks:

American Cotton Oil	Laclede Gas
American Sugar	National Lead
American Tobacco	North American
Chicago Gas	Tennessee Coal & Iron
Distilling & Cattle Feeding	U.S. Leather
General Electric	U.S. Rubber

Over the years, the list of stocks has changed continuously and has increased to a current size of 30 industrial stocks. (There are also three other Dow Jones averages made up of 20 transportation stocks, 15 utilities, and 20 bonds.) Such modifications over time are important, since a given company may become less representative of the whole market as the nature of the economy changes and some companies go out of existence. For example, the original railroad stocks would hardly tell us about the performance of, say, today's computer companies. As a result, only 2 of the 12 from 1896—American Tobacco (now American Brands) and General Electric—are still on the Dow Jones industrial average list.

The task of maintaining the average is further complicated by stock splitting. If one of the companies on the list decides to split its stocks, so that every $50 stock becomes two $25 stocks, simply averaging in the new price would artificially lower the average, whereas the real value of stock-holdings would stay the same. The publishers of the Dow Jones average handle all such changes by adjusting the divisor in calculating the average. The divisor has undergone almost continuous change since Charles Dow first added up the prices of the 12 stocks and divided by 12. "Calculating the Dow Jones Divisor" describes how the divisor is figured.

As you can see, the average is not a meaningful dollar amount; it is merely a useful index of changes in the stock market. It is a guide to overall shifts in the value of stocks, gaining usefulness from the long period of time it allows us to examine.

The Dow Jones average is sometimes criticized as a measure because it reflects only selected stocks but is taken to represent the whole market. (The companies on the list account for about one-fourth the total market value of all the companies listed with the New York Stock Exchange [NYSE].) In response to this concern, newspapers often also publish the average price of all shares traded on the exchange each day, a figure that represents a real dollar value. As a comparison, on December 31, 1970, the Dow Jones industrial average was 838.92, and the average price of a share on the NYSE was $50.23. Exactly ten years later, the Dow rested at 963.99, and the NYSE was $36.88, representing a 15 percent increase in the Dow and a 27 percent decrease in the average NYSE share of stock.

An interesting footnote to this discussion concerns my attempt to compile these figures. I spent three hours tracking down the 1980 closing price of a share on the NYSE. I called two local libraries, six stockbrokers, the U.S. Department of Commerce, the Securities and Exchange Commission, and a local newspaper—all with no success. Finally, the figure was obtained through a call to the research department of the New York Stock Exchange in New York. The most common explanation for not having the information was that it was a useless statistic.

So after all is said and done, why was passing the 1000 mark on the Dow so significant? No reason. It had no more real meaning than breaking the 4-minute mile (as opposed to the 4:01.24-minute mile) or rushing 100 yards in a football game (as opposed to 97 or 103 yards). It was just a nice, round number—a convenient milestone. Charles L. Booth of the Bank of New York put his finger on the real significance, saying it was "an impor-

CALCULATING
THE DOW JONES DIVISOR

For simplicity, let's suppose that each of the original 12 stocks composing the Dow Jones list had been priced at $100. The total value, $1200, would have been divided by 12 to get an average of $100. Now suppose one of those $100 stocks split into two $50 stocks. Simply adding the price of shares and dividing by 12 would give a new average of $95.83. To take account of the stock split, we divide the new total by something other than 12—we divide by something that will make the end result be the same as if there had been no stock split. In the case of our hypothetical example, we would change the denominator of the equation from 12 to 11.5.

Essentially the same procedure is used when stocks are added, deleted, or substituted in the list. Each time, the denominator of the equation is changed to whatever would keep the average the same at the time of the modification. With all the adjustments made since 1896, the denominator of the equation had evolved to 1.826 as of May 19, 1970. That meant that the Dow Jones industrial average at that time represented the sum of closing prices of one share each of the 30 industrial stocks in the list, divided by 1.826.

---

tant psychological breakthrough, encouraging people to believe the market will go higher" (*San Francisco Chronicle*, November 20, 1980).

CONSUMER PRICE INDEX

One of the most heated issues of the 1980 presidential race and of recent years generally has been *inflation*. In mid-1980, the *Christian Science Monitor* (June 6) described the beast this way:

Gasoline cost 30 cents a gallon, a nice 3-bedroom home was $20,000, and you could drive away in a new car for under $3,000. Those were "the good old days"—barely 10 years ago. Since then, America has discovered double-digit inflation. Higher and higher prices have deflated the value of savings and eroded the buying power of U.S. workers.

All of us have a personal experience of things getting more expensive, and we usually describe the state of affairs by comparing prices of specific items. Thus, the house that cost $20,000 now sells in the neighborhood of $100,000. Whenever the talk of inflation gets serious, however, it usually involves references to "a shift in the Consumer Price Index (CPI)." The mention of "double-digit inflation," in fact, refers to an annual rate of increase of 10+ percent in the CPI. But what is the Consumer Price Index, anyway?

The U.S. Department of Labor (1978:1) describes the index as a measure of "the price change of a constant market basket of goods and services over time." It was first published on a regular basis in 1919, in response to actions by the Shipbuilding Labor Adjustment Board of World War I, as a way of determining appropriate wages in shipyards around the country. To determine the relative costs of living in different cities, the Bureau of Labor Statistics surveyed 12,000 families in 92 cities to find out what they spent their money on. Then the Bureau began monitoring the prices of such items in retail stores. Essentially the same method is used today.

Since consumption patterns change over time, the Bureau conducts a quarterly Consumer Expenditure Survey to update what people spend their money on. Around 6,000 households are interviewed for this purpose each quarter. In addition, another 4,800 households are selected each year to keep two one-week expenditure diaries. This is the way the Bureau determines what prices are the most relevant in determining the overall cost of living in America and—equally critical—what proportion of the total cost each item represents.

Over the years, eight major categories have been measured. They are shown in Table 1.1, along with the percentages of the whole they have made up over time.

Further specifications are made within each major category. Food and alcoholic beverages, for example, is broken down as shown below. I have also shown the percentage of the whole cost of living that each area represented as of December 1977.

Food and alcoholic beverages	18.813%
Food	17.718%
Food at home	12.235%
Cereals and bakery products	1.530%
Meats, poultry, fish, and eggs	3.943%
Dairy products	1.654%
Fruits and vegetables	1.759%
Sugar and sweets	.435%
Fats and oils	.360%
Nonalcoholic beverages	1.513%
Other prepared food	1.041%
Food away from home	5.483%
Alcoholic beverages	1.095%

(*U.S. Department of Labor, 1978:22*)

TABLE 1.1 Major Expenditure Categories Composing the Consumer Price Index, 1935–73 (percentage of total expenditures)

	1935–39	1952	1963	1972–73
Food and alcoholic beverages	35.4	32.2	25.2	20.4
Housing	33.7	33.5	34.9	39.8
Apparel	11.0	9.4	10.6	7.0
Transportation	8.1	11.3	14.0	19.8
Medical care	4.1	4.8	5.7	4.2
Entertainment	2.8	4.0	3.9	4.3
Personal care	2.5	2.1	2.8	1.8
Other goods and services	2.4	2.7	2.9	2.7

Source: U.S. Department of Labor, *The Consumer Price Index: Concepts and Content over the Years* (Report 517). Washington, D.C.: U.S. Government Printing Office, 1978:8.

Within such categories, the Bureau further specifies particular items: a loaf of white bread, a half-gallon container of whole milk, and so forth. Ultimately, about 400 items make up the list. These, then, are priced by field workers in cities across the United States, with adjustments being made at the most specific level to reflect local consumption patterns. (Specific brands, for example, should reflect local preferences.)

Finally, the consumer price index is expressed in relation to 1967 prices—a year chosen somewhat arbitrarily to give a point of comparison. The actual CPI figure represents the current cost of what would have cost $100 in 1967. Thus, the CPI at the close of 1980, 258.4, means that it cost $258.40 to purchase items that cost $100 in 1967.

The CPI was initially created to measure regional differences in the cost of living, and it still serves that purpose. At the same time, it gives us an indication of changes in the cost of living over time. In its first function, it is used by both government and private businesses to make cost-of-living pay adjustments for employees working in different areas of the country. In the second, it is used for the purpose of gauging pay raises over time.

UNEMPLOYMENT RATES

As hotly debated as inflation is *unemployment*. On a personal level, it's a clear enough fact: You are out of work and hurting financially. But what does it mean on an aggregated, statistical level? What does the nation's unemployment rate stand for? Here's a typical example of what you read in the paper every day:

Nearly 4 million young people who need work may not find jobs this year. This group is composed of women, dropouts, minority groups, and the poor.

A U.S. Bureau of Labor Statistics report for April showed a 16.2 percent jobless rate among young people (the adult jobless rate is 7.0 percent), with the rate among minorities much higher. (*Shipp, 1980*)

The rate of unemployment represents that fraction of the labor force that is not actually working. But who is the "labor force?" It's easier to say who *isn't* in it. Some groups excluded are: all people under 16 years of age and anyone not working for income by virtue of being a homemaker, in school, retired, unable to work for physical or other reasons, or institutionalized (in prisons, mental hospitals, etc.); or simply not needing or not wanting to work.

More concretely, the Labor Department determines how many people are employed and unemployed through the Census Bureau's monthly Current Population Survey of some 47,000 households sampled from across the country. In each interview, a determination is made as to whether individual household members were employed or unemployed during the survey week.

As defined by the survey, *employed* people are those "who, during the survey week, did any work at all as paid employees, or in their own business, profession, or on their own farm, or who worked 15 hours or more as unpaid workers in a family-operated enterprise." Also included are those who were temporarily away from work during the week by virtue of vacations, illnesses, and the like (U.S. Department of Labor, 1976:6).

Unemployed people, within the definitions of the survey, are those not working, available for work, and looking for work. In the last regard, anyone who made any specific effort to find work—for instance, registering with an employment agency—during the preceding four weeks is considered to be "looking for work." In addition to these people, the survey also considers as unemployed those people who are currently laid off and waiting to return to work plus those waiting to begin new jobs.

In this fashion, the number of employed and unemployed *civilians* is determined. Those figures are combined with monthly Department of Defense figures on military employment to create the total labor force. The *unemployment rate*, then, is the result of dividing the number of unemployed members in the labor force by the total labor force.

INTELLIGENCE QUOTIENT (IQ)

Many other economic measures have become household words without being clearly understood by those who read about them daily. But economics is not the only source of such measures in modern American life. IQ is a good example.

The abbreviation IQ stands for *Intelligence Quotient*. It is intended to represent a person's intelligence relative to others of the same age. This determination is based on any of several "IQ tests," the most widely used of which are the Stanford-Binet Intelligence Scale and the Wechsler Adult Intelligence Scale and the children's version of the Wechsler.

Intelligence testing was developed primarily in the early 1900s in France by Albert Binet and was standardized by a U.S. psychologist, Lewis Terman, at Stanford University—hence the Stanford-Binet test. IQ tests are sometimes administered in a one-on-one situation by a psychologist and sometimes in mass-administration classroom settings, though the individually administered tests are considered more accurate. The tests may contain over 200 items and measure such verbal abilities as comprehension, information, and vocabulary, and may include such nonverbal tasks as arithmetic, finding missing elements of pictures, putting together story panels, doing puzzlelike constructions, and so forth.

A good deal of controversy has surrounded the interpretation of IQ scores. The chief issue concerns the extent to which the tests measure what we are born with or what we learn as we grow up; in other words, whether they measure intelligence or education. To the extent that they measure the latter, scores on such tests will largely reflect a person's socialization. More specifically, people growing up in, say, deprived urban ghettos will do poorly since, it is charged, the tests were prepared to measure abilities more common to the white middle-class.

Probably the truth in this matter lies between the two positions. Unquestionably, cultural factors enter in. (A person who has learned only the rudiments of reading and writing, for example, will not do very well.) And at the same time, the tests undoubtedly measure more than socialization, since people of similar cultural backgrounds perform differently on the tests. Similarly, IQ tests do *not* measure achievement, though they probably measure the potential for achievement to some degree. Thus, IQ scores are positively related to measures of achievement—most closely, scholastic achievement, as you might imagine.

The tests are scored in such a fashion that a person's final score is based on an age-group average of 100 (something like the Consumer Price Index). For instance, suppose the average test score for your age group was 154, and you scored 198. Your IQ would be $100 \times (198/154) = 129$, where the average is, by definition, 100.

CRIME RATES

A major concern of many Americans these days is the growth of crime, especially in large cities. We hear frequently of crime rates going up by some percentage and some cities being more crime-ridden than others, but it's not always clear what such reports mean. One powerful way of presenting the prevalence of crime, for example, is to show how often crimes occur. Consider this 1980 report in the *San Francisco Chronicle* listing crimes in selected cities around the San Francisco Bay Area in 1979.

City	One crime every
San Francisco	7.43 minutes
Oakland	12.74 minutes
Sunnyvale	83.65 minutes
Walnut Creek	176.02 minutes

(Carroll, 1980)

Now here's the question: Which of these four cities is the most "crime-ridden" and which the least? At first glance, it certainly looks as though the answers were San Francisco and Walnut Creek, respectively. Crimes occur almost twice as frequently in San Francisco as in Oakland, and less than half as frequently in Walnut Creek as in Sunnyvale. However, ask yourself what other piece of information might be relevant in understanding the crime situation in these four cities.

If you thought population size was relevant, you were right. The four cities vary greatly in population. Let's suppose, hypothetically, that 1 person in 1000 everywhere is a mugger. If City A were twice as large as City B, we'd expect twice as many muggings in City A as in City B. But since City A had twice the population of City B, there would also be twice as many potential victims. Ultimately, that would mean your chances of being mugged would be the same in both cities. For this reason, it makes more sense to compare crime *rates*: the number of crimes per 1000 people, for example. Table 1.2 presents the four-city comparison in terms of crime rates.

As you can see in Table 1.2, the crime *rates* of the four cities give a somewhat different picture. Whereas San Francisco at first seemed much worse off than Oakland, we now see that Oakland actually had a somewhat higher crime rate than San Francisco. Similarly, Walnut Creek's crime rate turns out to be slightly higher than Sunnyvale's.

TABLE 1.2   Crimes Rates in Four Cities, 1979

City	Number of crimes	Population	Crimes per 1000 population
San Francisco	70,745	659,176	107.3
Oakland	41,269	344,686	119.7
Sunnyvale	6,283	108,953	57.7
Walnut Creek	2,986	51,004	58.5

Source: Jerry Carroll, "The Growing Fear of Crime in U.S." Copyright *San Francisco Chronicle*, October 23, 1980. Reprinted with permission.

There are other things to be known about crime statistics, and we'll return to them in Chapter 9. To complete your overview, however, let me give you just a little more general information.

Most of the crime statistics you will see in the mass media are derived from the Uniform Crime Reporting (UCR) program administered by the FBI in cooperation with some 15,000 law-enforcement agencies in the country. The system was initiated in 1930 by the International Association of Chiefs of Police, and Congress authorized the FBI to serve as a national clearinghouse for the statistics collected. For the most part today, local law-enforcement agencies report their crime statistics to statewide programs, and the states compile and pass on their data to the FBI. The FBI then publishes the national data, primarily in its annual *Uniform Crime Reports.*

One of the necessary ingredients in such a system is a standardized view of what constitutes a "crime." This was accomplished by the Committee on Uniform Crime Records of the chiefs' association, as the FBI explains:

Seven offenses, because of their seriousness, frequency of occurrence, and likelihood of being reported to police, were selected to serve as an Index for evaluating fluctuations in the volume of crime. These crimes, known as the Crime Index offenses, are murder and nonnegligent manslaughter, forcible rape, robbery, aggravated assault, burglary, larceny-theft, and motor vehicle theft. (1978:1)

These, then, are the offenses counted in reports that crime rates have increased or (rarely) decreased. Note that the list does not include all crimes, any more than the Dow Jones industrial average includes all industrial companies. Rather, each of these selected measures is intended as a reflection of the total phenomenon (crime, the economy) from which it is selected. This is a fundamental measurement issue that we'll return to frequently in the book, particularly in Chapter 4.

Finally, notice another phrase in the FBI statement that is more important than it may appear: "likelihood of being reported to police." The crime statistics are limited to those index crimes that are reported to police—and, as we'll see in Chapter 9, the number of crimes committed far exceeds the number reported. Moreover, the likelihood of reporting varies with the crime, the victim, and the relationship between victim and offender, further complicating matters.

THE MOST ADMIRED MAN/WOMAN IN THE WORLD

Who do you suppose is the most admired man or woman in the world? In late April 1946, pollster George Gallup asked a sample of American adults: "What person living today in any part of the world do you admire the most?" The following were the most frequently mentioned (listed in order of frequency):

Douglas MacArthur	Henry A. Wallace
Dwight D. Eisenhower	Thomas E. Dewey
Harry S. Truman	Harold Stassen
Mrs. Franklin Roosevelt	James Byrnes
Winston Churchill	(*Gallup, 1972:584*)
Herbert Hoover	

Two years later, Gallup repeated the question, asking separately for men and women. In the 1948 polls, Harry Truman and Eleanor Roosevelt led their respective races for national admiration. Since 1948, Gallup has been periodically asking Americans to name their most admired man and woman. The male competition has most typically been won by the sitting president of the United States, and the female division has usually gone to a first lady (current or former) or to a non-American head of state, such as Golda Meir, former prime minister of Israel. In 13 of the first 14 times the question was asked, however, the same woman won: Eleanor Roosevelt.

Heading the list as "most admired" man or woman doesn't mean that a majority of the American people admire you, however. Since the question is asked in an open-ended format, so that a wide variety of names are given by respondents, 8 or 10 percent of the responses is often enough to qualify a person as "most admired." Finally, it bears underscoring that, while these votes are cast for the most admired people "in the world," all

RESEARCH
AND COMMUNICATION

One of the essential functions of research is communication. It is not sufficient that the researcher learn something about the world; the knowledge needs to be communicated to others so they may act on it appropriately. That communication function, moreover, depends on a partnership between the researcher and the consumer of research.

Here's how Mary Wilhite and Ida Unsain (1979)* described that partnership in connection with nursing:

> *The sophisticated practitioner and researcher should be able to read study reports, apply relevant findings, and generate new research. These nurses—the consumers of research journals—should be able to rely on the integrity of the reports, particularly on the accuracy and appropriateness of the statistics used and on the implications derived from the study findings. They should also be able to understand the statistics they read, or at least have easy access to references that will help them understand the statistical method. If everyone concerned—authors, editors, educators, and individual nurses—shares the responsibility for this understanding, perhaps nurses will read, comprehend, and apply the findings of nursing research.*

These comments apply equally to students in the social sciences, social work, business, law, public health, education—virtually every field. The mission of this book is to provide you with the level of understanding Wilhite and Unsain speak of.

SOURCE Mary J. Wilhite and Ida C. Unsain, "Statistical Reporting: How Accurate? How Appropriate?" *Nursing Research*, September–October 1979:259.

*Parenthetical source notes in Real World Research boxes refer to bibliographical information given at the end of the boxes, rather than to the general Bibliography.

the votes are cast by Americans. Similar studies conducted in other countries would surely produce different results.

These several examples should illustrate the range of concerns that prompted this book. My purpose—to empower you in reading, evaluating, and using the results of social science research—is elaborated on in "Research and Communication," above.

A PREVIEW OF THE BOOK

The purpose of this first chapter has been to introduce you to the orientation of the book—to present the logic and techniques of social science research with the research consumer in mind. The remainder of the book will treat those subjects in detail.

Chapter 2 will take you into the fundamental logic of social research. Here, you'll see the logical foundation upon which specific research techniques are based. In part, I suspect, you'll find that the logic of social research is just about what you would expect, and it will make perfectly good sense to you. The logic of other areas, however, will not necessarily be immediately apparent, and you'll have to look a little deeper into the matter to see where the sense lies. You should emerge from the chapter well equipped to begin learning about specific forms of research.

In Chapter 3, we're going to examine the wide variety of research designs available to social scientists. We'll look at the advantages and disadvantages of qualitative and quantitative research methods, studies done at one point in time and those done over time, studies of individuals and of groups, and so forth. My purpose is to alert you to general strengths and weaknesses of the different designs so that you'll be able to guard against inappropriate or misleading research conclusions and weigh the relative merits of studies that reach contradictory conclusions.

Chapter 4 deals with the issue of *measurement*. We've already discussed measurement briefly in this chapter; in Chapter 4, we'll look at the steps involved in moving from a general concept (e.g., intelligence) to a concrete, specific measurement device (e.g., items on the Stanford-Binet test) and back again. In particular, we'll look at some standards of measurement quality and some common errors made in research.

We often want to draw conclusions about groups that are too large to observe directly in their entirety. For example, people want to predict the outcome of elections but are unable to interview all voters in advance of polling day. Sampling is a common form of social research in such cases. Chapter 5 will lay out the main logic and techniques for selecting a sample of people so that observations of the sample will give a good estimate of the total population from which they are selected.

Chapters 6 through 9 will deal with specific data collection methods commonly used in social research: survey research, experiments, field research, and the analysis of existing statistics. In each of these chapters, I first introduce you to the fundamental logic and techniques involved in the particular method, and then I focus on the relative strengths and weaknesses of that method compared with other alternatives. Ultimately, you should know what to look for in evaluating conclusions based on a particular research method. So when you are confronted, for example, with a research report drawing conclusions on the basis of a national survey, you'll know what to look for in the report to determine whether it was a good survey or a bad one and whether survey research was the appropriate method to study the topic under examination.

In Chapter 10, we'll focus on a field that has become increasingly common in recent years: *evaluation research*. Here the research is intended to determine the consequences of some form of program. Suppose someone comes up with an innovative method for teaching calculus to sixth graders. It would be useful to know whether the program really does what it's supposed to do, and whether it has unanticipated consequences as well. Evaluation research does just that.

Chapters 11 and 12 deal with the analysis and reporting of social research data. In Chapter 11, we'll take a brief overview of common methods of analyzing data that appear in research reports. As in other parts of the book, I'll focus on the relative strengths and weaknesses of various methods so you'll know what to look for in evaluating a particular example of that method and in determining whether the most appropriate method has been used.

Chapter 12 covers statistics. In my years of teaching research methods and writing research methods textbooks, I have become fascinated with the fear and loathing many students bring to the subject of statistics. I want to bust through any such fear you may have. If you are going to be an informed consumer of social research, you'll have to confront statistical analyses from time to time. If you think you don't like statistics, I suppose that's bad news. But the good news is that the fundamentals you need to know aren't really so complicated, as you'll see in Chapter 12.

If you and I have both done our jobs in all these chapters, you should reach the end of the book having enhanced your ability to separate reliable and meaningful research findings from junk, and you will be able to add to the process of inquiry as an informed consumer. This is one of the many ways you can make a real contribution to the quality of life in the society and the world you live in.

THE DESIGN OF RESEARCH PROJECTS

The four chapters making up Part One of this book lay out the general issues and options of structured social inquiry. Chapter 2 looks at the fundamental logic of inquiry and lays the groundwork for the chapters that follow.

Chapter 3 describes the various research designs available to and commonly used by social researchers. We'll see that each has particular strengths and weaknesses.

Measurement is a fundamental issue in any kind of research. Chapter 1 has already raised some of the questions appropriate to measurement, and Chapter 4 will present the answers.

Whereas how to measure is discussed in Chapter 4, Chapter 5 looks at who or what to measure. In Chapter 5, we'll see that a variety of sampling techniques have been developed to make research regarding large numbers of people both possible and accurate.

THE LOGIC OF
SOCIAL RESEARCH

INTRODUCTION

In a sense, this book grows out of a fundamental human activity: *inquiry*. A good chunk of our time and attention is devoted to finding out the way things are and why. For example, substantial portions of your life have been addressed to learning why some people are your friends and others aren't, and how you can tell one group from the other. Similarly, a good part of your childhood was devoted to learning which behaviors were acceptable and which weren't. We want to learn the way things are, we want to understand why they are that way, and we'd like to be able to predict the future on the basis of our understanding. In particular, we'd like to be able to predict the consequences of the various actions available to us. Will people laugh if I eat the peas with my knife? Will I find more happiness as a poet, a lawyer, or a nude dancer? There are a great many things we need to know to get through life.

This chapter is devoted to an examination of the *ways* we know things. We'll begin by looking briefly at the various sources of understanding available to humans. We'll see the roles played by personal experience, tradition, and authority, for example, and we'll touch on some of the more common errors we make in finding out about the world.

Science is one important way of knowing, and so most of the chapter has to do with science. My purpose is to touch on aspects of scientific inquiry that you need in order to fully grasp the logic of social science. We'll see that science is founded on two major pillars: *observation* and *reason*. Then we'll look into some of the fundamental issues of social science. We'll see that social science is a study of the way things are rather than the way they ought to be, although it can be difficult to maintain that division in practice. We'll look at the kinds of social regularities that interest social scientists, learn about the nature of variables and the process of generalizing our conclusions, and see how *intersubjectivity* is the key to what is normally called *objectivity* in science.

As we'll see, explanatory social science is based on a model of human behavior that implicitly assumes individuals have no freedom, that people are controlled by the forces of their environment. Determinism is some-times a troublesome issue for students when it's allowed to lurk in the background, so I'll bring it up front for examination.

Finally, the chapter concludes with a scrutiny of science in theory and in practice. Scientists are human, and we don't always follow the ideal tenets of scientific methods. Nonetheless, science does offer special protections against error in inquiry, and I want you to come away from this chapter with an appreciation of what those are and why.

SOURCES OF UNDERSTANDING

You already understand a great number of things—some things pretty thoroughly and others only partially. And there are undoubtedly some things you don't understand at all. In the discussion to follow, we'll be less interested in *what* you understand than in *how* you came to understand it—that is, the *source* of your understanding. It's true in life generally that there are many different sources for your understandings, and this often produces contradictory explanations of things.

VARIATIONS IN EXPLANATIONS

To illustrate the variety of explanations that people create for the way things are, let's look at a concrete social issue that concerns social scientists as well as people in general: deviance. Why is it that in any society some people break the rules and transgress against themselves and others? Why do some people become burglars, alcoholics, drug addicts, murderers, and the like?

Pat Lauderdale and James Inverarity (1980:16) note that there has been a progression of theories for explaining deviance.

1. Aristotelian (antiquity). Deviance was associated with punishment inflicted on individuals by the gods. Logic revealed that some individuals were by nature deviant.
2. Medieval scholastic. Deviance was thought to have been created by the devil (or some similar religious or spiritual entity). The demonic entity possessed or manipulated the deviant.
3. Physiological. Deviance was felt to be related to the surface characteristics (exterior) of individuals, regardless of whether the researcher thought the cause was biological or psychological. Physiognomy, craniology, cranioscopy, phrenology, or a general conception of ugliness served as the frame of reference.
4. Biological. Deviance was thought to be rooted in the biochemistry of the person. The emphasis was on the inner characteristics (interior) of individuals.
5. Economic. Deviance was related to economic conditions. For example, drunkenness was associated with prosperity and burglary with depression.
6. Psychological. Deviance was initially viewed as a consequence of events in the individual's biography, be it situational frustration or an arrested stage of psychosexual development. Recent views propose a modified frustration-aggression perspective, a series of reinforcement theories, or a modeling explanation of deviance.*

Lauderdale and Inverarity present this list of explanations as alternatives to sociological explanations, which offer social structure and social processes as the reasons for deviance. Aside from their specific differences, these several explanations also illustrate the different sources of explanations. For a great many years, common people explained deviance in terms of the Aristotelian or scholastic views: Deviance was either a punishment from the gods or the devil's wile. People believed these explanations because they had been *taught* them. The explanations had the weight of tradition and the authority of the church behind them. As we'll see shortly, both tradition and authority are common sources of what we "know."

The physiological view of deviance has enjoyed support of various kinds. Though many disciplines have claimed scientific status for their points of view, there is a persistent sense among people that you can often tell who the deviants are "just by the way they look." Biological explanations have varied in content and source. Some—such as research into the effects of blood sugar levels, xyy chromosomal structures, and so on—originate in biological science. Other "biological" explanations—such as com-

*Reprinted with permission of the University of Minnesota Press, from *From Apolitical to Political Analyses of Deviance* (Minneapolis, 1980), p. 16. Copyright 1980 by the Unversity of Minnesota, University of Minnesota Press.

mon beliefs in people having "bad blood"—are rooted more in emotions and gossip.

Finally, the economic and psychological models of deviance have roots both in scientific research and in day-to-day experiences and observations. It makes sense that people will steal when they are starving, for example, and careful scientific observation demonstrates the accuracy of the conclusion.

There are, then, several sources of our explanations for things. Let's look at each briefly, ending with science as a source of understanding.

PERSONAL EXPERIENCE AS A SOURCE OF UNDERSTANDING

Many of the things we understand about the world around us come directly from our personal experiences in and of it. Certainly, you learned about your parents that way. From your very beginnings, you were finding out what their habits were, what they expected of you, and what they were likely to do when you acted in various ways. This is probably how you learned what cats do when you pull their tails. Some people learn about hot stoves this way.

Personal experience is a primary source of understanding. In fact, the "show me" attitude has a high status in America; we take pride in thinking for ourselves, making up our own minds, and insisting on the facts. At the same time, very little of what we understand really comes from personal experience. Let's see where it does come from.

TRADITION AS A SOURCE OF UNDERSTANDING

A great deal of what you "know" falls into the category of things "everyone knows," things that are "obvious" and "have always been that way." Don't stand under a tree during a lightning storm—right? It's better for a husband to be a couple of years older than his wife—right? Excessive masturbation will adversely affect your later sex life—right? Most politicians lie and cheat—right?

But how do you know such things? Not by personal experience, I'd wager, although you may have had experiences you felt confirmed what you'd already learned through tradition. You know such things because you've been taught them as things everyone knows, as things that have been true for a long time. **Tradition** is an important source of understanding for all of us; we give up finding out for ourselves in favor of accepting what has always been believed.

AUTHORITY AS A SOURCE OF UNDERSTANDING

Authority operates somewhat like tradition as a source of understanding. Much of what we know is based on what we are told by people who "ought to know." There are no palm trees growing on the moon—right? How on earth do you know that? You "know" that because NASA and *Newsweek* both said so. It was even in the *New York Times.* Neil Armstrong brought back snapshots to prove there were no palm trees within sight of the Apollo capsule. How do you know that crime rates have gone up? The FBI said so, or at least your local newspaper said the FBI said crime rates went up. How do you know that Russia invaded Afghanistan in 1980? You read it in the newspapers and saw it on the TV news—right?

The source of much of what we "know" lies with people and organizations that possess authority in one field or another. In small rural communities, professionals such as doctors or lawyers may be paid special attention in most matters, even those far removed from medicine or the law. Political leaders are often accorded such authority. In some societies, the old possess authority; in some, religious leaders have it. In any event, much of what we "know" hinges on what those in authority have told us.

PUBLIC OPINION AS A SOURCE OF UNDERSTANDING

The simple weight of general agreement can constitute a sort of authority in the sense that I've been discussing it above. Much of what we "know" is a function of what everyone around us seems to "know." Peer groups have a special conforming pressure that's wielded among friends and close acquaintances. If all your friends think that inflation is going to get worse in the months to come, you're probably going to take on that view yourself. And more impersonally, **public opinion** (often measured by social scientists, as we'll see in Chapter 6) is also a source of understanding for us. The progressive loss of public support for the war in Vietnam is probably a good example: Once the tide of opinion turned, the tide itself became a cause of change.

As we'll see later, public opinion is an important focus of the social sciences, and it can explain a good portion of what we see around us in society. If people share the opinion that a gasoline shortage is just around the corner, they may act accordingly and actually create a shortage by hoarding. However, this does not prove that a shortage would have occurred without the hoarding. In other words, public opinion can be wrong.

COMMON ERRORS IN UNDERSTANDING

One area of special interest in this book is the trouble we sometimes get into in attempting to understand the world: the errors we make in inquiry of all sorts. There are problems inherent in each of the sources of understanding mentioned above.

When we set out to discover the way things are all by ourselves, we often make mistakes. Sometimes we observe inaccurately, for example. I may begin forming an impression that Albanians are superstitious when the superstitious people I just encountered are really Bulgarians. Sometimes we spin out explanations for people's opinions when we misunderstood what they said in the first place.

As these illustrations also indicate, our inquiries often go astray through the common practice of **overgeneralization,** observing one or two instances of something and taking it to be a rule of nature. And having reached a general conclusion about the way things are, we often have a tendency to only observe, or at least pay the most attention to, things that substantiate our previous conclusion. Having concluded that Yale students are jerks, a Harvard student may only notice jerky Yalies and ignore the clever ones. This practice, which psychologists call **selective perception,** creates havoc with inquiry.

There are equally severe dangers lurking within tradition as a source of understanding as well. The fact that everyone has always believed something scarcely makes it accurate. After all, everyone once believed the world flat, believed witches to be the source of bad harvests, and believed criminal behavior to reflect the work of the devil. Without saying everything traditionally believed is false, we can still say that tradition is a powerful force operating against inquiry. Those things "everyone knows and has always known" seem so certain that only fools would question them. And such fools are all too rare.

Authority can be equally problematic in this respect. First, persons with authority can make mistakes and do. Yet others are often hesitant to challenge people with clout. Second, people with authority in one field often make pronouncements in other fields. When then-President Nixon heard that his own blue-ribbon Presidential Commission on Pornography and Obscenity reported no relationship between pornography and sex crimes, Nixon simply responded that they were wrong. Since he was president of the United States, many people probably believed him.

Public opinion is no safer a source of truth. General agreements among people represent just that: agreements. And people can agree on things that are inaccurate as well as on things that are accurate. If there were a special truth value in public opinion, we'd do surveys to ask people for a cure for cancer.

SCIENCE AS A SOURCE OF UNDERSTANDING

The purpose of the preceding comments is not to rule out personal experience, tradition, authority, and public opinion as valid sources of understanding. Much of what you have learned from these sources is probably accurate. However, I want to draw your attention to their shortcomings, so

FIFTY-NINE CENTS ON THE DOLLAR

During this century, women have become much more active in the labor force. This trend has been particularly dramatic among married women. Between 1940 and 1977 alone, the participation of married women in the labor force increased from 16.7 to 47.1 percent (U.S. Bureau of the Census, 1978:404). Moreover, over time, women—like all workers—have been earning more and more. At the same time, however, the ratio of men's to women's incomes has stayed relatively constant, with women earning about 59 percent as much as men overall.

The relatively lower wages paid to women have been explained in terms of many factors. Overall, women are more likely to be part-time employees, and they are more likely to work temporarily, often leaving work to assume full-time family responsibilities. Similarly, women generally hold lower status jobs in comparison to men: Men are physicians while women are nurses, for example. In addition, it is argued that women in general have less formal job training and less on-the-job experience. All these factors quite reasonably affect incomes—but are they the only reasons for the relatively lower incomes of women?

Researchers at the University of Michigan (Levitin, Quinn, and Staines, 1970) undertook a national survey on occupation and employment to examine in

that you will be in a position to appreciate some of the special characteristics of science as a source of understanding. As we'll see, scientific research often provides views of the world that contradict what people otherwise understood to be the case. This is illustrated in "Fifty-nine Cents on the Dollar."

THE BASES OF SOCIAL SCIENCE

In this section, we are going to look more deeply into the nature of social science as a way of knowing about the world. I want to raise a number of issues that are sometimes sources of misunderstanding for the consumers of research.

detail the charge that women are discriminated against in income. They began their analysis of the data by selecting half the men surveyed and by studying carefully the relative importance of different factors in determining their incomes. They considered the type of occupation, years of experience in it, education and special training completed, and many other relevant factors. Out of those factors they were able to construct a complex equation they felt would predict the income a given person might expect to receive.

When the researchers applied the equation to the qualifications of the men not used in the construction of the equation, their income estimates were off by only about $30 a year (thus reassuring them that they had discovered the determinants of different income levels). When the same equation was applied to the qualifications of the women surveyed, however, the researchers found that those women actually earned over *$3000 a year less* than their qualifications predicted.

This research clearly demonstrates, then, that women earn less money than men for reasons other than those commonly offered to explain the discrepancy. This illustrates a key aspect of science that we'll examine shortly: Explanations not only must make sense; they must correspond to what really happens in the world.

SOURCES U.S. Bureau of the Census, *Statistical Abstract of the United States, 1978.* Washington, D.C.: U.S. Government Printing Office, 1978: Teresa Levitin, Robert Quinn, and Graham Staines, ''Sex Discrimination Against the American Working Woman.'' Report of the Institute of Social Research. Ann Arbor: University of Michigan, 1970.

THE DUAL FOUNDATIONS OF SCIENCE

Science is sometimes described as **rational/empirical** or **logico-empirical.** Each of these terms points to the two foundations of science: *observation* and *logic*. On the one hand, scientists make observations of the world; thus science is empirical. On the other hand, they make sense out of what they observe; hence the logical/rational quality of science. Moreover, both aspects are necessary, as we see from some classic studies of soldiers' morale during World War II. Samuel Stouffer (1949) observed (to his surprise, incidentally) that the morale of black soldiers assigned to northern training camps was no higher than that of those assigned to southern camps. This was a strange finding in view of the much greater prejudice and discrimination directed against blacks in the South than in the North. Stouffer was able to suggest reasons for the finding. Take a moment to see if you can think of any logical reasons, then read what Stouffer suggested:

1. Stouffer suggested that black soldiers would probably compare their lot in life with that of black civilians. In the South, where blacks were generally treated very badly, the soldiers were at least treated better than civilians. In comparing themselves with black civilians, then, the soldiers training in the South would have relatively high morale. In the North, on the other hand, there were more opportunities for blacks generally. Thus, the black civilians a soldier compared himself with would probably be working in well-paying defense jobs, enjoying far greater freedom than soldiers. For this reason, Stouffer suggested, the black soldier training in the North might be more likely to feel he had a crummy lot in life.

2. Furthermore, since most blacks lived in the South at the time of the war, those who were assigned to northern camps would be away from home, family, and friends and thus might be more lonely or depressed than those trained in the South, who would be more likely to be near home.

The point of this example is that observation alone is not science. The scientist must make sense—or seek to make sense—of what is observed.

On the other hand, logical explanations are worthless in science unless they can be tested by observation in what is generally referred to as **empirical verification.** In some realms of life, conclusions about reality are accepted without observations to support them. For instance, the Christian belief in heaven and hell, plus the belief that worldly acts determine one's subsequent address, are accepted without any supporting observations. The same is true of the Hindu belief in karma. In science, however, empirical verification is essential to the acceptance of a statement about what's so. It is never sufficient in science to figure out what would happen under certain circumstances without also finding or creating those circumstances and seeing if it really does happen.

In the aftermath of the 1965 Watts rioting in Los Angeles, for example, many social scientists sought to discover the causes of the violence. H. Edward Ransford was one of them. Ransford (1968) looked at a body of theoretical literature dealing with extreme political behavior, and he found reason to believe that blacks who felt "socially isolated" and "powerless" should have been the most likely to participate in the rioting. If you think about it, you'll see that the idea makes good sense. To complete the examination, however, Ransford undertook an interviewing project in which black residents of Watts were asked questions relating to their feelings of isolation and powerlessness, on the one hand, and their willingness to engage in violent protest on the other. Once the data had been collected and analyzed, Ransford found his hunches confirmed.

Walter Wallace has provided a pretty realistic model of how science operates. He sees science as a circle made up of theories, hypotheses, obser-

FIGURE 2.1
An image of science. Adapted from Walter Wallace, *The Logic of Science in Sociology* (Chicago: Aldine-Atherton, 1971).

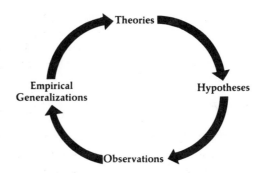

vations, and empirical generalizations. His image of science is presented in Figure 2.1.

A significant feature of Wallace's model is that science can begin anywhere. To explain the diagram, let's begin at the bottom. A scientist might make observations regarding something—say, different forms of prejudice. An **empirical generalization** consists of finding a common pattern running through all the several observations. In this case, let's suppose that most of the prejudices observed were held by people with little education.

This empirical generalization might lead the researcher to develop a general **theory**—a system of logical explanation that links several elements into a meaningful whole. Here, the theory might link prejudice to the lack of education, specifying the aspects of education, both formal and informal, relevant to prejudice. The theory would draw on what is already known about education and about prejudice, including perhaps psychological, economic, and other factors.

Once developed, the theory would offer a fairly general explanation of how education relates to prejudice. Such a theory would, therefore, suggest certain things about social life that had not been observed previously. The theory might suggest that people with a liberal arts education would be less prejudiced than those with, say, an engineering education. Such an expectation is called a **hypothesis,** as shown in Figure 2.1. As Wallace's model suggests, the next step in the wheel of science is to make more observations: The researcher might undertake a study to find out if liberal arts graduates are less prejudiced than engineers. Those new observations, in turn, might only partially confirm the hypothesis. Let's say that liberal arts graduates were less prejudiced against racial and ethnic minorities, but both they and engineers were equally prejudiced against women. These new empirical generalizations would require modifications to the theory, producing new hypotheses, and so forth.

It is essential that you realize the importance of both observation and reason in science. All too often, that which seems to make good sense simply turns out not to be true. That was certainly the case in Stouffer's study of morale among black soldiers. It was also true in regard to explanations for why women earn less money than men.

The interplay between logic and observation is what distinguishes science from systems of philosophy, morality, and belief.

THEORY—NOT PHILOSOPHY, MORALITY, OR BELIEF

Since the social sciences deal with subject matter that is often highly charged emotionally, it is necessary at the outset to make it clear that social science does not represent specific positions on the matters studied. Thus social scientists may study marijuana use, but social science has no position as to whether that use should be legal or illegal. Social scientists study people's attitudes and behavior regarding abortions, to take another example, yet social science is neither pro nor con on the question.

Social science presents theories, which, as we've just seen, are systems of explanation about the way things are, not the way they ought to be. At the same time, you should realize that social science is not unrelated to questions of philosophy, morality, belief, and the like. On the one hand, social science research often challenges established beliefs. It is often argued, for example, that capital punishment is an important deterrent to serious crimes, such as murder. However, comparisons of murder rates in states with and without capital punishment deny the deterrent effect; if anything, states with capital punishment have higher murder rates. This does not mean that social science research has concluded that capital punishment should be abolished; it means only that capital punishment doesn't seem to deter murder.

Finally, you should realize that social scientists—as individuals— have philosophical, moral, and other points of view, and they act on those points of view in words and deeds. Often, moreover, their points of view are affected by what they have learned as social scientists. So although science is not about philosophy, morality, or belief, it is definitely relevant to such types of thought.

Ultimately, science is devoted to discovering regularities in the world and explaining why those regularities exist. Let's see what kinds of social regularities make up our everyday lives.

SOCIAL REGULARITIES

Some people express unhappiness with the idea of a "science of human behavior," feeling that humans are somehow above or beyond the sort of scientific explanation and prediction we routinely exercise on other animals and on inanimate objects. This is an issue we'll return to again in this chapter.

At base, the feasibility of scientific studies of human behavior depends on the existence of *regularities* in our behavior. Without regular patterns of behavior, social science would be impossible. As it turns out, we are in fact pretty regular creatures.

Consider commute-hour traffic: It's an excellent example of human regularity. It starts, builds, peaks, and subsides at the same times weekday after weekday. When one person gets sick and stays home from work, it's as though someone else fills in. Birth rates offer another example of human regularity. If the birth rate in a society is 17.3 births per 1000 population this year, next year's birth rate will be very close to 17.3—even though those babies will be produced primarily by a different group of women. Even when birth rates increase or decrease in the long term, year-to-year differences are relatively slight.

On the whole, then, we humans are a pretty regular lot, so social scientists have plenty to study. Even unexpected, bizarre, out-of-the-ordinary behavior often serves to shed light on the regularities it violates. In fact, pattern violations often serve to draw attention to the existence of the patterns, since we are often unconscious of our most regular patterns. Suppose you came across a young woman smoking a stubby black cigar. That sight would be so bluntly out of the ordinary that you would be reminded of the norm in American society that women don't smoke cigars.

There is an important sense in which social scientists study patterns of regularity rather than people; people figure in only as the evidence of those patterns. Let's see how that works.

A VARIABLE LANGUAGE

There's a relatively simple experiment done in high school physics labs that you may have seen. To observe a form of subatomic particle activity called Brownian Movement, radioactive material is placed in a small, glass-topped chamber, and the chamber's temperature is lowered with dry ice. The lowering of the temperature causes the air in the chamber to form a cloud—the chamber is called a cloud chamber—and the subatomic particles emitted from the radioactive material leave traces in the cloud. Suddenly you can observe directly the erratic paths taken by powerful particles far smaller than the eye can see.

Social research is analogous to the cloud chamber procedure. We are interested in discovering and understanding social patterns that are usually only "visible" in the form of the behaviors of individual humans, but we are not ultimately interested in those individuals per se. No demographer is really interested in whether Mary Smith had a baby because her husband wanted to prove his masculinity to the guys in the bowling league or because her own mother was agitating for a grandchild. But all demographers are interested in such reasons if they represent social patterns *in general.*

Put somewhat differently, individual human beings are the "carriers" of what social scientists study, and the "what" is variables. A **variable** is a set of related characteristics; for example, gender is a variable made up of the characteristics male and female. These characteristics often go by the technical term **attributes.** Thus, variables are composed of sets of attributes.

Other examples of variables studied in social research include age, race, education, prejudice, religiosity, alienation, liberalism, conservatism, social participation, and so forth. If we were to study student success in college, some of the variables we'd probably consider would be major, grade-point average, hours spent studying, quality of precollege education, parents' education, IQ, and so on.

Social research is aimed at discovering the relationships that exist among variables, and those variables can usually only be observed in the form of humans. For example, prejudice, as I've mentioned above, is negatively related to level of education. All else being equal, as people become more and more educated, they become less and less prejudiced. Notice, however, that the people in this example are simply the cloud chamber that lets us see the relationship between the two variables: education and prejudice.

This is what Paul Lazarsfeld has called the "variable language" of social research. If you can fully appreciate this view of what social research is all about, it will spare you a great deal of confusion later on. When I just said "as people become more and more educated, they become less and less prejudiced," it's quite possible that some disconfirming examples came to your mind. You may have thought of someone you know who has little or no education but is as tolerant as they come. Or you may have brought to mind an educated bigot you've had the displeasure of meeting. As long as you think social scientists are out to explain people, such examples are a problem. When you realize that our attention is on the relationships among variables, such examples merely indicate that the relationships do not operate all the time or that they are sometimes overridden by other variables.

GENERALIZATION AND SPECIFICITY

There are two characteristics of science that seem to contradict each other: **generalization** and **specificity.** On the one hand, scientists strive for the most general conclusions available. It would be less satisfying and less useful to discover that education reduces prejudice among white, middle-class Americans than to discover it applies to everyone. In this sense, generalization is a goal of science.

At the same time, science proceeds most effectively—even in the pursuit of generalization—when scientists are scrupulously specific in noting the nature and limitations of particular findings. Be clear, however, that these qualities of science do not contradict each other. The opposite of generalization is limitation. The opposite of specificity, on the other hand, is vagueness.

This aspect of science is significant to you as a consumer of social research in many ways. First, the specific details presented in research reports can aid you in drawing your own conclusions about the implications of the study findings. Suppose you are the head of a juvenile delinquency rehabilitation project, and you've just come across a report on the effectiveness of a new rehabilitation program. If the report has been presented with appropriate specificity, you'll be able to make an educated guess as to whether it might work with the particular juveniles in your program. Specificity in research reports can also assist you in making sense out of seemingly conflicting research results. Finally, any research report that lacks specificity should be taken with caution.

INTERSUBJECTIVITY

The final foundation of science that I want to discuss here is related to the issue of generalization. I'm sure you've heard references to *objectivity* in science. Recognizing that the results of scientific research often hinge on the many decisions that go into the specific design and execution of a study, we are concerned that we discover what's "really" so rather than things that might be products of the researcher's conscious or unconscious biases.

In practice, there is no way of determining whether a research conclusion is objectively true. Ultimately, every research finding is inseparable from the particular details of the study producing it. This situation is not as bad as it seems, however. In place of objectivity in science, we look for **intersubjectivity:** a research finding being repeated in studies conducted by different researchers. Do different researchers, having different feelings in the matter and using slightly different methods, arrive at the same conclusion? If a research conclusion is intersubjectively true, we assume it is "objectively" true. If Candidate A announces that his or her political poll indicates victory, we are likely to be a little dubious. If Candidate B then announces another poll that also shows Candidate A the likely winner, this intersubjective confirmation strengthens our confidence in the conclusion.

The term **replication**—the repeating of studies—is often used in this connection. Replication is important to science by guarding against misleading research conclusions that were produced by factors other than the apparent ones. If the same conclusion keeps issuing from study after study, we speak of a "weight of evidence" building up in support of the conclusion. Specificity enters back into the matter in that researchers must report their research findings with sufficient detail that other researchers can replicate them—either exactly the same or with small changes in order to test the generalizability of the conclusion.

These, then, are some of the fundamental bases of science. They apply as much in social science as in any other science. At the same time, some of the norms of science in general create special problems in the study of humans. We're going to turn now to a consideration of one such problem.

DETERMINISM AND HUMAN BEHAVIOR

In this section of the chapter, I want to discuss an issue, touched on earlier, that can be problematic for people as they begin dealing with social science— the deterministic nature of scientific explanation.

THE IMPLICATIONS OF SCIENTIFIC EXPLANATION

As we'll see, science has two major purposes: description and explanation. This is as true for social science as for physics and biology. On the one hand, scientists describe the nature of reality: For example, demographers describe the number of women in a population who have babies during a given year, economists determine the percentage of unemployed among the labor force, political scientists measure the percentage of voters casting votes for Ronald Reagan or Jimmy Carter, and so forth. While people sometimes complain about being put in "pigeon-holes" by such counting procedures, it is seldom really much of a problem for anyone.

Explanation, on the other hand, can be more problematic. To show you how that is, let me take a short detour into some simple experiments in the natural sciences. Suppose, as a biology student, you placed a plant on a table near a window in your lab. After a few weeks, you would discover that the plant has begun leaning toward the window. This phenomenon is referred to as *heliotropism:* As a part of their biological make-up, plants tend to grow toward the rays of the sun.

Or, as a psychology student, suppose you replicated Pavlov's classic experiments on conditioned reflexes among animals. For a few weeks, you'd ring a bell just prior to feeding a laboratory dog. After a while, you'd discover that the dog began salivating as soon as it heard the bell, whether there was food coming or not. The salivation would represent a conditioned reflex.

The purpose of these examples is to have you notice two things. First, notice how the plant and the dog had nothing to say about the behaviors being studied. We don't imagine that either had any freedom in the matter. The plant grew toward the sun because of its genetic structure, and the dog started salivating at the sound of the bell because the psychologist implanted an association between the bell and food. Second, notice that you probably weren't particularly bothered by either of those explanations. I would doubt, for example, that you muttered, "But the plant *wanted* to lean toward the window."

Now let us return to the earlier examples from the social sciences. In addition to observing, social scientists also seek explanations for *why* some women had babies while others didn't, *why* some people were unemployed while others were employed, *why* some voters chose Reagan while others chose Carter. These "why" questions are potentially problematic because of the nature of the answers given. As in the physical sciences, social scientists offer **deterministic** explanations: Human behaviors are conceptualized and studied as though they were determined by forces and factors beyond the control and often beyond the awareness of the human actors involved.

In the case of the heliotropic plant, we conclude that the plant's behavior was *determined* by forces in its *environment* (the sun); we make no assumptions about the plant "choosing" its behavior or even being conscious of the environmental forces pushing it around. The dog, too, was an unaware victim of its environment (the food, bell, and psychologist). Similarly, social scientists find environmental explanations for why women did or didn't have babies, why workers were employed or unemployed, why voters went for Reagan or Carter. Women have babies, for example, because of cultural norms, peer pressure, and so forth. You will never find a social scientist concluding that "17 percent of the women had babies because they wanted to."

A RUBE GOLDBERG VIEW OF DETERMINISM

The determinist model is one of *cause* and *effect*. Everything you see happening is caused by and causes other things; everything is connected to everything else in a complex system. An amusing illustration of this view is found in the ingenious creations of Rube Goldberg (1904–64). Goldberg's cartoons presented a simultaneous view of long, related circles of events. Figure 2.2, a drawing similar to Goldberg's, is an example of what I mean.

A painter might accidentally bump into a stepladder, knocking down the can of paint atop the ladder; the paint would pour onto a cat, who would screech in surprise, startling a nurse, who would let go of her baby carriage, which would roll into a table and tip over a glass of milk, which would spill on the ground, to be slipped on by a man carrying a bowling ball, who'd drop the bowling ball, which would startle the painter into bumping the ladder . . . The chain of events goes on and on.

A deterministic view, like Rube Goldberg's drawings, says that everything you do has many consequences, and everything that happens in the universe fits into an endless chain of interrelated events. This is the model currently used in ecological explanations of the physical world. As biologist Garret Hardin has said, the first law of ecology is: "You can't do just *one* thing." In ecosystems, everything is related to everything else; nothing is independent.

Similarly, Figure 2.2 depicts a deterministic system of human behavior. Suppose that you are the nurse in the drawing. *Why* did you let go of your baby carriage? You were forced to do it by the cat's screeching. The cat's screeching determined your action. But wait a minute. What caused the cat to screech? Look at the figure for a moment, and you'll see that *you* did. Can you see how the nurse in the figure was the cause of the whole thing? By letting the baby carriage run into the table, and so spilling the milk, which made the man slip, and so forth, the nurse caused the cat to screech! So you can see from this fanciful illustration the deterministic foundation of explanatory science. Nothing "just happens." Everything has causes, including the things *you* feel, think, and do.

DETERMINISM VERSUS FREE WILL

Crudely put, the explanatory model employed by social scientists denies individual freedom. Fundamentally, there is no place for volition, or "free will." Even when social scientists are unable to predict or explain behavior totally (which is usually the case), the implicit assumption is that more knowledge would produce fuller explanation and prediction. This is the same model employed by natural scientists. However, when we are dealing with people, it becomes problematic.

There appear to be three main objections to determinism in explaining human behavior. First, it contradicts our experience of things. Each of us has countless experiences of "choosing" from among alternatives. You may have debated whether to read this chapter at this time—maybe you had a chance to do something with friends—and you feel you chose to read the chapter. Nobody forced you to take this course, in fact, and you probably feel that you chose to do it. (If the course is required for your major, you feel you chose that major.) To be sure, we experience some limits on our freedom—you can't flap your arms and fly away—but I doubt that anyone feels totally controlled in everything.

The second objection to applying a deterministic model to human behavior has to do with its implications for credit and blame. If your behavior is determined by forces beyond your control, that means you can't take credit for any of the things you've achieved. For example, I'm the first

FIGURE 2.2
A Rube Goldberg
view of determin-
ism.

member of my family ever to attend college. How can I take any credit for that within a model that says I went to college because of forces and factors in my environment that pushed and pulled me into doing it? I can't. By the same token, the deterministic model implies that people are not to blame for the bad things they do. This view is probably familiar to you. Whether criminals are "to blame" for their crimes has become an ideological issue in America. Liberals—often supported by social science research— argue that criminals are the products of bad environments or of unjust social systems. Even if everyone would agree that a certain person was totally rotten, this view suggests that it was all a result of environmental forces and factors that the person couldn't control.

Third, the deterministic model raises fears about how we would behave if we really accepted it as a true statement of the way things are. Since whether you graduate from college or not will be determined by forces and factors beyond your control, why should you work hard? Why should you study? If you really accepted the deterministic model that social scientists use, wouldn't you simply give up, curl up in a corner and suck your thumb, watch TV, or something like that? In discussing this issue with literally thousands of students, I've found this concern to be the most powerful objection to the deterministic model employed by social scientists in studying human behavior.

In a moment, I'll return to the concern about "how you'd behave." First, I want to make sure you realize the full implications of the model social scientists use to explain human behavior.

THE FULL IMPLICATIONS OF THE DETERMINISTIC MODEL

The deterministic model is a foolproof trap. You cannot think of anything you have ever done that cannot be explained in terms of the deterministic model. You cannot think of anything you have ever done wholly out of your free will.

Think of something you feel you "chose" to do. How about the fact that you are reading this sentence, this chapter? You could have been doing something else, right? No one is holding a gun to your head. Let's use that example as a vehicle for discussing the issue.

Answer this: *"Why* are you reading this chapter?" Let me guess some of the answers you might give if we were discussing this face-to-face. "Because it was assigned by my methods instructor." "Because I wanted to learn something about social science." "Because my friend told me it was interesting." Whatever answer you might give, I suggest that you have trapped yourself by your reason. That reason is the "force" causing you to read the chapter. You didn't choose after all; there's no free will involved. You were *determined* to read the chapter because of that factor. *Given* that factor, you *had* to read the chapter.

"What!!" you object. Let's suppose you said your reason for reading the chapter was that your instructor assigned it. Even so, you protest, you still could have gone to the movies instead, right? Just having it assigned didn't "force" you to read it. But why did you "choose" to read it then? If we were having this discussion, you might reply, "Because I want to get a good grade in the course." *Aha!* Now I see you were determined to be reading this chapter because (1) your instructor assigned it, and (2) you want to get a good grade. Anyone can see that, with those two forces operating, a person would *have* to read the chapter. "NO!!" you shout. "I still could have gone to the movies." Then, I respond, why are you reading this chapter?

The point of this fictitious dialogue is that you'd have another reason to explain why you were reading the chapter, and I'd respond that the now-expanded set of reasons was the cause of your action, but not your free-will choice. You are hung by your reasons. We are all so reasonable about why we do things that it certainly looks as though the factors and forces embodying those reasons determine the way we turn out. Specifically, explanatory social science operates on a model that assumes we are determined by forces and factors rather than making free choices. The implications of the model are even worse than I've indicated. At some point in our dialogue, you would probably say something like, "Although I may be determined to read the book because of my desire to do well in college, aren't I the one who chose to go to college and who made a commitment to doing well?" No luck. The question now becomes, "Why did you decide to go to college, and why did you make a commitment to doing well?" Again, you'd have reasons for having your reasons. "I want to please my parents." "Why do you want to please your parents?" "Because . . . "

You can see where this leads. If your reasons determined why you are doing what you are doing right now, you have earlier reasons for having your current reasons, and reasons to account for the earlier reasons. If you reflect on it, you'll see that the string of reasons extends back into the past without a beginning in sight. Trace the reasons back to the way you were at birth, and I'll ask why you were that way.

The deterministic process we are beginning to see in its full implications ought to extend into the future as well as back into the past. There are no grounds for expecting it to cease today. All the things you are doing now, all the things true about you, all the past reasons that have gotten you to this spot—all those things will presumably determine what you do next. And what you do next will contribute to the forces and factors determining what you do after that.

Implied in the deterministic model, then, is a full dose of predeterminism as well. This suggests that your whole future has been laid out already. Your grade in this course, whether you graduate or not, your postcollege career, your failure or success in life would seem to be already determined. The time, place, and circumstance of your death would appear to be already determined within the assumptions of the deterministic model that social science is based on.

I think it's important to confront these implications before launching into the logic and techniques of social science research. Otherwise, when you get engrossed in studies of what causes juvenile delinquency, why some people are more religious than others, which background factors produce liberalism and which produce conservatism, and so on, there's a good chance that some part of your mind will begin wondering if the logic of the research doesn't pretty much deny individual freedom of action. So, I want to start out with the recognition that it *does*. While we're usually too polite to say that, it's so. "Why Are People Religious?" illustrates the way this issue crops up in the process of social research. At the same time, I

WHY ARE PEOPLE RELIGIOUS?

The issue of religion is an intensely personal one for many people. It involves their relationship with God, gods, or godness. Ask a religious person why he or she is religious, and you'll probably get a profound and heartfelt response. Sociologists have spent considerable time and effort seeking their own answers to this question.

Charles Glock and his colleagues (1967) sought the causes of religiosity through a national survey of Episcopalian church members. A lengthy questionnaire asked a great many probing questions about the nature of church involvement. The explanations that the researchers arrived at were quite different from those that church members themselves would give. Their analysis followed Wallace's model for science as a circle of activities (see Figure 2.1).

The researchers began with a set of observations. Women were more religious than men. Old people were more religious than young people. Those without families were more religious than those who were married and had children. Finally, lower-class church members were more religious than upper-class members.

Eventually, the researchers arrived at an empirical generalization that linked these disparate observations: In each case, those with less social status were more religious than those with more status. This was obviously the case in terms of social class (measured in terms of education and income). It didn't stop there, however. Men are more highly esteemed in America than women and get more of the benefits of society. We are a youth-oriented society, in which the elderly are often viewed as a deprived minority. Finally, our society generally expects people to marry and form families; those who fail to live up to these expectations are regarded as somewhat odd. Moving from this empirical generalization, the researchers developed a theory of church involvement.

Coining the term *social deprivation*, the authors suggested that people who

---

realize that the idea of determinism is not a comfortable one. So let's take the sting out of this bee.

DEALING WITH THE ISSUE OF DETERMINISM

To start, I haven't said that the deterministic point of view is "true" or that it represents some ultimate reality. I have simply described the model that were deprived of status in the secular society turned to the church as an alternative source of gratification. This explanation coincided with the traditional role of the church to "comfort the weary and the heavily laden," leading the researchers to speak of a *comfort theory* of religiosity. Hypotheses generated from that theory were tested and confirmed.

Taken together, the several factors described above provided a powerful explanation of church involvement. The table below indicates the level of church involvement (ranging from 0 to 1) for groups of church members experiencing differing degrees of social deprivation. At the extremes, those scored 0 were young, upper-class, married men with children (while none of the respondents had all these characteristics, those scored 1 lacked only one); those scored 8 were lower-class, elderly women with no husbands or children. As you can see, church involvement increased steadily and strongly with an increasing degree of deprivation.

Level of church involvement	SOCIAL DEPRIVATION								
	0	1	2	3	4	5	6	7	8
Mean score:	—*	.23	.31	.36	.45	.51	.60	.62	.72

*Note: No one was scored 0.

Though this study provided a powerful, scientific explanation for why some people are more religious than others, it was a source of controversy. In particular, it suggests that something as profoundly personal as religiosity is a matter not of choice but of social causes largely beyond the control of the people involved. This illustrates the way in which the deterministic model conflicts with our personal experience of why we are the way we are.

SOURCE Charles Y. Glock, Benjamin B. Ringer, and Earl Babbie, *To Comfort and to Challenge.* Berkeley: University of California Press, 1967.

lies at the heart of explanatory social science. You don't have to believe it in order to study social science or to be a social scientist. Probably few social scientists would align themselves with the position that human behavior is ultimately, totally determined. Certainly even those who accept the position intellectually deny it in their own behavior. They work hard to get ahead, they agonize over decisions among alternatives, they worry about and plan for the future.

Why do social scientists use a deterministic model of explanation, then? Mainly, we do it because *it works*. In practice, we find that a great deal of people's behavior (not to mention attitudes, beliefs, etc.) can be accounted for in terms of environmental forces and factors. However none of our explanations accounts for *all* behavior. Some of the sting of the deterministic model, then, is drawn off by our failure to account fully for behavior.

Similarly, it is clear that—even if determined—any given human behavior is the product of a very large number of factors. Your reading this chapter may have been determined by 237,576,887 different factors. Again, the enormous complexity of the causal model seems to reduce the threat posed by the deterministic view lying at the base of social science.

Finally, a word is in order regarding the concern about the implications of fully accepting the deterministic model as truth rather than as a convenient tool for scientific explanation. If you are concerned about how you might change if you accepted that view, just ask yourself: "*How would I change if I fully accepted as true the belief that I had no personal control over my thoughts and actions?*"

Maybe you'll find the answer by returning to the Rube Goldberg-like cartoon in Figure 2.2. Suppose that you are the nurse in the drawing. Why did you let go of your baby carriage? If you look back at the explanation on page 37, you'll recall that, ultimately, the nurse in the figure was the cause of the whole thing. The point is that, if you take the deterministic model totally seriously, you can still choose how to see your part in the system. You can experience yourself as the cause of it all *or* as its effect. Both experiences fit equally well with the facts; each is equally true. That's the heart of the joke that lies behind our unvoiced fears and unhappiness with the deterministic model of human behavior that is so essential to explanatory social research.

Science, then, is based on a deterministic model that contradicts our notions of free will. Despite that "rudeness," it provides a useful way of understanding human behavior. I want to conclude this chapter by cautioning you that scientists do not always pursue the model "scientifically."

SCIENCE IN THEORY AND PRACTICE

You will have seen by now that the scientific method has definite advantages over other methods of understanding, such as personal experience, tradition, and authority. Though it does not absolutely guarantee against error, it offers substantial safeguards.

PROTECTION AGAINST ERRORS

Above all else, scientific procedures call for consciousness and diligence in observation and anaylsis. Many of the errors we make in everyday life are due to sloppiness or inattentiveness. What color socks did your methods instructor wear at the last meeting of your class? What color did *you* wear, for that matter? In everyday life, we only semiconsciously observe what goes on around us. That's not bad, but it's important to realize that it produces questionable measurements.

A very simple value of science is that the scientist is expected to make observation a conscious activity. You say, "Now I will observe X," and you plan how best to make the measurements, determine what measuring instruments are appropriate, plan a schedule of observations, and consciously make and record your observations on schedule. Simply making observations conscious and deliberate is a powerful element in science but one that is often overlooked.

Consciousness by itself cannot guarantee success, however. Scientists make mistakes even when they are observing consciously and deliberately. Scientists make errors of logic in interpreting the results of their observations. Though the second pillar of science is "making sense" of what is observed, scientists sometimes make nonsense. When that happens, another safeguard of science sometimes intervenes: the scientist's colleagues. Science is organized as an open, public enterprise, and scientists are expected to share their research procedures and findings with one another, even those who have made mistakes they will later regret. Thus, scientists keep each other honest.

SCIENTISTS ARE HUMAN

Scientists—social as well as natural or physical scientists—are human beings, susceptible to the full range of human frailties. And those human frailties can get in the way of scientific research. A scientist may become attached to a particular research conclusion, for example. Imagine that a cure for cancer were named after you. How would you feel if a colleague published a paper arguing that your potion didn't cure cancer after all? Scientists often feel like that and sometimes act in accordance with their feelings.

Secondly, scientists have prejudices within their scientific disciplines. Some scientific viewpoints enjoy more favor than others at any given time, and papers presenting unfavorable points of view may wait a long time for publication. The holders of unpopular viewpoints may have trouble getting university appointments or research grants. In all these respects, scientists are similar to other humans.

On the other hand, the elements of science we have been examining in this chapter provide a counterbalance to the various human frailties. If scientists are not perfect, they are nonetheless supported by their training and by their colleagues in being better at inquiry than might otherwise be the case.

When all is said and done, scientists are like investigative detectives. Science is about finding the answers to questions. Although it is tempting to reduce scientific inquiry to a set of steps to be followed, there is no such recipe that does justice to this way of learning about the world. At the same time, there are certain procedures that separate science from other forms of inquiry. In the remainder of this book, we'll be looking at some of the logic and skills that support social scientists in coming to grips with human social behavior.

It is essential for you as a consumer of social research to be familiar with both the logical fundamentals and the specific techniques of social science. In the first place, such familiarity will make it easier for you to understand research reports and make use of their findings. And at the same time, you can guard against being misled by the mistakes that social scientists themselves sometimes make.

☑ CONSUMER'S CHECKLIST

The main purpose of this chapter has been to lay out the logical fundamentals of social science research to prepare you to read research reports. The points covered in the chapter also represent issues you should check out in evaluating any particular study.

- Has the researcher generalized from personal experiences that may not be typical of other people?
- Has the researcher relied on things traditionally believed true but never proven?
- Has the researcher relied on the pronouncements of authorities rather than on hard evidence? In particular, has an authority in one field been taken as authoritative in another?
- Has public opinion been treated as data or as a source of truth?
- Are you convinced that the researcher has observed accurately? What opportunities exist for errors to have been made?
- Has the researcher overgeneralized from relatively few observations? What evidence is there that the observations are broadly typical rather than isolated instances?
- Has the researcher been guilty of selective observation? Has a conclusion been reached and special attention paid to subsequent

observations that support the conclusion while contradictory observations have been ignored?

- Does the research report offer a sound, logical explanation for the findings discovered and the conclusions reached?
- Are the researcher's logical explanations backed up by empirical verification?
- Have the researcher's personal beliefs, philosophies, and morality intruded into the observations and explanations?
- What are the key variables under study by the researcher? What attributes compose each of those variables?
- Are the researcher's findings of general applicability or are they limited to a narrow portion of life?
- Has the researcher been specific in describing the details of the research procedures? Would it be possible for another researcher to replicate the study?
- How does the deterministic model of human behavior figure into the researcher's view of what is being studied? Does it get in your way as you read and respond to the research report?

KEY WORDS

Tradition	Empirical verification	Attribute
Authority	Empirical generalization	Generalization
Public opinion		Specificity
Overgeneralization		Intersubjectivity
Selective perception	Theory	Replication
Rational/empirical	Hypothesis	Determinism
Logico-empirical	Variable	

MAIN POINTS

1. Personal experience is a common source of our understanding of the world around us.
2. Many of the things we know about the world merely reflect tradition—things "everyone has always known."
3. Authorities—people with special expertise—also are a source of what we "know."

4. All of us are susceptible to the impact of public opinion: We tend to believe what everyone else around us believes.
5. Each of the above sources of understanding is susceptible to error. We can be misled by each.
6. Sometimes we simply observe things inaccurately.
7. Overgeneralization refers to reaching general conclusions on the basis of relatively few observations.
8. Selective perception means paying attention to things that confirm what we believe and ignoring things that contradict what we believe.
9. Science is based on the twin foundations of logical explanation and empirical observation. Science is sometimes described as rational/empirical or logico-empirical.
10. A theory is a system of logical explanation that links several elements into a meaningful whole.
11. A hypothesis is an expectation about the world that we derive from a theory.
12. Empirical verification refers to making observations to test the accuracy of a theory or a hypothesis.
13. Empirical generalizations are general patterns found among diverse observations.
14. Science deals with theories about the way things are rather than philosophies, moralities, or beliefs about the way things should be.
15. Social science discovers and explains regularities in social life.
16. A variable is a logical set of attributes. For example, sex is a variable comprising the attributes male and female.
17. Scientists are interested in the relationships among variables. People figure in as the carriers of these attributes.
18. Generalization is the quality of science wherein research findings apply to a large portion rather than a limited portion of life.
19. Specificity refers to the reporting of specific details making up a research project. The opposite of specificity is vagueness.
20. Intersubjectivity is the quality of scientific research wherein researchers with different points of view should arrive at the same conclusions. What is sometimes referred to as objectivity is really a matter of intersubjectivity.
21. Explanatory social science is based on a deterministic model of human behavior.
22. The deterministic model conflicts with our common belief in free will.
23. Scientists do not necessarily believe that people lack free will, but the scientific model they use makes that assumption.
24. The scientific method provides safeguards against errors in inquiry, but it is not foolproof. Scientists also make mistakes.

? REVIEW QUESTIONS

1. Look through the Letters to the Editor section of your local newspaper and find examples of errors of inquiry based on:
   a. Selection perception
   b. Overgeneralization
   c. Inaccurate observation
2. When Charles Darwin published his findings on natural selection and evolution, many objections were voiced by religious leaders. Discuss those objections in the light of what we've discussed in this chapter.
3. Make a list of ten things you "know" on the basis of tradition alone.
4. Make a list of ten things you "know" on the basis of authority.
5. Although science is based on openness to new ideas, scientists have often been very resistant to ideas that contradicted current scientific theories. Can you think of any such ideas that are rejected by scientists today?
6. For each of the following variables, suggest a set of attributes that could be used in measuring that variable.
   a. Political affiliation
   b. Prejudice
   c. Age
   d. Education
   e. Employment status
7. Find a newspaper report on a research study. What are the key variables discussed?
8. Recall "Fifty-nine Cents on the Dollar" (pp. 26–27). Make a list of all the factors that you think might account for the different incomes of men and women.
9. Think of some action you took today and describe the causal chain that would explain your action in a deterministic model.
10. Notice something happening around you today that puzzled you. Map out a research project that might result in your understanding it.

SUGGESTED READING

Babbie, Earl. *Survey Research Methods* (Belmont, Calif.: Wadsworth, 1973), Chapter 3. An application of the basic ideas developed in this chapter to the method of survey research. This short discussion should further clarify your understanding of the characteristics of science and social science as these appear in practice.

Campbell, Donald and Julian Stanley. *Experimental and Quasi-Experimental Designs for Research* (Chicago: Rand McNally, 1963). A somewhat different approach to the logic of social science than has been presented in this chapter. The authors begin with the logic of the controlled experiment and show how it is approximated in other social research designs.

Franklin, Billy and Harold Osborne (eds.). *Research Methods: Issues and Insights* (Belmont, Calif.: Wadsworth, 1971), Parts One and Two. An excellent collection of papers dealing with various aspects of social research. The selections in Parts One and Two provide a variety of stimulating perspectives on the general logic of social research, asking whether social science is "scientific," where it fits into our comprehensive understanding of people, and the links between theory and research in the social sciences.

Glazer, Myron. *The Research Adventure: Promise and Problems of Field Work* (New York: Random House, 1972). An informal biography of social research. I've included this book among the more technical and theoretical references to give you a flavor of what social inquiry is like in the flesh.

Wallace, Walter. *The Logic of Science in Sociology* (Chicago: Aldine-Atherton, 1971). An eminently readable overview of the logic connecting the several stages of social research. This remarkable little book leads you around the unending circle of observation to generalization to theory to hypothesis to observation and on and on.

RESEARCH DESIGN

INTRODUCTION

So far, I have been talking about social research as though there were one way of doing it. In fact, there are a great many ways social scientific inquiry is carried out.

We'll begin this chapter by looking at some of the different purposes that stimulate research. Sometimes, researchers are interested in only opening up an area of inquiry, sometimes the purpose is precise description, and sometimes it's explanation. We'll see examples of each purpose and examine the key elements to be evaluated in each.

Next, we'll look at the distinction between qualitative and quantitative research. Quantitative research—that dealing with numbers—reflects the traditional image of science, and most social scientific research is quantitative in nature. At the same time, numbers and complex statistical analyses are not necessary for a piece of research to be highly scientific and valuable.

Three of the key dimensions of variation in social research design concern "who" is studied, "when," and "what." We'll look at the "who" in terms of what researchers call the *unit of analysis*, the fundamental element that is observed, described, and manipulated analytically for the purpose of understanding it. Secondly, we'll see that it's possible to study social processes as they occur over time, but it's also possible to make observations at one point in time and still make inferences about processes. Finally, we'll see that social science addresses a wide variety of subjects and look at some examples of various research designs.

In all this, I have two aims of my own. On the one hand, I want to enable you to avoid being misled by defective research. There is no question that many published research conclusions should not be taken at face value. On the other hand, I want to build your appreciation for the tremendous value of social scientific research. Much research is first rate, and the potential for social scientists' contribution to the quality of life is great indeed. Without an informed and empowered audience, however, even good research is unlikely to have much impact. Thus, even if you never design and conduct studies of your own, you can become a full partner in the social scientific enterprise.

THE PURPOSES OF SOCIAL RESEARCH

One of the first things to ask yourself about a research report concerns the researcher's purpose. Research is undertaken for a wide variety of purposes. Political candidates, for example, may commission political polls to find out how they are doing in their races. Sometimes poll results are released for the purpose of swaying the electorate. Such an impact is called the **bandwagon effect,** implying that voters will want to get on the winning side.

The bandwagon effect is often used in product marketing research, also. During the 1980–81 professional football season, for example, the Schlitz Brewing Company sponsored several beer-preference studies, live on television, during the half-time period of major games. The first of these tests illustrates the design of all. The subjects for the study were 100 beer drinkers. All 100 had indicated they preferred Miller Hi-Life beer, and they were referred to as "loyal Miller drinkers." Each of the subjects was given two unmarked glasses of beer: One contained Miller, the other Schlitz. Each subject tasted the two beers and at a signal—live on national television—each threw a switch indicating his or her choice. In the first test, 50 subjects picked Miller and 50 picked Schlitz. As the announcer pointed out, fully 50 percent of the "loyal Miller drinkers" preferred Schlitz. In a later test measuring Schlitz against Budweiser, when the percentage picking Schlitz dropped to 37, viewers were still reminded that 37 percent of "loyal Budweiser drinkers" preferred Schlitz.

No matter how few subjects chose Schlitz, the implication of the results was that Schlitz tasted so good that even a large number of those loyal to another brand would have to admit Schlitz's superiority in a blind tasting. But consider another possibility: What would have happened in the experiments if all the beers examined tasted pretty much the same? Probably about half the subjects would have picked one and half the other in each experiment—whether the subjects reported normally drinking Miller, Budweiser, or even Schlitz, for that matter. (In fact, if you watched the TV presentations, you may have wondered why the researchers never tested a group of "loyal Schlitz drinkers.")

Quite obviously, this research was undertaken to sell more Schlitz; the research design was cleverly construed for that purpose. If the research purpose had been to find out which beers are most preferred by American beer drinkers, a different design would have been appropriate. A larger number of subjects would have been chosen with no reference to beer preference. Then, they would have sampled several different brands and indicated their preferences. If a large number of brands were to be compared, a system could be devised such that a given subject would compare only a few brands, and all the brand comparisons would be made by the group of subjects as a whole. The conclusion to be drawn from this research design would be that X percent preferred Schlitz, Y percent preferred Miller, and so forth.

If the purpose of the research had been to determine the extent to which beer drinkers who identify themselves with a particular brand can actually distinguish that brand from others, the original research design could have been augmented slightly. Each subject would have been asked what brand of beer he or she preferred. Those stated preferences could have been compared with the beers chosen in the course of the experiment. Research conclusions in this instance would have been something like "X percent of the loyal Schlitz drinkers chose another brand, Y percent of the loyal Budweiser drinkers did so, and so on."

The Schlitz half-time experiments highlight the importance of knowing the purpose of a research project—in advertising, this usually means who has sponsored the research. Now let's look at some of the research purposes that social scientists often have in designing studies.

EXPLORATION

Often, social research is undertaken for the purpose of **exploration**—opening a line of inquiry in a previously unresearched area. Such exploratory studies typically are small in scale, open-ended in design, and tentative in conclusion. Here's an example.

I'm sure you've heard about female college students having sex with their professors for the purpose of improving their grades. In one version of this story, the calculating coed is getting through school substituting sex for study, while the other version has an unscrupulous professor taking advantage of the students at his mercy. In recent years, the latter version has drawn a lot of attention in the context of the women's liberation movement. It's not surprising, therefore, that social scientists would turn their attention to the issue.

Dick Skeen (1981) provides a good example of an exploratory study of the issue of student-faculty sex. Here's how he began his research:

Through word of mouth, I found 38 informants, most of them graduate students and faculty members. They provided the names of 111 people they knew had been involved in at least one such affair recently. I picked as diverse a sample as I could from the initial roster and asked (usually through the informants) 31 people to participate in confidential, in-depth interviews structured around a list of open-ended questions. Of those, 25 agreed — 11 students and 14 professors.

Skeen's interviews yielded a very different pattern from the predominant stereotypes of student-faculty sexual affairs. Typically, he found the relationship originating in the faculty member's taking notice of a student because of her scholarly excellence. Out of this grew friendship, then dating, then sex, and, in two cases, marriage. In none of the 25 cases studied did Skeen find either faculty exploitation of students or students trading sexual favors for grades.

This is a good example of an exploratory study in that it yields insights contrary to what was previously assumed, and it points to directions of further research. It does not provide a definitive statement on the subject, so you should be careful not to conclude, on the basis of the information provided, that the traditional stereotypes of student-faculty sex are never or rarely found in reality. We do not know that the 25 students and faculty interviewed by Skeen are representative of all those who engage in student-faculty sex, either in the Denver area where the interviews were conducted, or in other regions of the country. Perhaps the interview situation led the subjects to "clean up" the facts. Nonetheless, Skeen's study has real value. It might very well be the first step in a series of studies getting ever closer to a definitive appraisal of the situation. Exploratory studies serve an important function within research.

DESCRIPTION

Another purpose of research is **description,** discovering the state of affairs in some area. A perfect example is the U.S. Census, mandated in the

Constitution to determine the number of citizens residing in the several states. The various public opinion polls—Gallup, Harris, Roper, and others—have a primary purpose of description. For example, a July 1954 Gallup Poll asked Americans for their attitudes toward admitting the People's Republic of China to the United Nations. Of those surveyed, 7 percent favored admission, 78 percent opposed it, and 15 percent were undecided. In May 1971, the description of that state of affairs was quite different. On the eve of the opening of U.S.-Chinese relations, 45 percent of those interviewed in a Gallup Poll favored admission, 38 percent were opposed, and 17 percent were undecided (see de Boer, 1980:270).

There are two keys to description as a research purpose: *measurement* and *sampling*. In the first instance, descriptions are only as good as the ways in which variables are defined and measured. For instance, economists and others are often interested in learning the current unemployment rate in the nation. As we saw in Chapter 1, the definitions of *labor force* and *unemployed* are specific and reasonably complex. Without specificity of definition and measurement, the conclusion that "8 percent are unemployed" would be meaningless. Changing the definitions would directly change the percentage of "unemployed."

Consider an even more ambiguous concept. What percentage of the U.S. population is happy? If we define *happy* as having smiled at least once, probably 100 percent would be judged happy. If we define it as smiling all the time, then the percentage probably would drop to zero. The descriptive statistics depend directly on the definition of what is described. Terms like *conservative, religious, alienated,* and so forth do not have specific, agreed-upon definitions that would warrant quantitative descriptions, so you should always be wary of statements such as "45 percent of the population are conservative." We'll return to this issue in Chapter 4.

Descriptive research also hangs importantly on the issue of sampling. We are seldom interested in knowing about the attitudes or circumstances of the particular people the researcher happened to study. But if research descriptions can be taken to reflect on a meaningful population—such as all American voters—that's a different matter. Whether research observations *can* be taken to reflect on meaningful populations depends on the manner in which those observed were chosen for observation. We'll examine this in some detail in Chapter 5.

EXPLANATION

A step beyond determining the percentage unemployed would involve a determination of the factors accounting for a person being out of work: education, age, sex, race, occupation, and the like. The purpose of such a study would be an **explanation** of why some people are employed and others unemployed. A descriptive study of voting intentions during the

1980 presidential campaign would have reported the percentages planning to vote for Reagan or for Carter. Explanatory studies would go a step further in explaining the reasons for the choices.

Let's look at another example in more detail. Paul Benson is a researcher interested in citizens' evaluations of the police, since public support or lack of support for the police is important to a society in many ways. To examine the issue, Benson undertook a telephone survey of St. Louis residents. One questionnaire item was used to determine respondents' assessments of the police: "Overall, how would you rate the police service in the two or three blocks around your home—outstanding, good, adequate, inadequate, or very poor?" (Benson 1981:52) Over 90 percent of the respondents answered "adequate" or better. This near-consensus notwithstanding, Benson was able to shed some light on why a minority had a dim view of the police's performance. Negative views were common among those who:

• doubted the honesty and integrity of police officers.
• saw crime rates as increasing in their neighborhoods.
• felt alienated from public officials in general.
• were lower class.
• were nonwhite.

Going beyond the relationships between these individual variables and assessments of the police, Benson examined combinations of effects. As a result, he suggests "that the distrust of nonwhites toward law enforcement officials may be ameliorated to some degree by a perception of police honesty and integrity." (1981:62)

Like descriptive studies, explanatory ones also involve issues of sampling and measurement, though less critically. As we'll see in Chapter 4, it is possible to discover the causes of something even when we can't agree on how to measure it. For instance, it is more reasonable to report the causes of conservatism than to specify the percentage of people who are "conservative." The explanatory purpose of research is illustrated in the Real World Research box entitled "Occupation and Wife Abuse."

Though somewhat less demanding in terms of sampling and measurement, explanatory research entails an additional consideration: degree of relationship. When we say that two variables are related to one another—age and conservatism, for example—we must also say how "strongly" they are related. If everyone over 50 was a Republican and everyone under 50 was a Democrat, we'd conclude there was a very strong relationship between age and political affiliation. If the percentages were 37 percent for those over 50 and 36 percent for those under 50, however, we'd conclude there was little or no difference. But where, between those extremes, does the relationship between the variables become "real," "strong," "important," and so on? Much of the discussion in Chapters 11 and 12 will deal with this knotty issue.

As you can see, social research can have a variety of purposes underlying it, and those purposes have important implications for what's critical in the research design and what isn't. In evaluating a research report, you should find out what purpose the researcher has in conducting and reporting the inquiry. Something that is quite logical given one purpose may not be excusable in another case.

All the examples we've been looking at so far have one thing in common: They involve **quantitative** (statistical) research. In my choice of examples, I have reflected the overall orientation of contemporary social scientific research. However, sometimes quantitative research is not appropriate.

QUALITATIVE VERSUS QUANTITATIVE RESEARCH

When Erving Goffman (1976) set out to discover the ways women are subordinated to men in American advertising, he found no need for quantitative measurements and statistical analyses. Instead, he brought together a large collection of advertising layouts and looked for different ways men were subtly and implicitly presented as superior. In some of the photos, for example, the men pictured were simply bigger than the women. In others, men were higher—a man standing and a woman sitting, for instance. Often, the men appeared in professional roles with the women as assistants (e.g., physician and nurse). These were but a few of the subordination formats discovered by Goffman. Goffman's study of "gender advertisements" provides an excellent example of **qualitative** research.

Anthropological field work is another form of social science research that is typically qualitative rather than quantitative. Colin Turnbull's examination of the Ik tribe living near the Kenya-Uganda border offers a powerful example. The creation of a national game reserve had destroyed the nomadic way of life traditional to the Ik. Encouraged to become farmers, the Ik tribesmen were given drought-ridden, unproductive land. As food became scarcer, as starvation drew nearer, social norms and ties began disintegrating. At the time Turnbull lived among the Ik, they had become isolated individuals lacking any sense of mutual support. They were, as Turnbull concluded and demonstrated in powerful first-hand accounts, a people who had given up society itself. Even family members seemed to care little for the well-being of one another, as brought home by Turnbull's story of little Adupa.

Her stomach grew more and more distended, and her legs and arms more spindly. Her madness was such that she did not know just how vicious hu-

OCCUPATION
AND WIFE ABUSE

Family violence is a topic of increasing concern for many Americans, particularly social workers and police. A large percentage of police calls involve marital discord, typically husbands abusing their wives. In each specific case, there are idiosyncratic reasons for the trouble, but Roger Petersen undertook an explanatory analysis to uncover some of the general reasons for wife abuse.

Petersen suggests there are two major explanations for wife abuse. On the one hand, it is argued that the pervasive sexism in American society is the root cause. The marriage contract is regarded as a "hitting license" in the norms of American society, according to this view. At the same time, others argue that wife abuse is more a function of unemployment, poverty, and other stresses. According to the latter view, the stress associated with economic problems produces frustration, and that frustration results in violence. If there is any truth to this explanation, we would expect to find wife abuse more common among people lower in economic status. In a partial test of this explanation, Petersen examined the frequency of abuse among a sample of 602 married women in Maryland, categorized according to their husbands' occupations.

In general, the table indicates wife abuse is more common at the lower rungs of the social ladder than near the top. This table does not present a complete analysis or explanation for wife abuse; it is only a part of Petersen's examination. Employment stability, home ownership, and other relevant variables were also ex-

---

mans could be, particularly her playmates. She was older than they, and more tolerant. That too was a madness in an Icien world. Even worse, she thought that parents were for loving, for giving as well as receiving. Her parents were not given to fantasies, and they had two other children, a boy and a girl who were perfectly normal, so they ignored Adupa, except when she brought them food she had scrounged from somewhere. They snatched that quickly enough. But when she came for shelter they drove her out, and when she came because she was hungry they laughed. . . . (*1972:131*)

As with Goffman, Turnbull's qualitative format for research and presentation were perfectly suited to the subject matter. No numbers could communicate as effectively the destruction of social bonds among the Ik.

There is a place for both quantitative and qualitative research in social science. Ideally, the two can be brought to bear simultaneously on the

Husband's occupation	Percentage abused	Number in category
Professional, technical	6%	(117)
Management, administration	4	(82)
Sales, sales managers	3	(41)
Clerical	6	(16)
Craftsmen	7	(101)
Semiskilled workers	15	(27)
Transport-equipment workers	18	(22)
Laborers	20	(35)
Service workers	19	(16)
Self-employed	16	(32)
Police, military	9	(23)

amined, with results pointing in the same direction. Moreover, the frustration of economic problems is only a part of the story. As Petersen shows, wife abuse is a response to frustration that is learned: Those who witness wife abuse as children are more likely to practice it as adults.

Petersen's analysis is a good illustration of the explanatory purpose of social research.

SOURCE   Roger Petersen, "Social Class, Social Learning, and Wife Abuse." *Social Service Review*, September 1980: 390–406. Table is adapted from author's Table 4 on p. 398. Copyright 1980 by the University of Chicago Press. Reprinted by permission of the publisher.

same topic. Each orientation has its particular strengths and weaknesses. We shall return to this topic in Chapter 8 on field research—a largely qualitative enterprise. At this point, I want to draw your attention to one fundamental distinction between the two orientations, to assist you in appraising the value of particular qualitative or quantitative research reports.

Quantitative research requires more specificity than qualitative research. Thus, for example, Turnbull could conclude that the Ik lacked compassion for one another and illustrate the point profoundly and powerfully. To quantify the observation, it would be necessary to specify the concrete actions that represented a lack of compassion. Then a researcher could look for and count actions fitting the definition. We might decide, for example, that giving someone else food constitutes an act of compassion, whereas refusing food to someone who asked for it would be an act lacking compassion. This format might allow us to determine and report that 76 percent of the observed actions lacked compassion. We might also report that women were compassionate in 38 percent of their actions, compared to 21 percent for men.

Very often, the specificity required for quantification seems to drain much of the life out of what is being studied. Quantification often seems to produce superficial measures. At the same time, however, unspecified qualitative measurements hang heavily on subjective interpretation and individual judgment. Can we be sure, for example, that you and I would have agreed with Turnbull that Adupa was more tolerant than her playmates? Perhaps his idea of tolerance differs from yours or mine. The relative strengths and weaknesses of qualitative and quantitative research methods represent a two-edged sword that will follow us through this book.

UNITS OF ANALYSIS

One of the first questions you should ask in examining a research report is: Who or what is it talking about? In most social research reports, individual humans are the focus of the investigation, but that's not necessarily always the case; sometimes families, cities, corporations, or innumerable other subjects are the focus.

Social researchers use the term **unit of analysis** to refer to who or what is the basic element being analyzed. When a political pollster reports that "73 percent of the voters say they will vote," the researcher has presumably examined a number of voters (say, 1000), asking each if he or she will vote. Each voter was then classified as "planning to vote" or "not planning to vote," and the number planning to vote (say, 730) was divided by the total studied in order to calculate the percentage planning to vote. In this example, the individual voter was the unit classified in terms of voting plans and counted in reference to that classification for the purpose of arriving at the research conclusion. Thus, in this example, the individual voter was the unit of analysis.

The unit of analysis is not always immediately apparent. Consider these three hypothetical research conclusions drawn from a survey of families in a city:

1. Thirty percent of the heads of families are college graduates.
2. Twenty-six percent of the children live in families headed by college graduates.
3. Thirty-two percent of the families contained at least one college graduate.

In (1) above, the unit of analysis is the individual (family head). Suppose 1000 families were surveyed in the study, providing data on 1000 heads of families. If 300 of those family heads were college graduates, we'd arrive at the conclusion reported. In (2), individuals are again the units of analysis—this time children. Let's say there are 1900 children living in the 1000 families surveyed. For each child, we'd ask whether the person heading that child's family was a college graduate. If that were so for 494 of the children, then we'd report the conclusion shown. Finally, in (3), families are the units of analysis. In each of the 1000 families, we would look at the educational levels of all family members to see if any were college graduates. Presumably, 320 families turned up a college-educated member.

Here are some examples from real research reports. See if you can determine the unit of analysis in each.

- ... women watch TV more than men because they are likely to work fewer hours outside the home than men. ... Black people watch an average of approximately three-quarters of an hour more television per day than white people.
  (*Hughes, 1980:290*) [individuals]
- Of the 130 incorporated U.S. cities with more than 100,000 inhabitants in 1960, 126 had at least two short-term nonproprietary general hospitals accredited by the American Hospital Association.
  (*Turk, 1980:317*) [cities]
- The early TM organizations were small and informal. The Los Angeles group, begun in June 1959, met at a member's house where, incidentally, Maharishi was living.
  (*Johnston, 1980:337*) [groups, organizations]
- However, it appears that the nursing staffs exercise strong influence over ... a decision to change the nursing care system. ... Conversely, among those decisions dominated by the administration and the medical staffs. ...
  (*Comstock, 1980:77*) [groups]
- In 1958, there were 13 establishments with 1,000 employees or more, accounting for 60 percent of the industry's value added. In 1977, the number of this type of establishment dropped to 11, but their share of industry value added had fallen to about 48 percent.
  (*York and Persigehl, 1981:41*) [companies]
- Though 667,000 out of 2 million farmers in the United States are women, women historically have not been viewed as farmers, but rather, as the farmer's wife.
  (*Votaw, 1979:8*) [individuals]

In conducting social research, it is essential that you recognize the unit of analysis appropriate to your inquiry. As a consumer of research, you must know who or what the researcher is drawing conclusions about to understand and evaluate research reports.

THE ECOLOGICAL FALLACY

The significance of the unit of analysis extends to the thrust of the research. Sometimes studies are done using one unit of analysis, and conclusions are drawn about other units of analysis. In a classic statement of what is called the **ecological fallacy,** W. S. Robinson (1950) pointed out that certain correlations found to exist at the group level might not apply at the level of individuals; the fallacy lies in assuming that group patterns necessarily reflect comparable patterns in individuals.

For example, in Chapter 9 we are going to look at a classic study of suicide by Emile Durkheim, the great French sociologist. Durkheim found that nations and regions with predominantly Catholic populations had lower suicide rates than those with predominantly Protestant populations and concluded that Catholics were less likely to commit suicide than Protestants. As Robinson pointed out, however, it is possible that the people committing suicide in those Protestant countries were Catholics. By the same token, if we were to discover that cities with large Albanian populations had high crime rates, that would not necessarily mean that the Albanians were committing the crimes. In Chapter 9, we'll see some of the ways of avoiding the ecological fallacy in the analysis of group data. For now, the point is the importance of knowing the unit of analysis in a study.

THE TIME DIMENSION

Time is another critical variable in research design. Some studies are oriented primarily toward describing the state of affairs at one point in time; others aim at explaining processes that occur over time. Appropriately, some study designs involve making observations and measurements at one point in time, while others involve observations made more than once. As we'll see, the correspondence between purpose and design is not perfect.

CROSS-SECTIONAL STUDIES

Studies that have one-time description as their purpose are usually referred to as **cross-sectional studies.** We've already seen examples of this in earlier discussions—Goffman's examination of gender advertisements, for example. Censuses and public opinion polls provide descriptions of states of affairs at particular points in time.

When Bruce Hackett and Seymour Schwartz (1980) visited rural communes in America, their purpose was to describe whether and how such alternative lifestyles handled the issue of energy conservation. It was a cross-sectional study, documenting the present state of affairs. When John Viga (1981) wanted to find out about mobility among business executives, he conducted a cross-sectional survey of executives and asked them questions about their mobility. When W. Doyle Gentry and colleagues (1981) wanted to find out the national status of medical psychology, a cross-sectional study of psychology programs was the appropriate vehicle.

Cross-sectional studies are by far the most common in social research, though they have the disadvantage of capturing only a "snapshot" of the process of social life. Most of the things we are interested in learning about take place over time, however. Let's turn now to some of the research designs aimed specifically at gathering information about changes over time, known collectively as **longitudinal studies.**

TREND STUDIES

Polls and censuses also offer examples of studies of processes over time. By comparing cross-sectional snapshots, we can observe trends over time; such studies are called **trend studies.** For example, Tom Smith reviewed 125 Gallup Polls between 1946 and 1976 to discover trends in attitudes toward "America's most important problem."

Remarkable shifts have occurred in the ranking of problems over the last four decades. At the end of World War II concerns dealing with reconversion to a peacetime economy, shortages, the termination of price controls, the lingering fears of a return of the Great Depression combined to make economics the dominant problem. As the Cold War heated up in 1947 and 1948, however, more and more attention shifted to foreign affairs. This trend was briefly broken in 1949, when the passing of the immediate postwar crises and the onset of America's first postwar recession swung concern back to economics. (Smith, 1980:166)

These are the kinds of observations available from the vantage point of a trend study. Going beyond gross variations, Smith was able to look at and compare opinion trends among men versus women; among blacks versus whites; among young, middle-aged, and older groups; in different regions of the country; and so forth. Such comparisons, moreover, allowed Smith to speculate intelligently about the reasons for opinion shifts.

To take another example, Howard Bahr (1980) was interested in learning about changes in family life in middle America during this century. This interest was facilitated by several classic sociological studies of Muncie, Indiana (called "Middletown" in the studies) by Robert and Helen Lynd (1929, 1937). In 1924, the Lynds conducted two surveys of high school students. In 1977, Bahr surveyed Muncie high school students, asking many of the same questions asked fifty years earlier. Many differences appeared in the generational comparison. In 1924, for example, 32 percent of the boys and 68 percent of the girls cited their parents as their chief source of sex education. In 1977, the respective percentages had decreased to 18 and 35. Asked to cite two qualities most desirable in a mother, 57 percent of the 1924 boys and 52 percent of the girls said she should be "a good cook and housekeeper." The impact of the women's movement was evident in the 1977 survey, as the percentages giving ths answer had decreased to 41 percent for the boys and 24 percent for the girls.

PANEL STUDIES

Whereas trend studies are based on comparisons of populations or subpopulations at different particular points in time, **panel studies** follow the same individuals (the *panel*) through experiences over time. There's a special strength to this form of study design. Here's an example.

One of the lessons of political polling has been that many voters make up their minds before the beginning of a presidential campaign, which raises questions about the impact of candidate campaigning. This conclusion is supported by trend studies of voting intentions over the course of campaigns. Although there are shifts over time, stability is usually the most apparent characteristic. Thus, it appears that few voters change their minds over the course of the campaign.

Steven Chaffee and Sun Yuel Choe (1980) challenged the view that most voters make their minds up in advance by following a panel of Wisconsin voters over the course of the Carter-Ford campaign of 1976. The panel study revealed something the trend studies missed: Carter-to-Ford and Ford-to-Carter switches cancelled each other out in the aggregated figures, thus making overall intentions appear more stable than they were. In fact, only 29 percent of the panel could be characterized as "precampaign deciders."

Most experiments (see Chapter 7) are panel studies. Experimental subjects are observed at the start of the study, they are exposed to an experimental stimulus (something expected to change them), and then they are observed again. In this way, it is possible to observe the changes that occur for specific individuals.

Though panel studies are, in many ways, superior vehicles for studying the kinds of processes that interest social scientists, they are, except for experiments, less common than you would imagine. This is true because of a variety of logistical considerations. Panel studies, requiring several waves of data collection, cost more money and take longer. Subjects must be persuaded to cooperate more than once. Panel members dropping out during the course of the study—called **panel attrition**—presents a complication in the analysis of data and the generalizability of the study findings, since those who remain in the study may not be typical.

INFERRING CHANGE FROM CROSS-SECTIONAL STUDIES

Although social processes are most logically studied through longitudinal studies, it is sometimes possible to make reasonable inferences about changes over time on the basis of data collected at only one time. Quite often people of different ages are compared for the purpose of inferring changes that occur over the course of the life cycle. For example, when old people are found to be politically more conservative than young people, it is concluded that people get more conservative as they grow older. Similarly, old people have been found consistently more religious than young people, hence the conclusion that people tend to get more religious as they age. The attitudes of freshmen might be compared with those of seniors for the purpose of inferring the attitudinal effects of the college experience. New and old employees in a corporation might be compared for the purpose of inferring the effects of working there.

The advantages of inferring change from cross-sectional studies rather than conducting longitudinal ones are obvious. Each of the examples I have given involves processes taking place over the course of years, even lifetimes. I suspect the disadvantages will also be pretty obvious to you. Whenever processes are inferred from cross-sectional differences, it is usually possible to think of other explanations that could have produced the observed differences. If college seniors are found to be more intellectually sophisticated than freshmen, for example, that difference may not reflect the effects of college. Perhaps admissions standards have been lowered in recent years, producing a less sophisticated freshman class. The seniors may, in fact, be no more sophisticated than when they entered as freshmen, and the new freshmen may not change during their college years, either.

Whenever a researcher draws a conclusion about processes over time on the basis of cross-sectional data, you should regard the conclusion with caution. I am not saying you should discount such conclusions, only that you should take time to ask yourself what else might account for the differences observed. This issue is illustrated in the Real World Research box entitled "Television and Trust in Government."

WHAT CAN BE STUDIED?

Given that individual people are the most frequent units of analysis for social research, there are a great many things that can be studied about

TELEVISION AND
TRUST IN GOVERNMENT

We've seen examples of researchers inferring changes over time from cross-sectional studies. As a more general matter, all explanatory conclusions drawn from cross-sectional data involve inferences of process. To take only one recent example, David Berman and John Stookey (1980) have discovered that the more television adolescents watch, the more negative their feelings about local, state, and federal government. Focusing more closely into the relationship, Berman and Stookey found police shows and the news were the primary source of television's impact. Think about it for a minute, and you'll see that these observations make sense. However, Berman and Stookey's assumption—that a process occurs over time in which people watch TV and that it has a subsequent impact on their attitudes toward government—is based on data from one point in time.

Berman and Stookey point out that the causal order in this instance is unclear. Their suspicion, in fact, is that news telecasts probably influence adolescents' attitudes toward government, and those attitudes in turn will affect the kind of entertainment shows they select, including police shows. This illustrates a fundamental issue whenever longitudinal processes are inferred from cross-sectional data.

SOURCE David Berman and John Stookey, "Adolescents, Television, and Support for Government." *Public Opinion Quarterly*, Fall 1980:330–340.

people, as previous examples have illustrated. First, researchers often examine such "objective" characteristics as sex, age, employment status, education, and so forth. They also study people's beliefs, attitudes, and general orientations (such as prejudice, conservatism, etc.). Behavior is often studied, either directly or by asking people to report on it.

Relationships are another unit of analysis in social research: mother-son pairs, marriages, doctor-patient relationships, and the like. Each of these can be examined in various aspects. Marriages, for example, can be studied in terms of how old they are, whether they are religiously or racially mixed, whether created in religious or civil ceremonies, and so forth.

A wide variety of characteristics can be studied when groups, organizations, and whole societies are the units of analysis. As one illustration, here are the characteristics that the Population Reference Bureau (1980) reports for all the nations of the world:

Population
Birth rate
Death rate
Rate of natural increase
Number of years to double population
Population projected for 2000
Infant mortality rate
Total fertility rate
Population under age 15 (%)
Population over age 64 (%)
Life expectancy at birth
Urban population (%)
Projected ultimate population size
Per capita gross national product

"Who," "when," and "what" are critical elements in the design of research. In the chapters to come, we'll examine some of the other elements more fully.

EXAMPLES OF VARIATIONS IN RESEARCH DESIGN

I want to conclude this chapter with examples of diverse social science research designs to insure that you have a broad appreciation of the wealth of possibilities available for understanding the nature of our social life. To do this, let's take a look at the February 1981 issue of the *American Sociological Review*.

FIRING CORPORATION EXECUTIVES

Capitalism is an economic system based on property interests. As Karl Marx and others have pointed out, the concentration of property control has important implications for the whole society—especially for its social class system. If a relatively few people control the means of production and act strictly on the basis of their own economic interests, the tendency is for "the rich to get richer and the poor to get poorer."

The modern corporation has provided an interesting contrast to the Marxist view. In particular, incorporation has typically resulted in a separation of ownership from control. The corporate officers—those in charge of the day-to-day operations—usually own only a small fraction of the corporate stock. As John Kenneth Galbraith has written, "The decisive power in modern society is exercised not by capital but by organization, not by the capitalist but by the industrial bureaucrat" (1971:xvii). Does this mean that profit has been replaced by something else as the main thrust of American corporations?

David James and Michael Soref (1981) wanted to find out. To do so, they decided to examine the 300 largest industrial corporations in America, in terms of 1964 sales. They then reviewed business media to learn which of the 300 firms had fired their chief officers during 1965. But how would you do that?

James and Soref began by checking the listings of chairmen, presidents, and chief executive officers of the 300 corporations. Comparing the 1965 and 1966 editions of *Moody's Industrial Manual*, they were able to determine that 110 corporations had had a change in leadership. But which executives were *fired*? To answer this next question, the researchers researched business periodicals such as the *Wall Street Journal, Fortune*, and the like. Some of the executives in question had retired, some had resigned to take other positions, and so forth.

Having determined which corporations fired their executives, James and Soref were able to look for factors related to such firings. After a complex, statistical analysis weighing several different explanatory models, they concluded that those corporations that failed to produce profits were the most likely to dismiss the people presumably responsible. In other words, profits were still a chief determinant of corporate policy.

MODERNIZATION AND POLITICAL CHANGE

Michael Hannan and Glenn Carroll begin their report on modernization and political change with the following timely observation:

> Competitive national politics have not thrived in the postwar period. The number of countries with multiparty politics has declined while the number of one-party and military regimes has risen each year. (1981:19)

Such changes of political systems in far-off lands affect us all, so the issue addressed by Hannan and Carroll is of vital interest. It has been widely assumed in the West that, as developing nations modernize economically, they are likely to develop Western, multiparty political systems. The authors set out to find out if the assumption was true.

Nations were the units of analysis for this study. Of the 140 nations in existence in 1950, the researchers were able to get full information on 90 of them, so the study focused on those 90 nations. Political changes occurring between 1950 and 1975 were the key variable under study. For purposes of this research, four political systems were considered: (1) nations with no political parties (e.g., Libya, Jordan); (2) military regimes (e.g. Ghana, Ethiopia); (3) one-party states (e.g., China, U.S.S.R.); and (4) multi-party states (e.g., U.S.A., England). A nation was judged to have changed its political system if it moved from one of these forms to another or from colonial status to one of the four forms.

The shifts were measured and analyzed in two ways. With nations as the units of analysis, the authors sought to account for differences between 1950 and 1975 political systems. The authors also analyzed "transition sequences" as the unit of analysis, looking into the patterns of political shifts occurring during the 25-year period. The African state of Benin, for example, moved from colonial status to a one-party state to a military regime to one-party to military to one-party to military to one-party to military to one-party status. This change in unit of analysis proved important, since the study of transition sequences yielded somewhat different conclusions than the study of nations. For instance, "Countries with high per capita GNPs are less likely to change political forms, whatever the form" (Hannan and Carroll, 1981:30). The researchers ultimately concluded that the conventional view regarding economic and political development seems essentially correct.

SOCIAL CLASS AND CRIME

One of the generally accepted conclusions in the social scientific study of crime is that criminal behavior is more typical of the lower class than of the middle or upper classes. A great many explanations make sense of this observed relationship. However, recent journal articles have called that conclusion into question. John Braithwaite (1981) set out to settle the issue. Whereas most examinations of the relationship between social class and crime have individuals as the unit of analysis, Braithwaite took as his units of analysis the previous studies.

Braithwaite found that, of 53 studies of social class and juvenile crime, "44 showed lower class juveniles to have substantially higher offense rates than middle class juveniles" (1981:38). Of 46 studies of adult crime and social class, all showed higher rates for lower-class subjects. Other studies measured social class in terms of the areas in which people lived, regardless of their own social class. In 57 studies of juveniles and 13 studies of adults, all showed higher crime rates for residents of lower-class areas. The weight of evidence, then, suggests that the traditional conclusion was sound.

Braithwaite's analysis also sheds light on the recent challenges to the traditional conclusion. Specifically, when the measure of criminal behavior is based on self-reports of crime rather than on official records, the relationship between crime and class becomes cloudier.

LABELING MENTAL RETARDATION BY IQ

As I mentioned in Chapter 1, IQ measures have generated a great deal of controversy. People debate what they mean and what they don't mean. Richard Berk, William Bridges, and Anthony Shih (1981) begin their analysis with a novel question: So what? For all the debating over IQs, does the measure ever affect people's lives significantly?

As it turns out, the researchers found one area where IQ tests matter heavily: the placement of students in classes for the educable mentally handicapped. This conclusion was based on a study of a sample of 6292 students sent to school counseling personnel for testing. The researchers examined the various data compiled on each student and determined that IQ test results weighed heavily in the class placement recommendations made by the counselors.

THE 1890 GHOST DANCE

During the late 1800s, a religious movement called the Ghost Dance arose among many American Indian tribes. Following a period during which the native Americans had been widely dispossessed by the westward-expanding whites, the movement focused on a belief in a time when the buffalo would return to the prairies and the Indians, led by their heroic ancestors, would regain control over their lands. The Ghost Dance has been immortalized in sociology and anthropology as an example of what is called a *revitalization movement.*

Russell Thornton recently set out to discover what factors determined whether or not particular tribes participated in the Ghost Dance. His first decision involved the definition of a tribe. This was complicated by the fact that American Indian tribes have been artificially divided and combined by the U.S. government over the years. For the purpose of continuity in his research, Thornton fairly closely followed the tribal identifications used by earlier researchers studying the Ghost Dance. Historical records were also used to determine which tribes had participated in the movement. Of the 70 tribes studied, 45 had participated and 25 hadn't.

Tribes, then, were the unit of analysis in this study. They were characterized by a number of variables potentially relevant to their participation in the Ghost Dance movement. Among other things, Thornton found that small tribes were much more likely to participate than large ones. Those who had experienced a loss of population between 1870 and 1890 were especially likely to participate, and those with the greatest loss were the most likely. Also, the recentness of first contact with European settlers was influential: Participation in the Ghost Dance was more typical of those tribes with recent contacts. Of the 13 large tribes whose initial contacts with European settlers had predated 1700, for example, none joined in the Ghost Dance.

Though historical in content, this study touches on a subject of current relevance. Revivalist movements are common in developing nations around the world. Thornton's analysis begins to uncover some of the factors that interact with one another in producing revivalist participation.

These few research reports, along with the many examples presented throughout the chapter, should give you an appreciation for the range of possibilities available in the design of social research. We will never really leave the topic of research design in this book, since all the topics to be taken up in subsequent chapters can be seen as issues of design.

✓ CONSUMER'S CHECKLIST

When you first start reading a research report, you should orient yourself by noting some basic features of the study design and its purposes. Here are some questions you might ask.

- Who conducted the research? Who paid for it? What motivated the study?
- What is the purpose of the study: exploration of a topic, precise description, explanation, or what? (Note: many studies represent a combination of these purposes.)
- What is the unit of analysis? (Note: some studies utilize more than one unit of analysis, and it's important to be aware of what is being analyzed at each step.)
- Do the questions addressed by the researcher relate to a single point in time or reflect a process occurring over time? Have data been collected appropriate to this? Are cross-sectional observations being used to infer longitudinal processes?
- If longitudinal data have been collected, are they comparable across the different points in time? Have members of a panel dropped out during the course of the study, for example? Have comparable sampling methods been used and comparable measurements been made at the different points in a trend study?
- Overall, is the study design chosen the most appropriate for the questions raised? If not, do the shortcomings invalidate the conclusions reached?

KEY WORDS

Bandwagon effect	Qualitative research	Longitudinal studies
Exploration	Unit of analysis	Trend studies
Description	Ecological fallacy	Panel studies
Explanation	Cross-sectional stud-	Panel attrition
Quantitative re-	ies	
search		

MAIN POINTS

1. The purpose of a research project is sometimes a reflection of its spon-sor's interests.
2. Exploration—gaining some initial information and insights into a topic—is a common purpose of social research.
3. Some research has the primary purpose of description: discovering and documenting the state of things.
4. Explanation goes a step beyond description to find the reasons things are the way they are.
5. The discovery of relationships among variables is the basis for explana-tion.
6. Quantitative research methods involve the creation and manipulation of numerical data and sometimes complex statistical analyses.
7. Qualitative research methods are nonnumerical—for example, observ-ing a social event and then detailing what happened and perhaps suggesting why.
8. The unit of analysis in a research project is that unit about which data are collected and manipulated and about which conclusions are drawn. Individuals are usually, though not always, the units of analy-sis in social research.
9. The ecological fallacy is the mistaken assumption that relationships discovered at the group level are necessarily true at the individual level.
10. Cross-sectional studies collect data at one point in time.
11. Longitudinal studies collect data at more than one point in time.
12. Trend studies examine changes in some population over time.
13. Panel studies collect data from the same subjects at different points in time.
14. Panel attrition refers to subjects dropping out of a panel study before it's complete.

15. Sometimes it's possible to infer changes over time from the analysis of cross-sectional data.
16. In the study of individuals, social scientists can examine beliefs, attitudes, general orientations, "objective" characteristics, and behaviors.

? REVIEW QUESTIONS

1. Design an experiment that would objectively determine what kind of cola drink people prefer.
2. When Candidate X's campaign team releases poll results indicating that the voters favor Candidate X, we tend to question the validity of the results. What information would you want to know in order to assure yourself that the results are valid.
3. If a research report concludes that "56 percent of the students at State University are politically conservative," what information would you want in order to evaluate that conclusion?
4. Suppose a researcher has used qualitative methods to study unemployment in a society. Discuss the inherent limitations of that study.
5. Review the discussion of Goffman's study of gender advertising (p. 55). Describe some of the ways quantitative methods could have been brought to bear on the topic.
6. Review the list of six examples of research statements illustrating different units of analysis (p. 59). Rewrite each statement so as to represent a different unit of analysis. (Note: you will have to make up data in the new statements.)
7. Make up a research example that would illustrate the ecological fallacy.
8. Look through your local newspaper and find a report of a cross-sectional study and one of a longitudinal study.
9. Suppose that a researcher wanted to find out if continuing membership in a particular labor union makes workers increasingly liberal. How could that be tested through the analysis of cross-sectional data?
10. List ten variables that might be measured in a study of families.

SUGGESTED READING

Bart, Pauline and Linda Frankel. *The Student Sociologist's Handbook* (Morristown, N.J.: General Learning Press, 1976). A handy little reference book to assist you in getting started on a research project.

Written from the standpoint of a student term paper, this volume is a particularly good guide to the periodical literature of the social sciences that's in your campus library.

Hammond, Phillip (ed.). *Sociologists at Work* (New York: Basic Books, 1964). A collection of candid research biographies written by several eminent social science researchers, discussing the studies that made them eminent. A variety of research motivations and designs are illustrated in these honest reports of how the research actually came about and unfolded. Take two chapters every four hours to relieve the discomfort of believing that social seience research is routine and dull.

Miller, Delbert. *Handbook of Research Design and Social Measurement* (New York: David McKay, 1977). A useful reference book for introducing or reviewing numerous issues involved in design and measurement. The book also contains a wealth of practical information relating to foundations, journals, and professional associations.

Stouffer, Samuel. *Social Research to Test Ideas* (New York: Free Press of Glencoe, 1962). A stimulating and inspirational posthumous collection of research articles by one of the giants of social research. In these reports, you will see how an ingenious man formulates an idea, designs the perfect study for testing it, is prevented from conducting the study, and then devises another feasible method for testing the same idea. Especially enlightening are Paul Lazarsfeld's introduction and Chapter 6, in which Stouffer reports on the effects of the Great Depression on the family.

MEASUREMENT

INTRODUCTION

As I've indicated earlier, the dual foundations of scientific research are observation and explanation. In science, observation typically takes the form of **measurement.** In this context, measurement is an operation resulting in standardized classifications of the attributes of whatever is being observed. When a physicist "observes" the weight of an object, for example, the resulting measurement is, say, "20 grams." In this case, measurement is the operations the physicist undertook in order to arrive at that representation: placing the object on a scale and noting the weight indicated. When a psychologist "observes" a person's IQ, the measurement operation involves the administration of an IQ test, as discussed in Chapter 1.

In this chapter, we're going to examine the various ways in which social scientists make measurements. As I indicated earlier, the ways measurements are made are inseparable from the conclusions drawn from those measurements. When you read that the unemployment rate for a city is 10 percent, that number is meaningless unless you know how people were characterized as employed or unemployed, or even omitted from the measurement altogether. Does the unemployment rate reflect people who are retired, for example, or people who are too sick to work, high school students, or housewives? This chapter will deal with all the decisions that must be made in the process of scientific measurement.

We'll begin with the relationships connecting and distinguishing observations, concepts, and definitions, and we'll see the role played by definitions. With this foundation, we'll examine two key processes: *conceptualization* and *operationalization.*

Several levels of measurement are made by scientists. Recall the Chapter 1 discussion of variables. The different levels of measurements concern what distinguishes the attributes making up a variable. Sometimes the attributes are simply different ("male" and "female"), and sometimes one attribute is "more" than another ("college graduate" represents more education than "high school graduate"). As we'll see, there are other relationships among attributes as well.

The levels of measurement are important to your assessment of research conclusions, and I'll discuss that. Then we'll look at some of the other ways to evaluate the quality of measurements. Finally, we'll briefly examine some of the more complex measurements that social scientists often use: indexes, scales, and typologies.

CONCEPTS, TERMS, AND DEFINITIONS

As we have noted, *observation* is a general term for the act of noticing or perceiving things. But where observation is pretty much an automatic and unconscious act in ordinary life, it is conscious and deliberate in science. And where people often make mistakes in everyday observations, there are special guards against error in scientific observation.

CONCEPTS

Although it seems possible to "just observe," all observations actually depend on and reflect **concepts:** mental images that organize, summarize, and classify what is observed. Take the concept *social class,* for example. Listen to these varied uses of the notion:

Researchers have issued a health warning for the wealthy — the upper-class lifestyle may make some of them more susceptible to cancer.

A report in the current Journal of the American Medical Association shows a higher incidence of cancer of the pancreas among people of the upper socio-economic bracket. (*San Francisco Chronicle,* January 9, 1981)

No democracy in the world can eliminate the class struggle and the omnipotence of money. It is not this that makes democracy important and useful. The importance of democracy is that it makes the class struggle broad, open and conscious. (*Lenin, 1912:47*)

One of the characteristics of modern urban-industrial society is the creation of a segment of the lower class sometimes referred to as the "welfare class." . . . Government welfare programs, such as Aid to Families with Dependent Children (AFDC), serve as the basic income maintenance program for this segment of the population. (*Weed, 1980:151*)

Regardless of the subjective attitude of one or another class or social stratum, production has always exerted a determinative influence on all other fields of endeavour. Economic relations based on the position of a class or group vis a vis the means of production and its results have always been the substructure of the entire system of social relations, their "driving axle." (*Medvedev, 1981:48–49*)

Since middle class children have higher aspirations for success, it may be that middle class school failures suffer from a greater discrepancy between aspirations and expectations of occupational success. And it has been shown that children with a great discrepancy between aspirations and expectations are more likely than others to engage in delinquency. . . . (*Braithwaite, 1981:50*)

TERMS

These varied examples suggest a broadly shared belief in the reality of social class. It is important to realize, in the case of such apparent consensus, that *social class* is nothing more than a **term** or name used to represent a concept that many people have created in their minds. In a very important sense, social class does not really exist. You can't touch it or hear it or say what color it is. Social class doesn't weigh anything. It is only a pair of words chosen to represent an idea.

Since the beginning of social affairs, people have noticed the inequalities that characterize our relationships with one another. Some people are stronger than others and dominate them on that basis. In other regards, some people are wealthier than others, possess higher political authority, command larger armies, or seem to stand one above the other in countless ways. We have noticed, moreover, that social inequalities are not limited to individuals but characterize relations among groups or types of people. Landowners have exercised power over their tenants, factory owners over workers, white planters over black slaves, and so forth. As a result of such observations, the general term *social class* was coined as a convenient reference to such social inequalities in general.

Concepts such as *social class* have a convenience value, then. Having one term to represent a variety of concrete observations obviously simplifies communication. There is an additional value, however. The analysis of general concepts such as *social class* allows us to discover the extent to which inequalities of money, say, correspond to inequalities of political power, prestige, and other concrete observations gathered under the same conceptual umbrella.

DEFINITIONS

It is important here that you fully understand the seemingly paradoxical role of **definitions** in social research. On the one hand, definitions are essential if research findings are to be communicated meaningfully. If I tell you that my research indicates that upper-class people are more conservative than lower-class people, that doesn't tell you anything of value unless you know what I mean by upper- and lower-class and by conservative. Even though most of the terms social scientists use have some common-language meanings, they are typically ambiguous in everyday usage. Thus, it is essential that definitions be given to specify exactly what is meant by the terms used.

Unfortunately, rigorously specifying and defining terms can suggest that the definitions given are "right" or "true." You should know from the start that you cannot evaluate research findings on the basis of whether the research has used the "correct" definitions. The best you can do is determine whether the definitions and measurement techniques were *appropriate* or *useful* to the research question at hand.

To turn the matter around again, however, social scientists have developed some conventions for definition and measurement. *Household, labor force,* and *unemployed* are examples of terms that have pretty commonly accepted technical definitions—those developed by the U.S. Census Bureau. Though the accepted definitions are not the "true" ones, they have a special utility since experienced researchers and experienced consumers learn them and since, with them, comparisons can be made from study to study.

To summarize with an example, there is no "true" answer to the question of whether independently wealthy people who do not work and have no interest in working should be counted as "unemployed." But most research purposes in the area of employment make it appropriate to omit such people from the labor force altogether. The conventional definitions of *labor force* and *unemployed* do omit such people. This is not to say that some research purposes might not make it appropriate for them to be counted.

Social scientific research is inseparable from the analysis of concepts. Take a moment to look back at the Braithwaite quotation above. Here are some of the terms he uses that represent social scientific concepts:

middle class
aspirations
school failures
expectations
occupational success
delinquency

I imagine that each of these terms means something to you, although you might feel a little uncertain about precisely what the writer intended in some cases. I want you to realize that each of the terms is only a convenient way of referring to mental images that each of us has and that we use to bring together a variety of observations. Your observations, mine, and Braithwaite's are all different. Whether we mean the same thing in using one of these terms, then, is a crucial question in scientific research and one that is addressed through the research process called *conceptualization*.

CONCEPTUALIZATION

Concepts are the chief content of our thoughts and communications. Look at the preceding sentence, for example. *Concepts, chief, content, our, thoughts,* and *communications* all represent concepts. I know these words represent more or less the same thing to you as to me, or I wouldn't have used them. At the same time, it's certain that you and I mean something at least slightly different by each of them. While normal conversation proceeds relatively well in the face of such differences, they can be a problem.

Frances Inzer and Mary Jo Aspinall describe the problem inherent in nurses judging the recovery of patients in a hospital. *Ambulation* is the ability to walk. But how much do you have to walk to be judged ambulatory?

For example, one nurse may have recorded that the patient was increasing in ambulation when he could walk from the bed to the chair, whereas another nurse may have stated he achieved this goal when he could walk the length of the corridor. Without specificity, recordings are unreliable as indicators of patient progress. (*Inzer and Aspinall, 1981:178*)

The need for specifying concepts crops up in many areas of life, as "Setting World Records" illustrates. It is particularly important in the area of social research.

In introducing and using terms representing concepts, a researcher must specify exactly how those terms are being used. Braithwaite's re-

SETTING WORLD RECORDS

During 1978–79, the Bubble Yum company sponsored a contest to see who could blow the biggest bubble-gum bubble. Susan Montgomery of Fresno, California, won a place in the *Guiness Book of World Records* with a bubble of 19.25 inches in diameter. Get out a yardstick and you'll have a good idea of the size of the winning bubble. If you got the idea that you might like to challenge the champ, you'll need a little more information.

According to the *Guiness Book of World Records* (1980:454), "Each bubble in the competition was blown using 3 pieces of gum only, and all measurements were taken on a horizontal rather than a vertical basis, to eliminate any elongation due to gravity." Notice the potential arguments that the latter specification would divert.

I'll bet you've never heard of world record holder Anton Christy of Jaffina, Sri Lanka. In 1979, she set the world's record for balancing on one foot: 31 hours, 45 minutes. Before setting your stopwatch and putting on your soft shoe, you'd better know that "the disengaged foot may not be rested on the standing foot nor may any sticks be used for support or balance" (1980:451).

The specification required in connection with world records is similar to the specification required in social research. Unless a researcher's concepts are fully specified, the conclusions drawn from the analysis of those concepts are meaningless.

SOURCE Norris McWhirter, *Guiness Book of World Records.* New York: Bantam Books, 1980.

search cited above focused on crime. But his idea of crime might differ from yours. Recognizing that possibility, he writes: "For the purposes of this review, crime is defined as behavior punishable, but not necessarily punished, under a specific legal prohibition" (1981:37). Notice how this specification handles the question you might have had: "Do you have to get caught for it to be a crime?"

In brief, **conceptualization** involves a refinement and specification of what a particular term will and won't mean. It is the process of specifying and clarifying mental images. The great methodologist Paul Lazarsfeld suggested (1972:17–18) that the conceptualization process includes these main steps:

1. We begin to express our original mental imagery in words, giving examples to illustrate what our imagery includes.
2. As we verbalize about our mental concept, we uncover many dimensions or aspects of it. Lazarsfeld says that "as the discussion of the concept expands, the number of eligible indicators increases."
3. Once we have expanded the parameters of our concept, it is next necessary to narrow down the focus for the purpose of actually undertaking research.

The importance of conceptualization notwithstanding, Edward Grabb points out that social scientists do not always come through. Here's what he has to say about the concept of social class, which we've been examining.

Researchers in social stratification regularly discuss the "working class," the "middle class," or the "capitalist class," apparently secure in their belief that such terms have a clear meaning for both themselves and their audiences. Yet, even a brief examination of existing studies reveals considerable disparity in the definition . . . of the class concept.

Much of the disagreement may be due to the use of a variety of empirical indicators of class, such as income, education, or occupational status. The inconsistency in the choice of measures and category cutting-points sometimes makes comparisons of findings and the accumulation of evidence difficult. (*Grabb, 1980:359–360*)

The disparities in what is meant by *social class* can be seen in the examples presented earlier (pp. 72–73). In the *Chronicle* article, for example, the focus is on "lifestyle." The quotation from Lenin gives little indication of how social class is used, but a study of Marxist-Leninist theory would clarify this somewhat. For Medvedev, a contemporary Soviet scholar, social class refers to the relationship of a mass of people to the means of production in a society—workers, factory owners, and so on. For Weed, class is a function of income and dependency on the welfare system for that income. Braithwaite's report, finally, is a review of past studies of crime and class, so his specification of the concept is simply his assessment of how earlier researchers had conceptualized it. He says:

Those relatively low on the social class continuum (sometimes referred to as the lower class, sometimes as the working class, sometimes as the low socioeconomic status group) are those who have unskilled or semiskilled occupations, or, in some cases, are the unemployed. In the case of juveniles, the [measure of] social class is almost always based on parents' occupations. (*1981:37*)

In reviewing a research report, then, it is important that you discover how the researcher has conceptualized the variables under study. What does the researcher have in mind when he or she refers to *prejudice, liber-*

alism, ambition, or even such seemingly straightforward concepts as *educated, old,* or *successful.* Conceptualization is the first step in the development of a social research measurement. Let's see what follows next.

OPERATIONALIZATION

Operationalization is the process of devising actual measurement procedures, detailing the steps, or operations, to be followed. Suppose we are planning to do a study in which we want to know how educated people are. In the conceptualization process, we might narrow our focus down to years of formal schooling. As our operationalization, we might settle for the following questionnaire item:

Please indicate below the highest level of school you've completed.

0 1 2 3 4 5 6 7 8	9 10 11 12	13 14 15 16	Masters Doctorate
Elementary school	High school	College	Graduate studies

Or, when Holsti and Rosenau set out to measure the attitudes of "a sample of American leaders in all walks of life" (1980:4), they operationalized leaders as people listed in *Who's Who in America.* They selected a sample of people from that source and mailed questionnaires to them.

Operationalization is an essential step in doing research since you need to decide how you will make your observations and measurements. It is equally important for the consumers of research. All too often, researchers will describe their variables one way and actually measure them some other way. Unless you know precisely how variables were measured, you can't really assess the meaning and implications of the research conclusions.

Recall the discussion of Braithwaite's (1981) review of research on social class and criminality. Braithwaite defined crime as behavior that was punishable under the law, whether the criminal was actually punished or not. That specification narrowed the meaning of the term *crime* and ruled out some other possible definitions. Still, this conceptualization doesn't tell us how to actually measure criminal behavior—that is, how to tell who has committed crimes and who hasn't. Since Braithwaite was reviewing the research of others, the operationalization of criminal behavior was something to look for in studies rather than to decide on. What he found was very interesting for our present discussion.

Essentially, Braithwaite found two operationalizations of crime used in the studies he reviewed: (1) official police records and (2) self-reports from people being studied. The latter method has much to recommend it: You can select a sample of people for study, measure their social class in some fashion, and ask them (with a little more tact) if they have ever committed a crime. In all the studies where criminal behavior was operationalized in the form of official police records, Braithwaite discovered that lower social status was associated with higher crime rates. Where the operationalization took the form of self-reports, the results were mixed and, overall, inconclusive. Braithwaite explains:

> ... while we know that lower class youth are more likely than middle class youth to get into trouble with the police and the courts, a number of studies have shown that, when interviewed, lower class youth do not *report* that they have been in trouble with the police or courts more frequently than do middle class respondents. ... Similarly, lower class youths tend to score higher on "lie" scales with self-report measures. ... Perhaps when confronted by unfamiliar white middle class researchers with their probing questions, lower class respondents are more suspicious and defensive than their middle class counterparts. (*1981:47*)

Therefore, if you know that juvenile delinquency has been measured through self-reports, in weighing the research findings you should take into account the fact that lower-class youth are less likely to admit having committed crimes. Does this mean that official police records provide a superior operationalization? Not necessarily. Before you continue reading, take a minute to think of some of the problems inherent in using official police records.

Recall that Braithwaite conceptualized criminal behavior as committing crimes, whether the individual was punished or not. Official police records are limited to those who are apprehended and/or convicted. This fact makes a difference in terms of the relationship between class and crime. It is often contended that the lower classes are more susceptible to arrest than the middle and upper classes, just as blacks are more susceptible to arrest than whites. Moreover, once arrested, poor people are more likely to have a weak legal defense and more likely to be convicted. Results based on official police records, therefore, are somewhat contaminated by the practices of the criminal justice system. Knowing that allows you to evaluate the research results accordingly. In either case, you stand the risk of being misled if you don't know how variables were actually operationalized.

DIMENSIONS AND INDICATORS

Lest I mislead you into thinking that every variable needs *one* operationalization, I want to remind you of the earlier discussion of concepts and dimensions. Prejudice, for example, includes attitudes toward racial and ethnic minorities, toward members of the opposite sex, toward old people or young people. It also includes a football player calling all tennis players pansies, Republicans calling Democrats communists, Democrats calling Republicans fascists, and even the ugly things sociologists sometimes say about psychologists. None of these is a truer example of prejudice than the others. Each is an equally good example in general—though you may have a specific research interest that makes some more appropriate than others for you to focus on.

When we move from conceptualization to operationalization, it's necessary to identify indicators for the various **dimensions,** or aspects, of the variables to be studied. An **indicator** is an empirical observation that can be taken as evidence of particular attributes of a variable. Sometimes a single indicator will suffice (e.g., male or female as an indicator of gender), but more often it's necessary to find more than one indicator. It's essential if there are several dimensions to a given concept. Let's look at some examples of operationalizations in social research.

Lewis Killian illustrates the difficulty of measuring concepts that, on their face, seem straightforward and obvious. Discussing black progress in the United States, he says:

The standard indicators of progress toward equality in education, income, and occupation are crude, variable, and often contradictory, despite the fact that they have been sanctified by complex data-processing equipment and sophisticated tests of statistical significance. (1981:46)

For example, whereas the number of elected black officials has increased, Killian points out that they generally hold the lower levels of political office. Moreover, he notes, such gains also reflect "the persistence of residential segregation." That is, the increase in numbers of black voters does not balance the disproportionate power of large corporations and influential industries.

Events of the past 10 years suggest that the oil companies, the dairy industry, the automobile manufacturers, and the hidden empire of crime each has more real political clout than do all the black citizens of the United States. (Killian, 1981:46)

When Charles Glock and Rodney Stark (1965) set about studying religiosity, they fully recognized that religion meant different things to different people. As a result, they began by conceptualizing the most common dimensions of the concept. They specified five dimensions:

1. *Ritual:* Participating in the religious events and practices prescribed by one's religion—for example, attending church, praying, taking communion.

2. *Belief*: Accepting one's religion's doctrines regarding reality—for example, believing in the existence of God, believing in reincarnation, believing in the divinity of Jesus.
3. *Knowledge*: Simply knowing about one's religion—its history, beliefs, and practices.
4. *Experience*: Having religious experiences, such as communication with supernatural beings, visions, and seizures.
5. *Consequences*: Living one's secular life in accord with the teachings of one's religion.

In their subsequent empirical research, each of these dimensions was operationalized in the form of questionnaire items administered to respondents. The ritual dimension, for example, was measured in part by asking people how often they attended church. The empirical research showed that these dimensions of religiosity definitely reflected different aspects of "being religious" as they were caused by different factors and had different implications.

Thompson and Brown, to take a different research focus, wanted to explain differences in men's and women's reactions to illness. To do that, they characterized their subjects in terms of their use of medical facilities. They used three measures:

First, Mechanic's . . . Response-to-Illness scale was selected, since it has been widely cited as a measure of tendency to adopt the sick role. Respondents are asked what they would be most likely to do in four hypothetical illness circumstances, such as "when you have been feeling poorly for a few days." They may answer "do nothing," "consult a physician," "take bed rest," and "take medication." . . .
 The second measure of illness behavior was the number of office visits to the prepaid clinic during the past twelve months, and was obtained from clinic records. The third measure was the number of health-related visits during the past twelve months, as reported by the patient. This measure included visits both inside and outside the prepaid system, for example, to chiropractors, naturopaths, psychologists, and psychiatrists. (*1980:408–409*)

In 1957, Professor Fei Hsiao-t'ung, the great Chinese sociologist, journeyed to Kaihsienkung, a rural Chinese village, to determine whether the quality of life had improved since the Communist revolution of 1949. Fei had previously studied village life in Kaihsienkung in 1936. In a relatively poor agricultural village, rice production seemed an appropriate measure of quality of life.

Have the agricultural cooperatives been adequately managed?
 The achievements not only approach the limits of the possible, they are also very great: the average per *mou* unhusked rice yield in 1936 was 350 catties; after collectivization, in 1956, it had reached 559 catties, an increase of over 200 catties. (*Fei, 1957: 43*)

Despite these figures, Fei found dissatisfaction among the villagers: They did not feel their quality of life had particularly improved. Looking more deeply into the matter, and recalling his 1936 research, Fei examined the other occupational activities of the villagers. In 1936, many had engaged in the raising of silkworms and the manufacture of silk, which provided them with added income. In 1956, he found that rice production was virtually their only source of income—hence their lot had not improved all that much.

These are a few examples of ways social scientists operationalize some of the concepts they wish to study. Realize, however, that operationalization is sometimes less clear-cut and deliberate than in these examples. This is often the case with qualitative research, as we can see from the research of Bernard Lefkowitz, who wanted to explore a relatively unstudied economic phenomenon—people who have voluntarily dropped out of the labor force. It was sufficient for Lefkowitz to describe his subjects as follows:

They were older than college or graduate-school age, and they hadn't reached their traditional retirement age. Some were planning to stop work. Others had stopped working. A few had gone back to work. Some had been fired and refused to look for another job, some had just walked out. (1979:24–25)

Though they got there in a variety of ways, Lefkowitz's subjects had all chosen to drop out of the mainstream occupational system in America, where occupation is typically the key to your identity. Given the nature of Lefkowitz's study, it was not appropriate for him to create a rigid specification of the variable.

Before moving on to more refinements of the measurement process, I want to look at a confusion that often arises in relation to conceptualization and operationalization. As researchers specify and operationalize their concepts, creating refined measures, the concepts and measures can seem more real than the observations that started the research.

THE CONFUSION OVER DEFINITIONS AND REALITY

It is important to remember that, although observations and experiences are real, our concepts are only mental creations, images that summarize collections of seemingly related observations and experiences. The terms associated with concepts are merely devices created for purposes of filing and communication. The word *prejudice* is an example. Ultimately, that word is only a collection of letters and has no intrinsic meaning. We could have as easily created the word *slanderice* to serve the same purpose.

Very often, however, we fall into the trap of believing that terms have "real" meanings, separate from the context in which they were devised. That danger seems to grow stronger when we begin to take terms seriously and attempt to use them precisely. And the danger is all the greater in the presence of experts who appear to know more than you do about the terms. It's very easy to yield to the authority of experts in such a situation.

Once we have assumed that terms have real meanings, we begin the tortured task of discovering what those real meanings are and what would constitute a genuine measurement of them. Figure 4.1 illustrates this process. We make up conceptual summaries of real observations because the summaries are convenient. They prove to be *so* convenient, however, that we begin tricking ourselves into thinking they are real. The process of regarding as real those things that are not is called **reification.** The reification of concepts in day-to-day life is very common.

Bearing in mind that concepts, terms, and operational measures are merely useful mental devices for making sense out of what we observe, let's look at some of the useful distinctions that researchers make.

LEVELS OF MEASUREMENTS

Social scientific measurements are of four levels of rigor: nominal, ordinal, interval, and ratio. The distinctions among these four levels concern the relationships connecting the attributes composing a variable. Figure 4.2 presents a graphic portrayal of the different levels of measurement.

NOMINAL MEASURES

A **nominal** variable is one comprising attributes that are simply different from each other. Gender is such a variable, made up of the attributes male and female. Race, religion, political party affiliation, and region of birth are a few more common social variables at the nominal level of measurement. The nature of nominal measures will become clearer as we move on to more rigorous measures that have characteristics nominal measures do not have.

ORDINAL MEASURES

Sometimes attributes represent **ordinal** measures—"more" or "less" of the variable. In the physical sciences, the "hardness" scale is the classic example: All substances can be arranged in progression of relative hardness

FIGURE 4.1
*The process of
conceptual en-
trapment.*

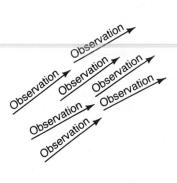

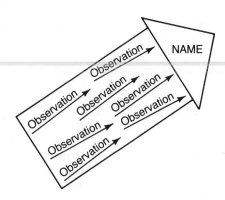

1. Many our observations in life seem to have something in common. We get the sense that they represent something more general than the simple content of any single observation. We find if useful, moreover, to communicate about the general concept.

2. It is inconvenient to keep describing all the specific observations whenever we want to communicate about the general concept they seem to have in common, so we give a name to the general concept—to stand for whatever it is the specific observations have in common.

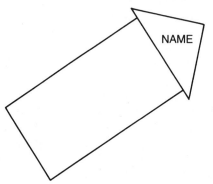

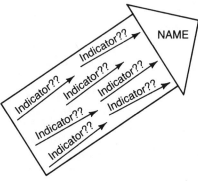

3. As we communicate about the general concept, using its term, we begin to think that the concept is some*thing* that really exists, not just a summary reference for several concrete observations in the world.

4. The belief that the concept itself is real results in irony. We now begin discussing and debating whether specific observations are "really" sufficient indicators of the concept.

FIGURE 4.2
Levels of measurement.

Nominal Measure Example: Sex

Female   Male

Ordinal Measure Example: Religiosity

"How important is religion to you?"

Low   High

Interval Measure Example: IQ

Ratio Measure Example: Income

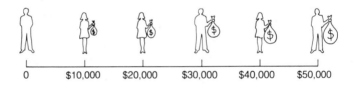

0    $10,000 $20,000 $30,000 $40,000 $50,000

on the basis of which substances scratch which. No numbers are needed to represent the relative hardnesses.

In the social sciences, the frequently used *Likert item* is a good example of an ordinal measure. This is the questionnaire item that consists of a statement such as "The United States should contribute more to foreign aid" and the responses: "Strongly agree," "Agree," "Disagree," and "Strongly disagree," or something similar. Notice that the four responses are arranged from most to least agreement with the statement, or from most to least support for foreign aid. While the categories in an ordinal measure are arranged in order, the "distance" between adjacent categories is not necessarily the same.

INTERVAL MEASURES

An **interval** measure has the additional quality that adjacent categories are a uniform distance from one another. The Fahrenheit and Celsius scales of temperature are classic examples. They are constructed in such a way that the distance between 20 and 30 degrees, for example, is the same as between 50 and 60 degrees. In social research, IQ tests have been constructed in the same fashion. What interval variables lack, however, is a *true zero*. As you know, zero degrees Fahrenheit does not represent a total lack of heat (though zero degrees Kelvin does). By the same token, an IQ score of zero would not represent a total lack of intelligence. Both zero degrees Fahrenheit and zero IQ are just arbitrary positions on the scales.

RATIO MEASURES

Ratio measures have all the qualities of nominal, ordinal, and interval measures—plus a true zero. There are numerous examples of this in social research: age, population sizes, years of schooling to name just a few. There are more ratio than interval measures in social science research.

As you review research reports, it's important for you to recognize the levels of measurement represented by the variables under study. As we'll see, different levels of measurement are appropriate (or inappropriate) to different analytical techniques.

THE SIGNIFICANCE OF LEVELS OF MEASUREMENT

The importance of these distinctions appears in the context of data analysis. The different levels of measurement allow or disallow certain statistical techniques.

About all that can be said about data collected in terms of a nominal measure is how many of something there are in each category, either in raw numbers or as percentages of the whole. It makes no sense to talk about the median religion, for example. At this level, we can't compare two people who report different religions except to say that they are different. One is not more or less than the other. With ordinal measures, more-less comparisons are appropriate. With interval measures, we can add and substract scores since there's a uniform unit separating adjacent points on the measure. Finally, ratio measures permit multiplication and division. We can speak of one person being twice as old as another, for example, whereas we cannot say one is twice as intelligent as the other on the basis of IQ test scores. In Chapter 12, when we consider statistics, we'll look a little more deeply into this issue. Before leaving the issue of levels of measurements, I want to make two nearly contradictory points.

First, the researcher has a certain degree of latitude in choosing the level of measurement to be employed in regard to a particular variable. For instance, age was described above as a ratio measure, but in some social research circumstances it might make sense to treat it as nominal. Economists, for example, sometimes measure the percentage of a population that is economically "dependent." All people over 65 or under 16 might be combined to represent that part of the population that is largely dependent on the rest economically. Thus, age would be measured as two nominal categories: dependent and nondependent.

Age might also be treated as ordinal. Many of the physical, social, and psychological changes that occur over the course of the life cycle, for example, are related to ordinal categories: infancy, childhood, adolescence, young adulthood, middle age, and old age. Though I can't think of any way age could be used as an interval measure, it is a technical possibility.

Second, constructing a variable at a certain level of measurement does not insure that the variable will behave at that level. The example of age as an ordinal rather than ratio measure is a good example. In general, people become more conservative as they grow older. If you were to test that relationship, measuring age as a precise-to-the-year ratio variable, you would undoubtedly find that the relationship doesn't work that way. Forty-two-year-olds are not necessarily more conservative than forty-one-year-olds. The relationship between age and conservatism would probably be more evident if age were treated as ordinally arranged life-cycle categories.

EVALUATING MEASUREMENT QUALITY

When someone mentions the "quality" of a measurement, one of the first characteristics that comes to mind is **precision.** Somehow, "earned $12,376" seems better than "earned between ten and fifteen thousand." I suppose that, all else being equal, that would be so. For the most part, however, precision is not the key to quality in social research. The nature of relationships linking social variables—linking income and political orientation, for example—can be discovered without the need for as much precision of measurement as you might imagine. Although rich people are generally more conservative than poor people, there is unlikely to be much difference between those earning $12,000 and those earning $12,050 a year. Broader income categories, however, show definite differences, as Table 4.1 indicates.

I make this point regarding precision for two reasons. On the one hand, I don't want you to dismiss out of hand research findings that are based on less precise measurements than you might expect. Instead, you must examine the measurements that have been made and decide if they

TABLE 4.1   Income and Political Orientation

Question: "Regardless of the party you may favor, do you lean more toward the liberal side or the conservative side politically?"

Income	Percentage conservative
Less than $5000	27%
$5000–$9999	30
$10,000–$14,999	35
$15,000–$19,999	38
$20,000–$29,999	42
$30,000 and over	47

Source: Adapted from Everett Carll Ladd, "Conservatism: National Review." *Public Opinion*, February-March 1981: 21. Copyright 1981 by the American Enterprise Institute. Reprinted with permission of the publisher.

were appropriate to the task set for them. On the other hand, I want to warn you against placing too much confidence in research findings that are bedecked with apparent precision. Such precision can distract you from more significant errors that have been committed. The two types of error that you should focus your attention on concern *validity* and *reliability*. Let's look now at each of those criteria of quality in measurement.

VALIDITY

Simply put, **validity** is a matter of whether a measurement measures what it is supposed to measure. We can ask people how often they attend church services and call that a measure of religiosity, but does it "really" measure religiosity? Though I have just emphasized that there is no "true" definition or measure of any variable, I want to show you how it is still reasonable to ask whether a given indicator is a "valid" measure of a particular concept. There are three major aspects to the test of validity.

First, social scientists sometimes speak of *prima facie validity*, sometimes called *face validity*. This means that an indicator is a reasonable representation of some concept just "on its face." Asking people if they attend church is at least somewhat relevant to religiosity; therefore, it has prima facie validity. By contrast, asking people about their church attendance is not obviously a measure of their political affiliation, even though churchgoers as a whole are somewhat more conservative than non-churchgoers. Going to church may be related to political orientation, but it is not a measure of it.

Second, the validity of a particular indicator as a measure of some concept should be weighed against other concepts the indicator might reasonably reflect. Church attendance, for example, may also reflect a more general tendency to join organizations. This problem crops up often in connection with studies of differences between men and women. Numerous studies show that boys do better in mathematics than girls do. But what does gender actually reflect in this case: differences in the natural abilities of males and females or differences in the ways they are brought up? The implications of this distinction are crucial. Although I can't give you a handy rule of thumb for determining the answer to such a question, the beginnings of an answer can be found in the final thing I want to say about the general issue of validity.

Recall that the terms associated with our mental concepts are labels of convenience for representing sets of similar, concrete observations. (Notice that we are now testing the appropriateness of such concrete observations as *indicators* of concepts.) If we have five potential indicators of a concept, we can use the empirical connections among the five to test each as an appropriate indicator. Here's how it works:

1. Suppose we want to measure antifemale sexist attitudes, and we have five possible indicators. We've asked people to agree or disagree with each of the following statements:
   a. Women are silly and irrational.
   b. Women are stupider than men.
   c. Women are too emotional for positions of responsibility.
   d. A woman's place is in the home.
   e. Men and women have unchangeable biological differences.
2. Each of these attitudes could be taken to indicate anti-female prejudice.
3. If each does, then a very prejudiced person will agree to all, and a very unprejudiced person will disagree with all. Even in between those extremes, people who agree with one statement should be more likely to agree with another than are those who disagreed with the first. For example, people who agreed that "women are silly and irrational" should be more likely to agree that "women are stupider than men" than those who disagreed that "women are silly and irrational."
4. By comparing the patterns of responses that people give to these five statements, we can determine statistically the extent to which agreement with one item is related to agreement with the others.
5. Now suppose that all the items except (e) are related to one another. But suppose that those who agreed that men and women are irrevocably different biologically were not more prejudiced on the other statements than were those who denied the biological differences. We could conclude on that basis that statement (e) measures something other than is measured by the other four items. As we looked back at the other four, we'd reconfirm our feeling that they were good indicators of antifemale prejudice. Hence, item (e) must not be a good indicator of it.

MEASURING HEALTH HAZARDS

Here's an example illustrating the problem of reliability. Jeffrey Sacks and his colleagues focused their attention on Health Hazard Appraisal (HHA), part of a preventive medicine program to be used by physicians in counseling their patients. Sacks wrote: "Given knowledge of clinical, historical, and lifestyle parameters, risk multipliers can be applied to the baseline risks for an individual to compute a chance of death and an overall measure of risk. . . . A physician can then counsel the patient accordingly" (1980:730). In other words, by knowing patients' life situations, a physician could advise them on their potential for survival and how to improve it. All this depends, of course, on the accuracy of the information gathered on each patient.

To test the reliability of the patient information, Sacks and his colleagues undertook a test-retest study of 207 subjects. All subjects completed a baseline questionnaire soliciting data on their characteristics and behavior. Follow-up questionnaires were administered about three months later, and the results of the two studies were compared. Overall, only 15 percent of the subjects reported the same information in both studies.

Almost 10 percent of subjects reported a different height at follow-up examination. Parental age was changed by over one in three subjects. One parent re-

We'll look again at this test of validity shortly in the section on indexes, scales, and typologies. For now, you should note that, although there are no ultimately "true" measures of concepts, we can test the validity of potential indicators. Researchers should examine validity in selecting measures, and consumers of research need to ask whether such an examination substantiates the wisdom of the measurements made.

RELIABILITY

Reliability could be defined in simplistic terms as consistency or dependability. Whereas a valid indicator measures what it purports to measure, a reliable one can be counted on to measure what it says time after time.

The question is: Would a particular measurement technique produce the same result if the same thing could be measured repeatedly. Let me *portedly aged 20 chronologic years in three months. One in five ex-smokers and ex-drinkers have apparent difficulty in reliably recalling their previous consumption pattern.* (1980:730)

Some subjects erased all trace of previously reported heart murmur, diabetes, emphysema, arrest record, and thoughts of suicide. One subject's mother, deceased in the first questionnaire, was apparently alive and well in time for the second. One subject had one ovary missing in the first study but present in the second. In another case, an ovary present in the first study was missing in the second study—and had been for 10 years! One subject was reportedly 55 years old in the first study and 50 years old three months later. You have to wonder if the physician-counselors could have had nearly the impact on their patients as their patients' memories did.

Of course, all these inconsistencies could have been cleared up with a little more investigation. We could find out "for sure" if the last-mentioned subject was 55 or 50. We could sort out all the hide-and-seek ovaries, mothers, and arrest records. The point is that virtually every study you'll be reading will contain such errors, and there'll be no follow-up study to determine what they are. It is vital, therefore, that you scrutinize every measurement technique employed with an eye to its likely reliability.

SOURCE   Jeffrey J. Sacks, W. Mark Krushat, and Jeffrey Newman, "Reliability of the Health Hazard Appraisal." *American Journal of Public Health*, July 1980:730–732.

illustrate this with an extreme example. Earlier we discussed church attendance as a potential indicator of religiosity. Suppose we asked people "How many times have you attended church in your life?" What would be the problem with that? Well, except for those who have never attended church and those who have attended every day of their lives, people would not be able to answer this question very accurately; they'd have to give a very rough estimate. If you were able to ask me this question, then ask it again without my remembering having been asked before—and without remembering my earlier answer—it is likely that I would give different answers (different estimates) each time. This exemplifies a measurement technique that would *not* be very reliable.

As a general rule, it is difficult to test for reliability in a single study, though it is not impossible. In the simplest case, you might simply collect the same information twice. If you were studying corporations, for example, you might interview the personnel officer and ask "How many employees are there?" Later on, you say: "Oh, I've forgotten how many employees you said there are." The problem is this: If you get two different answers, you will have learned that the measurement technique is unreliable, but you end up not knowing how many employees there are. Over the course of research in a given area, the community of researchers discover measures that appear relatively reliable and those that seem unreliable. This is why you will often find researchers citing each other's research and indicating that they are using measures previously used by others. This is another value of the standardization of definitions and measures.

The Real World Research box entitled "Measuring Health Hazards" takes up the issue of reliability in a different situation.

Be clear that reliability does not guarantee validity. Here's an illustration my students have found to clarify the point. One day, I bought a small, inexpensive mail scale. I was a little uneasy about whether a cheap scale would be very accurate. I put a letter on it and saw it register exactly 1 ounce. I repeatedly took the letter off the scale and put it back on. Imagine my delight when I found it registering exactly one ounce each time. What did that little experiment demonstrate? It demonstrated that the scale gave me a *reliable* measure of the letter's weight—it was the same at each testing. It did not demonstrate that the measurement was *valid*, however. Conceivably the letter could have weighed 2 ounces and the cheap scale only registered half the "true" weight of objects. How would you test the validity of the measurements given by the scale? All you could do would be to measure the letter on other scales—preferably better ones— and find that they agreed with the first or with each other. Notice how this test of validity parallels the early one concerning antifemale prejudice.

We'll return to the issues of validity and reliability throughout this book as they are fundamental issues. In the discussions of different data collection techniques, we'll see that validity and reliability even conflict with one another. For now, you should have developed a basic sensitivity to the two concepts as part of your training as an informed consumer of research. We'll conclude our discussion of measurement with a brief overview of the more sophisticated measurement techniques often employed by social researchers.

INDEXES, SCALES, AND TYPOLOGIES

By now, you should have gotten a pretty good idea about the difficulty of making measurements appropriate to concepts. Except for trivial cases, any indicator you could think of for any concept could be brought into question in terms of validity and/or reliability. Almost any measurement technique will result in misclassification of some of our observations—we will classify some liberals conservative and some conservatives liberal, some religious people irreligious and some irreligious ones religious. One powerful solution to this dilemma is to construct **composite measures** combining several indicators: indexes, scales, and typologies.

INDEXES

Although the term **index** is used in many ways, most social science uses involve the combining of several indicators into a single, composite measure. We have already discussed a number of indexes in this book: The Consumer Price Index, the Dow Jones average, and IQ tests are examples. Glock and Stark (1965) have combined indicators of their several dimensions of religiosity into a composite index. Similarly, social class is typically measured as a composite of several indicators: typically, measures of education, income, and occupation.

When Edward Grabb wanted to measure cynicism among American adults, he considered each of the following seven questions:

1. Generally speaking, would you say that most people can be trusted, or that you can't be too careful in dealing with people?
2. Would you say that most of the time people try to be helpful, or that they are mostly just looking out for themselves?
3. Most people really don't care what happens to the next fellow. Do you agree or disagree?
4. Do you think most people would try to take advantage of you if they got a chance, or would they try to be fair?
5. In spite of what some people say, the lot of the average man is getting worse, not better. Do you agree or disagree?
6. It's hardly fair to bring a child into the world the way things look for the future. Do you agree or disagree?
7. These days a person doesn't really know whom he can count on. Do you agree or disagree?
   (1979:40)

Grabb felt that each of these items reflected cynicism on the face (prima facie validity). When he examined the empirical relationships among the several items, the results confirmed his view that all were indicators of the same variable. To get an overall measure of cynicism, then, Grabb assigned each respondent one point for each "cynical" response, thereby resulting in each person getting an overall "score" ranging between zero (no cynical responses) and seven (cynical on all seven). The scores, thus constructed, were taken as indications of how cynical each respondent was—or as an index of cynicism.

SCALES

One of the shortcomings of simple, cumulative indexes is that they fail to take account of differences in "strength" of the items comprised in them. For example, the cynicism item (4) that speaks of others taking advantage of us seems, on its face, a more cynical sentiment than that reflected in item (3), which simply holds that others don't care. In the index, however, each item was given the same weight.

Scales are composite measures that take account of the different strengths of the indicators being combined. To take a simple example, suppose we wished to create a measure of illegal drug use among a sample of high school students. Suppose, further, that we asked the students whether they had ever tried each of the following: heroin, marijuana, and alcohol (having limited the study to students too young to drink alcohol legally). Those three questions could produce nine different response patterns, but if you think about it a moment, you'll see that we'd probably only get four. Those four probable response patterns are shown below.

Simple index score	Alcohol	Marijuana	Heroin
3	Yes	Yes	Yes
2	Yes	Yes	No
1	Yes	No	No
0	No	No	No

As indicators of illegal drug use, these three items clearly represent different degrees of severity (as reflected in punishments, for example): heroin highest, marijuana next, and alcohol the mildest. Notice how unlikely it would be for us to find a student who had used heroin and marijuana, but had never used alcohol, for example. These items have the advantage that if we know *how many* drugs a student used, we know—with almost perfect accuracy—*which* drugs were used.

Scales—created through a variety of different statistical techniques—have two advantages over simple indexes. First, scaling techniques insure that intensity structures such as that illustrated above are present among the indicators. Typically, the researcher will have access to several indicators and choose those that exhibit an intensity structure. Second, when scales are created, it is sometimes appropriate to modify some scores from what they would be if simple index scores were assigned. In the drug-use example, if we did find someone who used heroin and marijuana but not alcohol, we'd score that person 3 anyway—assigning that person to the "highest" drug-use category.

The scale design described above was developed primarily by the great Israeli methodologist Louis Guttman. Usually called a *Guttman scale*, it is one of the most common types of scale used in the social sciences. Increasingly common is the *factor scale*, based on factor analysis. We will discuss this and other composite measures in Chapter 12.

TYPOLOGIES

Both indexes and scales have the quality of *unidimensionality*, measuring only one dimension. This is somewhat more true of scales than indexes for the reasons already discussed. Sometimes reality is not unidimensional, however. In such cases, it's often appropriate to create **typologies,** multidimensional sets of categories created from two or more variables.

Earlier in this chapter, I spoke of social class as being typically measured as a composite of education, income, and occupation. It's possible to construct social class indexes and scales because those three indicators are empirically related to one another: People with much education tend to have much income, those with little education little income, and so forth. At the same time, such relationships are never perfect. There are always exceptions, and sometimes those exceptions deserve special study. Consider the following table:

	EDUCATION	
	High	Low
INCOME High	A	B
INCOME Low	C	D

In any empirical study, we would expect to find most people in cells A and D. Sometimes, however, it is useful to study what sociologists call *status inconsistency:* in this example, cells B and C. Take a minute to get an idea of the kind of person you would expect to find in cells B and C. Those in B have little education but high incomes, whereas those in C have high education but low incomes. The self-made, rags-to-riches stereotype fits into cell B; the unemployed English Ph.D. is an example of those in cell C. Obviously, these two cells represent quite different people, and a typology such as this one allows the examination of such differences.

These, then, are some of the composite measures used in the operationalization of social variables. You should now have a general grasp of the process of measurement; you will have a chance to exercise that new understanding in the chapters that follow.

☑ *CONSUMER'S CHECKLIST*

In this chapter, we've looked at several theoretical and concrete aspects of measurement in the social sciences. Here are some of the questions you might ask in reviewing the measurements undertaken in a research report you read.

- What are the names of the concepts under study?
- Has the researcher delineated different dimensions, if there are any, of those concepts?
- What indicators have been chosen as measures of those dimensions and concepts?
- For each indicator, is it a valid measure of the concept intended?
  a. Is the indicator, on its face, a reasonable measure of the concept?
  b. What else could the indicator be a measure of?
  c. What steps have been taken to test the validity of the indicator(s) used to measure each concept?
- Is the indicator a reliable measure? What steps, if any, have been taken to insure its reliability?
- What's the level of measurement used in the case of each variable: nominal, ordinal, interval, or ratio? Does it seem the appropriate level of measurement given the research question?
- Have composite measures been used?
  a. For each, is it an index, a scale, or a typology?
  b. Is it the appropriate form of measure?
  c. How have the items been chosen for inclusion in the composite index?

KEY WORDS

Measurement	Indicator	Validity
Concept	Reification	Reliability

Term	Nominal measure	Composite measure
Definition	Ordinal measure	Index
Conceptualization	Interval measure	Scale
Operationalization	Ratio measure	Typology
Dimension	Precision	

MAIN POINTS

1. Concepts are mental images that organize, summarize, and classify what we observe.
2. Terms are the names we use to stand for our concepts.
3. Definitions are specifications of the meanings to be associated with particular terms.
4. Conceptualization is the process of specifying concepts (mental images), indicating what will be included and what excluded in the use of the concept in a particular research project.
5. Operationalization is the process of specifying concrete observations that will be taken as indicators of a concept.
6. In operationalization, it is important to be clear which dimension is being operationalized.
7. Indicators are concrete observations taken to represent concepts.
8. As concepts are specified, terms defined, and operational measures devised, there is a tendency to regard the concepts as more real than the concrete observations.
9. Always remember: Observations are real; concepts are mental creations.
10. Nominal measures merely distinguish attributes as different from one another.
11. Ordinal measures arrange attributes as more or less than each other.
12. In interval measures, attributes are separated by equal intervals.
13. Ratio measures are like interval measures, with the addition of a true zero.
14. Specific statistical techniques require that variables be of a particular level of measurement.
15. Precise measurements are not necessarily accurate.
16. Validity is the quality of a measurement actually measuring what it purports to measure.
17. Face validity (prima facie validity) means that a measurement obviously—on the face of it—seems to measure what it is said to measure.
18. Reliability is the quality of consistency in a measure. If the same

measurement were made more than once, it would yield the same result each time.

19. An index is a composite measure created from the combination of several indicators.
20. A scale is a composite measure that takes account of the differing intensities of indicators.
21. Indexes and scales are unidimensional measures of variables.
22. A typology is a classification system that combines more than one dimension.

? REVIEW QUESTIONS

1. Look through a research journal and pick an article. Identify a concept in the article. How has it been conceptualized and operationalized?
2. Find a newspaper article reporting research data. Identify two variables and identify their levels of measurement.
3. Write four statements presenting education as (1) a ratio variable, (2) an interval variable, (3) an ordinal variable, and (4) a nominal variable.
4. Suppose a researcher were going to study the variable education. List several dimensions of the variable and suggest ways of operationalizing each.
5. A researcher measures "civic participation" by asking people whether or not they voted in the last election. What are some reasons this might not be a valid measure?
6. The following have high status. Describe the dimension of status each would rank high on.
   a. a millionaire
   b. a professor
   c. a priest
7. Suppose a researcher measures the "lawlessness" of cities in terms of the number of murders committed. What are some problems of validity and reliability in that measurement?
8. Select a concept of interest to you. Define it. Describe the aspects you want to include and exclude in your conceptualization. Then suggest an operational measure of the concept.
9. Suppose a researcher wants to measure delinquency among a group of juveniles. What problems are inherent in using arrest records as the operational measure? What problems are inherent in asking the juveniles to report on their own delinquent behavior?
10. Review the dimensions of religiosity presented by Glock and Stark (pp. 80–81). Suggest an operational measure for each dimension.

SUGGESTED READING

Gould, Julius and William Kolb. *A Dictionary of the Social Sciences* (New York: Free Press of Glencoe, 1964). A primary reference to the social scientific agreements on various concepts. Although the terms used by social scientists do not have ultimately "true" meanings, this reference book lays out the meanings social scientists have in mind when they use those terms.

Lazarsfeld, Paul and Morris Rosenberg (eds.). *The Language of Social Research* (New York: Free Press of Glencoe, 1955), Section I. An excellent and diverse collection of descriptions of specific measurements in past social research. These 14 articles present extremely useful accounts of actual measurement operations performed by social researchers as well as more conceptual discussions of measurement in general.

Oppenheim, A. N. *Questionnaire Design and Attitude Measurement* (New York: Basic Books, 1966). An excellent and comprehensive treatment of the construction of questionnaires and their relation to measurement in general. Although the illustrations of questionnaire formats are not always the best, this comes the closest of any book available to being the definitive work on questionnaires. Its coverage ranges from the theoretical to the nitty-gritty.

Wallace, Walter. *The Logic of Science in Sociology* (Chicago: Aldine-Atherton, 1971), Chapter 3. A brief and lucid presentation of concept formation within the context of other research steps. This discussion relates conceptualization to observation on the one hand and to generalization on the other.

SAMPLING

INTRODUCTION

In November 1980, Ronald Reagan was elected president of the United States with 50.8 percent of the popular vote, as against 41 percent for Jimmy Carter and 6.6 percent for third-party candidate John Anderson. This election outcome was widely regarded as an "upset" for political pollsters, none of whom had predicted such a wide margin for Reagan. How far off were the polls? Compare the final preelection Gallup poll—based on interviews conducted October 30 through November 1—with the actual results shown at the top of page 103.

When George Gallup released his findings on November 2, he warned that political polls could give only an estimate of probable election outcomes, not a precise prediction of the results. He pointed out, moreover, that, in all the final election polls since 1936, the last estimate had been off

	Final Gallup poll	Actual voting
Reagan	47%	50.8%
Carter	44	41.0
Anderson	8	6.6
Other	1	1.6
	100%	100%

by an average of 2.4 percentage points. As things turned out, the 1980 poll was off by 3.8 percentage points, somewhat more than the average (Ladd and Ferree, 1981).

Whether you feel the 1980 Gallup "error" was a large one or a small one, there's one other aspect of the poll that you might find a little startling. In 1980, nearly 100 million Americans voted (U.S. Bureau of the Census, 1981). How many interviews do you suppose the Gallup organization conducted in order to come within 4 percentage points of the actual result? Fewer than 2000. In this chapter, we are going to find out how it's possible for social researchers to pull off such wizardry.

We've been talking a lot about observation in recent chapters. Those discussions have omitted the question of *what* or *whom* will be observed. If you think about it for a minute, you'll see that a social researcher has a whole world of potential observations. Yet nobody can observe everything. A critical part of social research, then, is the decision as to what will be observed and what won't. If a researcher wants to study voters, for example, which voters will be studied? That's the subject of this chapter.

Sampling is the process of selecting observations. We'll begin with a brief examination of the purpose of sampling, then look at the history of social scientific sampling. As you'll see, this aspect of research has evolved over time.

The key section of this chapter discusses the logic and the skills of probability sampling. Probability sampling techniques—involving random sampling—make it possible for a researcher to generalize from relatively few observations to a much wider population. We'll examine the requirements for generalizability. As you'll discover, random selection is a scientific procedure, not the haphazard choosing people often have in mind when they say "selected at random."

Although probability sampling is central to social research today, we'll take some time to examine a variety of nonprobability methods as well. Though not based on random selection, these methods have their own logic and can provide useful samples for social inquiry. We'll examine both the advantages and the shortcomings of such methods and see where they fit within the social scientific enterprise.

THE PURPOSE OF SAMPLING

Most of what you and I "know" is based on partial observations. You've probably noticed that traffic gets pretty heavy between, say, 7:00 and 9:00 on weekday mornings. But I doubt that you've been out in rush-hour traffic *every* morning. And though you probably believe there's a rush hour in all major cities, I know you can't have observed a very large percentage of all those rush hours everywhere. You probably have some ideas about college textbooks, though I know you haven't read them all. You probably have a different opinion of "romance" magazines—again without observing them all.

In almost every social research question you can imagine, it would be impossible to make all the observations relevant to answering it. Suppose, for example, that you want to learn something about American college students. There are approximately 10 million of them. You couldn't possibly hope to observe that many people individually. Inevitably, you would observe only a tiny fraction of the population you wished to learn about.

There is an obvious danger in drawing conclusions about a broad class of phenomena based on observations of only some of them. If you were to interview students where you attend school, there's no assurance that those students would be "typical" of all American college students. Indeed, the ones you interviewed might not even be typical of your school. Perhaps you chose particularly studious students, or perhaps you leaned toward athletes. In either case, you wouldn't really be able to talk about college students in general.

The purpose of sampling in social science is to select a set of people or things for study who—taken together—have the same characteristics as the larger group from which they were selected. Since about 52 percent of American college students are men (U.S. Bureau of the Census, 1979:164), the sample chosen for observation should be about 52 percent men. Both the sample and the total population of students should have the same age, ethnic distribution, and regional representation; public and private schools should be represented in the same proportions in the sample as in the population, as should the proportions of junior colleges, four-year colleges, and universities.

Ultimately, the sample chosen for observation should be a miniaturized version of the whole. When it has that character, we speak of the sample as being *representative*. If the sample is representative of the population from which it is selected, then whatever is learned about the sample may reasonably be assumed to apply also to the population. For example, CBS News and the *New York Times* interviewed a sample of 12,782 voters as they left the polls on November 4, 1980. Fifty-four percent of the men and 46 percent of the women said they voted for Reagan (*Public Opinion*, 1981:42). It is assumed, therefore, that more men than women (by approximately the percentages mentioned) voted for Reagan among the electorate as a whole.

Representation, then, is the purpose of sampling. Selecting samples that fulfill that purpose, however, is an involved business. The sampling procedures used by social researchers today are the current stage in an evolution of techniques that has seen rocky times. Since the history of sampling is instructive, let's take a momentary historical diversion.

THE HISTORY OF SAMPLING

Sampling in social research has developed hand-in-hand with political polling. This is the case, no doubt, since political polling is one of the few opportunities social researchers have to discover the accuracy of their estimates. On election day, they find out how well or poorly they did.

PRESIDENT ALF LANDON

You may have heard about the *Literary Digest* in connection with political polling. The *Digest* was a popular news magazine published in America between 1890 and 1938. In 1920, the *Digest* editors mailed postcards to people in six states, asking them who they were planning to vote for in the presidential campaign between Warren Harding and James Cox. Names were selected for the poll from telephone directories and automobile registration lists. On the basis of the postcards sent back, the *Digest* correctly predicted that Harding would be elected. In the elections that followed, the *Literary Digest* expanded its polling operations, and correct predictions were made in 1924, 1928, and 1932.

In 1936, the *Digest* conducted their most ambitious poll: Ten million ballots were sent out to people listed in telephone directories and on lists of automobile owners. Over two million responded, giving Republican contender Alf Landon a stunning 57 to 43 percent landslide over incumbent President Franklin Roosevelt. The editors modestly cautioned:

We make no claim to infallibility. We did not coin the phrase "uncanny accuracy" which has been so freely applied to our Polls. We know only too well the limitations of every straw vote, however enormous the sample gathered, however scientific the method. It would be a miracle if every State of the forty-eight behaved on Election day exactly as forecast by the Poll. (1936a:6)

Two weeks later, the *Digest* editors knew the limitations of straw polls even better. They were spared the miracle of all 48 states voting exactly as forecast: Voters gave Roosevelt a third term in office with the largest landslide in history, 61 percent of the vote. Landon won only 8 electoral votes to Roosevelt's 523. The editors were puzzled by their unfortunate turn of luck.

A part of the problem surely lay in the 22 percent return rate garnered by the poll. The editors asked:

Why did only one in five voters in Chicago to whom *The Digest* sent ballots take the trouble to reply? And why was there a preponderance of Republicans in the one-fifth that did reply? . . . we were getting better cooperation in what we have always regarded as a public service from Republicans than we were getting from Democrats. Do Republicans live nearer to mail-boxes? Do Democrats generally disapprove of straw polls? (1936b:7)

Certainly a part of the answer to these questions lay in the sampling frame used by the *Digest*: telephone subscribers and automobile owners. Such a sampling design would select a disproportionately wealthy sample, especially coming on the tail end of the worst economic depression in the nation's history. The sample effectively excluded poor people, and the poor people predominantly voted for Roosevelt's New Deal recovery program.

PRESIDENT THOMAS E. DEWEY

The 1936 election also saw the emergence of a young pollster whose name was to become synonymous with public opinion. In contrast to the *Literary Digest*, George Gallup correctly predicted that Roosevelt would beat Landon. Gallup's success in 1936 hinged on his use of quota sampling, which I'll say more about later in the chapter. For now, you need know only that quota sampling is based on a knowledge of the characteristics of the population being sampled: What proportion are men, what proportion women, what proportions are of various incomes, ages, and so on. People are selected for the purposes of matching the population characteristics: the right number of poor, white, rural men; the right number of rich, black, urban women, and so forth. The quotas are based on those variables most relevant to the study. By knowing the numbers of people with various incomes in the nation, Gallup selected his sample in such a fashion as to insure the right number of respondents at each income level.

Gallup and his American Institute of Public Opinion used this quota sampling method to good effect in 1936, 1940, and 1944—correctly picking the presidential winner in each of those years. Then, in 1948, Gallup and most political pollsters suffered the embarrassment of picking New York Governor Thomas Dewey over incumbent President Harry Truman. A number of factors accounted for the 1948 failure. First, most of the pollsters stopped polling in early October despite a steady trend toward Truman during the campaign. In addition, many voters were undecided throughout the campaign, and they went disproportionately for Truman when they stepped into the voting booth. More important for our present purposes, however, Gallup's failure rested on the unrepresentativeness of his samples.

Quota sampling—which had been effective in earlier years—was Gallup's undoing in 1948. Recall that this technique requires that the researcher know something about the total population (of voters, in this instance). For national political polls, such information came primarily from census data. In 1948, however, a world war, producing a massive movement from country to city, had radically changed the character of the American population from what the 1940 census showed. City dwellers, moreover, were more likely to vote Democratic, hence the rural-urban unrepresentativeness also underestimated the number of Democratic votes.

In 1948, a number of academic researchers had been experimenting with probability sampling methods. By and large, they were far more successful than those using quota samples. Today, probability sampling remains the primary method for selecting samples for social science research. Let's see how it works.

PROBABILITY SAMPLING

Most sampling in the social sciences is based on probability theory. While it's not necessary for you to have a full grasp of probability theory, you should know enough about the fundamental logic of **probability sampling** in order to understand the most standard sampling techniques.

THE LOGIC OF PROBABILITY

The fundamental principle of probability sampling is this: A sample will tend to be representative of the population from which it is selected if every member of the population has the same chance of being selected into that sample. This principle is perhaps easiest to understand in contrast to its opposites. Imagine that the students at your school are the population we want to study. Now suppose that we interview all the men and none of the women. Two things are evident: (1) The sample is hardly representative, and (2) individual students did not have the same chance of being selected. Men had a 100 percent chance and women had a 0 percent chance. Suppose that we selected the sample by standing in front of the library on a Tuesday afternoon and stopping students for interviewing. Again, the sample would not be representative: it would overrepresent students who studied at the library and underrepresent those who studied elsewhere or who didn't study at all. Moreover, the sample would overrepresent students with Tuesday-Thursday-Saturday class schedules and underrepresent those with Monday-Wednesday-Friday schedules.

RANDOM SELECTION The way to select a sample of students from your school that would represent the whole student body would be to insure that every student had an equal chance of being selected for the sample. Here's perhaps the most obvious way of **random selection.** Imagine lining up the entire student body, single-file, in a column stretching from one end of campus to the other. Then move down the line, flipping a coin on behalf of each student: Heads puts that student in the sample, tails leaves him or her out. This procedure would result in the selection of approximately half the student body into the sample, and each student would have had, unquestionably, the same chance of being selected.

You've probably heard references to *random sampling, random selection,* or *picked at random.* To accomplish such procedures feasibly, researchers typically use **random numbers,** numbers generated by a computer following the rule that each number be selected with no consideration given to what numbers had been previously selected. Each number has been given the same chance of selection as any other number, as though the computer had flipped a coin repeatedly to make its selections. Appendix C of this book contains a table of random numbers.

To select a sample of students, therefore, you might do the following. Make a list of all students at your school and number the list. Let's say there are an even 40,000 students. If you wanted a sample of 1000, you could go down the list of numbers in the table of random numbers and pick students whose numbers came up. To see what I mean, turn to Appendix C and run your finger down the first column. The first number is 10,480: you'd go to your student list and include the 10,480th student in your list. Next, you'd include student 22,368, then student 24,130. Notice that the next number in the table is 42,167; you don't have that many students listed, so just skip that number and go on to 37,570. You'd repeat this procedure until you had 1000 students in your sample. In this fashion, you would have selected a sample of students in such a way that each had the same chance of being chosen. As a result, what you learned about that sample of students would tend to apply to the whole population of students at your school.

SAMPLING ERROR Several times above, I mentioned that a probability sample would *tend* to represent the population from which it was drawn. The degree to which it does is primarily a function of the number of people selected into the sample. As an approximate rule of thumb, the following sample sizes will produce samples accurate within the number of percentage points indicated:

Sample size	Accurate within
100	10 percentage points
400	5 percentage points
1600	2.5 percentage points
6400	1.25 percentage points

This means that if 45 percent of the students at your school are men, a probability sample of 400 students would be likely to fall within 5 percentage points, plus or minus—somewhere between 40 and 50 percent men. When I say the sample "would be likely" to produce that degree of accuracy, the full, technical statement is that 95 out of 100 such samples would fall within the range indicated. If we were to select sample after sample from the school student population, 95 percent of those samples would have between 40 and 50 percent men in them. This is referred to as the 95 percent **confidence level,** and it's the standard most often used in references to **sampling error.** (I'll elaborate on this in the next section.) This is what pollsters work with in saying that an election is too close to call: If the apparent lead of one candidate over another could be simply a matter of normal sampling error, then it's unwise to draw any conclusions about who is "really" leading.

The point is that probability samples do not necessarily yield perfectly accurate representations of the population, but they are likely to come close. Moreover, how close is a function of the size of the sample selected. You should always check for the size of samples used in research projects, since these can vary a great deal—and the accuracy of the results with them. The Real World Research box entitled "How Many Rope-Skippers?" illustrates this.

HOW MANY ROPE-SKIPPERS?

William Myles and his colleagues (1981) were interested in learning whether rope-skipping might be a reasonable alternative to jogging and other forms of exercise for people who didn't get much exercise in the rest of their lives. To find out, they conducted a study of six different styles of rope-skipping, gauging the intensity of each as measured by heart rate.

Subjects performed each of the six styles three times for 2 minutes at a time. Their heart rates were measured after each 2-minute session. The tests were conducted over several days, with the order of the styles assigned at random. Ultimately, the researchers concluded that "the rhythm hop and the rhythm leap can be recommended for individuals up to middle age," contradicting previous research suggesting that rope-skipping is too strenuous for people who don't get much exercise in their other activities. However, the Myles study was based on *six* subjects, with no information given on how they were selected. The researchers wisely qualify their results by saying they "remain to be confirmed on a larger population" (1981:78).

SOURCE William S. Myles, Michael R. Dick, and Rita Jantti, "Heart Rate and Rope Skipping Intensity." *Research Quarterly for Exercise and Sport*, March 1981:76–79.

CALCULATING SAMPLING ERROR Notice that the accuracy of samples is a function of the *size* of the sample, not the *proportion* it represents of the total population. That's a point of common confusion, so let me make it clear. To determine the sex ratio among the more than 200 million Americans and come within 2.5 percentage points, you would need a probability sample of 1600. To achieve the same degree of accuracy in sampling a city's population of, say, 100,000, you would also require 1600 in your sample, despite the fact that the two proportions are very different: .000008 versus .016, respectively. The proportions are irrelevant because the probability theories upon which sampling is based assume that the populations involved are infinitely large; hence all sample sizes would represent 0 percent of the population. Only when the sample represents around 5 percent or more of the total population do researchers take account of the proportion selected.

There's one further element to be added to the determination of sampling accuracy. We define the accuracy of a sample by calculating the amount of error we can expect. The following formula allows you to calculate sampling error in probability sampling:

$$\sqrt{\frac{P \times Q}{n}}$$

P = some percentage (e.g., male)
Q = 1 − P
n = sample size

Take a simple example: a sample of 400 taken from a population that is 50 percent male. Inside the square root radical, we have (.5 × .5) divided by 400; the square root is .5/20 or 2.5. This is the sampling error.

Recall my earlier reference to confidence levels. The significance of the sampling error that we've calculated is that 95/100 such samples would produce an estimate of the percentage male that was within plus or minus 2 sampling errors of the true value. Let's take that step by step.

The sampling error calculated above was 2.5 percentage points. Twice that is 5 percentage points. Probability theory indicates that, if we selected a great many samples of 400 each from the population in question, 95 out of every 100 samples would have between 45 and 55 percent males in it (50 percent plus or minus 5 percentage points).

The range—in this case, 45 to 55 percent—is called the **confidence interval** in probability sampling. The 95-out-of-a-hundred is called the *95 percent confidence level* and, as indicated earlier, is the most commonly used level of confidence. It is not the only option, however.

The same body of probability theory states that 99.9 percent of all samples would produce estimates within plus or minus 3 sampling errors of the true value. In the present example, we'd say we were 99.9 percent confident that the true value was between 42.5 and 57.5 percent. All statements of sampling error should specify both the confidence level and the confidence interval. When no confidence level is specified, you can usually assume that the 95 percent level is being used.

George Gallup, through the well-known Gallup Poll, has done a great deal to educate the American public in the nature of survey methods and sampling error. A 1981 report on public opinion, for example, concludes with the statement:

These results are based on in-person interviews with 1545 adults, 18 and older, conducted in more than 300 scientifically selected localities across the nation during the period April 3–6.

For results based on a sample of this size, one can say with 95 percent confidence that the error attributable to sampling and other random effects could be 3 percentage points in either direction. (*Gallup, 1981:9*)

The sampling error formula also shows the influence of the percentage distribution in the population. A 50–50 split, as in the above example, produces the most sampling error. As the variable is skewed in one direction or the other, the sampling error is reduced. For example, blacks make up approximately 11 percent of the American population. A probability sample of 400 would—95 times out of 100—contain between 8 and 14 percent blacks, plus or minus 3 percentage points. Jews make up some 3 percent of the U.S. population. Samples of 400 would produce estimates of the percentage of Jews within plus or minus 1.7 percentage points. Take a minute to calculate these two examples, so that you get a better grasp of the relationships connecting percentage distributions, sample size, and sampling error. Notice that what matters here is the "skewedness" of the variable, that is, the proportion of Jews in the population. As stated earlier, it is irrelevant what proportion of all Jews is selected.

Sample size alone is not a guarantee of representativeness. When John F. Veiga set about discovering whether corporate executives who move from job to job do better than those who stay with the same firm, he based his conclusions on 1191 managers. Here's what Veiga said about his sample. What questions would you raise about the sample?

In a large-scale study of managerial careers done over the past few years, I surveyed all the managers up to the level of vice president in three major U.S. corporations. All three companies are in manufacturing. Each employs well in excess of 100,000 people and each has more than 40 domestic plant locations. (*1981:20*)

Here are some of the questions you should have asked. What were the three companies? How were they chosen? What do they represent? Do the findings of this study say something about large corporations in general? What, if anything, do they say about smaller corporations? Are the findings applicable to nonmanufacturing corporations—banks, insurance companies, advertising agencies, and so forth?

As we'll see in the next section, it is important to note what a researcher's sample has been selected from.

SAMPLING FRAMES

Probability theory, as we've seen, provides a theoretical basis for the selection of samples that very closely reflect the populations from which they are selected. Shortly, we'll look at some of the concrete selection techniques that accomplish that. There's an intervening matter, however, that often produces confusion in sampling and which is essential to the evaluation of samples.

For the most part, probability sampling comes down to the selection of elements from a list. To select a sample of students from your school, for example, we would need a list of their names. To select a sample of voters in a city, we would need a list of all the voters. These lists are called **sampling frames.** Everything that has been said about the representativeness of probability samples should now be revised slightly: Probability samples represent the sampling frames from which they are selected.

Ideally, a researcher will (1) have a research interest in studying some meaningful population, (2) find a sampling frame that lists all the members of that population, and (3) select a sample from that sampling frame. In practice, however, there are usually discrepancies between the populations and the sampling frames from which samples are selected. The student roster at your school will inevitably omit some students, and it will contain names of students who have dropped out of school. A list of registered voters will have the same kinds of discrepancies. Sometimes these discrepancies are few enough as to be trivial. Other times, however, the only available sampling frames are merely approximations of the populations the researchers are interested in. As one of the most common examples, researchers use a city's telephone directory as a sampling frame for studying the city's population, its voters, or the like. The very poor, the transient, and those who seek the privacy of unlisted numbers are all omitted from such a sampling frame.

Here are some examples of reports of sampling frames:

The data for this research were obtained from a random sample of parents of children in the third grade in public and parochial schools in Yakima County, Washington. (*Petersen & Maynard, 1981:92*)

Using the 1979 ASA *Guide to Graduate Departments of Sociology* and *The 1979 Directory of Sociology Departments*, 120 institutions with sociology departments were identified in the Pacific region. . . . Mail questionnaires were sent to the chairs of all 120 institutions in the region. . . . Chairs were asked to provide the following items of information on all members of their departments. . . . (*1981:108*)

The sample at Time 1 consisted of 160 names drawn randomly from the telephone directory of Lubbock, Texas. (*Tan, 1980:242*)

The data reported in this paper . . . were gathered from a probability sample of adults aged 18 and over residing in households in the 48 contiguous United States. Personal interviews with 1,914 respondents were conducted by the Survey Research Center of the University of Michigan during the fall of 1975. (*Jackman and Senter, 1980:345*)

This last example illustrates a common report on sampling in the research literature. While the statement doesn't tell us the precise sampling frame used, it cites an established research organization with well-developed sampling procedures. The University of Michigan, the National Opinion Research Center (NORC) at the University of Chicago, and other university research centers, as well as the national commercial polling firms such as Gallup, Roper, and Harris routinely use sampling methods of proven reliability. Research reports based on data collected by such organizations will often omit detailed descriptions of methods since such accounts are either known to many professional readers or can be obtained from other publications.

Sometimes research reports are vague as to the sampling frames and sampling techniques employed:

The data for this analysis come from a telephone survey of 5241 adult respondents in the St. Louis SMSA [Standard Metropolitan Statistical Area]. . . . Sixty study neighborhoods were selected to match, as closely as possible, existing police precincts and community boundaries. A detailed structured questionnaire was administered to a randomly selected group of respondents from each of these study areas. (*Benson, 1981:52*)

A random sample of households yielded 170 completed interviews. Though the sample is based on a random selection of households, it is somewhat purposive in the sense that a special effort was made to include youthful respondents, since it is among them that conflict with the police is believed to be most intense. Interviewers were instructed to interview an adult member of the household and a teenaged member, whenever possible. (*Mirande, 1981:71*)

Though the samples selected in these two studies may be excellent, the information provided doesn't allow us to judge. In the first, we know that telephone households were selected, but we don't know whether telephone directories were used—with the attendant problems that entails—or if one of the newer telephone sampling techniques was used. Consider, for contrast, this report: "All interviews were conducted by telephone, and sampling was based on a probability sample of area codes and telephone prefixes, followed by four random digits" (Chaffee and Choe, 1980:58). This latter technique avoids the underrepresentation of people with unlisted numbers.

In the second example, we know nothing about the list of households from which the random sample was selected. Did the researcher have a list of all households in the neighborhood being studied? How complete was the list?

See what questions and objections you might raise to the following report. The issue under discussion is which drugs are most frequently prescribed by American physicians.

Information on prescription drug sales is not easy to obtain. But Rinaldo V. DeNuzzo, a professor of pharmacy at the Albany College of Pharmacy, Union

University, Albany, N.Y., has been tracking prescription drug sales for 25 years by polling nearby drugstores. He publishes the results in an industry trade magazine, *MM&M.*

DeNuzzo's latest survey, covering 1980, is based on reports from 66 pharmacies in 48 communities in New York and New Jersey. Unless there is something peculiar about that part of the country, his findings can be taken as representative of what happens across the country. (*Moskowitz, 1981*)

The main thing that should strike you is the final sentence in the quotation presented—the casual comment about whether there is anything peculiar about New York and New Jersey. There is. These 2 states are hardly typical of the other 50 in terms of lifestyle, so we are hardly safe in assuming that residents in these large, urbanized, Eastern Seaboard states would necessarily have the same drug-use patterns as residents in, say, Mississippi, Utah, New Mexico, and Vermont.

Does the survey even represent prescription patterns in New York and New Jersey? In order to determine that, we would have to know something about the manner in which the 48 communities and the 66 pharmacies were selected. We should be wary in this regard in view of the reference to "polling nearby drugstores." As we've seen, there are several methods for selecting samples that insure representativeness, and unless they are used, we should not generalize from the study findings.

The issue of sampling frames is implicit throughout sample selection, so we'll see it appearing repeatedly as we discuss the actual techniques for probability selection.

TECHNIQUES OF SAMPLING

Although people often refer to *random selection,* that term is not terribly precise. Sometimes, it is used in reference to what might more accurately be called haphazard selection, as in those cases where interviewers stop passersby on a streetcorner with no rigorous plan for whom they'll stop. Even many of the acceptable probability selection methods are not literally random.

SIMPLE RANDOM SAMPLING In introducing the notion of probability selection, I gave examples of what is called simple random sampling. Flipping a coin or rolling dice in order to make selections are examples of simple random selection. The hypothetical example of numbering all the members of your school and selecting numbers from a table of random numbers is also an example. A **simple random sample,** then, is one in which every element in a population has the same chance of selection into the sample by virtue of selections being made through the use of random numbers.

In practice, simple random sampling is most typically done with computerized name lists. If the sampling frame is a computerized list, the computer can be instructed to generate a set of random numbers and print out the names associated with those numbers. This is obviously simpler than writing numbers beside names and looking up hundreds of numbers in a table.

SYSTEMATIC SAMPLING In practice, simple random sampling is seldom done. Instead, researchers are more likely to select **systematic samples:** taking every *k*th name from a list, every twenty-third name, for example. With few exceptions, this is a perfectly acceptable method. In fact, in some ways systematic sampling is superior to simple random sampling. If names are arranged alphabetically, for example, systematic sampling would assure a proper representation of the various sections of the alphabet, and to the extent that ethnic groups are slightly grouped alphabetically, systematic sampling improves ethnic representativeness. If the households in a city district are listed in geographical order (in a serpentine manner), a systematic sample assures geographical representativeness.

Systematic samples are usually initiated by a *random start*. If you are selecting every tenth element in a list, you begin by selecting a random number between 1 and 10, say 7. This is the first element in the sample. You then take every tenth element after it: 17, 27, 37, and so on.

STRATIFIED SAMPLING The advantage of systematic sampling is a function of grouping together similar elements before sampling and taking the correct numbers from each. If the student roster were first grouped by sex, for example, and then every thirty-fifth name was selected, we'd be assured of having the right numbers of men and women. The process of grouping similar people together before sampling is called *stratification,* and the sample a **stratified sample.** In sophisticated sample designs, several stratification variables may be used: Students might be grouped by sex, year, and grade-point average; city blocks might be grouped by average income of residents, racial composition, percentage of renters versus owners; and so on.

Once elements have been stratified for sampling, simple random samples can be selected within each of the separate subgroups or, more typically, a systematic sample can be selected across the stratified list.

MULTISTAGE CLUSTER SAMPLING Unfortunately, many populations of interest to researchers are not listed anywhere. Although your college maintains a list of its students, there is no one list of all American college students. Nor is there a list of all faculty members, all voters, all physicians, and so on. It is this lack of lists that gives rise to the approximation mentioned earlier: selecting a sampling frame that somewhat reflects the population of interest—telephone directories as lists of households, for example. A more complex sample design offers a generally superior solution to this problem. A *cluster sample* is one in which natural groupings (clusters) of elements are selected through some probability selection method, and then the elements making up each selected cluster are subsampled. Some examples will clarify this procedure.

Although there is no single list of college students, there are lists of colleges. It would be possible, therefore, to select a sample of colleges, get the student lists from each of the colleges selected, and then select samples of students from each of those lists. Though there is no list of city households, the U.S. Census Bureau provides lists of census blocks (usually the same as city blocks). In a high-quality city household sample, the researcher will select sample blocks, send people into the field to make lists of the households on each of those blocks, and then select samples of households from each block. Here's a good example:

Interviews were conducted with a random sample of 600 adolescents aged 13 through 17. A multistage sampling design involving the random sample of census tracts, blocks, and dwelling units was used. Selected dwelling units were screened for teenagers. If a teenager lived in a selected home, he or she was interviewed. If more than one youth lived in the selected dwelling, a random procedure based on age and sex was used to choose the respondent. If the initial unit was not the home of a 13- to 17-year-old, interviewers used a preestablished decision rule to select another unit on the block. (*Berman and Stookey, 1980:331–332*)

This sample design is called a **multistage cluster sample** (sometimes just called a cluster sample). It is multistage for the obvious reason, and the clusters are the natural groupings—colleges, blocks—that are sampled at the first stage of sampling. In the city household study, the researchers first listed the census tracts comprised in the city and selected a random sample of tracts. For each of the tracts selected, they listed the census blocks making up each tract and then selected a random sample of blocks from each. Once they had identified their sample of census blocks, they visited each and listed all the dwelling units they found there. Finally, they selected a sample of dwelling units on each selected block. This household sample design is also called an **area probability sample.** Figure 5.1 gives a graphic review of part of the process.

Typically, cluster samples also involve considerable stratification. Colleges could be stratified by region of the country, private or public sponsorship, size, and other characteristics. Then the lists of students could be further stratified as described earlier.

There is much more to be said about cluster sampling, but we don't need to go into further details here. Few researchers will undertake a complex cluster sample without knowing what they are doing, so you will usually not have to critique the fine points of cluster sampling.

FIGURE 5.1
Multistage cluster sampling.

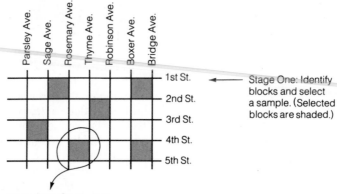

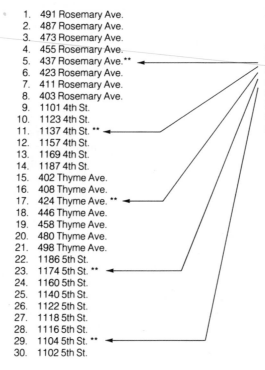

Stage One: Identify blocks and select a sample. (Selected blocks are shaded.)

Stage Two: Go to each selected block and list all households in order. (Example of one listed block.)

1.	491 Rosemary Ave.
2.	487 Rosemary Ave.
3.	473 Rosemary Ave.
4.	455 Rosemary Ave.
5.	437 Rosemary Ave.**
6.	423 Rosemary Ave.
7.	411 Rosemary Ave.
8.	403 Rosemary Ave.
9.	1101 4th St.
10.	1123 4th St.
11.	1137 4th St. **
12.	1157 4th St.
13.	1169 4th St.
14.	1187 4th St.
15.	402 Thyme Ave.
16.	408 Thyme Ave.
17.	424 Thyme Ave. **
18.	446 Thyme Ave.
19.	458 Thyme Ave.
20.	480 Thyme Ave.
21.	498 Thyme Ave.
22.	1186 5th St.
23.	1174 5th St. **
24.	1160 5th St.
25.	1140 5th St.
26.	1122 5th St.
27.	1118 5th St.
28.	1116 5th St.
29.	1104 5th St. **
30.	1102 5th St.

Stage Three: For each list, select sample of households. (In this example, every sixth household has been selected starting with #5, which was selected at random.)

All of the sampling techniques we have looked at have the same basic purpose: to achieve representative samples. Sometimes, however, it is appropriate to select samples that are purposely unrepresentative, as the Real World Research box entitled "Disproportionate Sampling" illustrates. You'll see, however, that special precautions are needed in such cases.

COMPLETION RATES

Probability theory makes numerous assumptions that are not met in practice. For the most part, these discrepancies are of little consequence. One, however, can matter a great deal.

The calculation of sampling error, as discussed above, assumes that observations will actually be made of all the elements selected into a sample. In most cases, this means that all the people selected must be reached and must agree to participate. In practice, this is almost never the case. Whether interviewers visit people in their homes, call them on the telephone, or mail questionnaires to them, some will refuse to participate; others will be unreachable. The problem with a less-than-complete response rate is that those not responding may be different from those who respond. Thus, the study results will be misleading. This effect is called **nonresponse bias.** Because of this danger, any report on sampling methods should also include a report on **completion rates,** in some cases called *return rates* or *response rates*. Here are some typical examples:

Fifty-three percent, or 2,282 of the questionnaire recipients, completed and returned the survey instrument. (*Holsti and Rosenau, 1980:6*)

The response rate for originally selected youth was 81 percent. (*Berman and Stookey, 1980:332*)

The response rate was just under 70 percent, which is within the normal range for national surveys conducted by the Survey Research Center in recent years. (*Jackman and Senter, 1980:344*)

The question you are probably asking is, "What is a sufficiently high completion rate?" Unfortunately, there is no answer to the question, except for 100 percent. This doesn't mean that nothing less than 100 percent is acceptable. As a rule of thumb, interview surveys that achieve 85 percent or higher completion rates would generally be regarded as successful in that regard. A 70 percent return rate in a mail questionnaire survey is quite high as such studies go. I would guess, moreover, that most researchers would regard a 60 percent return rate in a mail survey as sufficient. Fifty percent would probably be regarded as worth analyzing and reporting, whereas return rates lower than 50 percent probably need some additional justification. This last comment raises a more fundamental point.

DISPROPORTIONATE SAMPLING

Sometimes it's appropriate to select a sample in such a way that it isn't representative of the population—on purpose. It was appropriate, for example, when the *Harvard Business Review* decided to survey its subscribers on the issue of sexual harassment at work. Here's how Collins and Blodgett explained the matter:

We also skewed the sample another way: to ensure a representative response from women, we mailed a questionnaire to virtually every female subscriber, for a male/female ratio of 68% to 32%. This bias resulted in a response of 52% male and 44% female (and 4% who gave no indication of gender)—compared to HBR's U.S. subscriber proportion of 93% male and 7% female. (1981:78)

You should have noticed a couple of things in this quotation. First, it would be nice to know a little more about what *"virtually* every female" means. Evidently, they didn't send questionnaires to all female subscribers, but there's no indication of who was omitted and why. Second, the use of the term *representative* is at variance from the normal usage in social science. What they mean, of course, is that they want to get a substantial or "large enough" response from women, and **oversampling** is a perfectly acceptable way of accomplishing that.

By sampling more women than a straightforward probability sample would have produced, they have gotten enough women (812) to compare with the men

A relatively high completion rate doesn't assure a representative sample, nor does a low completion rate necessarily deny one. What do you suppose would be persuasive that a sample was a good representation of the population?

Often it's possible to test the representativeness of a sample. Suppose you had selected a sample of the students at your school. Chances are the school administration will have some data about the student body already: sex ratio, average age, and so on. Whatever data are available regarding the population characteristics can be used as a test of the representativeness of the sample.

Here's another excellent way of handling the problem of non-response. In a study of the impact of the Three Mile Island nuclear crisis on workers, Stanislav Kasl and his colleagues achieved a 61 percent re-

(960). Thus, when the authors report, for example, that 32 percent of the women and 66 percent of the men agree that "the amount of sexual harassment at work is greatly exaggerated," we know that the female response is based on a substantial number of cases. That's good. There's a problem, however.

To begin, subscriber surveys are always problematic. In this case, the best the researchers can hope to talk about is "what the subscribers to *Harvard Business Review* think." In a loose way, it might make sense to think of that population as representing the more sophisticated portion of corporate management. Unfortunately, the overall response rate was 25 percent. Although that is quite good for subscriber surveys, it is a low response rate in terms of generalizing from probability samples. Beyond that, however, the disproportionate sample design creates a further problem.

When the authors state that 73 percent favor company policies against harassment, that figure is undoubtedly too high, since the sample contains a disproportionately high percentage of women, who are more likely to favor such policies. In fact, when the researchers report that top management is more likely to feel that claims of sexual harassment are exaggerated than are middle and lower-level management, that finding is also suspect. As the researchers report, women are disproportionately represented in lower management. That fact alone might account for the apparent differences in different levels of management. In short, the failure to take account of the oversampling of women confounds all survey results that don't separate findings by sex.

SOURCE G. C. Collins and Timothy B. Blodgett, "Sexual Harassment . . . Some See It . . . Some Won't." *Harvard Business Review,* (March-April 1981): 76–95.

sponse rate. To test for nonresponse bias, they undertook a follow-up study.

Toward the end of data collection, a separate small methodological study was conducted with a random subset of 125 workers who until them were classified as non-respondents. Those 58 who were brought into the study under these special effort circumstances (mostly the "no contacts," but also a few "refusals") were found to be broadly representative of the other respondents, both on sociodemographic characteristics as well as the various indicators of impact. (1981:473)

The whole purpose of representativeness in samples is to justify generalization from the samples to the larger populations from which they were drawn. Let's now look at some of the rules of generalization.

GENERALIZING FROM SAMPLES

There are two kinds of generalization that social scientists commonly want to make from studies of samples: descriptive and explanatory. Let's consider them separately, since the requirements for each are somewhat different.

DESCRIPTIVE GENERALIZATIONS

Whenever the U.S. Census Bureau undertakes a sample survey and asks respondents whether they are employed, looking for work, or not even looking, the purpose of that questioning is to generalize from the sample to estimate the unemployment rate prevailing in the population as a whole. The purpose is descriptive generalization: The researchers wish to describe the sample (percent unemployed, for example) and infer that the same description would hold for the total population.

Whenever Gallup polls a sample of voters and asks them which candidate they would vote for "if the election were held today," the purpose is again descriptive generalization. No one cares how Gallup's particular sample would vote, but everyone is interested in the estimate of how the electorate as a whole would vote.

Ironically, descriptive generalizations are more difficult than explanatory ones. Valid descriptive generalizations depend directly on the nature of the measurements used—as we saw in Chapter 4—and on the representativeness of the samples. Whenever a research report purports to describe characteristics of a population on the basis of a sample from that population, you should check all the elements that typically go into a representative sample: an appropriate sampling frame, a probability sampling design, a high completion rate, and any tests of representativeness.

Even when the sample is found to be somewhat unrepresentative of the population, it is possible to draw meaningful and accurate inferences from it. Typically, this is done by **weighting.** Suppose, for example, that we wanted to find out how your student body felt about increasing the proportion of the athletics budget that went to women's sports. Imagine that we select a sample of 1000 students and find 52 percent opposed to the proposal and 48 percent in favor. (To simplify the illustration, we'll pretend there are no undecided students.) In evaluating our study design, however, we discover that we have underrepresented women in the sample. Whereas the student body is 50–50, we have selected 550 men and 450 women—unlikely with good sampling techniques but possible. We could make a statistical adjustment that would give women their proper representation: By multiplying every woman's responses by 1.22 (550/450), we could statistically create 550 women to match the 550 men. Table 5.1 illustrates the way this adjustment works.

TABLE 5.1   Unweighted and Weighted Results, Attitudes toward Increasing Women's Sports Budget (hypothetical)

	Men	Women	Total
Unweighted			
In favor	90	390	48%
Opposed	460	60	52%
TOTAL			
550	450	100%	100%
Weighted			
In favor	90	477	52%
Opposed	460	73	48%
TOTAL	550	550	100%

Notice that weighting the sample in order to compensate for misrepresentations can change the overall results of the study. In this case, a slight majority of the student body is in favor of the proposal, whereas the raw, unweighted results pointed in the opposite direction.

It is interesting, in this context, to note that another of the problems discovered by political pollsters in 1948 was that they had not handled the "undecided" voters appropriately. In the preelection polls, it was simply assumed that the undecideds would ultimately vote in the same proportions of Democrat and Republican as those who had declared themselves. In fact, more of them voted for the Democrat, Truman. Since then, Gallup and the other pollsters have taken great pains to weight their results to take account of past voting patterns and other variables.

In summary, descriptive generalizations depend directly on the representativeness of the samples selected. Good sampling methods should produce representative samples, and any distortions found to exist can often be adjusted for by weighting.

EXPLANATORY GENERALIZATIONS

There is an irony in the distinction between descriptive and explanatory conclusions to be drawn from social research. On the one hand, the explanatory findings—explaining *why* things are the way they are—seem intellectually superior to simple description. Knowing why there's crime, inflation, or war seems more important than simply measuring how much there is. In the present context of generalizing from samples to populations, however, explanation is easier to justify than description.

Whereas descriptive inferences are directly affected by the representativeness of the sample, explanatory inferences are not. Let's look again at the hypothetical illustration of attitudes toward the women's sports budget. We've already seen that the descriptive conclusions can be turned around by the unrepresentativeness of the sample. Weighting the sample appropriately switched the majority from opposition to support. Suppose we wanted to explain why people favored or opposed shifting more money into the budget for women's sports.

Table 5.1 leaves little doubt that sex is a powerful determinant of attitudes about the proposal. Women are far more likely (390/450 = 87%) than men (90/550 = 16%) to favor the proposal. Though the unrepresentative sample misled us as to the overall student body opinion, it did not conceal the causal process at work.

To distort the descriptive generalization, then, it was necessary for the sample to underrepresent women. To distort the explanatory generalization, it would have been necessary to have too many "opposed" women and too few "favorable" ones, or the converse misrepresentation of men. Even though too few women were picked in this hypothetical example, it is likely that those selected reflected the correct proportion of female opinions on the issue.

As a consumer of research, then, you must be able to evaluate the representativeness of a sample in terms of the purposes of the study. In general, you can afford to be somewhat more generous in the case of explanatory findings than in the case of descriptive ones.

This completes our examination of probability sampling methods. You should now be prepared to read about and understand the samples selected by other researchers and even to select simple samples yourself. At this point I want to spend a few minutes examining some other sampling methods, since not all social research uses probability sampling.

NONPROBABILITY SAMPLING

Although probability sampling is the primary sampling method used in social research—especially when rigorous description is the purpose—there are situations when other methods are appropriate. In this section, we'll examine some **nonprobability sampling** methods—ones that are not based on random selection: purposive sampling, snowball sampling, and quota sampling.

PURPOSIVE SAMPLING

Sometimes, the research purpose is such that the researcher should simply choose what to observe on the basis of his or her own judgment. This is called a **purposive,** or **judgment, sample.**

Suppose you wanted to do a study of community leaders in a small town. You'd be well advised to make your own decision as to whom to include, based on what you mean by "community leader"; there's no probability sampling method that would point to the people you want to study.

Often, purposive sampling is used in situations where the researcher wants to study all the people or things appropriate to the inquiry: studying all of a small town's community leaders, for example. If you've studied all of Babbieville's community leaders, you have no problem of generalization about that particular group. If you wanted to study community leaders in general, however, it might be appropriate to define the category in such a way that you could create a list of such people in many communities and select a probability sample.

Purposive sampling can be an appropriate and legitimate method for getting subjects appropriate to a research objective. At the same time, it is important that you learn to recognize where the researcher has simply selected whoever is available, rather than having a specific purpose in mind. Consider this report on the sampling design in an examination of knowledge and opinions regarding nutrition and cancer among medical students and family physicians:

The fourth-year medical students of the University of Minnesota Medical School in Minneapolis comprised the student population in this study. The physican population consisted of all physicians attending a "Family Practice Review and Update" course sponsored by the University of Minnesota Department of Continuing Medical Education. (*Cooper-Stephenson and Theologides, 1981:472*)

After all is said and done, what will the results of this study represent? They cannot distinguish medical students from family physicians in the United States or even in Minnesota. Who were the physicians who attended the course? We can guess that they were probably more concerned about their continuing education than other physicians, but we can't say that for sure. Ultimately, we don't know what to do with the results of a study like this.

SNOWBALL SAMPLING

Often, the only way to locate people appropriate for study is through referrals. Suppose you wanted to study the people who participated in a student demonstration. There's no list available for sampling.

If you knew a few people who had participated in the demonstration, you could ask them to tell you the names of others they knew were there. You could then study those newly named participants and ask them to give you the names of others who were there. This unfolding process yields what is called a **snowball sample:** the selection of relevant subjects through referrals from other subjects.

Here's how Letitia Anne Peplau set about selecting a sample of gay men and women:

Recruiting research participants—our first task—wasn't always easy. Many lesbians and gay men distrust psychologists and feel maligned by a profession that only recently removed homosexuality from its catalog of mental disorders. To recruit as diverse a sample as possible, we spread word of our research throughout the Los Angeles area. We got in touch with homosexual organizations in the community and at universities, ran advertisements in homosexual publications, and used informal social networks. Ultimately, 127 lesbians and 128 gay men took part in our study in 1976 and 1977. (1981:29)

Like the purposive sample, the snowball sample leaves the researcher with a problem regarding generalization. Since you don't know what people are included in the larger population of interest, a snowball sample leaves you with a question as to whether the people you've located and observed are representative of the larger population. In fact, you can assume that you've discovered the most visible members, perhaps the most active ones. In that event, your sample is definitely not representative.

All these problems notwithstanding, a snowball sample may be the most appropriate means of selecting relevant observations. The choice may be between learning something of questionable generalizability or learning nothing at all.

QUOTA SAMPLING

I've already mentioned this last type of nonprobability sampling method. **Quota sampling** was the method that served George Gallup so well in 1936—and caused him troubles in 1948. Here's how the method works.

A representative sample is one that has the same characteristics as the population it is intended to represent. If the population is made up of half men and half women, then the same should be true of the sample. As we've seen, a probability sample will produce that relationship. Going a step further, stratification insures representativeness in the variables that the sample is stratified on. Quota sampling works on a similar principle.

Let's return to the example of sampling a college student body. For simplicity, let's assume we want to pick a sample of 1000. Assume further that we have a good deal of information about the student body's characteristics. We know not only that half are women but further that 30 percent of the women are first-year students and that 10 percent of those are black. This means that 1.5 percent of the whole student body are first-year black women. Suppose that, say, 2 percent are first-year black men; 1.2 percent are second-year black women; and so on.

Imagine a complex table—called a **quota matrix**—giving a breakdown of all such subcategories of students, indicating the percentage each represents within the whole student body. A quota sample would be created through the selection of people to fit—in proper proportions—each of the categories. For a sample of 1000, then, we'd pick 15 first-year black women, 20 first-year black men, 12 second-year black women, and so forth. The total sample, so constructed, would be representative of the larger population in terms of the variables used in selecting it. And to the extent that those variables were related to the variables to be studied (political attitudes, for example), the sample should be representative in terms of those variables as well.

In a somewhat different approach, we might select some fixed number of respondents in each of the quota categories and then weight the results, as discussed earlier.

In either event, there is a range of options available for the selection of individuals to represent the various quota categories. This is the source of both the advantage of quota sampling—you can select people who are readily available—and also the danger—they may be unrepresentative in terms of variables other than those involved in the quota matrix. Ultimately, the problem with all forms of nonprobability sampling is that we don't know whether the sample is representative or not. The major strength of probability sampling is that we can calculate how accurate the sample findings are likely to be in representing the larger population.

Among all the aspects of social research design, sampling is the most amenable to concrete evaluation. Whereas measurements, for example, can be judged as relatively good or bad, sampling procedures can sometimes be judged right or wrong.

☑ *CONSUMER'S CHECKLIST*

As you've seen, sampling is a critical element in most social research. With an infinite number of observations to be made, the researcher must select a set that will reveal something useful about social life in general. Here are some questions to assist you in seeing if the researcher has been successful.

- Was sampling appropriate to the research purpose and situation? As we've seen, sometimes it's appropriate to study all the relevant elements, and sometimes it's appropriate to sample.

- If sampling was appropriate, were probability sampling methods called for, or would a purposive, snowball, or quota sample have been appropriate? Has the proper sample design been used?
- What is the population that the researcher wishes to draw conclusions about? Is the researcher's primary purpose description or explanation? If it is description, rigorous probability methods are called for.
- If a probability sample has been selected, what sampling frame has been used? Is it an appropriate representation of the population of interest to the researcher? What elements of the population have been omitted from the frame, and what extraneous elements have been included?
- What are the specific sampling techniques employed: simple random sampling, systematic sampling, or cluster sampling? Has the researcher stratified the sampling frame prior to sampling? Have the stratification variables been chosen wisely; that is, are they relevant to the variables under study?
- How large a sample was selected? What range of sampling error would such a sample size normally provide? Is that degree of accuracy appropriate to the research purpose, especially if the purpose is descriptive?
- What completion rate has the study achieved? Is it relatively high or low in terms of justifying generalizations from the sample to the population?
- What additional indications of representativeness has the researcher provided? Has it been possible to compare the sample and the population in terms of age and sex profiles, for instance?
- Ultimately, the question to answer is whether you can trust the sample design to have provided a sample of observations from which you can safely generalize to some larger, meaningful population, and whether the researcher has provided you with sufficient details for reaching your judgment.

KEY WORDS

Sampling	Confidence interval	Multistage cluster
Probability sampling	Sampling frame	sample
Random selection	Simple random sam-	Completion rate
Random number	ple	Weighting
Confidence level	Systematic sample	
Sampling error	Stratified sample	

Area probability
    sample
Oversampling
Nonresponse bias

Nonprobabilty sam-
    pling
Purposive (judgment)
    sample

Snowball sample
Quota sample
Quota matrix

MAIN POINTS

1. The purpose of sampling is to select a set of elements from a population in such a way that what we learn about the elements can be generalized to the population from which they were selected.
2. In social research, the elements selected are typically individual people, though this need not be the case.
3. Many sampling techniques have been developed in connection with political polling, where the accuracy of the samples can be compared to election-day results.
4. Probability sampling is the primary sampling method used in current social science research.
5. The fundamental principle of probability sampling is that every element in the population has the same chance of selection.
6. Equal probability of selection can be achieved by the use of random numbers.
7. Random samples provide approximations of the populations from which they are selected, but they are seldom 100 percent accurate.
8. Probability theory provides methods for calculating how accurate a probability sample is likely to be in approximating the population it was selected from.
9. The result of this calculation is called the sampling error.
10. Reports of sampling error must include the confidence interval and the confidence level.
11. A sampling frame is the list of elements that a sample is selected from.
12. Probability samples can only approximate the population of elements contained in the sampling frame.
13. Simple random sampling is a technique in which the elements of a population are numbered, a set of random numbers is selected, and those elements having the random numbers selected are included in the sample.
14. Systematic sampling is a technique in which every kth element in a list is included in the sample. Usually, systematic sampling is an acceptable substitute for simple random sampling.
15. Stratification is a technique in which the elements of a population are

grouped according to certain characteristics, and then a random or systematic sample is selected from each grouping.

16. In cluster sampling, natural groupings (clusters) of elements are listed and sampled. Then the elements contained in each selected cluster are listed and subsampled.

17. Once a good sample has been selected, it is important that a high percentage of those selected actually participate in the study; in other words, that there be a high completion rate.

18. Sometimes weighting techniques are employed for the purpose of adjusting for unrepresentative samples.

19. Purposive sampling is a nonprobability technique in which the researcher makes his or her own judgment as to which elements are the most appropriate to the study's objectives.

20. A snowball sample is a type of nonprobability sample in which subjects are selected through referrals by other subjects.

21. Quota sampling is a nonprobability sampling technique in which subjects are selected according to their characteristics so as to fill out a picture of the distribution of characteristics in the total population.

22. While often appropriate, nonprobability sampling methods do not allow the calculation of sampling error as probability samples do.

? REVIEW QUESTIONS

1. Turn to any page of your local telephone directory. Using the random number table in Appendix C, select a simple random sample of 25 listings from the page.

2. On the same page, select a systematic sample (with a random start) of 25 listings.

3. Describe some of the ways a researcher can test for nonresponse bias.

4. What is wrong with the following statement? "The findings of this study are considered 95 percent accurate."

5. Assume that a researcher has conducted a political poll among a probability sample of 800 people. Sixty percent of the respondents favor candidate Smith. Calculate the sampling error and write a statement reporting the confidence interval at the 95 percent confidence level.

6. In your own words, describe why the *Literary Digest* erroneously predicted that Alf Landon would defeat Franklin Roosevelt in 1936.

7. Describe a situation in which a purposive sample would be appropriate.

8. Given the discussion of snowball samples and the example cited, what kinds of situations necessitate this sampling design?

9. If a researcher wanted to conduct a survey of medical school faculty members teaching in departments of pediatrics, what kind of sampling design would be the most appropriate? Give a brief description of how the sample might be selected.
10. A researcher conducts a political poll by selecting a sample of names from the telephone directory. What's wrong with that sampling frame?

SUGGESTED READING

Kish, Leslie. *Survey Sampling* (New York: John Wiley, 1965). Unquestionably the definitive work on sampling in social research. If you need to know something more about sampling than was contained in this chapter, this is the place to go. Kish's coverage ranges from the simplest matters to the most complex and mathematical. He is both highly theoretical and downright practical. Easily readable and difficult passages intermingle as Kish exhausts everything you could want to or need to know about each aspect of sampling.

METHODS OF OBSERVATION

By now, you will have developed a general sense of the various ways social scientists do research. The several examples we've considered point to some of them. In Part Two, we'll spend a chapter on each of five commonly used techniques for making scientific observations. My purpose is to make you aware of the relative strengths and weaknesses of each, so that you'll be better equipped to assess the results of research you read about.

Survey research is probably the most popular method of social research today. Basically, it involves the administration of standardized questionnaires to large samples (hundreds or thousands) of people. We'll look at that method in Chapter 6.

Chapter 7 addresses the research method that probably comes first to mind when people think of scientific research: experiments. This technique is commonly used in social research, and we'll look at the logic of the specific experimental formats that have been developed.

Field research, discussed in Chapter 8, represents a method of research you've been doing all your life. It involves the direct observation of social processes in their natural setting. As you'll see, however, it is not simply a matter of common sense. Scientific field researchers have found problems intrinsic in this activity, but they have also found ways of handling those problems.

Chapter 9 looks at the analysis of existing statistics. It is often possible for researchers to examine social issues without doing any original observation. In our society, great masses of data are collected and reported every day, in all areas of life, and these data can be subjected to scientific analysis. It is important, however, that the researcher—and consumers of such analyses—be aware of certain potential dangers in that activity.

Finally, Part Two concludes with a discussion of evaluation research. This is not a separate method of observation, since it may utilize surveys, experiments, field research, or the analysis of existing data. Rather, evaluation research represents a particular research purpose: assessing the impact of social interventions. Chapter 10 will examine the ways in which that purpose is put into practice and some of the problems that crop up in the process.

CHAPTER 6

SURVEY RESEARCH

INTRODUCTION

Survey research is probably the most used method in quantitative social research. We've already looked at a number of surveys in the illustrations of various aspects of study design. In this chapter, you'll see how survey methods are used for a variety of research and other purposes.

We will turn first to an overview of the different faces of survey research: surveys, censuses, and polls. Next, we'll take a close look at questionnaire construction and the pitfalls you must know about in order to spot problems in the studies you read about. We'll see the critical importance of question wording and other aspects of the design of research instruments. Then we'll look briefly at the logistics of administering questionnaires through the mail, by phone, face to face, and in other ways. As you'll see, there are some definite advantages and disadvantages to each method.

One of the important developments in connection with survey research has centered around the possibility that data collected for one purpose can be reanalyzed for different purposes by other researchers. During the 1960s, data archives began springing up, chiefly in American universities. Structured like conventional libraries, data archives are filled with data sets generated by past surveys, and researchers can check studies out and reanalyze them in a form of research called secondary analysis.

Let's get started by looking at the most popular social research method.

SURVEYS, CENSUSES, AND POLLS

Three terms are used with some degree of confusion. **Survey** is a general term used for a research effort in which data are collected from individuals by means of questionnaires. The term **poll** usually refers to surveys designed to collect attitudes and opinions, primarily for descriptive purposes. The Gallup Poll is a foremost example. A **census** has two specific characteristics. First, censuses typically collect demographic data: population characteristics such as age and sex distributions, employment data, and the like, as contrasted with the attitudes and opinions typically measured by polls. Second, the term *census* is usually reserved for studies in which whole populations are studied, as contrasted with surveys conducted among samples of people. The decennial census conducted by the U.S. Census Bureau is a prototypical example of this research form.

In addition to being a comprehensive term, survey usually implies *sample* survey. And—in contrast to polls—surveys typically have more in-depth, explanatory purposes. Thus, academic social scientists often conduct surveys for the purpose of determining the underlying causes of such things as prejudice, political orientation, alienation, and so forth. For the purpose of this discussion, I'll use the term *survey research* to include censuses and polls.

EARLY SURVEYS

Survey research is a very old research technique. Ancient Egyptian rulers conducted censuses for the purpose of rationally administering their domains. Jesus was born away from home because Joseph and Mary were journeying to Joseph's ancestral home for a Roman census.

A little-known survey was attempted among French workers in 1880. A German political sociologist mailed some 25,000 questionnaires to workers to determine the extent of their exploitation by employers. The rather lengthy questionnaire included such items as:

Does your employer or his representative resort to trickery in order to defraud you of a part of your earnings?

If you are paid piece rates, is the quality of the article made a pretext for fraudulent deductions from your wages? (*Marx, 1880:208*)

The survey researcher in this case was not George Gallup but Karl Marx. Though 25,000 questionnaires were mailed out, there is no record of any being returned.

At about the same time, the sociologist Max Weber is reported to have employed survey research methods in his work on the link between "the Protestant ethic" and the "spirit of capitalism." In his classic work, Weber argued that early Protestantism—as opposed to Roman Catholicism—held worldly success to be a sign of God's favor and of the successful person's destiny for salvation after death. As a result, early Protestants worked hard, saved their money, accumulated capital, and invested it in ever greater economic achievement. Thus, Weber contended, were the seeds of modern capitalism planted. For the most part, Weber based his conclusions on comparative historical studies. However, he also studied Protestant and Catholic factory workers to provide confirming data at the individual level (see Lazarsfeld and Oberschall, 1965).

CONTEMPORARY SURVEY RESEARCH

Contemporary uses of survey research have taken place in three different arenas. The ongoing research conducted by the U.S. Census Bureau is one. In addition to the decennial censuses mandated by the Constitution, the Census Bureau conducts many sample surveys on a variety of topics. Their continuing Current Population Survey, for example, is a valuable source of data about the American population.

Second, the several commercial polling companies, such as Gallup, Harris, Roper, and others, have both pioneered methodological techniques and generated masses of data available for secondary analysis. During times when research funds were not available to support academic surveys, the commercial polling companies were able to continue experimentation with sampling methods, question wording, data collection techniques, and other aspects of survey research.

Finally, survey research has come of age within most American universities: Columbia, Harvard, Chicago, Michigan, Wisconsin, North Carolina, U.C.L.A., and U.C. Berkeley are especially strong in this regard. Two sociologists are most responsible for the development of survey research as a tool for the social sciences: Samuel A. Stouffer at Harvard and Paul F. Lazarsfeld at Columbia.

Stouffer's pioneering work largely represented attempts to apply empirical methods of social research to social problems, beginning with analyses of the effects of the Depression in America and the collection of data regarding the status of black Americans during the 1930s. With the advent of World War II, Stouffer directed the Information and Education Branch of the U.S. Army, bringing together a group of rising social scientists to examine issues relevant to the successful prosecution of the war. During the McCarthy era of the early 1950s, Stouffer conducted national surveys to examine the effects of the anticommunist crusade.

Paul Lazarsfeld came to America from a European intellectual background. Like Stouffer, he was interested in the study of social phenomena such as leadership, communications, economic behavior, and the professions. In the examination of such topics, Lazarsfeld continued the development of rigorous techniques for applying empirical research methods to social issues. In the area of political behavior, for instance, Lazarsfeld felt it important to examine voting as a process rather than a single event. To do this, in the 1940s he designed and executed panel studies, a longitudinal method discussed in Chapter 3. When we get to the logic of data analysis in Chapter 11, we'll focus on the elaboration method developed by Lazarsfeld as a logical format for understanding the nature of relationships among variables.

The heart of survey research is the **questionnaire:** a standardized set of questions asked of a relatively large number (hundreds or thousands) of people. *Questionnaire* is typically used as the generic term for this research tool; questionnaires used in interview surveys are sometimes called **interview schedules.** Where appropriate, I'll distinguish between the two.

QUESTIONNAIRE CONSTRUCTION

Questionnaires are part of the observation/measurement aspect of survey research. We observe people, if you will, by asking them questions and "observing" their answers. Put differently, we provide a stimulus and measure their responses to it. The stimulus is as much a part of the measurement as the response it produces.

There are two keys to a successful questionnaire, both generally relating to the goals of validity and reliability. First, the questions asked should generate the information desired. If you wish a *valid* measure of people's prejudice, then the questions you ask should tap prejudice and not something else. Second, to be *reliable*, the questions you ask must tap the same thing in each person being observed. For example, sociologists of religion have learned that questions determining people's knowledge of the Bible reflects religiosity in some people but education in others; therefore, they are not a reliable measure of religiosity.

OPEN-ENDED AND CLOSED-ENDED QUESTIONS

In the most straightforward form of observation in survey research, the researcher asks (in a questionnaire) a question, and the respondent provides an answer. Consider, for example, a common Gallup Poll question, first asked in 1935 and repeated periodically ever since:

What do you regard as the most vital issue before the American people today?

In 1935, in the wake of the Great Depression, "employment" was the most frequent answer given, followed by "economy in government." The terms *employment* and *economy in government* were made up by Gallup after the fact as categorizations of the actual responses volunteered by the survey respondents. In other words, some respondents answered "jobs," some said "putting people back to work," and so forth. Gallup combined all these into a category called *employment* (Gallup, 1972:5).

This type of survey question is called an **open-ended** question. As the name suggests, the question is asked and respondents answer in their own words. Subsequently, the researcher combines similar responses into categories. The categorization process is called **coding.**

You must be conscious of a danger in the coding of open-ended responses. Since research conclusions will often hinge on the way responses are coded, the coders may unconsciously interpret responses in such a way as to confirm a preferred conclusion. Thus, if you are of the opinion that religious people are more prejudiced than irreligious people, when you code the responses of a religious person, you may see prejudice that you might have overlooked in other questionnaires.

This danger has two aspects. On the one hand, if all coders have the same biased view of the subject matter being coded, the coded data will, obviously, be biased. Respondents may, overall, seem more liberal than they "really" are, for example. On the other hand, if coders disagree, the standardization of data—a central strength of survey research—is not achieved. The agreement among coders in how they code responses is referred to, appropriately, as *reliability*. Notice how this usage corresponds to our earlier discussions of reliability.

Though open-ended questions are used frequently in survey research, it is my sense that most questionnaire items provide respondents with both questions and answers. The following is an example of a **closed-ended** question used in an interview survey.

Some people say that you should vote only if you want to. Others say that everybody has a duty to vote. What do you think: that you should vote only if you want to or that it is a duty? (*Bybee et al., 1981:75*)

In this instance, the researchers have made it clear that they are interested in only two possible answers: Voting is either a matter of choice or a duty. If (in an interview setting) a respondent were to say something like, "Well, I think you should do what's good for the country," he or she would be asked to pick one of the two positions suggested. No coding is required when closed-ended questions have been successfully executed.

Consider these closed-ended questions regarding people's trust in government, used to measure the consequences of the 1970 election of a black man, Maynard Jackson, as mayor of Atlanta:

How much of the time would you say you can trust city government—always, most of the time, some of the time, or never?

On the whole, while your city government officials are working for the public, how would you compare them to, say, people in business—would you say they are more honest, about the same, or less honest? (*Abney and Hutcheson, 1981:95*)

In each case, the answers desired by the researcher were provided, and respondents were asked to choose which best represented how they felt. Those who gave some other answer were asked to pick one of those provided.

In the context of an interview schedule, closed-ended questions have the answers integrated into the questions themselves, like those above. In questionnaires that respondents complete themselves—**self-administered questionnaires**—the answers are simply presented in a form to allow easy marking. For example:

Overall, how important would you say the freedom of the press is for the protection of our democracy?

☐ Essential
☐ Very important
☐ Quite important
☐ Only slightly important
☐ Not at all important

There are two criteria for the answer categories of a closed-ended question: They should be **exhaustive** and **mutually exclusive.** The first criterion means that the item should offer all the relevant answers. Even though respondents may not feel their views are perfectly represented by the answers offered, they should be able to find one that comes close. The questions quoted above satisfy this criterion. The mutual exclusion criterion means that no respondent should find more than one response equally appropriate. Notice how the items quoted above offer mutually exclusive responses. For example, it would not make sense for you to think city officials were, in general, both "more honest" and "less honest" than other people.

People sometimes complain about the artificiality or superficiality of survey research, citing closed-ended questions as an example of what they mean. A set of response categories sometimes seems like an attitudinal straitjacket, severely limiting the attitudes you can express. Without question, the responses provided by the researcher will not exhaust the range of attitudes people have, and many respondents will only be able to approximate their attitudes in picking one of those provided in the list.

Nevertheless, there are good reasons for using closed-ended questions. As a practical matter, not having to code responses makes the processing of data easier, faster, and cheaper. In fact, if the whole questionnaire is closed-ended, you could ask respondents to put their responses on an optical-scanning sheet by blacking in the spaces corresponding to specific answers to specific questions.

The reasons for closed-ended questions are not only logistical, however. In one sense, they guarantee a greater fidelity to the respondents' feelings. In combining open-ended responses into categories, it is often necessary for the researcher to make interpretations, and those interpretations may be wrong. How would you interpret the answer of the respondent who said, "Well, I think you should do what's right for the country" in response to the question on voting as choice or duty? I suppose I'd assume it meant that voting was a duty, but I can think of interpretations that would point the other way. In coding, then, there is a danger of misrepresenting people's attitudes. Closed-ended questions force the respondents to make the interpretations. By the same token, a set of responses also assists the respondent in correctly interpreting what the researcher wants to know.

Closed-ended questions provide for standardization and allow respondents to be combined and contrasted to paint an overall picture of how the public feels. Suppose that Atlanta voters had simply been asked whether they felt government officials were honest or not? One person might have answered "sort of," another "less honest than ministers," and another "more honest than salesmen." It would not be possible to know which of these three had the highest or lowest assessment of officials' honesty, let alone make any overall statements about public feelings.

As you can see, there are trade-offs involved in the choice of open-ended or closed-ended questions. As a general rule, open-ended questions are preferred in exploratory studies, when the range of answers to a particular line of questioning is unknown. If the range of relevant responses is fairly well understood, or if a particular subset of those responses is desired, then closed-ended questions are best.

Often it is appropriate to use both formats. It is wisest to ask the open-ended question first, however; otherwise, the list of answers will affect the open-ended answers people give. I once presented respondents with a list of community problems and asked them to tell me whether they considered each a "major problem," a "minor problem," or "not a problem." Then I asked them—in an open-ended question—what they considered the biggest problem facing the community. Few respondents cited problems other than those I had listed.

QUESTIONS AND STATEMENTS

Though I have spoken of "asking questions" as the observational method of survey research, most questionnaires actually contain at least as many statements as questions. Researchers provide statements and ask respondents to agree or disagree, approve or disapprove, and so on. Consequently, we usually refer to questionnaire *items,* which include both questions and statements. The most commonly used format for statements in place of questions was developed by Rensis Likert, and such items are called **Likert items.** Here are some typical examples:

Policemen in your neighborhood are basically honest.

(1) Strongly agree
(2) Agree
(3) Neutral
(4) Disagree
(5) Strongly disagree

A person can't get any satisfaction out of talking to the public officials in your community.

(1) Strongly agree
(2) Agree
(3) Neutral
(4) Disagree
(5) Strongly disagree
  (Benson, 1981:53)

This format has the advantages attributed earlier to closed-ended questions. In addition, the answers make the dimensionality of the variable clear to respondents. Whereas we would be hard pressed to rank-order "pretty much" and "largely" as descriptions of how honest respondents felt police were, there is no doubt as to the order of the five answers shown above. Furthermore, using this format consistently with a long list of statements allows for some comparisons across the statements. With a set of racial-ethnic stereotypes, for example, we would be in a position to tell which stereotypes were the most widely accepted and which the least. This format also is useful in the construction of composite measures, which we will return to in Chapter 11. There are a great many other formats for questionnaire items, and researchers are creating new ones all the time.

COMMON PROBLEMS IN QUESTIONNAIRE ITEMS

In this section, I want to focus attention on common problems that crop up in questionnaire items. You should be on the lookout for these whenever you read the report of a survey.

UNCLEAR TERMS Quite often, survey researchers create questionnaire items that seem clear and unambiguous to them, but the items contain references or terms that will not be clear to respondents. This commonly happens when the researcher has only a superficial understanding of the topic. "What do you think about the proposed antiballistic missile system?" may evoke the counterquestion: "*Which* proposed antiballistic missile system?" Asking someone's attitude toward "China" is still somewhat ambiguous—some will think of the People's Republic on the mainland and others will think of the exiled government on Taiwan.

RESPONDENT NOT COMPETENT The same problem can arise when the researcher knows "too much" about the topic. If you've spent the past ten years in deep study of American foreign policy, you may distinguish between our approach to Czechoslovakia and our approach to Poland. Asking a national sample of American adults which approach they feel the more appropriate to our relations in Eastern Europe will produce nothing of value. Many people would say they didn't know. Unfortunately, many would give an answer—so they wouldn't look stupid—and their "opinions" would be made up on the spot.

In a political poll in Honolulu years ago, I asked a sample of voters whether they were familiar with each of 15 political figures. One of the names was Tom Sakumoto. Nine percent of the sample said they were familiar with him. Of those, about half said they had read about Tom in the newspapers, and half said they had seen him on TV. Some characterized him as a liberal, others as a conservative. Some liked him, others weren't impressed. The one thing no one mentioned about Tom was that he was made up! There was no political figure of that name in the state. Nonetheless, a substantial portion of the sample provided information about him.

People very often answer questions they have no interest, knowledge, or competence in. Unfortunately, in the survey results answers that are meaningless are indistinguishable from answers that are meaningful. Student newspapers, for example, occasionally ask a sample of students on campus how they feel the student government ought to spend its money.

"Administration" never receives many votes because nobody wants to "waste" money on administration. That response, however, points to the respondents' lack of knowledge about organizational budgeting and operations, ignoring such things as postage, telephone, rent, supplies, equipment, and other items that are essential to the provision of those activities deemed more worthy.

I don't mean this discussion of incompetence to sound elitist. The point is that researchers often ask questions no one is really competent to answer. Unfortunately, we often find it hard to say "I don't know." In reviewing survey results, therefore, you must ask whether the respondents are likely to be competent to answer the questions asked of them.

DOUBLE-BARRELED QUESTIONS   Sometimes researchers ask a **double-barreled** question—one that is really two questions. "Do you support the continuation of NASA's exploration of space, or do you think we should reduce taxes instead?" will be unanswerable for some respondents. Some will oppose the space program but feel that tax money should be spent on domestic problems. Others will feel the money should go toward foreign assistance, and others toward military spending.

LONG ITEMS   The danger of double-barreled questions increases with long items. Sometimes inexperienced researchers create items that are essentially paragraph-long statements of a position, prefaced with "Some people believe" and concluding with "Do you agree or disagree?" In almost every case, such items will contain parts you agree with, parts you disagree with, and parts you don't care about.

NEGATIVE TERMS   I have always warned students against using negative terms in writing questionnaire items, and you should be wary of surveys that have used them. The problem here is simple: Respondents may miss the negation and misinterpret the item by 180 degrees. "The United States should not ratify the Strategic Arms Limitation Treaty" will have some people agreeing with the statement when they meant to agree with the treaty, and others will disagree incorrectly. Double negatives— "The United States should not withdraw from the United Nations"—will probably miss as often as they hit.

Here's a place where introspection can assist you in evaluating research. If you read a research report and find you initially misread or misinterpreted an item, don't just condemn yourself as a sloppy reader; ask whether some of the respondents in the survey might have made the same error. It is the responsibility of the survey researcher to create items that generate clear, meaningful responses. If respondents make mistakes, that's the researcher's responsibility.

BIAS IN QUESTIONNAIRES

My comments here are intended to open up a can of worms you need to deal with. I have used the term *bias* even though I know it may initially mislead you. In the abstract, *bias* takes the meaning here of "slant"—like bias in a nail you are driving. In a survey item, **bias** means the slanting of answers. Some aspects of the item will encourage people to answer in a certain direction. Bias, then, is at odds with validity.

BIASED QUESTIONS   Let's take some simple examples first. If a pollster were to ask, "Don't you agree with most people that Tom Sakumoto would make a fine mayor, given his years of experience and dedication working for UNICEF?" that item is likely to drive more people into Tom's camp than "Do you favor Tom Sakumoto or Sam Smith for mayor?" The first item is clearly biased, by suggesting that everyone else favors the candidate and by lauding his experience and dedication to a worthy cause.

Bias can be more subtle, however. Earlier, I mentioned possible ambiguity over the meaning of China. Specifying the *People's Republic of China* and the *Republic of China* will not resolve the confusion for everyone. *Red China* or *Communist China* will pierce the confusion for Americans, but the terms *Red* and *Communist* will bias the item for some respondents. Identifying office holders with their title can slant favor in their direction. "How good a job do you feel the president is doing?" has to buy the incumbent a few points. The Real World Research box entitled "Presidential Popularity and Question Order" presents some other aspects of this problem.

IS BIAS INEVITABLE?   Now here's the bad news. No matter how you word a question, that wording will affect the responses generated by it. Hadley Cantril provided us with the classic example of this in the early days of World War II. With war breaking out in Europe, Americans were wondering whether the United States would end up in the war. Cantril conducted two national surveys to find out what Americans as a whole thought about the prospects. Both samples were well designed, and cross-checking the characteristics of those selected in them indicated that each sample provided a representative cross-section of the total population. In one survey, Cantril asked, "Do you think that the United States will succeed in staying out of the war?" Most respondents (55 percent of those with an opinion) said "yes." In the other survey, respondents were asked, "Do you think the United States will go into the war before it is over?" Most (59 percent of those with an opinion) said "yes." Obviously, their opinions were shaped by the way the question was asked (reported in Selltiz et al., 1959:564).

PRESIDENTIAL POPULARITY AND QUESTION ORDER

In late 1939, the Gallup Poll asked a sample of Americans "In general, do you approve or disapprove of Franklin Roosevelt as President?" (63.5% approved, 34.5% disapproved.) Gallup has been asking some version of that question periodically ever since, and the results have provided a month-to-month barometer of presidential popularity.

In polls through 1955, this question was asked near the conclusion of interviews, after a number of other questions had been asked of respondents. Since that time, however, the question has usually been asked at the outset of the interview. The impact of this shift in question order was the subject of a 1979 article by R. Darcy and Sarah Slavin Schramm.

Darcy and Schramm suggested that more favorable responses were likely to be obtained when the question was asked first and less favorable responses when it had been asked after respondents had been questioned about the various problems of the country and the world. In January 1968, an exception was made to the post-1955 pattern, and respondents were asked whether they approved or disapproved of Lyndon Johnson's job as president—after having been asked questions about the Vietnam War, wage and price controls, and who they preferred for president in the upcoming election. That procedure, Darcy and Schramm argued, probably lowered Johnson's apparent popularity.

More recently, Lee Sigelman (1981) reported on a test of the Darcy-Schramm conclusion. In a telephone survey among a statewide sample in Kentucky, two forms of the same questionnaire were used. All respondents were asked the same 48 questions, but half were asked for their approval or disapproval of President Carter's performance as the first question, while the other half were asked that question at the end of the questionnaire. Here's what Sigelman found:

Presidential question asked:

	First	Last
Approve	42.5%	45.7%
Disapprove	37.9	43.0
No opinion	19.6	11.3
	100%	100%
n (number of respondents)	(337)	(328)

These data indicate, contrary to the Darcy-Schramm contention, that presidential popularity appears somewhat higher when the presidential question is asked last. Look at the table for a minute and see if you can spot the most significant piece of information in it.

Not only is approval higher in the second form, but so is disapproval! The key difference between the two forms is in the percentages giving no opinion. When the presidential question was asked at the outset, 19.6 percent (nearly one in five) had no opinion; when asked last, only 11 percent had no opinion.

Here's what Sigelman found when he excluded those with no opinion:

Presidential question asked:

	First	Last
Approve	52.8%	51.5%
Disapprove	47.2	48.5
	100%	100%
n =	(271)	(291)

As you can see, the order of the question did not substantially affect the degree of approval or disapproval of Carter as president. As Sigelman pointed out, the difference of one percentage point could easily have resulted from sampling error.

In this case, question order most affects whether people voice an opinion at all. This is a matter of consequence since the press commonly reports the percent who *approve* of the president as the summary measure of popularity. When those with no opinion are subtracted from the president's approval, the popularity level is automatically decreased.

This example should alert you to the complexities involved in the effects of question wording. It is by no means a settled matter, but one you should be sensitive to as a consumer of research.

SOURCES George Gallup, *The Gallup Poll*. New York: Random House, 1972:196. Copyright 1972 by Random House, Inc. Reprinted with permission of the publisher. R. Darcy and Sarah Slavin Schramm, "Comment on Kernell." *American Political Science Review* (1979) 73:543–545. Lee Sigelman, "Question-Order Effects on Presidential Popularity." *Public Opinion Quarterly*, Summer 1981:199–207. Data are adapted from Table 1 on page 202.

In this example, it would appear that both forms of the question biased responses. A less biased form would have been "Do you think the United States will go into the war or stay out of it?" Still, the results produced would not be exactly the same as if the question were "Do you think the United States will stay out of the war or go into it." All else being equal, the first alternative will garner slightly more support than the last. I will discuss how you can deal with bias a bit later in this section.

SENSITIVE ISSUES   Norman Bradburn and Seymour Sudman did extensive research on the impact of question form on responses. Using eight different forms of a questionnaire with matched national samples, the researchers asked respondents questions about gambling, drinking, and sex. Take a minute to think about how you'd go about finding out how often people get intoxicated. One of the ways used by Bradburn and Sudman was to ask, "In the past year, how often did you become intoxicated while drinking any kind of beverage?" (1979:18). Respondents were given a set of eight answers ranging from "never" and "once a year or less" through "several times a week" and "daily." The reported frequency of intoxication was increased when the question was prefaced by the statement "Occasionally, people drink on an empty stomach or drink too much and become intoxicated." The frequency was further increased when respondents were allowed to give their own (open-ended) responses in place of the set of eight answers. And finally, when the researchers first asked respondents to supply their own term for intoxication and then used that wording in the question, even higher frequencies were reported.

Since there is no way of determining how often the respondents actually got intoxicated, we don't know which form of the question provided the most accurate reports. Other questions give a clue, however. Similar variations in question structure and wording were used in asking respondents how much they drank during the year. For example, respondents were asked to estimate how many times they had drunk beer during the year and about how many beers they had drunk each time on the average. The responses were converted into estimates of the number of ounces consumed in a year. When the question on annual beer consumption was asked in a longer, open-ended format, the responses produced an estimate of 2016 ounces of beer per year. When a shorter and closed-ended form was used, the resulting estimate was 1176 ounces—considerably less. When the researchers turned to the U.S. Brewers Association for national sales figures, the resulting estimate was that an average adult drank 3982 ounces of beer annually. Since the latter figures are based on actual sales rather than on respondents' recollections, we might assume that 3982 is the best estimate. This suggests that both of the survey formats underestimated consumption but that the longer, open-ended question came closest to the mark (Bradburn and Sudman, 1979:23).

DEALING WITH BIAS   I've pursued this topic at length because I want you to be especially sensitive to the structure and wording of questionnaire items. I'll close the discussion with observations that can be useful to you in dealing with this situation.

First, all the effects I've reported are stronger in certain situations than in others. They are stronger when the respondent is not really competent to answer and must guess. Questions asking for age and sex, for example, will be less susceptible to these problems than those asking, say, "How many miles have you driven in your lifetime?"

Second, all the effects discussed are stronger when the information to be reported is "sensitive"—especially when there is a **socially desirable** response. Surely, the intoxication reports were depressed by respondents' awareness that getting drunk frequently is looked down upon. (Ironically, so is never getting drunk.) For years, George Gallup was troubled by the fact that postelection surveys always showed a higher voter turnout than the official voting statistics. When asked, "Did you vote?" more people said "yes" than was true. Eventually, Gallup began asking, "Did you happen to have a chance to vote?"—a form that produces more accurate data.

In summary, then, you should be wary of data derived from questions that respondents are probably incompetent to answer accurately. Be warier still if the alternative answers vary in social desirability. The wording and format of items in a questionnaire have an important impact on the answers people give. It is essential that you study the questionnaire items upon which findings are based. At the same time, the manner in which the questionnaire is administered to respondents can influence responses as well. Let's see how that happens.

QUESTIONNAIRE ADMINISTRATION

Questionnaires can be administered to respondents in several ways, and you are likely to come across studies in the literature representing each of those methods. Fundamentally, there are two methods, with several variations: (1) an *interview survey*, in which an interviewer reads the questionnaire items to the respondent and writes down the answers given, and (2) the *self-administered questionnaire*, which is designed for the respondent to read and complete.

MAIL QUESTIONNAIRES

Perhaps the most common method of administering a survey is through the mail. You've probably received such questionnaires. There are several reasons why this method is so common; mainly they concern time and money. There are several things you should be sensitive to in reading reports of mail surveys.

SAMPLING FRAME First, how was the sample selected? To mail a questionnaire, you must select a sample such that their addresses are available to you. Sometimes, this leads to the use of a sampling frame that is convenient rather than one that really represents the population of interest. Telephone directories, for example, give addresses for most people, and they may be used for sample selection even when they're not appropriate to the research purpose.

RESPONSE RATES In any mail survey, you must be sure to find out what the completion rate was: How many questionnaires were mailed out, and how many were returned? I noted earlier, most professional survey researchers would probably agree that mail surveys that produce more than 70 percent completion have done quite well; over 60 is pretty good, but anything under, say, 50 percent ought to be questioned as to its representativeness. In particular, researchers who have achieved a low return rate should provide you with some additional evidence of representativeness, as discussed in Chapter 5.

Sometimes it's possible to examine the representativeness of a sample even when there are no data available to describe the whole population. When Holsti and Rosenau set out to study American national leaders, they selected their sample from *Who's Who in America*, as I described in Chapter 5. They mailed their questionnaire to a sample of 4290 people. Two months later, 1899 had replied. To increase their return rate, the researchers mailed another questionnaire (and plea for participation) to those who had not responded. Another 383 responded to the second mailing.

Fifty-three percent, or 2,282 of the questionnaire recipients, completed and returned the survey instrument. The return rate may have been adversely affected by the length of the questionnaire and the atmosphere of distrust toward social science surveys prevalent in recent years. As a partial test of sample representativeness we compared responses to the two mailings. We assumed that those who had to be prodded a second time sufficiently resembled those who did not respond at all. If the 383 second-mailing respondents differed significantly from their 1,899 counterparts in the first mailing, concern that the sample was biased would have been heightened. In fact, we found little difference in the responses of the two groups. (*Holsti and Rosenau, 1980:6-7*)

This was one of many ways the quality of survey data can be tested. If the second-wave respondents had been more conservative, say, than the first-wave respondents, we might have suspected that those who didn't respond at all were more conservative yet. We wouldn't know that for sure, but it would be a reasonable suspicion. That would suggest, then, that the overall survey results would reflect more liberal attitudes than were present in the whole population from which the sample was originally selected.

INCOMPLETE ANSWERS   In mail surveys, more than in interviews, respondents will leave some questions unanswered. Even if 60 percent of a sample have returned their questionnaires, 10 or 20 percent of the respondents may have failed to answer a particular question. All forms of incompletion need to be taken into account in assessing the representativeness of survey results. A perfect sample can be selected and its value seriously undermined by a low response rate and/or a large percentage of questions left unanswered. In reviewing the results of a mail survey, then, you should pay attention to the number of responses that particular findings are based on. In the case of unanswered questions, you need to ask yourself what kinds of people—with what kinds of situations, attitudes, and so on—would have been likely to leave the questions unanswered.

AUSPICES   As a rather different consideration, you should pay attention to the **auspices** under which the questionnaires were mailed to respondents; that is, who was conducting the study? It is essential that the study's auspices not become a biasing factor. Surveys sent out from "The National Association for Free Enterprise" or "Clergy in Support of Abortions" are likely to produce biased results. People with opinions in opposition to the sponsor of the survey are unlikely to even participate; in fact, many may throw away the letter unopened.

FACE-TO-FACE INTERVIEWS

The face-to-face interview is one of the classic forms of questionnaire administration. The sample is selected in such a way that the respondents' geographical locations (typically, their residences) are known. The interviewer then visits the respondent, introduces the study, and asks for permission to conduct the interview. If the respondent agrees, the interviewer reads the questionnaire items one at a time and writes down the answers given by the respondent.

ADVANTAGES   There are several advantages to this method. In comparison with sending questionnaires through the mail, this method typically produces a much higher completion rate. This method provides for another kind of completeness as well. In mail surveys, respondents often skip questions: Sometimes they simply miss the question, other times they choose not to respond, for a variety of reasons. Interviewer administration reduces this problem significantly, since the interviewer will be trained to ask all questions and can persist, at least gently, in getting answers that the respondent might have left out otherwise.

Finally, the interviewer is a guard against misunderstandings. Respondents sometimes totally misunderstand the intent of questionnaire items, and they give answers that aren't even in the ballpark. When this happens in a self-administered questionnaire, that response simply can't be used. When an interviewer is administering the questionnaire, however, such misunderstandings can be detected and corrected on the spot. Similarly, interviewers can probe for more complete answers than respondents might initially give. Asked "What do you think is the most important problem facing people in this neighborhood?" a respondent might say "housing." It would not be clear if the reference was to the quality, cost, short supply, or some other problem of housing. An interviewer could continue with "Could you say a little more about that?"

Interviewers also offer the advantage of being able to collect information aside from that solicited by the questionnaire itself. Information about the quality of the respondent's house and neighborhood, how the respondent dresses and acts (friendly, nervous, hostile, etc.) can be collected by an interviewer more easily than through questions to be completed by the respondent.

DISADVANTAGES In addition to logistical problems of time and money, interview surveys have some disadvantages. First, the presence of the interviewer can somewhat suppress the respondent's expression of facts and views. This is particularly the case for items with a social desirability component. Suppose you are a young single person being interviewed by an older woman who reminds you somewhat of your mother, and she asks "About how many times, if any, have you had sex during the past month?" Regardless of your actual performance, you'd probably squeak "never" nervously and worry that she could tell if you were lying. "How often do you brush your teeth?" "After every meal, ma'am." Any kind of behavior that is socially, morally, or legally prohibited or expected is likely to change in frequency when an interviewer is asking the questions. Clearly, an anonymous, self-administered questionnaire is the preferable method for such subjects, as people will feel somewhat safer about admitting behaviors that are embarrassing to them.

Generally unacceptable attitudes are also dampened by the presence of an interviewer. Few interview respondents will admit to deeply prejudiced feelings, for example. Whenever prejudice is to be studied in an interview survey, by the way, it is important that interviewers and respondents be matched in terms of race, to make it somewhat safer for the respondent to express any prejudices he or she might have.

The second general problem created by the interviewer is more fundamental. Recall that a major strength of survey research is standardization: Every respondent is asked exactly the same questions, in exactly the same words. Thus, the measurements are consistent from one respondent to another. In this respect, the interviewer is an intervening factor. An interview is a social interaction, and all of us interact differently with different kinds of people. We have different expectations about them, and we shape our behavior accordingly, to at least some extent.

In the typical interview survey, there will be many interviewers: some men and some women; some young and some old; representing different income groups, races, political attitudes, educations, and so forth. As a result, all respondents are not presented with the same stimulus. To complicate matters further, interviewers will react differently to different kinds of respondents. The danger, then, is that the responses collected in the survey may represent the various interactions of specific interviewers with specific respondents more than the simple "facts."

The solution to this problem lies in the selection and training of interviewers. Typically, interviewers will be picked on the basis of apparent blandness and lack of threat in their general appearance. They are instructed to dress in ways that make no particular statement. Neither punk-rock haircuts nor tuxedos would be appropriate, since each makes a statement about who the interviewer is and what he or she will approve or disapprove of. Similarly, interviewers are trained to behave neutrally, adding nothing. It is vital that questionnaire items be read just as they are written. If the interviewer paraphrases the items in his or her own words, the rewording will change the meaning somewhat, perhaps a lot—and we've already seen how significant question wording is.

EXPERIENCE This information may not seem directly applicable to you as a consumer of research. Few research reports will tell you much about the methods of selecting and training interviewers, so you'll have to judge that quality by other clues. First, if the research was conducted by an established research organization—Gallup, Harris, Roper, NORC, the University of Michigan, and the like—you can be sure that the researchers were well aware of the problems and were experienced in handling them. However, some troubles will slip through even in those instances, since new interviewers are being added to interviewing staffs all the time.

If an interview survey has been done by people who apparently have little experience with the method, you should be more wary. This is not to say that they will have done badly, just that you can't be as sure they haven't. Be especially wary of interview surveys conducted by volunteer interviewers who are personally wrapped up in the subject of the survey. Campaign workers, for example, are a bad source of interviewers for political polls. Even if they don't cheat for their candidate, it is likely that they will inadvertently communicate their feelings to respondents.

In summary, there are definite advantages to using interviewers rather than self-administered questionnaires, and there are dangers as well. Figure 6.1 summarizes the particular strengths of the two methods. These strengths and weaknesses are both modified somewhat by the telephone interview.

FIGURE 6.1
Two survey meth-
ods and their
strengths.

Self-Administered
Questionnaire

Face-to-face Interview

Large samples
Inexpensive
Good for sensitive issues
No interviewer effects

High completion rates
Fewer unanswered questions
Fewer misunderstandings
Interviewer can make observations

TELEPHONE INTERVIEWING

Telephone interviewing has become quite popular in recent years. It retains many of the advantages of interviews over mail questionnaires while reducing the costs of interviewing substantially. Though it is still true that this technique omits those people who do not have telephones, this has become a smaller and smaller percentage of the population. The U.S. Bureau of the Census (1979:582) estimates that 97 percent of all households had telephones in 1978.

The potential bias produced by unlisted telephone numbers has been erased through a technique that has advanced telephone sampling substantially: **random-digit dialing** (explained in Chapter 5). Chaffee and Choe report surveying a random sample of Wisconsin adults as follows:

All interviews were conducted by telephone, and sampling was based on a probability sample of area codes and telephone prefixes, followed by four random digits. Three callbacks were tried before a number was abandoned. Within households, adults were selected randomly according to a predetermined schedule. (1980:58)

A survey method sure to become more popular in the years to come is **computer-assisted telephone interviewing (CATI).** Though there are variations in practice, here's what it can look like: The interviewer sits in front of a computer terminal and its video screen. The central computer randomly selects a telephone number and dials it on behalf of the telephone headset the interviewer is wearing. On the video screen is an introduction ("Hello, my name is . . . ") and the first question to be asked ("Could you tell me how many people live at this address?"). The respondent answers the phone, and the interviewer says hello and introduces him- or herself and the study. Then the interviewer reads the first question as displayed on the screen and types the respondent's answer

COMPUTER-ASSISTED TELEPHONE INTERVIEWING (CATI)

It seems likely that computer assisted telephone interviewing will become more and more popular in the years to come. Developed largely at the University of California's Survey Research Center in Berkeley, it is now being adapted for use by the U.S. Census Bureau.

An advertising brochure from the commercial research firm Audits & Surveys, Inc. details some of the advantages of CATI. Respondents can be selected randomly by the computer. The order of questions making up the questionnaire can be rotated automatically to avoid any biases due to question order, and the order of possible answers to particular questions can also be rotated.

As soon as respondents answer questions, their responses are typed into the computer by the interviewer, and the growing body of data can be analyzed continuously. Moreover, the computer maintains a continuing check on unacceptable answers, insisting on acceptable ones. If a series of numerical answers is supposed to total 100 percent, the computer checks the arithmetic automatically.

The company points to several cost savings as well:

- Elimination of printed questionnaires
- Reduced interviewing time
- Automatic editing and cleaning (finding and correcting errors)
- Automatic coding on all structured questions
- No keypunching
- No hand tabulations

These are some of the reasons you are likely to be reading more and more reports on CATI surveys in the future.

SOURCE Advertising brochure from Audits & Surveys, Inc., One Park Avenue, New York, NY 10016.

into the computer terminal. The respondent's answer is immediately stored within the central computer. The second question to be asked instantly appears on the video screen, and the interview continues.

This is not science fiction. This method is being used increasingly by commercial survey firms, as the Real World Research box entitled "Computer-Assisted Telephone Interviewing" indicates. It suggests that survey technology is still evolving, and that you can expect to come in contact with new methods in the years to come.

I want to conclude this section with a discussion of some common survey types that almost always spell trouble.

ALMOST-ALWAYS-BAD SURVEYS

The general popularity of survey research has been a mixed blessing. Though this popularity has produced numerous useful innovations, it has also generated a lot of inadvisedly cut corners. Here are a few of the surveys you are likely to come across that you should be wary of.

DEAR OCCUPANT   An advantage of interviewer surveys is that you can select a sample of addresses without knowing the residents' names; the interviewer will make a personal contact with them. On the other hand, mailing questionnaires to a sample of addresses, adding "Occupant" or "Resident" to the mailing label, will almost always yield an extremely low return rate. Be aware that political figures often conduct surveys of their constituents in this fashion, and they usually generate return rates of less than 5 percent. If you read that your senator's survey achieved a "relatively high" 4 percent return, bear in mind that it's a terrible return rate anyway. Do not trust the results to represent anything, unless the respondents have been compared carefully with the population they are intended to represent.

MAGAZINE QUESTIONNAIRES   A similar problem crops up in the case of questionnaires published in magazines and newspapers. Not only do they usually generate low return rates, but those who respond clearly differ from those who do not. For the most part, you can assume that people who take the trouble to clip the questionnaire out of the magazine, fill it out, find an envelope to fit it, address the envelope, put postage on it, and mail it care more about the issue under discussion than the average person. Also bear in mind that, even under the best of circumstances, the respondents only represent readers of the particular magazine. If the readers of *National Review* seem to take conservative positions on political issues, that's only to be expected because *National Review* is a conservative magazine. A survey of *New Republic* readers would seem to indicate that "people" are liberal.

RADIO CALL-IN OPINION POLLS   Every now and then, radio stations get the idea of polling their listeners, usually with the declared intention of informing public officials as to how the "people" feel about things. "Do you think we should declare war on Albania?" Listeners then begin stuffing the telephonic ballot box. These polls can appear credible because they may bring in hundreds, even thousands, of responses. The problems of representativeness are many, however. First and foremost, the respondents are limited to people who were listening to the particular radio station at the time of the poll. This number is further reduced by those who could get to a telephone to call in and further reduced by those who don't care enough to express an opinion. Then the results are further distorted by those who cared enough to call more than once. The machine politician's dictum to "vote early and often" usually carries the day with call-in polls.

STREETCORNER INTERVIEWS "Man and woman in the street" interviews are still sometimes offered as evidence of public opinion. Many people have not yet learned about probability sampling, and it can seem to them that representative opinions can be obtained by stopping people on a busy streetcorner. Rather than simply dismissing such polls, you should consider the location where the interviews were conducted and try to get some idea of the kinds of people who would have passed that corner during the time the interviews were being done: mostly construction workers? college students? housewives? blacks? whites? See if you can understand something about the responses reported by understanding the nature of the misrepresentations in the sample. This won't tell you anything about public opinion on the issues reported, but it'll sharpen your critical faculties.

I'm going to conclude our examination of survey research with a look at secondhand data.

SECONDARY ANALYSIS AND DATA ARCHIVES

Survey data are almost always processed by computer. The questionnaire data are transformed into punched cards or a comparable format for processing. This aspect of survey research has opened up an aspect of the method of considerable import. Suppose I undertake a survey, interviewing a couple thousand respondents. That survey could easily cost $200,000. Perhaps I got a foundation grant to pay for the survey. Now let's suppose you are interested in the same subject area I've studied, but you can't raise the money for your own survey. Quite possibly you could answer your research questions through an analysis of the data I collected. This is called **secondary analysis.**

Here's a simple example of how secondary analysis can work. Let's say my survey aimed at discovering what kinds of people voted for Reagan and what kinds for Carter in 1980. I would have asked people whom they voted for, of course, and then several questions dealing with such matters

FIGURE 6.2
Two kinds of librar-
ies.

Books

Survey Data

as their age, sex, education, religion, political party, income, occupation, and so forth. In my analysis, I could determine what kinds of people voted for the two candidates and perhaps figure out why.

Now suppose you want to test the long-observed relationship between religious and political affiliations in America. Traditionally, Protestants have been disproportionately Republican, while Catholics and Jews have favored the Democratic Party. Let's imagine you want to find out if that's still true. If you had access to my data, you could answer your question easily by checking the political party affiliations of the Protestants, Catholics, and Jews in my sample. That additional analysis would cost virtually nothing.

In recognition of this great potential, several universities collaborated during the 1960s to create a national system of **data archives,** modeled after lending libraries but containing sets of survey data rather than books. Students and faculty at participating schools request data sets through the mail, usually paying only the nominal costs of reproducing the cards or magnetic tapes containing the data. Two of the major archives today are the Inter-University Consortium for Political Research at the University of Michigan and the Roper Center at Williams College.

Some of the survey analyses you will find reported in the journals are in fact secondary analyses of data originally collected by some other researcher for some other purpose. Here's an example:

This research draws principally upon national surveys undertaken by the Center for Political Studies (CPS) during the fall of 1972, 1974, 1976, and 1978. Embedded in the extensive interviews that composed each of these studies were questions that enable an analysis of the pocketbook and sociotropic perspectives on presidential popularity. (*Kinder, 1981:4*)

Few researchers would be able to afford the time and money to conduct four national surveys in order to examine the bases for presidential popularity over time. The Inter-University Consortium for Political Research was able to supply data for Kinder's analysis from surveys originally undertaken by the Center for Political Studies.

The chief problem with secondary analysis lies in the arena of measurement—assuming that surveys have been done on the topic of interest among samples from relevant populations. Since the original researcher did not have the secondary analyst's interests in mind in designing the questionnaire items, they may provide only approximate measures. On the other hand, several data sets may provide different approximate measures, and if they coincide in the conclusion they produce, we can have more confidence in that conclusion. Despite these shortcomings, secondary analysis is a powerful tool in the social sciences today, and you should be able to evaluate studies reporting such inquiries.

☑ CONSUMER'S CHECKLIST

A survey has the special quality of being explicit in its procedures. Survey reports, therefore, should provide you with adequate information for evaluation. Here are some of the things you should look for.

- Check all the relevant sampling questions discussed in Chapter 5.
  a. What population is of interest?
  b. What sampling frame has been used?
  c. How was the sample selected?
  d. What was the sample size?
  e. What percentage of surveys and items were completed?
  f. Have tests of representativeness been undertaken?
- For each variable:
  a. Has the variable been clearly conceptualized?
  b. Which questionnaire item(s) have been used to measure it?
  c. If closed-ended items have been used, were the answer categories appropriate to the variable? Were they mutually exclusive and exhaustive?
  d. If open-ended items have been used, how have the answers been categorized? Has the researcher taken precautions to avoid coding answers in such a way as to confirm a preferred conclusion?
- For each questionnaire item:
  a. Does the item contain any unclear or ambiguous terms?
  b. Are the respondents capable of providing the data asked of them?
  c. Is the item double-barreled?
  d. Does it contain negative terms that may confuse respondents?
  e. Are there any biased terms in the item? Is there anything about the item that might encourage one response over another?

f. Is one response more socially desirable (or undesirable) than the others? What's the likelihood that respondents have shaded their answers in order to look good?

- As a general rule, it's a good idea to test the interpretation of each survey response by asking yourself if different frames of mind might have produced that response. If people say they are opposed to the government funding of NASA, for example, does that really mean they are against the space program? Maybe they are opposed to big government in general and might support private funding of space exploration.
- How has the questionnaire been administered? How does the choice of administration method interact with the other concerns expressed above? For example, have sensitive questions been asked in an interview survey?
- If the study reports a secondary analysis, were the data originally collected by a respected survey team? How well do the items analyzed really measure the variables of interest to the researcher?

KEY WORDS

Survey
Census
Poll
Questionnaire
Interview schedule
Open-ended question
Coding
Closed-ended question

Self-administered questionnaire
Exhaustive
Mutually exclusive
Likert items
Double-barreled question
Bias

Social desirability
Auspices
Random-digit dialing
Computer assisted telephone interviewing (CATI)
Secondary analysis
Data archive

MAIN POINTS

1. Survey research involves the administration of questionnaires—standardized sets of questions—to a large sample (hundreds or thousands) of people.
2. Survey research takes many forms, including polls and censuses.
3. Polls typically focus on the measurement of opinions.

4. Censuses are a form of survey that makes measurements by questioning all members of a population.
5. Survey research dates back at least to the early Roman censuses mentioned in the Bible.
6. Today, surveys are a popular method of research at most universities.
7. Questionnaire items must be evaluated in terms of both validity and reliability, as discussed in Chapter 4.
8. Open-ended questions ask respondents to answer in their own words.
9. Closed-ended questions provide a set of answers for the respondents to select among.
10. Though open-ended questions allow respondents to give answers that more accurately express their opinions, they must be coded later, and the coders may misunderstand or misrepresent what the respondents meant.
11. Closed-ended questions do not require coder judgments, but none of the answers may really represent what respondents want to say.
12. Every set of closed-ended responses must be exhaustive and mutually exclusive.
13. Many questionnaire items are in the form of statements with which respondents can agree or disagree.
14. Likert-type items utilize a standardized set of responses such as "strongly agree," "agree," "disagree," and "strongly disagree."
15. Some common problems to look for in questionnaire items are: unclear terms, respondents not competent to answer the questions, double-barreled questions, long and confusing items, and negative terms.
16. Emotionally charged terms can bias respondents' answers.
17. The order of questions in a questionnaire can affect responses.
18. Respondents may not answer sensitive questions honestly because of what they regard as socially desirable responses.
19. Ultimately, the way any question is worded will affect the responses people give.
20. Questionnaires can be administered three ways: Respondents can complete the questionnaires themselves, interviewers can ask the questions in a face-to-face situation, or interviews may be conducted over the phone.
21. Self-administered questionnaires can be administered by mail, allowing the study of large samples at a relatively low cost.
22. Self-administered questionnaires are generally better than interviews when sensitive issues are involved.
23. Interview surveys generally have a higher response rate than mail surveys.
24. While the presence of an interviewer adds a potential influence on how people answer questions, interviewers can insure more complete

responses with fewer mistakes, and they can make direct observations of the respondents and their circumstances.

25. Increasingly, telephone interviews are being conducted through computerized systems called computer-assisted telephone interviewing (CATI).

26. The following types of surveys are almost always useless: "Dear Occupant" surveys, magazine questionnaires, radio call-in opinion polls, and streetcorner interviews.

27. Data archives are libraries for the storage and circulation of survey data.

28. Data archives support secondary analysis: the reanalysis of survey data by someone other than those who collected the data originally, and usually for a different purpose.

? REVIEW QUESTIONS

1. Discuss the relative strengths and weaknesses of open- versus closed-ended questions.

2. Critique the following questionnaire item:

   Where do you get most of your news about world events?
   ☐ Radio
   ☐ Newspapers
   ☐ News magazines

3. Critique the following questionnaire item:

   On the whole, what do you think about politics?

4. Critique the following questionnaire item:

   Which of the following best describes your opinion on the Equal Rights Amendment?
   ☐ I am in favor of its ratification.
   ☐ I believe it is a good idea.
   ☐ I am opposed to its ratification.
   ☐ Women deserve rights equal to men's.
   ☐ I don't think it will be ratified.

5. Critique the following questionnaire item:

Do you agree or disagree that the history of international relations teaches us that we can't trust the commies?

☐ Agree
☐ Disagree

6. Critique the following questionnaire item:

The United States government should cut back defense expenditures and spend more on foreign aid.

☐ Agree
☐ Disagree

7. A local radio station sets aside 15 minutes for listeners to call in and say whether they are in favor of gun control or opposed to it. Discuss the problems of generalizability inherent in the study.

8. Suppose that a researcher wants to study juvenile delinquency by asking high school students to report any crimes they have committed. Discuss the relative advantages of using a self-administered questionnaire versus face-to-face interviews.

9. Make up a questionnaire item that reflects the problem of social desirability.

10. Discuss the advantages and disadvantages of secondary analysis.

SUGGESTED READING

Babbie, Earl. *Survey Research Methods* (Belmont, Calif.: Wadsworth, 1973). A comprehensive overview of survey methods. (You thought I'd say it was lousy?) This textbook, although overlapping somewhat with the present one, covers aspects of survey techinques that are omitted here.

Glock, Charles (ed.). *Survey Research in the Social Sciences* (New York: Russell Sage Foundation, 1967). An excellent collection of essays on the use of survey methods in the several social sciences. This book is especially useful in illustrating the somewhat different ways different disciplines regard and utilize a given research method. The chapters also provide extensive bibliographies, citing examples of survey projects.

Hyman, Herbert. *Secondary Analysis of Sample Surveys* (New York: John Wiley, 1972). A comprehensive overview of secondary analysis. Hyman examines the role of this method within the broader context of social scientific inquiry, discusses methods of secondary analysis, and provides many illustrations.

Hyman, Herbert. *Survey Design and Analysis* (New York: Free Press of Glencoe, 1955). An old but classic and important overview of survey methods. Although incomplete or outdated in its treatment of available survey techniques, it provides an excellent statement of the logic of survey in social research, illustrating the logic with several research examples. Paul Lazarsfeld's foreword is especially important.

Lazarsfeld, Paul, Bernard Berelson, and Hazel Gaudet. *The People's Choice* (New York: Columbia University Press, 1948). An old but classic survey. This panel survey, conducted in Erie County, Ohio, examined the ways voters reached their final presidential preference during the 1940 election campaign. I have cited this example of survey research for its historical value and because its methodological and substantive values remain current after several decades.

Stouffer, Samuel. *Communism, Conformity, and Civil Liberties* (New York: John Wiley, 1955). Another old but classic survey. This massive survey examined the impact of (Joe) McCarthyism on the attitudes of both the general public and community leaders, asking whether the repression of the early 1950s affected support for civil liberties. Like *The People's Choice*, this book maintains its methodological and substantive importance today.

EXPERIMENTS

INTRODUCTION

Say the word *research* to most people, and pictures of scientists in white coats standing around in laboratories filled with complex equipment will come to mind. For the most part, those pictures relate only to some of the research conducted in the natural sciences. Social research is seldom if ever done under such conditions.

Social scientists do undertake experiments, however. Those experiments take many forms, and we're going to look at some of them in this chapter. We'll begin with an examination of the basic elements of the "classical" experiment: the groups of subjects examined, the nature of testing, and the focusing on a single variable.

With this basis, we'll examine some of the problems of validity that the classical experiment solves. Then we'll look at additional problems and the designs that would handle those problems, and I'll describe two very different examples. To broaden your view even further, I'll conclude with a discussion of "natural" experiments: analyzing events that occur on their own—for example, earthquakes—as though they were part of an experiment. Seeing how that is possible further elaborates the logic of the basic experiment. So let's take a first look at that logic.

THE CLASSICAL EXPERIMENT

In Chapter 6, we saw how survey research is a method for discovering what's so in the world. Once data have been collected regarding the way things are, the survey analyst can manipulate the data (as we'll see in Chapter 11) in order to discover relationships among variables. In experiments, by contrast, the experimenter manipulates the conditions under which the data are collected. In a sense, the experimenter puts information into the situation under study.

There are three elements to the classic experimental model, and we're going to examine each of these in turn. Then I'll say something about placebo effects, which should complete your fundamental understanding of this research method.

INDEPENDENT AND DEPENDENT VARIABLES

A **dependent variable** is one that is caused by another. The values of the dependent variable depend on some other variable. The "other" variable in this case is called the **independent variable**. Its values are taken as given. Here's an example.

When Chaffee and Choe (1980) set out to discover whether early commitments to a particular political party would insulate voters from the effects of a mass media campaign, that research question implicitly included an independent and a dependent variable. The independent variable was called *precommitment*—whether people had made a precampaign commitment to a particular party. Some voters had made such a commitment, and others hadn't. That was taken as a starting point in the study. In addition, some voters were affected by the political mass media campaign, while others were not. This variation, was hypothesized to be caused by or depend (partly) on whether the voters were precommitted. Hence, being affected by the mass media campaign or not being affected was the dependent variable.

Experiments have the purpose of explaining the relationships existing among independent and dependent variables—the impact of particular independent variables upon particular dependent variables. This can be approached in a couple of ways. First, we can see the purpose of explanatory analyses as uncovering the causes of some dependent variable. On the other hand, we can see it as finding the consequences of some independent variable.

In the context of experiments, one particular independent variable is called the **experimental stimulus.** An experimental stimulus is some event or condition that is believed to have a consequence or impact on the dependent variable. The purpose of the experiment is to discover the consequences (or lack thereof) of the stimulus. Here's a brief example.

Many preliterate societies and fundamentalist Christian groups have a healing practice known commonly as the laying on of hands. Essentially, the healer enters a relaxed meditative state and instills that relaxed state in patients by touching them in deliberate ways. Patricia Heidt (1981) was interested in exploring this phenomenon, which she called the *therapeutic touch,* in modern nursing. Particularly, could the anxiety level of cardiovascular patients be reduced in this fashion?

Ninety volunteer patients were selected for the study. A questionnaire was administered to each patient for the purpose of measuring anxiety. Patients with matching anxiety scores were then divided into three groups, and Heidt interacted with the patients individually as follows.

For the patients in one group, the "therapeutic touch" (TT) group, she explained: "I am studying how nurses use their hands to assess and treat areas of physical discomfort in their patients. I am going to use my hands and pass them over your body in a way that has been taught to me" (1981:34). She then entered into a relaxed, meditative state and passed her hands over parts of the patient's body.

In the second group, the "casual touch" (CT) group, Heidt explained:

I am studying how nurses use their hands to assess and treat areas of physical discomfort in their patients. I am going to take your pulse over your heart and at your wrist, and near both ankles. This is going to take longer than usual because it is part of a research project. This does not mean that there is anything wrong; it is simply part of a standardized procedure. (*1981:34*)

She then proceeded to take the patient's pulses as described.

The final group of patients received no touch (NT group). In speaking to them, Heidt said "I am studying how nurses assess and treat physical discomfort in their patients. I am going to spend some time talking with you about how you are feeling today. Can you tell me how you are feeling right now?" (1981:34).

Subsequent to her interactions with the patients, Heidt's assistants returned and measured their anxiety levels once more. The data thus collected pointed to substantially lower levels of anxiety in those receiving the therapeutic touch than either those receiving the casual touch or no touch. The latter two groups did not differ very much in their levels of anxiety after the experiment.

This example illustrates the main elements of an experiment. Subjects are assigned to experimental and control groups (in this case, there were two control groups). A dependent variable (anxiety) is measured prior to the experiment, an experimental stimulus (the therapeutic touch) is administered to the experimental group, and the dependent variable is measured among all groups afterward. The experimental and control groups are then compared in terms of changes to the dependent variable. Let's take another example to get more deeply into these several elements.

MEASURING THE IMPACT OF ROOTS

Let's suppose for the moment that you and I wanted to find out if the television special *Roots* had any effect on white people's feelings about blacks. In such an inquiry, "seeing the show" would be the experimental stimulus. Essentially, we'd find out if those who saw the show had better feelings about blacks than those who didn't.

In practice, we would probably arrange for a group of people, none of whom had seen the show, to come to our laboratory. We would administer some test of antiblack prejudice to all the subjects. Then we'd show *Roots* to half the subjects and not show it to the other half. Afterward, we'd measure prejudice for both groups. If those who saw *Roots* were less prejudiced than those who didn't, we'd conclude that the experimental stimulus—seeing *Roots*—had the effect of reducing prejudice and making people more egalitarian in their attitudes.

This was the interest motivating Sandra Ball-Rokeach and her colleagues (1981). Following the media success of the original *Roots*, they decided to study the impact of *Roots II*. Rather than bringing people into the laboratory, however, the researchers chose to observe the effects of the stimulus in the real world. (This is an example of a "natural experiment," which we'll discuss later.)

Four large samples of respondents were selected in Washington state, and a combination of interviews and mail surveys provided the measurements of attitudes, as well as telling the researchers who had seen the show and who hadn't.

You may be interested in the results of the study. On the whole, the researchers found that people with egalitarian attitudes (as measured prior to the showing) were more likely to watch *Roots* than those with less egalitarian attitudes. This illustrates the matter of **self-selection** that often confounds social research. The show itself, however didn't seem to have any effect. That is, people who watched the show did not seem more egalitarian afterward than they were before. Table 7.1 illustrates this research design.

In the diagram, I have represented two groups of subjects in the study. As you can see, group I comprises those who watched *Roots II*; group II is those who did not. Recall that, in this case, people selected themselves into

TABLE 7.1   An Analytical Diagram of the Study of *Roots*

Group I

Level of egalitarianism (A)	Watched *Roots II*	Level of egalitarianism (B)

Group II

Level of egalitarianism (C)	Didn't watch *Roots II*	Level of egalitarianism (D)

one of the two groups. The diagram also contains four measurements of egalitarianism, represented by the letters A, B, C, and D. A is the level of egalitarianism initially measured among those who ended up watching the show. B is their level of egalitarianism after the show. C and D represent the comparable measurements for those who didn't watch the show.

The key analyses in this study design revolve around the comparison of levels of egalitarianism. If *Roots II* had had the desired impact, that would have been evidenced by a greater egalitarianism in measurement B than in measurement A. In contrast, the levels of egalitarianism found in measurements C and D would have been about the same. (We'll return to the significance of this in a moment.)

Now, what results do you think would have led to the conclusion that the researchers actually reached? Recall that there were two conclusions: (1) Egalitarian people were more likely to watch the show, and (2) watching the show didn't affect people's attitudes. First, finding that measurements A and B were essentially the same would point to the conclusion that the show had no impact on those who watched it. Finding that measurement A indicated a greater egalitarianism than measurement C, on the other hand, would tell the researchers that people with egalitarian attitudes were more likely to watch the show.

In this extended example, we have seen all the primary elements of the classical experiment, so let's take just a minute to review what those are.

PRETESTING AND POSTTESTING

Since experiments test for the impact of an experimental stimulus, this implies a change over time. Such changes are typically tested for by making measurements before the administration of the stimulus (a **pretest**) and afterward (a **posttest**). In the example, this is represented in the measurements of egalitarianism.

Notice the importance of this aspect of the classical experiment. If we only measured egalitarianism after the showing of the program and discovered those who watched the show to be quite high—even in comparison with those who had not watched it—we could be misled in concluding that the show affected attitudes. Indeed, in the example, those who watched the show were more egalitarian after the show than those who didn't watch it. As we've seen, however, they started out that way, and the show itself seems to have had no impact. That's the important function played by the pretest–posttest comparison.

EXPERIMENTAL AND CONTROL GROUPS

In the context of experiments, people also talk about **experimental groups** and **control groups.** Most simply put, the former is the group of subjects who are exposed to the experimental stimulus; the latter are not exposed to it. These are groups I and II, respectively, in Table 7.1— the experimental group saw the show, and the control didn't.

The role of the experimental group is obvious. The function of the control group has been illustrated in part already. Those people who didn't watch *Roots* give us a basis for evaluating anything that happened (or didn't happen) to those who did watch it. We've seen an analogous situation in the discussion of survey research in Chapter 6.

Recall the Atlanta study of black and white attitudes toward government focusing on the election of a black mayor in Atlanta. Abney and Hutcheson (1981) found that black trust in government didn't change at all, while whites became less trusting of government. Analogous to a control group here were the national opinion data introduced by the researchers. Over the course of this longitudinal study, people across the nation were becoming less and less trustful of government officials. The whites of Atlanta looked very much like the mainstream of American voters. The Atlanta blacks—by staying at a constant level of trust in government—gave evidence that the election of a black mayor enhanced black feelings about their elected officials. The "improvement" was simply canceled out by whatever was producing a nationwide decline in trust. Without the national comparison, the conclusion would have been that the election of a black mayor created a problem for whites without benefiting blacks. The control groups in experimental designs serve that same sort of function.

There are many ways of choosing experimental and control groups. In this regard, the *Roots* example is not a useful one, since subjects selected themselves into one of the two groups by watching or skipping the show. In the classical experiment, subjects are assigned to the experimental or control groups in one of two ways.

For years, the most common method was by **matching.** From a common pool of subjects, the researcher would select pairs of subjects who were as much alike as possible in terms of specified, relevant variables. Then, typically, one of the pair would be selected at random for the experimental group and the other for the control. The process would be repeated for successive pairs of subjects. Once the process was completed, the two groups would be very similar in overall characteristics.

There are problems with matching, however. First, the researcher must make a decision as to which variables are the relevant ones for matching. Errors are likely to result in groups that are not comparable to one another in ways that count. Second, it is a tedious process and one that will only approximate success in most cases: You'll end up with potential subjects who simply don't match with anyone else. Matching subjects on more than a few variables can be difficult if not impossible.

Increasingly, in recent years, experimenters have been creating experimental and control groups simply through **randomization.** Through some probability selection method—simple random, systematic, stratified, and the like—the pool of subjects is divided into two groups. Unless the overall pool of subjects is quite small (recall the discussion of sampling error in Chapter 5), the two groups will, in the aggregate, match one another. This method is, of course, much simpler, and it does not require that the researcher decide what variables to match on. (If you are clear which variables are relevant, though, you might stratify prior to sampling.)

The final step in this process occurs during the pretesting stage. The assumption in matching or random selection is that the two groups will start out essentially the same in terms of the dependent variable. Then any differences found in the posttest can be attributed to the impact of the experimental stimulus. If the group assignments do not produce the expected similarity, that will be learned in the pretesting, and it can be taken into account in comparing the posttest results. Thus, in the *Roots* example, it still would have been possible for the experimental group to increase in egalitarianism from their relatively high starting point and for the control group to stay at their initially low score.

Now you have the essential elements of the classical experiment: stimulus, dependent variable, pretest, posttest, and experimental and control groups. The function of each will become even clearer as we continue our discussion, looking at variations on the theme. Before moving on, however, let me draw your attention to a problem that often crops up in experiments, and we'll see how the basic logic of the model can handle it.

THE PLACEBO EFFECT

You've probably heard references to "sugar pills" in medicine. In the case of many diseases, the power of suggestion is sufficiently strong that patients get better without any "real" medical treatment. In the stereotypical case, the physican gives the patient a bottle of a "powerful, new superdrug." The patient, properly impressed, takes the pills and recovers. The pills, however, contain nothing but sugar. Such a phony treatment is called a *placebo*, and the recovery of the patient is attributed to a **placebo effect.**

Aside from providing some welcomed recoveries and a wealth of cute medical anecdotes, the placebo effect presents a problem for experimentation. When medical researchers are testing a genuine new drug, what are they to conclude if the experimental group benefit from it? Can we be sure that the treatment has genuine value or have we seen only a placebo effect?

Medical experimenters typically handle this problem by creating experimental and control groups and not telling the subjects which group they are in. Any placebo effects, then, should be seen about equally in both groups, and any extra improvement found in the experimental group can reasonably be attributed to the treatment.

An additional precaution is sometimes required. How do we know if the patient has "improved"? Often this determination is made by those administering the experiment. To the extent that the determinations require qualitative judgments ("Is patient less depressed?"), there is a danger that the researcher's judgment might be unconsciously biased by the desire to have the new drug succeed. In a **double-blind** design, neither the subjects nor those judging changes in the patients know which is the experimental group and which the control.

On the whole, the placebo effect seems less intrusive in social experiments than in medical research. This is due to the fact that, as we'll see shortly, social experimenters are more typically comparing the effects of several different stimuli rather than evaluating a single one. Nonetheless, it is important to be aware of the problem presented by the placebo effect and the methods developed for dealing with it. In the checklist for this chapter, I've suggested that you look for possible placebo effects in reports of experiments.

The Real World Research Box entitled "Preexperimental Designs" summarizes some of what we've learned about classical experiments and provides a useful context for the next section, in which I am going to describe some of the ways the validity of experimental findings may be challenged. We'll see how the classical model guards against some challenges, and we'll look at a more advanced model that guards against others.

EXPERIMENTAL PROBLEMS AND EXPERIMENTAL DESIGNS

In this section, I want to look at some variations on the model of the classical experiment. I have two purposes. On the one hand, I want to prepare you for as wide a variety of experiments as possible. Second, you can more fully grasp the fundamental logic of experimentation by understanding other study designs. These comments around will be organized around some of the problems that can challenge the conclusions drawn on the basis of experimental data. It will be useful for you to know these problems, of course, as you begin reading reports of social experiments.

This approach is greatly facilitated by the work of Donald Campbell and Julian Stanley (1963) in a truly excellent book on research design, and an updated treatment by Thomas D. Cook and Campbell (1979). In these books, Campbell, Stanley, and Cook discuss in depth problems of internal and external validity and describe experimental designs appropriate to solving those problems.

PROBLEMS OF INTERNAL INVALIDITY

The problems of **internal invalidity** refer to the possibility that the inferences drawn by the experimenter may not be an accurate reflection of what has actually occurred. Campbell and Stanley (1963:5–6) point to eight problems of internal invalidity. I want to look at each of those eight problems, seeing how the classical experimental design—particularly through the presence of a control group—deals with each.

1. HISTORY Historical events may take place that confound the changes observed within the experiment. The Atlanta study of trust in government (see pp. 140–41) illustrates this situation. It could have looked as though the election of a black mayor damaged whites' faith in government. As it turned out, the change observed among Atlanta whites paralleled changes occurring across the nation.

The Atlanta example also points to the way this problem is handled through the use of a control group. In the Atlanta case, the control group was the national population. In the conventional laboratory experiment, as we discussed earlier, equivalent experimental and control groups are established. The effects of historical events would affect both equally, and we'd be able to detect and compensate for the problem.

PREEXPERIMENTAL DESIGNS

Donald Campbell and Julian Stanley, in an excellent little book on research design, describe some sixteen different experimental and quasi-experimental designs. They begin by discussing three preexperimental designs—not to recommend them but because they are frequently used in less than professional research. I want to present these to you as a background against which to understand the value of the more complex designs we'll be looking at shortly.

In the first such design—the *one-shot case study*—a single group of subjects are measured on a dependent variable following the administration of some experimental stimulus. Suppose, for example, that we show *Roots* to a group of people and then administer a questionnaire that seems to measure antiblack prejudice. Suppose further that the answers given to the questionnaire seem to represent a low level of prejudice. We might be tempted to conclude that the film reduced prejudice. Lacking a pretest, however, we can't be sure. Perhaps the questionnaire doesn't really represent a very sensitive measure of prejudice, or perhaps the group we are studying was low in prejudice to begin with. In either case, the film might have made no difference, though our experimental results could mislead us into thinking it did. Part 1 of the figure opposite is a graphic presentation of the one-shot case study design.

The second preexperimental design discussed by Campbell and Stanley adds a pretest for the experimental group but lacks a control group. This design—which the authors call the *one-group pretest-posttest design*—suffers from the possibility that some other factor might cause a change in the posttest results (compared to the pretest). It looks like part 2 of the figure.

To round out the possibilites for preexperimental designs, Campbell and Stanley point out that some research is based on experimental and control groups but has no pretests. They call this design the *static-group comparison*. In this design, we might show *Roots* to one group and not to another and then measure prejudice in both groups. If the experimental group had less prejudice, we might assume the film was responsible, but we would have no way of knowing that the two groups had the same degree of prejudice initially. The static group comparison looks like part 3 of the figure.

Keep these three preexperimental designs in mind as we look at the potential problems of experimentation and some of the solutions to those problems.

1. THE ONE-SHOT CASE STUDY

Administer the experimental stimulus to a single group and measure the dependent variable in that group afterward. Make an intuitive judgment as to whether the posttest result is "high" or "low."

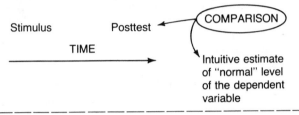

2. THE ONE-GROUP PRETEST-POSTTEST DESIGN

Measure the dependent variable in a single group, administer the experimental stimulus, and then remeasure the dependent variable. Compare pretest and posttest results.

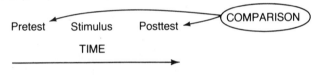

3. THE STATIC-GROUP COMPARISON

Administer the experimental stimulus to one group (the experimental group), then measure the dependent variable in both the experimental group and a control group.

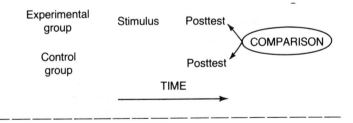

SOURCE Adapted from Donald T. Campbell and Julian C. Stanley, *Experimental and Quasi-Experimental Designs for Research*. Chicago: Rand-McNally, 1963. The figure is adapted from pages 6–13.

2. MATURATION People are continually growing and changing, whether in an experiment or not, and those changes may affect the results of the experiment. In a long-term experiment, the fact that they grow older (and wiser?) may have an effect; in shorter experiments, they will grow tired, sleepy, bored, or hungry, or change in other ways that may affect their behavior in the experiment.

Once again, the presence of a control group counteracts this problem The experiment should be designed in such a way that the effects of **maturation** would be present equally for the experimental and control groups. Differences in how they turn out can then be attributed to the experimental stimulus.

3. TESTING Often the process of testing and retesting will influence people's behavior, thereby confounding the experimental results. Suppose we administer a questionnaire to a group as a way of measuring their prejudice. Then we administer an experimental stimulus and remeasure their prejudice. By the time we conduct the posttest, the subjects will probably have become more sensitive to the issue of prejudice and will be more thoughtful in their answers. Possibly, in fact, they will have figured out that we are trying to find out how prejudiced they are, and, since no one likes to appear prejudiced, they will be on their best behavior and give answers they think we want or that will make them look good.

Again, the control is a protection against this problem. If testing has the effect mentioned, then both groups will show it, and that effect can be taken into account in evaluating the experimental results.

4. INSTRUMENTATION Thus far, I haven't said very much about the process of **instrumentation,** or the means of measurement, in pretesting and posttesting, and it's appropriate here to remind you of the problems of conceptualization and operationalization discussed earlier. If we use different measures of the dependent variable, how can we be sure that they are comparable to one another? Perhaps prejudice will seem to have decreased simply because the pretest measure was more sensitive than the posttest measure. Or if the measurements are being made by the experimenters, their standards or their abilities may change over the course of the experiment. Here we have the problem of reliability. The problems created by the different tests will be problems equally for both control and experimental groups.

5. STATISTICAL REGRESSION Sometimes it's appropriate to conduct experiments on subjects who start out with extreme scores on the dependent variable. If you were testing a new method for teaching math to hard-core failures in math, you'd want to conduct your experiment on people who have done extremely poorly in the subject previously. But consider for a minute what is likely to happen to the math achievement of such people over time without any experimental interference. They are starting out so low that they can only stay at the bottom or improve; they can't get worse. Without any experimental stimulus, then, the group as a whole is likely to show some improvement over time. (Referring to this phenomenon as **statistical regression,** or *regression to the mean*, statisticians often point out that a group of extremely tall people are likely to have children shorter than themselves, whereas a group of extremely short people are likely to have children taller than themselves.)

There is a danger, then, that changes occurring by virtue of subjects starting out in extreme positions will be attributed erroneously to the effects of the experimental stimulus. This problem will be detected in the control group.

6. SELECTION BIASES We discussed bias in selection earlier when we examined different ways of selecting subjects for experiments and assigning them to experimental and control groups. Comparisons don't have any meaning unless the groups are *comparable*. This should be a standard check for you in reading the reports of social experiments.

7. EXPERIMENTAL MORTALITY Although some social experiments could, I suppose, kill subjects, **experimental mortality** refers to the fact that subjects often drop out of an experiment before it is completed, the statistical comparisons and conclusions drawn can be affected by that. Suppose, for example, that you are doing an experiment involving an experimental and a control group, each with a pretest and posttest, to test the effects of *Roots* on antiblack prejudice. But now suppose that the bigots in the experimental group are so offended by the film that they tell you to forget it and leave. Those subjects sticking around for the posttest will have been less prejudiced to start with, so the group results will reflect a substantial "decrease" in prejudice.

In reviewing reports of experiments, therefore, you should look for reports on dropouts. If the mortality rate is substantial, the researcher should have checked on and reported the consequences of that. Pretest data, for example, can be used to compare the dropouts with those staying with the experiment. If the two groups don't really differ from one another, that lends weight to the conclusion that the experimental mortality won't affect the overall results.

8. SELECTION-MATURATION AND OTHER INTERACTIONS In addition to each of the individual sources of internal invalidity described above, it is possible that some combination of two or more sources may present a more sophisticated problem. Suppose, for example, that the experimental group had a lower boredom threshold than the control group. The selection problem (nonequivalent experimental and control groups) could combine with the maturation process to confound the experiment and produce misleading experimental results.

Cook and Campbell (1979:51–55) review these eight threats to internal validity and then examine some additional problems.

9. CAUSAL TIME-ORDER Though it is seldom the case in social research, there is a possibility of ambiguity as to the time-order of the experimental stimulus and the dependent variable. Whenever this occurs, the research conclusion that the stimulus caused the dependent variable can be challenged with the explanation that the "dependent" variable actually caused changes in the stimulus.

10. DIFFUSION OR IMITATION OF TREATMENTS In the event that experimental and control group subjects are in communication with each other, there is the possibility that experimental subjects will pass on some elements of the experimental stimulus. In that case, the control group becomes affected by the stimulus and is not a real control.

11. COMPENSATION As we'll see in Chapter 10, in experiments in real-life situations—such as a special educational program—subjects in the control group are often deprived of something considered to be of value. In such cases, there may be pressures to offer some form of compensation, and the control group is no longer a genuine control group. If one group of prisoners, for example, were granted conjugal visits in an attempt to improve morale, there might be pressure to give the control group (deprived of conjugal visits) something else—additional TV or athletics, perhaps.

12. COMPENSATORY RIVALRY In real-life experiments, the subjects deprived of the experimental stimulus may begin acting like an underdog and work harder. Suppose an experimental math program is the experimental stimulus; the control group may work harder on their math in the attempt to beat the "special" experimental subjects.

13. DEMORALIZATION On the other hand, feelings of deprivation among the control group may result in their giving up. In educational experiments, for instance, they may stop studying, act up, or get angry.

These, then are the sources of internal invalidity cited by Campbell, Stanley, and Cook. Aware of these, experimenters have devised designs aimed at handling some or all of them. The classical experiment, if coupled with proper subject selection and assignment, handles each of the eight basic problems of internal invalidation. Let's look again at that study design, presented graphically in Figure 7.1.

FIGURE 7.1
Another look at the classical experiment.

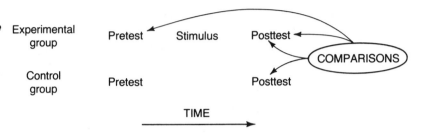

Experimental group   Pretest   Stimulus   Posttest

Control group   Pretest   Posttest

COMPARISONS

TIME

You'll recall that the Ball-Rokeach study sought to discover whether the television special *Roots II* had an impact on prejudice. That study differed from the classical experiment in that the researcher was not in a position to assign subjects to experimental and control groups, and you'll recall that those who watched the show started out less prejudiced than those who didn't watch it. Furthermore, it is worth noting that the show was not created specifically for the purpose of reducing prejudice.

To examine the classic experiment, let's consider a modification of the Ball-Rokeach study. Suppose we developed a black history film for the specific purpose of reducing prejuice in those who watched it. We would randomly select an experimental and a control group—with equal levels of prejudice—and we would then show the film to the experimental group. Finally, we would measure (posttest) prejudice among both groups.

If the black history film did indeed reduce prejudice, we should expect two findings from the experimental design shown in Figure 7.1. In the experimental group, the level of prejudice measured in the posttest should be less than was found in the pretest. In addition, when the two posttests are compared, less prejudice should be found in the experimental group than in the control.

This design guards against the problem of history in that anything occurring outside the experiment that might affect the experimental group should also affect the control group, and there should still be a difference in the two posttest results. The same comparison guards against problems of maturation as long as the subjects have been randomly assigned to the two groups. Testing and instrumentation can't be problems, since both the experimental and control groups are subject to the same tests and experimenter effects. If the subjects have been assigned to the two groups randomly, statistical regression should affect both equally, even if people with extreme scores on prejudice (or whatever the dependent variable is) are being studied. Selection bias is ruled out by random assignment of subjects. The problems of experimental mortality and the interaction of selection-maturation and other factors are more complicated, but the data provided in the study design offer a number of ways for dealing with them. Slight modifications to the design—administering a placebo to the control group, for example—can make the problems even more easily managed.

SOURCES OF EXTERNAL INVALIDITY

In addition to the problems of internal invalidity, there are problems of what Campbell, Stanley, and Cook call **external invalidity.** This second class of problems relates to the *generalizability* of experimental findings. Even if the results of the experiment are an accurate gauge of what happened during the experiment, do they really tell us anything about life in the wilds of society?

Campbell and Stanley (1963:16–22) describe four forms of this problem, and I want to present one of them to you as an illustration. The generalizability of experimental findings is jeopardized, as the authors point out, if there is an interaction between the testing and the experimental stimulus. Here's an example of what they mean.

Staying with the study of prejudice and the black history film, let's suppose that our experimental group—in the classical experiment—has less prejudice in its posttest than in its pretest, and its posttest shows less prejudice than that of the control group. We can be confident that the film actually reduced prejudice among our experimental subjects. But would it have the same effect whether the film was shown in theaters or on television? We can't be sure, since the film might only be effective when people have been sensitized to the issue of prejudice, as may have happened in the course of the pretest—and which is an example of interaction between the testing and the stimulus. The classical experimental design cannot control for that possibility; fortunately, experimenters have devised other designs that can.

THE SOLOMON FOUR-GROUP DESIGN The **Solomon Four-Group Design** (Campbell and Stanley, 1963:24–25) handles the problem of testing interaction with the stimulus. As the name suggests, it involves four groups of subjects, assigned randomly from a pool. Figure 7.2 presents this design graphically.

Notice that groups 1 and 2 in Figure 7.2 compose the classical experiment. In addition, group 3 is administered the experimental stimulus without a pretest, and group 4 is only posttested. This experimental design permits four meaningful comparisons. If the black history film really reduces prejudice—unaccounted for by the problem of internal validity *and* unaccounted for by an interaction between the testing and the stimulus— we should expect four findings:

1. In group 1, posttest prejudice should be less than pretest prejudice.
2. There should be less prejudice evident in the group 1 posttest than in the group 2 posttest.
3. The group 3 posttest should show less prejudice than the group 2 pretest.

FIGURE 7.2
The Solomon four-
group design.

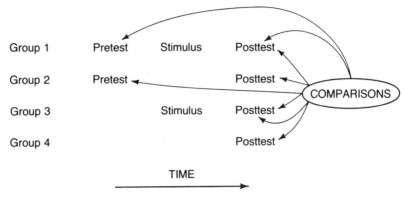

4. The group 3 posttest should show less prejudice than the group 4
   posttest.

Notice that findings (3) and (4) rule out any interaction between the testing
and the stimulus. And remember that the comparisons are meaningful
only if subjects have been assigned randomly to the different groups,
thereby providing groups of equal prejudice initially, even though preexperimental prejudice is measured only in groups 1 and 2.

   There is a side benefit to this research design, as the authors point
out. Not only does the Solomon four-group design rule out interactions
between testing and the stimulus, it provides data for comparisons that
will reveal the amount of such interaction that occurs in the classical experimental design. This knowledge would allow a researcher to review and
evaluate any prior research using that simpler design.

THE POSTTEST-ONLY CONTROL GROUP DESIGN This
last experimental design consists of the second half—groups 3 and 4—of
the Solomon design. As Campbell and Stanley argue persuasively, with
proper randomization, only groups 3 and 4 are needed for a true experiment that controls for the problems of internal invalidity as well as the
interaction between testing and the stimulus. With randomized assignment to experimental and control groups (which distinguishes this design
from the static-group comparison discussed earlier), the subjects will initially be sufficiently comparable on the dependent variable to satisfy the
conventional statistical tests used to evaluate the results, and it is not necessary to measure them. Indeed, Campbell and Stanley suggest the only justification for pretesting in this situation is tradition. Experimenters have
simply grown accustomed to pretesting and feel more secure with research
designs that include it.

   I trust that this discussion has given you a sense of the intricacies of
experimental design, its problems, and some solutions. There are, of

course, a great many other possible experimental designs in use, and you'll probably run into them in your reading of the research literature. Some involve more than one stimulus and combinations of stimuli. Others involve several tests of the dependent variable over time and the administration of the stimulus at different times for different groups. If you are interested in pursuing this topic, you should look at the Campbell and Stanley book, (see Suggested Reading) since such variations go beyond the scope of this discussion. Now I want to turn to a topic that we've touched on from time to time already.

TWO EXPERIMENTAL EXAMPLES

The problem of describing the logic of experimental design, as I have done, is that it can narrow your expectations of the experimental studies you will find reported in the literature. Therefore, I want to describe for you two very different experiments undertaken by social scientists in order to give you a broader view of what is possible. As you read these two examples, you should begin exercising your critical faculties as a consumer of experimental results.

OBSERVING HUMAN OBEDIENCE

One of the more unsettling clichés to come out of World War II was the German soldier's common excuse for atrocities: "I was only following orders." From the point of view that gave rise to this comment, any behavior—no matter how reprehensible—could be justified if someone else could be assigned responsibility for it. If a superior officer ordered a soldier to kill a small baby, the fact of the *order* was said to exempt the soldier from personal responsibility for the action.

Although the military tribunals that tried the war-crime cases did not accept the excuse, social scientists and others have recognized the extent to which this point of view pervades social life. Very often people seem willing to do things they know would be considered wrong by others, *if* they can cite some higher authority as ordering them to do it. Such was the pattern of justification in the My Lai tragedy of Vietnam, and it appears less dramatically in day-to-day civilian life. Few people would disagree with this sentiment, yet Stanley Milgram's now-famous study of the topic provoked considerable controversy.

To observe people's willingness to harm others when following orders, Milgram (1963, 1965) brought 40 adult men from many different walks of life into a specially designed laboratory setting. If you had been a subject in the experiment, you would have had an experience something like the following.

You would have been informed that you and another subject were about to participate in a learning experiment. Through a draw of lots, you would have been assigned the job of "teacher" and your fellow subject the job of "pupil." He would then have been led into another room, strapped into a chair, and had an electrode attached to his wrist. As the teacher, you would have been seated in front of an impressive electrical control panel covered with dials, gauges, and switches. You would have noticed that each of the switches had a label giving a different number of volts, ranging from 15 to 315. The switches would have had other labels, too, some with the ominous phrases "Extreme-Intensity Shock," "Danger—Severe Shock," and "XXX."

The experiment would run like this: You would read a list of word pairs to the learner and then test his ability to match them up. Since you couldn't see him, a light on your control panel would indicate his answer. Whenever the learner made a mistake, you would be instructed by the experimenter to throw one of the switches—beginning with the mildest—and administer a shock to your pupil. Through an open door between the two rooms, you'd hear your pupil's response to the shock. Then you'd read another list of word pairs and test him again.

As the experiment progressed, you'd be administering ever more intense shocks, until your pupil was screaming for mercy and begging for the experiment to end. You'd be instructed to administer the next shock anyway. After a while, your pupil would begin kicking the wall between the two rooms and screaming. You'd be told to give the next shock. Finally, you'd read a list and ask for the pupil's answer—and there would be no reply whatever, only silence from the other room. The experimenter would inform you that no answer was considered an error and instruct you to administer the next higher shock. This would continue up to the "XXX" shock at the end of the series.

What do you suppose you would have done when the pupil first began screaming? When he began kicking on the wall? Or when he became totally silent and gave no indication of life? You'd refuse to continue giving shocks, right? Of the first 40 adult men Milgram tested, nobody refused to administer the shocks until the pupil began kicking the wall between the two rooms. Of the 40, 5 did so then. Two-thirds of the subjects—26 of the 40—continued doing as they were told through the entire series—up to and including the administration of the highest shock.

As you've probably guessed, the shocks were phony, and the "pupil" was another experimenter. Only the "teacher" was a real subject in the experiment. You wouldn't have been hurting another person, even though you would have been led to think you were. The experiment was designed to test your willingness to follow orders, presumably to the point of killing someone. Which leads us to another aspect of Milgram experiment, as discussed in "Ethics and Experimentation."

EXPERIMENTING WITH COMPUTER DATING

In the folklore of courtship, there is a long and cross-cultural tradition concerning the desirability of the hard-to-get woman. Sages have advised young men to seek her out and win her heart, and young women, in turn, have been encouraged to play the part. By contrast, the too-easy woman is likely to be scorned, spurned, and slandered. But why, exactly, is that the case? That's the question that started Elaine Walster and her colleagues (1973) off on a winding and often frustrating search.

They began in a logical enough fashion: They asked a number of college men what they found so attractive about hard-to-get women. The answers came easily. If a woman could afford to play hard-to-get, she must be very popular and have desirable characteristics. Moreover, she was a challenge to male egos. Winning her brought fame if not fortune. Aside from the reports of college men, a number of psychological theories supported the desirability of the hard-to-get woman. People most appreciate those things they have to work hardest for. Also, sexual frustration can provide a strong motivation and hot passion. In short, everything supported the notion that hard-to-get women were especially desirable. But the researchers wanted a clearer understanding of the phenomenon.

In their initial experiment, the researchers showed pictures and biographies of teenage couples to a group of high school juniors and seniors. The key element in the biographies concerned the extent to which one member of the couple "liked" the other. Then students were asked how desirable the various partners pictured and described were. Everything suggested, of course, that those who were described as not caring very much for their partner would be the most desirable. Everything, that is, except the results of the experiment. Consistently, those described as caring very much were said to be the most desirable by the student subjects.

Back at the drawing boards, the researchers decided to approach the matter from a different direction and in a different fashion. This time, teaming up with a computer dating service, they hired as experimenters a number of women recently enrolled in the program. When the women began receiving calls and offers of dates from men matched with them, they had specific instructions on how to behave. Half the time, they were to pause three seconds before accepting, and half the time they were to accept right away. It was expected that the men would develop a greater liking for the dates who had subjected them to three seconds of being hard-to-get than for those who had been easy. Not so. It didn't seem to make any difference.

Getting increasingly frustrated with the repeated failures and again

ETHICS AND EXPERIMENTATION

For the most part, this book seeks to train you in methodological evaluations of research reports, and so I have concentrated on scientific critiques. At the same time, you should also be sensitive to ethical issues in research.

The cornerstone of social science research ethics is that no harm should come to the participants. There are many forms of potential harm, however.

A number of criticisms have been raised against the Milgram experiment, and particular concerns have been expressed about the effects of the experiment on the subjects. Many subjects seem to have personally experienced almost as much pain as they thought they were administering to someone else. They pleaded with the experimenter to let them stop giving the shocks. They became extremely upset and nervous. Some had uncontrollable seizures.

You should be sensitive to the issue of deception and ethics in this case since there is an ethical norm against lying to subjects. At the same time, experiments and other forms of social research often require various forms of deception. This is true of our second example, though it is not nearly as dramatic as in the Milgram experiment.

rethinking the problem, the researchers added two new dimensions. On the one hand, they wanted to rule out the actual experience of the date, forcing their subjects to react only to others' assessments of the woman. Second, they began to think that men's own self-esteem and self-confidence might matter. Specifically, they hypothesized that men lacking in self-confidence would be the most susceptible to the judgments of others that a woman was hard-to-get and thereby desirable. Here's how they tested that hypothesis.

This time, each man was given a standard test of self-esteem when he signed up for the dating service. All his data were entered into the computer, and the counselor then gave him a telephone number, saying it was that of a woman the computer had matched him with. The man then called the woman for a date and, after talking to her, reported his first impressions to the counselor. As you might guess, all the "dates" were members of the research team. Half the time, the "dates" accepted eagerly. The other half, they responded to the invitation saying "Mmmm (slight pause). No, I've got a date then. It seems like I signed up for that Date Match thing a long time ago and I've met more people since then . . . I'm really busy this week" (Walster et al., 1973:822). If the man suggested another time, she paused slightly and then agreed. If he didn't, she suggested getting together the next week and accepted whatever time he proposed.

Alas, no positive results were forthcoming from the new experiment. The men did not have a more favorable impression of the hard-to-get women than of the others, and their own level of self-esteem didn't make the difference. The desirability of the hard-to-get woman was now becoming an increasingly hard-to-get research finding. But the researchers persevered.

It next occurred to them that the experiment needed a heavier sexual component. After all, much of the folklore surrounding the hard-to-get woman had to do with sexuality and sexual attractiveness. So they set about adding sex to the study. How do you suppose you would do that? The researchers hired a prostitute as a new member of the research team. The subject were her clients or potential clients.

The easy-to-get condition was operationalized as the prostitute's normal mode of business. When playing hard-to-get, on the other hand, she would mix her client-subject a drink and warn him that she wasn't necessarily going to let him call her any time he wanted, adding that she was starting school soon and would only be able to see the men she liked best. She measured her perceived desirability on the basis of (1) how much she got paid by the man and (2) the number of times he called during the next month.

Though the experimentation was certainly getting more exciting, it didn't get any more successful. Being hard-to-get didn't seem to make the prostitute any more desirable. If anything, it seemed to put a chill on business.

At this point, the researchers concluded that the desirability of the hard-to-get woman was at least more complicated than they had imagined. Perhaps it only appeared under particular conditions. Not knowing what new dimensions to pursue, they went back to interviewing college men on the subject. But this time, there was an important difference in their questioning. Instead of merely asking what made the hard-to-get woman desirable, they asked about both the advantages and disadvantages she presented, and they repeated the expanded question in reference to the easy-to-get woman. It quickly became apparent that men perceived advantages and disadvantages in both kinds of women. Though there was certainly prestige to be gained by dating a woman generally regarded as hard-to-get, there was the accompanying danger that she'd stand her date up or call him a turkey in front of his friends. Eventually the full picture began to emerge.

A man was most likely to consider a woman desirable if she was impossibly hard-to-get for all other men but easy for *him*. Such a woman was subsequently labeled *selectively elusive*. Now the researchers were ready to conduct what would be the final experiments in the study.

They returned to the computer-dating gambit. Seventy-one college men were asked to participate in a test of computer matching as compared with random matching. Initially, each man completed a form describing himself. Then, later, he returned to the office to examine the files of some (fictitious) women in the study. Each man was given five folders, and each of the folders contained a woman's self-description plus her evaluations of five men, including the subject. Each of the self-descriptions was close enough to what the subject said about himself to make each woman a reasonable date. The five differed from one another as follows:

- One woman indicated she was willing to date any of the five men but was not very enthusiastic about any of them.
- One woman was enthusiastic about all the men, including the subject.
- One woman gave low marks to all the men *except* the subject, about whom she was really enthusiastic.
- The other two women were described, but the subject was told they had not returned to the office to evaluate the prospective dates.

Virtually every man in the experiment picked the selectively elusive woman: the one who liked them but didn't like any of the other men. They tended to reject the uniformly hard-to-get woman as too picky or stuck-up, and they tended to suspect the uniformly easy-to-get woman must have trouble getting dates. The selectively elusive woman was sometimes complimented for her good judgment. Some men simply said, "She made me feel good."

As I indicated at the outset of this section, the study of the hard-to-get woman has a special merit for my purpose here. It demonstrates nicely the pursuit of understanding in real-life social research. Failing repeatedly to confirm their hypothesis, the researchers returned again and again, rethinking their topic, adding new dimensions, and redesigning their observations. This is the process—often frustrating, always challenging—that can give social research the fascination and excitement of detective work. Notice also that this example involves the deception of subjects, as discussed in connection with the Milgram experiment. How do you feel about this? Could the experiment have been conducted without deception?

"NATURAL" EXPERIMENTS

Although we tend to equate the terms *experiment* and *laboratory experiment*, many important social scientific experiments occur outside of laboratories, often in the course of normal social events; these are known as **natural experiments.** Sometimes nature designs and executes experiments that we are able to observe and analyze; sometimes social and political decision makers serve this natural function.

Let's imagine, for example, that a hurricane has struck a particular town. Some residents of the town suffer severe financial damages, while others escape relatively lightly. What, we might ask, are the behavioral consequences of suffering a natural disaster? Are those who suffer most more likely to take precautions against future occurrences than those who suffer less? To find the answers to these questions, we might interview residents of the town some time after the hurricane. We might question them regarding their precautions before the hurricane and precautions that they are currently taking, comparing those who suffered greatly from the hurricane with those who suffered relatively little. In this fashion, we might take advantage of a natural experiment, which we could not have arranged even if we were perversely willing to do so.

A similar example may be taken from the annals of social research surrounding World War II. Following the end of the war, social researchers undertook retrospective surveys of wartime morale among civilians in a number of German cities. One of the chief purposes of this research was to determine the effect of mass bombing on the morale of civilians. The reports of wartime morale were compared for residents of heavily bombed cities and cities that received relatively little bombing. (Note: Bombing did not reduce morale.) We'll consider another form of natural experiment in some detail in Chapter 10: evaluation research.

Natural experiments—because the researcher must take things pretty much as they occur—raise many of the validity problems discussed earlier. Thus, when Stanislav Kasl and his colleagues chose to study the impact of the Three Mile Island (TMI) nuclear accident on the plant's workers, they had to be especially careful in the study design.

Disaster research is necessarily opportunistic, quasi-experimental, and after-the-fact. In the terminology of Campbell and Stanley's classical analysis of research designs, our study falls into the "static-group comparison" category, considered one of the weak research designs. However, the weaknesses are potential and their actual presence depends on the unique circumstances of each study. (*Kasl et al., 1981:474*)

The foundation of this study consisted of a survey of the people who had been working at Three Mile Island at the time of the accident. The survey was conducted five to six months after the accident. The survey questionnaire measured, among other things, workers' attitudes toward working at nuclear power plants. If the researchers had only measured the attitudes of TMI workers after the accident, they would have had no idea whether attitudes had changed as a consequence of the accident. They improved their study design by selecting another, nearby—seemingly comparable—nuclear power plant (abbreviated as PB) and surveyed workers there as a control group; hence their reference to a "static-group comparison."

Even with an experimental and control group, the authors were wary of potential problems with their design. In particular, they had to assume that the two sets of workers were equivalent to one another, except for the single fact of the accident. This could have been assumed if the researchers had been able to assign workers to the two plants randomly, but of course that was not the case. Instead, they needed to compare characteristics of the two groups and infer whether they were equivalent. Ultimately, they concluded that the two sets of workers were very much alike, and the choice of which plant they worked at was merely a function of where they lived.

Even granting that the two sets of workers were equivalent, the researchers faced another problem of comparability. They were not able to contact all the workers who had been employed at TMI at the time of the accident. The researchers discuss the problem thus:

One special attrition problem in this study was the possibility that some of the no-contact non-respondents among the TMI subjects, but not PB subjects, had permanently left the area because of the accident. This biased attrition would, most likely, attenuate the estimated extent of the impact. Using the evidence of disconnected or "not in service" telephone numbers, we estimate this bias to be negligible (< 1 percent). (1981:475)

This example points to both the special problems involved in natural experiments and the possibility for taking those problems into account. Social research generally requires ingenuity and insight, and natural experiments call for a little more than the average.

This concludes our examination of experimentation. I think the value of understanding the logic of experiments extends well beyond reading reports of experiments. What you have learned about this particular method should also be of use to you in evaluating other forms of research—surveys, for example.

☑ CONSUMER'S CHECKLIST

This chapter has presented both the power of the experimental model and also its potential weaknesses. We've seen some of the design features that can counteract those weaknesses, but researchers do not always utilize those features. As a result, you should ask the following questions as you read reports on social experiments.

- What is the primary dependent variable in the experiment? What effect is the experimenter trying to achieve?
- What is the experimental stimulus (or stimuli)?
- What other variables are relevant in the experiment?
- For each of these variables, check carefully how each is defined and measured. Check for problems of validity and reliability.
- How many experimental and control groups have been used in the experiment? How were subjects assigned to each? Has any test of comparability been made?
- What is the nature of the pretest and posttest measurements of the dependent variable? Again look for problems of validity and reliability.
- What is the chance of a placebo effect operating in the experiment? If this is a potential problem, has the researcher tested for it? If appropriate, has a double-blind design been used?
- Check for problems of internal validity, as listed below. If control groups have been used, were any of the problems detected? If there were no control groups, is there a chance that these problems might confound the research conclusions?
  a. *History:* Are the results a function of historical events occuring during the course of the experiment?
  b. *Maturation:* Are the results a function of subjects getting older, wiser, tired, and so on?
  c. *Testing:* Are the results a function of subjects being sensitized by the pretesting?
  d. *Instrumentation:* Are the results a function of using different measurements for the pretest and posttest?
  e. *Statistical regression:* Have "extreme" subjects been studied, so that they had only one way to change?
  f. *Selection biases:* Are the results a function of the way subjects have been selected for the experiment and/or assigned to experimental and control groups?
  g. *Experimental mortality:* How many subjects dropped out during the course of the experiment? Are the results a function of that?
  h. *Interactions of problems:* Has a combination of these problems interacted with one another to further confound things?

i. *Ambiguous causal direction:* Is there any doubt as to whether the stimulus causes the dependent variable or whether it might be the other way around?

j. *Diffusion or imitation of treatments:* Has there been any opportunity for members of the experimental group to communicate about the experiment with control group members?

k. *Compensatory treatment:* Has anything special been done to or for the control group to compensate them for missing out on the experimental stimulus?

l. *Rivalry:* Is there any evidence of the control group working to compete with the experimental group?

m. *Demoralization:* On the other hand, is there any evidence of the control group becoming demoralized as a result of being deprived of the experimental stimulus, thereby giving up and performing more poorly than they normally would?

• What precautions has the researcher taken to insure that the experimental results have external validity—that they apply in the real world as well in the laboratory? Can you see any problems not handled by the experimental design?

KEY WORDS

Dependent variable	Control group	Statistical regression
Independent variable	Matching	Experimental mortality
Experimental stimulus	Randomization	tality
ulus	Placebo effect	External invalidity
Self-selection	Double-blind	Solomon four-group
Pretest	Internal invalidity	design
Posttest	Maturation	Natural experiment
Experimental group	Instrumentation	

MAIN POINTS

1. An experiment is a research method involving the controlled manipulation of an independent variable to determine its effect on a dependent variable.

2. The key elements in a classical experiment are: a dependent variable measured in a pretest and a posttest, an experimental stimulus, and experimental and control groups.

3. Subjects are selected for study, and a pretest measurement is made of the dependent variable.
4. Subjects are assigned to either experimental or control groups.
5. Sometimes these assignments are made by matching subjects in terms of the dependent variable and other characteristics.
6. Matching is difficult when more than a few relevant variables are involved.
7. It is increasingly common for subject assignments to be made through random selection methods such as those discussed in Chapter 5.
8. Once assignments have been made, members of the experimental group are subjected to the experimental stimulus—an independent variable believed to affect the dependent variable. Members of the control group are not subjected to the stimulus.
9. Following the administration of the stimulus to the experimental group, a posttest of the dependent variable is undertaken among both groups.
10. The effect of the stimulus is determined by comparing the experimental and control groups in terms of any changes in the dependent variable between the pretest and the posttest.
11. The placebo effect is a change in the dependent variable purely as a consequence of subjects thinking they are receiving something that should change them. For example, medical patients sometimes improve when physicians give them sugar pills or some other bogus treatment.
12. The presence of a control group guards against the placebo effect as well as other problems of internal invalidity.
13. In a double-blind experiment, neither the subjects nor those administering the stimulus know who is getting the real stimulus and who is not.
14. There are several problems of internal invalidity—challenges to the assumption that the results of an experiment really represent the impact of the stimulus on the dependent variable.
15. Problems of external invalidity challenge the generalizability of the results from the experimental situation to real-life conditions.
16. The several problems of internal invalidity are handled by the Solomon four-group design.
    a. One group receives a pretest, the stimulus, and a posttest.
    b. One group receives a pretest, no stimulus, and a posttest.
    c. One group receives the stimulus and a posttest.
    d. One group receives only the posttest.
17. Experiments often raise ethical issues when they require deceiving subjects and when they have negative impacts on the subjects. This was seen in two examples—the Milgram experiment and the Walster et al. experiment on hard-to-get women.
18. A natural experiment applies the logic of the experimental model to real-life events, such as disasters.

1. Reread the discussion of the dating experiment. Identify the dependent variable, the experimental stimulus, and the experimental and control groups.
2. Evaluate the dating experiment in terms of each of the potential problems of internal invalidity.
3. Reread the discussion of the Milgram experiment. How does it differ from the classical experimental model?
4. Reread the discussion of the therapeutic touch experiment. What additional information would you want before accepting the conclusion that the therapeutic touch actually reduced anxiety?
5. Suppose that you wanted to determine whether receiving good grades on an exam leads students to work harder in the remainder of the course. Design an experiment that would allow you to make that determination.
6. Look over the research design you created in (5) above and discuss any ethical problems that might be involved.
7. Review the discussion of the Three Mile Island natural experiment. Pick three of the potential problems of internal invalidity and discuss them in connection with the TMI study.
8. Look through your local newspaper or a news magazine and find a report on an experiment. Critique the study in terms of one or more potential problems of internal invalidity.
9. Reread the discussion of the Milgram experiment and critique it in terms of the potential problem of external invalidity.
10. Design an experiment that would involve a possible placebo effect. How could you modify the experimental design so as to take account of the placebo effect?

SUGGESTED READING

Anderson, Barry. *The Psychology Experiment* (Monterey, Calif.: Brooks/Cole, 1971). An excellent overview of experimental methods, this readable little book begins with an examination of scientific inquiry in general, then describes the specific techniques available to the experimenter. Considerable attention is given to the analysis of experimental data.

Bales, Robert. *Interaction Process Analysis: A Method for the Study of Small Groups* (Reading, Mass.: Addison-Wesley, 1950). An old but classic overview of small-group research. Bales discusses the theory and techniques appropriate to the examination of social interaction in small groups undercontrolled laboratory conditions.

Campbell, Donald and Julian Stanley. *Experimental and Quasi-Experimental Designs for Research* (Chicago: Rand McNally, 1963). An excellent analysis of the logic and methods of experimentation in social research. This book is especially useful in its application of the logic of experiments to other social research methods.

Cook, Thomas D. and Donald T. Campbell. *Quasi-Experimentation: Design & Analysis Issues for Field Settings* (Chicago: Rand McNally, 1979). An updated and expanded version of Campbell and Stanley (above).

Graham, Kenneth. *Psychological Research: Controlled Interpersonal Interaction* (Monterey, Calif.: Brooks/Cole, 1977). A comprehensive treatment on the experimentation process, from initial curiosity to written report. This book presents psychological experimentation within theoretical, ethical, and technical contexts. It also gives a good guide to all the issues and problems that are likely to come up in the course of actual experiments.

FIELD RESEARCH

INTRODUCTION

Probably the most natural of social research methods is simply going to where something is happening and watching it. You and I have been doing this all our lives, and we've learned a lot from it. Newspaper reporters use that method in their work, as do social workers and professionals in many other areas. Called **field research,** this is the chief method used by anthropologists; it is also in common use by sociologists and other social scientists.

For example, here's some of what Bruce Hackett and Seymour Schwartz found when they set about studying energy use and conservation among young people who had moved to the country to take up a simpler lifestyle. These kinds of observations are available to those to take a first-hand look.

The sense of freedom from the demands of a steady job does not mean that individuals are independent of the cash economy. Most of the inland residents in our survey worked at occasional wage-paying jobs in nearby towns or at farms and ranches, and indicated that they would work more often if work were available. But the preferred ideal working situation is 2 or 3 days per week, not full-time. Men worked mainly in construction, automobile servicing and agriculture, while women worked mainly in agriculture (farm and ranch hands). Several people were self-employed in a variety of "cottage industry," craft or professional occupations. *(1980:167)**

The researchers were also able to correct what would have been a misconception if results were based on census data alone:

The rate of ownership of household appliances among those surveyed is much lower than that of the typical *poor* household in the nationwide survey conducted by Newman and Day. . . . Because of communal ownership in our sample, the number of households with direct access to several appliances was larger than the number of appliances. *(1980:168)**

Since field research is significantly different from the other research methods we are examining in this book, I'm going to organize this chapter differently. The success or failure of surveys and experiments hinges on particular technical procedures, so our examination has been organized around those. In preparing you to read and evaluate research reports on surveys and experiments, it has made sense to cover the same topics covered in training people to conduct research projects. To evaluate field research, however, the technical skills (e.g., note-taking techniques, filing systems, etc.) are, for the most part, meaningless.

Consequently, we'll begin with an overview of what field research is, how it's done, its special strengths, and the kinds of topics it's especially appropriate for. Following that introduction, I'm going to concentrate on some potential problems with field research—things you should look for in evaluating research reports. This is not to suggest that field research has more problems than other methods, only that it's easier to organize our examination that way. We'll look at problems of validity, reliability, sampling, and the other elements of scientific research. In addition, we'll look at the ethical problems of deceit in field research.

I'm going to conclude the chapter with a brief comment on other unobtrusive measures. I have two purposes in this. First, I want to prepare you to evaluate unobtrusive measures of all sorts. Second, I want to empower you as a more sensitive social observer. You'll find there are countless ways you can observe sociological patterns every day.

Now, let's take a look at the most frequently used unobtrusive measure employed by the social sciences.

*Reprinted with permission of the publisher from *Social Problems,* December 1980, pp. 165–178.

AN OVERVIEW OF FIELD RESEARCH

Field research often begins with work far from the field—in the library, for example. If you wanted to undertake field research on communication systems in gay bars, you might want to do a little research before simply leaping into action. There have been numerous studies on various aspects of the gay community, and you could profit from what has been done before. Often, this initial library research will lead to interviews with other scholars interested in the topic. By the same token, you might find it appropriate to collect some statistics relevant to your subject. That's the kind of prefield preparations that are typical in connection with field research.

DIRECT OBSERVATION

Eventually, the field researcher goes where the action is and observes it directly. If you were studying fundamentalist Christian revival meetings, you'd go to some and watch. If you were studying computer clubs, that's where you'd hang out. And because you were present at the scene of the action, you would need to make a decision whether to observe only or to participate in what you were studying. In your study of fundamentalist revivals, you could acknowledge yourself as an outside observer, or you could pretend to be a believer. We'll examine the various aspects of this issue in the section on personal involvement.

The sources of data for a field researcher are many. A major source is simply what the observer observes directly. At the revival meeting, for example, you'd watch the preacher preaching and watch the behavior of people in the audience. You might notice a lot of "incidental" things: how the audience dressed, their socioeconomic level, the racial/ethnic composition of the audience, and so on. Moreover, you would notice things you might not have anticipated—and would have missed if you had relied totally on predesignated questions.

In addition to direct observation, the field researcher quite often interviews people. (I'll have something to say a little later about sampling methods typically used in field research.) In your study of the fundamentalist revival, you might interview the leaders of the revival as well as some of the members of the audience.

QUALITATIVE ANALYSIS

With all these sources of data, the part of field research most difficult to describe concerns analysis. Field research calls for an essentially **qualitative** (nonnumerical) **analysis.** Throughout the process of observation, the field researcher engages in a parallel process of making sense out of what is being observed. As you prepared and reviewed your notes from an evening at the revival meeting, for example, you would be asking yourself what it all meant. We'll look into this process in more detail in the section entitled "The Logic of Inference."

Field research is particularly appropriate to ongoing events whose future course cannot be predicted with any certainty. Collective behavior— rallies, riots, panics, and the like—is perfect for field research. More generally, field research is appropriate to the study of interactions among people. If you wanted to study the nature of communications at an auction, you'd be well advised to go there, watch, and ask questions.

Field research has two particular strengths in comparison to other methods of research. First, by staying closer to the subject matter, it places fewer conceptual layers between the observer and the observed. As a result, field research is less susceptible to the charge of superficiality or artificiality sometimes lodged against other methods. Second, by taking place on the scene as the social events are unfolding, field research provides for greater flexibility than other methods. Methods such as surveys and experiments must be designed and laid out in advance, whereas the initial observations in field research provide feedback that restructures and redirects subsequent observations.

There are many other advantages to field research as well. It is relatively inexpensive in comparison with other methods. It's quick starting: You could begin a field research project right now. And it's easy to get started in. There is no complex body of technical skills to be mastered before you can begin doing recognizable field research, and you improve with continued practice. The Real World Research box entitled "Nonverbal Dentistry" provides another look at the kind of insights that just "being there" can offer.

To conclude this introduction to field research, I want to describe two examples that I think you'll find interesting and which will round out your initial grasp of the method.

STUDYING THE SATANISTS

As a part of a broad-based study of the "new religious consciousness," sociology graduate student Randy Alfred was given the task of studying and reporting on the Church of Satan. Pronouncing itself in league with Satan and opposed to Christ, the church is headquartered in San Francisco and operates under the charismatic leadership of Anton LaVey. You can probably imagine how you'd handle an assignment to study the local Methodist or Episcopalian congregation, but how would you go about studying the Satanists? Here's what Randy Alfred did:

NONVERBAL DENTISTRY

All sorts of things can be observed by simply watching people—means of communication, for instance. Gary Kreps (1981) points out to dental assistants that they communicate with patients in nonverbal ways.

The word *artifacts* refers to your total appearance based on your physical attributes (your size, shape, skin color and texture, hair style, hair color, etc.) as well as on the objects you carry and surround yourself with (your clothes, make-up, perfume, jewelry, eye glasses, cigarettes, books, files, charts, dental equipment, etc.). . . .

The term *kinestics* refers to your body movements and posture which often convey information about your attitudes toward involvement with patients in dental situations. . . .

Occulesics refers to your facial expressions and eye movements. Your face is a major source of emotional information for the patient. . . .

Paralinguistics is a form of nonverbal communication that is very closely related to verbal interaction. Paralinguistics refers to vocal cues and environmental sounds that accompany speech. Vocal cues include the rate, tone, pitch, volume, inflection, and expression of your voice. . . .

Tactilics—touching behaviors—comprise what is perhaps the most intimate channel of human communication. . . .

Proxemics, the use of space and distance in human interactions, are yet another form of non-verbal communication. . . .

Chronemics is often the most invisible and least recognized part of the dental practitioner's nonverbal communication pattern. Chronemics is the use of time in human interaction.

Take a minute to think of aspects of social life that you have special insights into. What descriptions could you report on the basis of your own experience?

SOURCE Gary L. Kreps, "Nonverbal Communication in Dentistry." *The Dental Assistant*, (January-February, 1981: 18–20.

I approached the group in April 1968 as an outsider and indicated an immediate interest in joining. My feigned conversion to Satanism was accepted as genuine and I made rapid progress in the group, as measured by my advancement in ritual rank, my being given administrative as well as magical responsibilities, and my appointment to the "ruling" body of the church.

From April 1968 to August 1969 I attended fifty-two of the group's weekly rituals, participating in all but eight of these early on. I was also present at twelve meetings of the ruling council, at twelve classes on various aspects of Satanism, and at six parties. (Alfred, 1976:183–184)

Alfred continued studying the church until 1973, having some 100 contacts with members, lasting a total of perhaps 600 hours and resulting in about as many pages of notes. In addition, he read books and articles about the group, including publications of the church itself. Right up until the end, he played the role of complete participant, concealing his research identity from those he was studying.

Alfred's total immersion in church life gave him insights into the nature of Satanism that would have been hard to gain from the outside. He was able to discover and distinguish the variety of motivations that led people to the group. Some were attracted by the prospect of sexual indulgence, some by the powers they might gain from magic. Others seemed primarily intent on rebelling against conventional religiosity and conventionality in general. Still others saw Satanism as a wave of the future, a new millennium. All told, Alfred found six distinct categories of reasons for joining the church.

Through his participation in the church—he ultimately became the official church historian—Alfred was able to learn details of rituals and other practices that would have been kept secret from outsiders. He was able to observe LaVey and other church leaders close up and was able to study the dynamics of interpersonal relations in the church. There simply would have been no other way of gaining such information.

In reading Alfred's report, you also have the sense that many of his analytical insights would have escaped an outsider. For example, the popular view of Satanism is one of total self-indulgence. Freed from all conventional social norms, Satanists would be expected to be completely hedonistic, indulging their every urge and desire. That is not what Alfred observed, however. In the case of sex, for example, Satanists limit sexual indulgence to those acts that don't hurt others against their will. LaVey further distinguishes between indulgence freely chosen and compulsive acts. Satanists should be free to indulge their desires, but they should not be run by those desires. By the same token, Satanists have a negative view of drug use. Even more unexpectedly, perhaps, LaVey strongly urges his followers to work hard at their jobs and succeed.

As a closing note, Alfred reports that he eventually found himself regreting his initial decision to conceal his research identity; he felt increasingly unethical. After all, he had been admitted into the inner circles of the church and given a position of trust and responsibility. As he approached the final stages of wrapping up and reporting the project, he went to LaVey to tell him the truth and to request permission to publish an article about what he had learned. LaVey indicated that he had suspected all along that Alfred was doing research. Did he feel Alfred had been unethical in attempting deception? Not at all: It was an appropriately satanic thing to do!

LIFE IN THE STREETS

The second example, Elliot Liebow's modern classic *Tally's Corner* (1967), differs from Alfred's study in many ways. There is an initial similarity, however. Like Alfred, Liebow, an anthropology graduate student, was assigned to his task as part of a larger research project. Liebow was hired to work on an ongoing study of child-rearing practices among low-income families in the District of Columbia. His task was to do field work among low-income adult males to fill out the picture created by numerous interviews with families.

Liebow prepared for the field work through a series of meetings with the project staff, learning the kinds of materials that were needed. He read the reports already written on the project. Then, he writes,

> Having partially digested the project literature, I told the director that I was ready to get started. He suggested a neighborhood that might be "a good place to get your feet wet." His instructions were: "Get out there and make like an anthropologist." (1967:245)

Arriving in the suggested neighborhood, Liebow discovered a white police detective scuffling with an angry black woman. Approaching two black male onlookers, Liebow asked them what happened. They answered cautiously. The conversation continued, warming somewhat as each expressed negative feelings about the police. Eventually convinced that Liebow was not himself a policeman, one of the men spent the next several hours talking to him over coffee.

Unlike Alfred, Liebow revealed his identity as a researcher and the purpose of his research from the start. Though recognized as an "outsider," he was accepted as a friend, and he became more and more a part of the streetcorner life as the research progressed. Like Alfred, Liebow soon found himself deeply involved in the lives of his subjects. He reports:

> I went to three different jails during this time, sat through one murder trial and two hearings in judges' chambers, testifying at one of them. I went to bondsmen's offices, to the United Employment Services, to the Blessed Martin de Porres Hostel (for homeless men) and into several private homes. (1967:245)

Whenever his new friends ran afoul of the law, Liebow's legal advice was sought and respected. He reports that he stayed in close touch with the project director about this participation, weighing the consequences of his actions for his research. There was certainly a danger that his own participation would change the character of the events and situations he had set out to study in the first place.

Liebow's description of his record keeping nicely illustrates the procedures described earlier in this chapter:

> Throughout this period, my field observations were focused on individuals: what they said, what they did, and the contexts in which they said them or did them. I sought them out and was sought out by them.
>
> My field notes contain a record of what I saw when I looked at Tally, Richard, Sea Cat and the others. I have only a small notion — and one that I myself consider suspect — of what they saw when they looked at me. (1967:248)

Ultimately, Liebow was able to gain a personal experience of street-corner life in a black, urban ghetto that few white people have. To an unusual extent, he was able to see and understand the men as they saw and understood themselves. He was able to learn their views and experiences of family life, employment, and—more to the point—unemployment.

These two short accounts scarcely do justice to the projects they describe, but they give you a concrete view of what field research entails. Both of the original reports are interesting and eminently readable, so you might like to read them for yourself.

In this section, we have seen some of the special strengths of field research. Those strengths come at a price, however. Let's turn now to some of the potential problems inherent in this method.

PROBLEMS OF VALIDITY AND RELIABILITY

You'll recall that validity concerns measurements actually measuring what they are supposed to measure rather than something else. Reliability, on the other hand, is a matter of dependability: If you were to make the same measurement again and again, would you get the same result? Let's see how field research stacks up in these respects.

VALIDITY

Against the backdrop of criticisms that survey and experimental measurements are often superficial and not really valid, field research has the appearance of providing more valid measures. Suppose it is important to categorize people in terms of their political views—how conservative or liberal they are, for example. In a survey, this might be accomplished by asking a series of questions about political issues or by asking people to agree or disagree with a series of political statements like the following:

Labor unions should be outlawed in the United States.
Heavy industries should be nationalized in the United States.
The very rich should pay a greater share of the costs of government than they now do.

Now suppose, by contrast, you were making a measurement of political views through a field research project. Let's imagine you want to characterize the politics of a woman who is running a large office. You could arrange to observe her interacting with those around her at work; listen in on political conversations she has with others; make a note of the associations she belongs to and whom she contributes money to. Does she write letters to public officials or to the editor of her paper (and what positions does she espouse in them)? Engage her in political conversations yourself. Eventually, you will have compiled a mass of observations regarding the woman's political orientation.

"Being there" is a powerful technique for gaining insights into the nature of human affairs. Listen, for example, to what a nurse reports—on the basis of her observations of and interactions with patients—about the impediments to patients' coping with cancer:

Common fears that may impede the coping process for the person with cancer can include the following:

- Fear of death—for the patient, and the implications his or her death will have for significant others.
- Fear of incapacitation—because cancer can be a chronic disease with acute episodes that may result in periodic stressful periods, the variability of the person's ability to cope and constantly adjust may require a dependency upon others for activities of daily living and may consequently become a burden.
- Fear of alienation—from significant others and health caregivers, thereby creating helplessness and hopelessness.
- Fear of contagion—that cancer is transmissible and/or inherited.
- Fear of losing one's dignity—losing control of all bodily functions and being totally vulnerable. *(Garant, 1980:2167)**

Observations and conceptualizations such as these are valuable in their own right. In addition, they can provide the foundation for further research—both qualitative and quantitative.

To bring this matter closer to home, take a minute to think about a friend or family member you know really well. In a sense, you have been doing a field research project with that person as the subject for some time. Think of all the information you have regarding your friend's political orientation. There's certainly no question about your assessment of that person's politics being superficial; the measurement you have arrived at would appear to have considerable validity.

Listen to what Joseph Howell had to say about "toughness" as a fundamental ingredient of life on Clay Street, a white working-class neighborhood in Washington, D.C.

Most of the people on Clay Street saw themselves as fighters in both the figurative and literal sense. They considered themselves strong, independent people who would not let themselves be pushed around. For Bobbi, being a fighter meant battling the welfare department and cussing out social workers and doctors upon occasion. It meant spiking Barry's beer with sleeping pills and bashing him over the head with a broom. For Barry it meant telling off his boss and refusing to hang the door, an act that led to his being fired. It meant going through the ritual of a duel with Al. It meant pushing Bubba around and at times getting rough with Bobbi.

June and Sam had less to fight about, though if pressed they both hinted that they, too, would fight. Being a fighter led Ted into near conflict with Peg's brothers, Les into conflict with Lonnie, Arlene into conflict with Phyllis at the bowling alley, etc. (1973:292)

Even without having read the episodes Howell refers to in this passage, you have the distinct impression that Clay Street is indeed a tough place to live. That "toughness" comes through far more powerfully than it would in a set of statistics on the median number of fistfights engaged in during a specified period of time.

The kinds of comprehensive measurements available to the field researcher tap a depth of meaning in our concepts—such as liberal and conservative—generally unavailable to surveys and experiments. Instead of defining concepts, field researchers will commonly give some detailed illustrations.

All of these advantages, however, depend on the researcher's good judgment and can be undercut by his or her biases. And because field research is less explicit than experiments and survey research, it is more difficult for the reader to assess the researcher's judgement and biases.

*Reprinted from *American Journal of Nursing*, vol. 80, no. 12, p. 2167, with permission of the publisher. Copyright 1981 by the American Journal of Nursing Company.

RELIABILITY

Though field research seems to have high validity, there is a potential problem in regard to reliability. We can't be sure, for example, that someone else would characterize your friend's politics the same way you did, even with the same amount of observation. Field research measurements—though in-depth—are also often very personal. How I judge your friend's political orientation depends very much on my own, just as your judgment would depend on your political orientation. Conceivably, you could describe your friend as middle-of-the-road while I'd feel I'd been observing a fire-breathing radical.

Be wary, therefore, of any purely descriptive measurements in field research. If the researcher reports that the members of a club are pretty conservative, know that such a judgment is unavoidably linked to the researcher's own politics. You can be more trusting of comparative evaluations: identifying who is more conservative than whom, for example. Even if you and I had different political orientations, we would probably agree pretty much in ranking the relative conservatism of the members of a group.

In any event, study the characterizations offered by field researchers to get a full sense yourself of what the people characterized are like. Even if you disagree with the researcher, you will be able to get some value out of the research.

In a sense, these questions also concern the issue of generalization. I want to look at that more directly now.

PROBLEMS OF GENERALIZATION

One of the chief goals of science is generalization. Social scientists study particular situations and events in order to learn about social life in general.

Generalizability is a problem for field research that crops up in three forms. First, as I've suggested above, the personal nature of the observations and measurements made by the researcher can produce results that would not necessarily be replicated by another, independent, researcher. If the observation depends in part on the particular observers, then it becomes more valuable as a source of insight than as proof of how "people" behave.

Second, because the field researcher gets a full and in-depth view of the subject matter, an unusually comprehensive understanding is possible. By its very comprehensiveness, however, it is less generalizable. Let's say you set out to understand fully how your city council operates. You study each of the members in great depth, learning about their ideological positions, how they came to public life, how they got elected, who their friends and their enemies are. You could learn about their family lives, seeing how personal feelings would enter into their public acts. After such an in-depth study, you could probably understand the actions of the council really well. But would you be able to say much about city councils in general? Your study would surely have provided you with some general insights, but you wouldn't be able to carry over everything you learned from the specific to the general. Having mastered the operations of the Dayton city council, you might not be able to say much about Cleveland's—though you would be in a position to organize a great study of the Cleveland city council.

In reviewing reports of field research projects, you should determine where and to what extent the researcher is generalizing beyond the specific observations to other settings. Such generalizations may be in order, but you need to judge that; nothing in this research method guarantees it.

Finally, there is often a problem of generalization even within the domain of what is being observed. As an illustration, let's imagine you were interested in learning about the Unification Church of Reverend Sun Myung Moon—the "Moonies." Suppose you were particularly interested in their recruitment practices: How does the group attract new members, what kinds of people are attracted, and so forth? One way to find the answers to such questions would be for you to express interest in the church yourself. By talking to members, attending meetings and retreats, you'd be able to get a first-hand experience of what you wanted to study. You could observe the way you were treated after expressing interest, and you could observe the treatment of other newcomers. By getting to know the other people who were considering joining the church, you would get an idea of the kinds of people who were joining.

Here's the problem of generalizability: Although you might talk to a number of church members, you couldn't be sure how "typical" they were. You might end up talking only to those people assigned the job of talking to potential recruits. Or perhaps you make your contact through your English class and meet mostly members majoring in the humanities and none majoring in the sciences. The potentials for biased sampling are endless. The same would apply to the new recruits you got to know: They might not be typical of new recruits in general.

Field researchers use several methods of selecting people to interview, and you should know something about each. George McCall and J. L. Simmons (1969:64–67) describe three common methods.

We have discussed *quota sampling* and *snowball sampling* in detail in Chapter 5. It is easy to understand their applicability to field research. If the group or social process under study has fairly clearly defined categories of participants, persons representing all different participation categories should be studied. In the study of a formal group, for example, you might wish to interview both leaders and nonleaders. Whenever representativeness is desired, you should use quota sampling and interview both men and women, young people and old people, and the like. A snowball sample would be appropriate in studying a loosely structured political group, for example. You might ask one of the participants whom he or she believed to be the most influential members of the group. You might interview those people and, in the course of the interviews, ask whom *they* believed to be the most influential. Your sample would "snowball" as each of your interviewees suggested others.

Finally, McCall and Simmons draw attention to the importance of **deviant cases.** Our understanding of fairly regular patterns of attitudes and behaviors is often improved through the examination of those cases that do not fit into the regular pattern. Thus, for example, you might gain important insights into the nature of school spirit as exhibited at a pep rally by interviewing those students who did not appear to be caught up in the emotions of the crowd, or those who did not attend the rally at all.

Aside from interviewing, there are other field research situations in which it may be possible to undertake a conscious sampling procedure. In a study of jaywalking, you might wish to make observations on a number of different city streets. You could pick the sample of locations through standard probability methods. More likely, you might employ a rough quota system, observing wide streets and narrow ones, busy streets and quiet ones, or including samples from different times of day or common types of pedestrians. In a study of the ways people interact at a bus stop, you would make observations at a number of different kinds of bus stops and other variations in the situation.

In practice, controlled probability sampling is seldom employed in field research. By and large, field researchers are more likely to employ what we have called a *purposive sample.* They select a sample of observations that they believe will yield the most comprehensive understanding of the subject of study, based on the intuitive feel for the subject that comes from extended observation and reflection. Nonetheless, understanding the principles and logic of more formal sampling methods is likely to result in more effective intuitive sampling in field research.

In evaluating this aspect of field research, bear in mind two stages of sampling. First, to what extent are the total situations available for observation representative of the more *general class* of phenomena the researchers wished to describe and explain? Are the three juvenile gangs they observed representative of all gangs? Second, are their *actual* observations within those total situations representative of all the *possible* observations? Have they observed a representative sample of the members of the three gangs? Have they observed a representative sample of the interactions that have taken place? Even when controlled probability sampling methods are impossible or inappropriate, the logical link between representativeness and generalizability still holds, and you need to be sensitive to that in evaluating field research reports.

THE PROBLEM OF PERSONAL INVOLVEMENT

Field research is sometimes referred to as **participant observation,** implying that the observer also participates in what is being observed. Actually, there is a range of variation on this dimension. Raymond Gold (1969) has discussed four different roles that field researchers may play in this regard: *complete participant, participant-as-observer, observer-as-participant,* and *complete observer.*

PARTICIPATION

Gold described the **complete participant** as follows:

The true identity and purpose of the complete participant in field research are not known to those whom he observes. He interacts with them as naturally as possible in whatever areas of their living interest him and are acceptable to him in situations in which he can play or learn to play requisite day-to-day roles successfully. (*1969:33*)

The complete participant, in this sense, may be a genuine participant in what he or she is studying (for example, a participant in a campus demonstration) or may pretend to be a genuine participant. In any event, if you are acting as the complete participant you let people see you *only* as a participant, not as a researcher.

Clearly, if you are not a genuine participant in what you are studying, you must learn to behave as though you were. If you are studying a group made up of uneducated and inarticulate people, it would not be appropriate for you to talk and act like a university professor or student.

PROBLEMS OF PARTICIPATION

Here let me recall your attention to an ethical issue involved in such a research situation. Is it ethical to deceive the people you are studying in the hope that they will confide in you as they will not confide in an identified researcher? Do the interests of science—the scientific values of the research—offset such ethical considerations? Social researchers themselves are divided on this issue. Although many professional associations have addressed the matter, the norms to be followed remain somewhat ambiguous when applied to specific situations.

Related to this ethical consideration is a scientific one. No researcher deceives his or her subjects solely for the purpose of deception, but rather in the belief that the data will be more valid and reliable, that the subjects will be more natural and honest if they do not know that the researcher is doing a research project. If the people being studied know they are being studied, they might modify their behavior in a variety of ways. First, they might expel the researcher. Second, they might modify their speech and behavior so as to appear more respectable than would otherwise be the case. Third, the social process itself might be radically changed. Students making plans to burn down the university administration building, for example, might give up the plan altogether once they learn that one of their group is a social scientist conducting a research project.

On the other side of the coin, if you are a complete participant, you may affect what you are studying. To play the role of participant, you must participate. Yet, your participation may importantly affect the social process you are studying. Suppose, for example, that you are asked for your ideas as to what the group should do next. No matter what you say, you will affect the process in some fashion. If you make a suggestion that is followed by the group, your influence on the process is obvious. If you make a suggestion that is not followed, the process whereby the suggestion is rejected may importantly affect what happens next. Finally, if you indicate that you just don't know what is to be done next, that may add to a general feeling of uncertainty and indecisiveness in the group.

Ultimately, *anything* that the participant observer does or does not do will have some effect on what is being observed; it is simply inevitable. More seriously, what you do or do not do may have an *important* effect on what happens. There is no way to completely prevent this effect, though sensitivity to the issue may provide a partial protection.

This problem frequently forms the basis of critiques of field research projects. For example, Leon Festinger and his colleagues (1965) wanted to learn something about a phenomenon fairly prominent in the 1950s. During a time of frequent flying saucer sightings, some people claimed to have made direct contact with visitors from outer space. One group, which Festinger and his colleagues would study, claimed that an arrangement had been made for a select group of Earth inhabitants to be picked up by a flying saucer and taken away just prior to the destruction of the planet. A core group of believers had arranged to be among those leaving Earth, and they had the task of persuading others to join them. Festinger's team signed up.

Especially fascinating to the researchers was the dilemma presented by failures. Indeed, the resulting book was entitled *When Prophecy Fails.* Several times, an arrangement was made for the group to be picked up and transported off Earth. They assembled at the designated spot, but nobody came, and the world didn't end. These were the times that most fascinated the researchers. What would the members do? As it turned out, the typical reaction was for the group to intensify its recruitment activities.

The intensified recruitment as a response to failure fit into the theory being developed by the researchers. But here's a question that concerned reviewers of the work: What assurance was there that the participant observers—acting as though they were 100 percent members of the group—were not subtly or even unconsciously encouraging or at least supporting behavior in line with their theory? It's a fundamental question to be addressed in field research, and one you should be conscious of in reviewing research reports.

"Where Psychologists Fit In" provides another example of the special insights available to those researchers who are also genuine participants in what they study.

LEANING TOWARD OBSERVATION

Because of these ethical and scientific considerations, the field researcher frequently chooses a different role from that of complete participant. In Gold's terminology, you might choose the role of **participant-as-observer.** In this role, you would participate fully with the group under study, but you would make it clear that you were also undertaking research. There are dangers in this role also, however. First, the people being studied may shift much of their attention to the research project rather than focusing on the natural social process, and the process being observed may no longer be typical. Or, conversely, you yourself may come to identify too much with the interests and viewpoints of the participants and lose much of your scientific objectivity.

The **observer-as-participant** is one who identifies himself or herself as a researcher and interacts with the participants in the social process but makes no pretense of actually being a participant. A good example would be a newspaper reporter who is learning about a social movement—for instance, the unionization of migrant farm workers. The reporter might interview leaders and also visit workers where they live, watch strawberry picking, go with an injured worker to the hospital, and so on.

At the other extreme, the **complete observer** is one who only observes a social process without becoming a part of it in any way. Quite possibly, the subjects of study might not realize they are being studied because of the researcher's unobtrusiveness. Sitting at a bus stop for the purpose of observing jaywalking behavior at a nearby intersection would be an example. While the complete observer is less likely to affect what is being studied and less likely to "go native" than the complete participant, he or she is also less likely to develop a full appreciation of the subject. Observations may be more sketchy and transitory. In every field research project, the researcher must decide on the proper balance of observation and participation.

Whenever you are reviewing a research report utilizing field research methods, then, it is essential that you discover the role played by the researcher. Having done that, you should take into account both the advantages and the disadvantages of that particular role.

WHERE PSYCHOLOGISTS FIT IN

Here's what John Linton is able to report regarding the way psychologists fit into the treatment of patients with spinal cord injuries:

By the time Mr. M. had become depressed, he had been seen by the psychologist and through the consultation service. Rapport had already been established, and the clinician had a predepression baseline against which to measure the patient's later observed depressive behavior. Medical patients often react negatively when "the shrinks" are called in. But this arrangement permitted Mr. M. to familiarize himself with the psychologist before he was in great felt need of psychological help. When help was needed, the patient felt less defensive and, since visits for psychological check-ups occurred from the beginning, less apt to feel that he was suddenly being seen as abnormal by the staff. (1981:234)

This aspect of medical treatment becomes evident to a researcher on the scene, whereas it might escape those removed from it. Notice what Linton has seen as a result of participating in the situation rather than merely observing it from afar.

SOURCE John C. Linton, "The Psychologist on a Spinal Cord Injury Team in a Community Medical Center." *Professional Psychology*, April 1981: 229–235.

THE LOGIC OF INFERENCE

We've talked a good deal about various aspects of making observations, but that's only part of the field research process. The other part has to do with making sense out of what has been observed. Put differently, this is a process of making **inferences** from data. There are two types of inferences to be made on the basis of field research observations: descriptive and causal.

Typically, the researcher will want to describe the people and events he or she has been observing. In addition to descriptions of specific elements, summary descriptions are also in order. What were the members of

Festinger's flying saucer group like on the whole? How old were they? How much education did they have? Were most of them men or women? The answers to questions like these are a fundamental part of the research report.

In the matter of description, you will do well to recall the earlier discussions of measurement and of sampling. How the researcher has defined variables and how observations have been sampled will directly affect the summary descriptions arrived at. I think you are already well enough versed in this that I won't pursue the issue.

The matter of causal inferences is trickier. We're dealing here with explanations for why things happened, what caused what, why people did the things they did, and so forth. The bottom line here is: Be careful of faulty reasoning. I want to draw your attention to an excellent book and mention a few guidelines for spotting logical errors in research reports. The book is Howard Kahane's *Logic and Contemporary Rhetoric* (1980). Here are some of the common errors Kahane warns of.

PROVINCIALISM All of us look at the world through glasses framed by our particular histories and current situations. There is always a danger, then, that the field researcher—or any researcher for that matter—will interpret people's behavior so as to make sense in terms of the researcher's own point of view. For example, the Christian researcher may see things in Christian terms, socialists in socialist terms, and so forth. If the researcher has failed to do so, you should attempt to get inside the subjects' points of view and see if the researcher's interpretations make sense in *those* terms.

HASTY CONCLUSION Researchers as well as other people are susceptible to this error. Whenever the researcher offers an interpretation of data, be sure to judge the "weight" of evidence leading to that interpretation. Is the conclusion essentially inevitable given the data lying behind it, or could other conclusions be reasonable?

QUESTIONABLE CLASSIFICATION Conclusions can only be reached through the classification of observations. Festinger and his colleagues concluded that group members responded to the failure of prophecies by intensifying their recruitment efforts. This conclusion depended on the classification of certain events as failures of prophecies and certain activities as an intensification of recruitment activities. Always scrutinize such classifications to see if they are warranted or if they might have been encouraged by their impact on the theories being developed.

QUESTIONABLE CAUSE Whenever a researcher suggests that X caused Y, ask yourself if that is necessarily the case. What else could have caused Y? Kahane (1980:63) gives several economic examples. If a business goes bankrupt, for instance, it is often concluded that the company's president must have lacked business skills—even when the bankruptcy occurred during a severe recession marked by a great many business failures.

SUPPRESSED EVIDENCE Field researchers, amass a great deal of information through direct observations, interviews, library work, and so on. Reaching conclusions requires dismissing information as much as selecting it. On the whole, the researcher will dismiss information that is "not relevant," but relevance is obviously a matter of judgment. It will be useful for you to take note of observations that do not figure in the conclusions reached, as well as observations not mentioned that you can reasonably assume were made. If a researcher concludes that members of a neo-Nazi group oppose blacks out of a fear of economic competition, for example, you would expect that most members are working class or lower-middle class. But if the researcher has provided no indication of the occupations of the members, you might well wonder about the conclusion.

QUESTIONABLE FACTS It's always useful to ask yourself whether it would be possible for the researcher to know the "facts" reported. This is especially relevant in the arena of motivations. Whenever the researcher tells you *why* someone did something, ask yourself whether the researcher's judgment is to be trusted in the respect. Kahane quotes one of Richard Nixon's critics as saying, in regard to the war in Vietnam: "The government had served notice to all but the blind that its intention was to win the war through escalation—even with nuclear weapons, if necessary" (1980:77). Kahane asks, reasonably enough, whether the critic could have really known whether the administration was willing to use nuclear weapons.

FALSE DILEMMA Research conclusions, like nonscientific opinions, often represent the selection of one position from among alternatives. Selecting one may seem to rule out the others, when this is not always necessary. Kahane offers as an example the statement "Economics, not biology, may explain male domination." Kahane comments:

This statement suggests that there are just two possibilities: either biology explains male dominance, or economic success does so. And it suggests that the second possibility, economic success, "may" (weasel word) be the true explanation of male domination. Yet there are many other possibilities, such as social custom, religious conviction, and various *combinations* of economic and biological factors. By tempting us to think of the cause of male domination as either economics or biology, the quote leads us to overlook other possibilities and thus to commit the fallacy of *false dilemma*. (1980:81)

INCONSISTENCIES This is obvious enough to need no elaboration. Keep your eyes open for contradictory evidence and/or conclusions.

These few examples of logical pitfalls may have sharpened your critical faculties somewhat, and I would heartily encourage you to read the Kahane book for more guidance and insights.

This completes our examination of field research. Just as I have said that field research skills improve with practice, the same may be said of evaluating research reports. Practice may not make perfect, but it certainly moves you in that direction. I'm going to conclude the chapter with a discussion that should improve your analytical skills even more.

UNOBTRUSIVE MEASURES

As we've seen, field research should be designed and executed so as to have the minimum impact on the behavior and events under study. In this, it contrasts with the other research methods we've examined so far. For all their strengths, surveys and experiments hardly fit unnoticed into the normal course of human affairs. The arrival of an interviewer on the doorstep obviously affects the respondent's behavior to some degree, and we've seen some of the protections developed to offset that problem.

In this respect, field research fits into a more general category that also includes content analysis and the analysis of existing statistics, which we'll look at in Chapter 9. All are examples of what Eugene Webb and his colleagues (1966) have called **unobtrusive measures.** The term refers to social research that has no impact on what is being studied. Whereas surveys, experiments, and "obtrusive" field research may influence the behavior of the people being studied, analyzing traffic accident statistics neither increases nor decreases accidents.

Webb and his colleagues, in a delightful and ingenious book, have played freely with the task of learning about human behavior by observing what people inadvertently leave behind them. Want to know what exhibits are the most popular at a museum? You could conduct a poll, but people might tell you what they thought you wanted to hear or what might make them look more intellectual and serious. You could stand by different exhibits and count the viewers who came by, but people might come over to see what you were doing. Webb and his colleagues suggest that you check the wear and tear on the floor in front of various exhibits. Those where the floor has been worn down the most are probably the most popular. Want to know which exhibits are popular with little kids? Look for mucus on the glass cases. To get a sense of the most popular radio stations, you could arrange with an auto mechanic to check the radio dial settings for cars brought in for repair. The possibilities are limitless. Like the investigative detective, the social researcher looks for clues, and clues of social behavior are all around you. In a sense, everything you see represents the answer to some important social scientific question—all you have to do is think of the question.

Though problems of validity and reliability crop up in unobtrusive measures like those mentioned above, a little ingenuity can either handle them or put them in perspective. I encourage you to look at the Webb book. It's enjoyable reading, and it should be a source of stimulation and insight for you in evaluating the research of others and in doing a little of your own.

☑ CONSUMER'S CHECKLIST

As we've seen, field research has special strengths and also some special problems. Here are some guidelines for evaluating how well a researcher has exploited the strengths and avoided the problems.

- Has the researcher placed this particular project in the context of previous research on the topic? Does this research add to, modify, replicate, or contradict the previous studies?
- What are the main variables under study?
  a. How have these been defined and measured?
  b. Are there any problems of validity in the way measurements have been made?
  c. Are there any problems of reliability?
  d. Is there any chance that the classification of observations has been influenced by how those classifications will affect the research findings and the researcher's hypotheses?
- If descriptive conclusions have been drawn—for example, the group's members were quite conservative"—what are the implicit standards of comparison being used?
- How much can the findings of the study be generalized to a broader sector of society?
  a. What has the researcher claimed in this regard?
  b. What is the basis for claims to generalizability?
  c. If people have been interviewed, what sampling procedure has been followed, and what are its implications for generalizability?
- What role did the researcher(s) play—observer and/or participant— in the events being studied?
  a. In what ways, if any, has the researcher's participation influenced what was being observed?

b. Is there any indication that the researcher has become "too involved" in the subject matter, losing his or her scientific objectivity?
c. What special insights has participation in the events given the researcher?
d. In what ways, if any, has the researcher's identification as a researcher changed the behavior of those being studied?

- Have the researcher's observations and interpretations been clouded or slanted by his or her own cultural background?
- Has the researcher been guilty of drawing hasty conclusions?
- Has the researcher provided you with any questionable facts? Be wary of items of information that are unlikely to be available to the researcher, especially reports of other people's thoughts and motivations.
- Can you find any problems of questionable classification?
- Are there examples of questionable causes?
- Has the researcher seemed to suppress evidence?
- Does the research report pose any false dilemmas? Be particularly wary of statements that spell out possible alternatives. Ask yourself if there are more.

KEY WORDS

Field research	Complete observer	Complete observer
Qualitative analysis	Participant-as-	Inference
Deviant cases	observer	Unobtrusive mea-
Participant observa-	Observer-as-partici-	sures
tion	pant	

MAIN POINTS

1. Field research involves the direct observation of social life in its natural setting.
2. Field research is an example of qualitative (nonnumerical) analysis.
3. Field research is especially strong in terms of validity—researchers can capture the depth and richness of events.
4. Reliability can be a problem since field research is based on the judgment of the researcher on the scene. Other observers might see things differently.

5. Because field research is so closely embedded in particular events, generalization to other situations can be a problem.
6. Field researchers must make decisions of what to observe from among the mass of possible observations.
7. When field researchers interview people as a part of their observations, they use three types of sampling, as discussed in Chapter 5: quota sampling, snowball sampling, and purposive sampling.
8. Often field researchers can gain special insights from the study of deviant cases—people and events that don't fit into the normal run of things.
9. Field researchers commonly participate in what they are studying.
10. The complete participant pretends to be a genuine member of what is happening and conceals his or her role as researcher.
11. The participant-as-observer participates fully but also acknowledges being a researcher.
12. While participation provides a source of insights denied mere observers, the researcher's participation can also affect what is being observed.
13. The observer-as-participant acknowledges being a researcher, interacting with the participants but not actually participating.
14. The complete observer does not interact with the participants at all but only observes what is happening.
15. Qualitative analysis depends on logical inferences, and the consumer of qualitative analysis must be wary of illogical reasoning.
16. Unobtrusive measures are ways of studying social life by observing the residue of behavior.

? REVIEW QUESTIONS

1. Review the discussion of the Church of Satan. Discuss the potential problems inherent in Alfred's decision to act as a complete participant.
2. Review the discussion of *Tally's Corner*. What additional insights do you think Liebow might have gotten if he had been black and had acted as a complete participant?
3. Pick a topic that social researchers might study and discuss the relative strengths and weaknesses of field research compared to survey research with regard to validity.
4. Compare field research and survey research, as in (3), with regard to reliability.
5. Suppose a researcher wanted to interview members of a radical political group. Suggest ways the researcher might utilize quota sampling, snowball sampling, and purposive sampling.

6. In the study of a radical political group as in (5) above, discuss how the analysis of deviant cases might be useful.
7. Suggest situations in which it would be particularly appropriate for a researcher to take on the role of:
   a. Complete participant
   b. Participant-as-observer
   c. Observer-as-participant
   d. Complete observer
8. In your local newspaper, find assertions that illustrate one or more of the following problems of logical inference.
   a. Provincialism
   b. Hasty conclusion
   c. Questionable classification
   d. Questionable cause
   e. Suppressed evidence
   f. Questionable facts
   g. False dilemma
   h. Inconsistencies
9. Think of an unobtrusive measure of the popularity of various diets.
10. Discuss the problems of validity and reliability inherent in the measure you suggested in (9).

SUGGESTED READING

Becker, Howard, Blanche Geer, Everett Hughes, and Anselm Strauss. *Boys in White: Student Culture in Medical School* (Chicago: Unversity of Chicago Press, 1961). An excellent and important illustration of field research methods. This study, involving continued interaction with medical school students over the course of their professional training, examines the impact of their experiences on their values and orientations. An informal biography of this project, by Blanche Geer, many be found in Phillip Hammond (ed.), *Sociologists at Work* (New York: Basic Books, 1964) and is also reprinted in McCall and Simmons (see below).

Lofland, John. *Analyzing Social Settings* (Belmont, Calif.: Wadsworth, 1971). An unexcelled presentation of field research methods from beginning to end. This eminently readable little book manages successfully to draw the links between the logic of scientific inquiry and the nitty-gritty practicalities of observing, communicating, recording, filing, reporting, and everything else involved in field research. In addition, the book contains a wealth of references to field research illustrations.

Lofland, John. *Doomsday Cult: A Study of Conversion, Proselytizaton, and Maintenance of Faith* (Englewood Cliffs, N.J.: Prentice-Hall, 1966). Another excellent illustration of field research methods in practice. This study examines the dynamic development of a deviant religious movement still active today. A shorter report of this study may be found in John Lofland and Rodney Stark, "Becoming a World-Saver: Conversion to a Deviant Perspective," *American Sociological Review* 30 (December 1965): 862–875.

McCall, George, and J. L. Simmons (eds.). *Issues in Participant Observation: A Text and Reader* (Reading, Mass.: Addison-Wesley, 1969). An excellent collection of important articles dealing with field research. The 32 selections cover most aspects of field research, both theoretical and practical. Moreover, many of the selections provide illustrations of actual research projects.

Shostak, Arthur (ed.). *Our Sociological Eye: Personal Essays on Society and Culture* (Port Washington, N.Y.: Alfred, 1977). An orgy of social scientific introspection. This delightful collection of first-person research accounts offers concrete, inside views of the thinking process in sociological research, especially field research.

THE ANALYSIS
OF EXISTING DATA

INTRODUCTION

The term **data-collection** is a common one in the social sciences. Typically, this means administering questionnaires, conducting experiments, making field observations, or something similar. In each of these instances, data collection really entails the "creation" of data where none existed prior to the research. As we'll see in this chapter, however, it is often possible for social scientists to study social life through an examination of already existing data.

We'll begin the examination with a classic example of this form of research: Emile Durkheim's *Suicide*. Though nearly a century old, this analysis of self-destruction still exemplifies what can be learned from a mass of dusty statistics and a keen imagination.

Following this opening example, I'll focus your attention on some of the keys to evaluating reports using existing data. We'll see that the issue of units of analysis is critical here, especially since aggregated statistics are often used to draw inferences about individuals. In this context, we'll examine the ecological fallacy.

Next, we'll examine the problems of validity and reliability in the analysis of existing data. We'll consider some general problems, and I'll draw your attention to particular problems associated with specific sources. I'll wrap up this part of the presentation with some comments on sources of existing data that you might want to use in undertaking analyses of your own.

I want to conclude the chapter with an extended example that points to many of the errors that can be made in the analysis of existing data. The example revolves around the issue of cost of living: Specifically, does it cost more to live on the island of Maui in Hawaii or in Washington, D.C.? The answer to that question meant hundreds of thousands of dollars in back pay for a group of federal employees. I was given the task of critiquing the government's research procedures as a witness in federal court in 1979. The errors uncovered are instructive well beyond the scope of the trial, and I think the discussion will assist you in evaluating social research in general.

STUDYING SUICIDE

Why do people kill themselves? Undoubtedly every suicide case has a unique history and explanation, yet all such cases could no doubt be grouped according to certain common causes: financial failure, trouble in love, disgrace, and other kinds of personal problems. Emile Durkheim (1897) had a slightly different question in mind when he addressed the matter of suicide. He was particularly interested in discovering the environmental conditions that encouraged or discouraged it, especially social conditions.

As he examined official government statistics, one of the first things that attracted Durkheim's attention was the relative stability of suicide rates. Looking at several countries, he found suicide rates to be about the same year after year. Clearly, the same group of people weren't committing suicide year after year, so Durkheim had to find another explanation for the stable figures.

The more he examined the available records, the more patterns of differences became apparent to Durkheim. All of these patterns interested him. He discovered, for example, that a disproportionate number of suicides occurred during the hot summer months, leading him to hypothesize that temperature might have something to do with suicide. If that were the case, we should expect to find higher suicide rates in the southern European countries than in the temperate ones. When he tested this hypothesis, however, Durkheim discovered that the highest rates were found in countries in the central latitudes, so temperature couldn't be the answer.

He explored the role of age (35 was the most common suicide age), sex (men outnumbered women around four to one), and numerous other factors. Eventually, a general pattern emerged from different sources.

In terms of the stability of suicide rates over time, for instance, Durkheim found the pattern was not *totally* stable. In particular, he found spurts in the rates during times of political turmoil, which had occurred in a number of European countries around 1848. This observation led him to hypothesize that suicide might have something to do with "breaches in social equilibrium." Put differently, social stability and integration seemed to be a protection against suicide.

This general hypothesis was substantiated and specified through Durkheim's analysis of a different set of data. The different countries of Europe had radically different suicide rates—the rate in Saxony (today part of East Germany), for example, was about ten times that of Italy—and the relative rankings of various countries persisted over time. As Durkheim considered other differences in the various countries, he eventually noticed a striking pattern: Predominantly Protestant countries had consistently higher suicide rates than Catholic ones. The predominantly Protestant countries had 190 suicides per million population; mixed Protestant-Catholic countries, 96; and predominantly Catholic countries 58 (1897:152).

It was possible, Durkheim reasoned, that some other factor, such as level of economic and cultural development, might explain the observed differences. If religion had a genuine effect on suicide, then the religious difference would have to be found *within* given countries. To test this idea, Durkheim first noted that the German state of Bavaria had both the most Catholics and the lowest suicide rates in that country, whereas heavily Protestant Prussia had a much higher suicide rate. Not content to stop there, Durkheim went on to examine the provinces composing each of those states. Table 9.1 shows what he found.

As you can see in both Bavaria and Prussia, those provinces with the highest proportion of Protestants also had the highest suicide rates. Increasingly, Durkheim became confident that religion played a significant role in the matter of suicide.

Returning eventually to a more general theoretical level, Durkheim combined the religious findings with his earlier observation about increased suicide rates during times of political turmoil. He then suggested, to put it most simply, that many suicides are a product of *anomie*—"normlessness," or a general sense of social instability and disintegration. During times of political strife, people might feel that the old ways of society were collapsing. They would become demoralized and depressed, and suicide was one answer to the severe discomfort. Seen from the other direc-

TABLE 9.1   Suicide Rates in Various German Provinces, Arranged in Terms of Religious Affiliation

Religious character of province	Suicides per million inhabitants
Bavarian Provinces (1867–1875)*	
Less than 50% Catholic	
Rhenish Palatinate	167
Central Franconia	207
Upper Franconia	204
Average	192
50% to 90% Catholic	
Lower Franconia	157
Swabia	118
Average	135
Over 90% Catholic	
Upper Palatinate	64
Upper Bavaria	114
Lower Bavaria	19
Average	75
Prussian Provinces (1883–1890)*	
More than 90% Protestant	
Saxony	309.4
Schleswig	312.9
Pomerania	171.5
Average	264.6
89% to 68% Protestant	
Hanover	212.3
Hesse	200.3
Bradenberg and Berlin	296.3
East Prussia	171.3
Average	220.0
40% to 50% Protestant	
West Prussia	123.9
Silesia	260.2
Westphalia	107.5
Average	163.6
32% to 28% Protestant	
Posen	96.4
Rhineland	100.3
Hohenzollern	90.1
Average	95.6

Source: Adapted from Durkheim, 1897, p.153.
*Note: The population below 15 years of age has been omitted.

tion, social integration and solidarity—reflected in personal feelings of being part of a coherent, enduring social whole—would offer protection against depression and suicide. This was where the religious difference fit in. Catholicism, as a far more structured and integrated religious system, would give people a greater sense of coherence and stability than would the more loosely structured Protestantism.

From these theories Durkheim created the concept of *anomic suicide*. Perhaps more importantly, he added the concept of *anomie* to the lexicon of the social sciences. Please realize that I have given you only the most superficial picture of Durkheim's classic study, and I think you'd enjoy looking through the original. In any event, this study gives you a good illustration of the possibilities for research contained in the masses of data regularly gathered and reported by government agencies.

UNITS OF ANALYSIS

As we have seen in the case of *Suicide*, the unit of analysis involved in the analysis of existing statistics is often not the individual. Durkheim was required to work with political-geographical units: countries, regions, states, and cities. The same situation would probably appear if you were to undertake a study of crime rates, accident rates, disease, and so forth. By their nature, most existing statistics are **aggregated:** They describe groups.

The aggregate nature of existing statistics can present a problem, though not an insurmountable one. For example, Durkheim wanted to determine whether Protestants or Catholics were more likely to commit suicide. None of the records available to him indicated the religion of those people who committed suicide, however, so ultimately, it was not possible for him to say whether Protestants committed suicide more often than Catholics. He *inferred* as much from the fact that Protestant countries, regions, and states had higher suicide rates than Catholic countries, regions, and states.

There's danger in drawing that kind of conclusion. It is always possible that patterns of behavior at a group level do not reflect corresponding patterns on an individual level. Such errors are said to be due to an ecological fallacy, which was described in Chapter 3. It is altogether possible, for example, that it was Catholics who committed suicide in the predominantly Protestant areas. You can probably come up with a story to support that possibility. Perhaps the Protestants in the areas Durkheim studied were more religiously intolerant than Catholics. If that were the case, we'd expect that Catholics in predominantly Protestant areas would be badly persecuted—perhaps leading them to despair and suicide. It would be possible, then, for Protestant countries to have high suicide rates without any Protestants committing suicide.

Durkheim avoided the danger of the ecological fallacy in two ways. First, his general conclusions were based as much on rigorous, theoretical deductions as on the empirical facts. Whenever our observations correspond with what we have predicted on the basis of reason, confidence in our explanations is increased. Second, by extensively retesting his conclusions in a variety of geographical locations, Durkheim further strengthened the likelihood that his conclusions were correct. Suicide rates were higher in Protestant countries than in Catholic ones; higher in Protestant regions of Catholic countries than in Catholic regions of Protestant countries; and so forth. The replication of findings added to the weight of evidence in support of his conclusions.

Durkheim's study of suicide had people—individuals and aggregates—as its units of analysis. The analysis of existing data is often based on units of analysis other than people. The Real World Research box entitled "Press Coverage of the Women's Movement" illustrates a very different unit of analysis.

PROBLEMS OF VALIDITY AND RELIABILITY

Whenever research involves an analysis of data that already exist, it is obviously limited to what exists. But what exists often isn't exactly what we are interested in, and our measurements may not be altogether valid representations of the variables and concepts we want to draw conclusions about. This is the chief disadvantage of analyzing data as opposed to creating original data specifically relevant to the question at hand. Let's look at the issue of validity in some real examples.

THE VALIDITY OF HEALTH INDICATORS

It is often difficult to know what social indicators represent. A variable that seems absolutely straightforward and meaningful may turn out to be a reflection of something altogether different. Here's an example.

Alain Colvez and Madeleine Blanchet (1981) were interested in the question of whether health in the United States was improving over time as commonly believed. Declines in death rates, especially in infant mortality, as well as a generally increasing life expectancy are typically pointed to as evidence that our national health is improving. Colvez and Blanchet point out, however, that such indicators measure survival but not health in any positive sense. Here's some of what the researchers found:

PRESS COVERAGE OF
THE WOMEN'S MOVEMENT

Starting in the late 1960s, American women began a concerted demand for equality with men. During the 1970s, the movement for women's liberation was widely reported in the press and was an issue discussed throughout the country.

Francesca M. Cancian and Bonnie L. Ross (1981) wanted to examine the relationship between the development of the movement and mass media coverage. A key question was whether the movement was a product of the media or whether the movement developed independently of the media. To find out, they undertook an analysis of press coverage of the women's movement. For a broad, historical view, they examined the period 1900–1977.

Data for the analysis were obtained from two indexes. The *New York Times* Subject Index lists and categorizes all articles published in that newspaper. The *Reader's Guide to Periodical Literature* provides a similar listing for 120 popular American periodicals. For each year of the period under study, the researchers calculated the percentage of articles listed under the headings "Woman" and "Women." The graph opposite summarizes the researchers' findings.

The data show two peaks in press coverage of women. Early in this century, press coverage was heavy during the time women were fighting for their right to vote. The 1970s saw another peak. During the 1940s, the *Reader's Guide* shows a smaller peak. According to the researchers, this represents a large number of articles describing the industrial jobs women assumed during World War II.

For the researchers, there is a significant lag between the beginning of the women's movement and the growth of press coverage. This seems to contradict the view that the movement was only a product of the media, though media coverage later supported the movement.

The researchers themselves point to some potential problems of validity inherent in their measurement of press coverage. Can you think what some of those problems might be?

According to data published by the United States National Center for Health Statistics, disability reported among the US population has increased substantially during the years 1966 to 1976. Among younger age groups, the increase in activity limitation involves visual and hearing impairments as well as asthma. In the middle age group (45–64), four causes increased in both sexes (diabetes, musculoskeletal disorders, hypertension, and diseases of the circulatory system other than hypertension and heart conditions); one cause affected

Coverage of Women in the New York Times and the Reader's Guide, 1900–1977

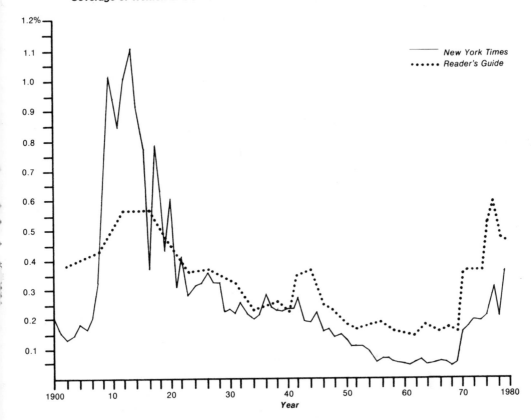

——— New York Times
•••••• Reader's Guide

SOURCE Francesca M. Cancian and Bonnie L. Ross, "Mass Media and the Women's Movement: 1900–1977." *The Journal of Applied Behavioral Science*, January-March 1981:9–26. The graph is taken from page 14.

men only (heart conditions) and one women only (malignant neoplasms). In the 65 and over age group, diabetes and circulatory diseases (excluding heart conditions and hypertension) increased significantly. Although the US population increased by 10 per cent, the number of persons permanently limited in their activities because of health conditions increased by 37 per cent with a much larger proportion of those disabled claiming to be unable to carry on their main activity. (1981:464)

A strong case, then, can be made for the position that the U.S. population is getting *less* healthy. As indicated above, this conclusion is based on national surveys conducted by the government for the purpose of learning how many people are disabled—defined as being limited in activities by virtue of health problems.

Before accepting the conclusion, however, can you think of any other explanations for the observations reported? Colvez and Blanchet suggest a few possibilities. First, it's possible that people's standards of health have risen over time, so that they might say they are too ill to work today, whereas they would have worked with the same condition years ago. Liberalized retirement plans allowing retirements based on health problems may have gone hand-in-hand with changing personal standards. All this notwithstanding, Colvez and Blanchet feel the apparent increase in disabilities is a genuine one, caused in part by environmental deterioration.

Ronald Wilson (1981), in a critique of the Colvez-Blanchet analysis suggests there are numerous reasons to wonder whether the disability data really measure disability. Wilson points first to studies indicating that medical interventions apppear to make matters worse rather than better. When the number of physicans and other medical facilities serving a population are increased, more illness is found. People who went undiagnosed and untreated earlier are now diagnosed and treated. Though this is a good thing, it does produce an *apparent* increase in the number of illnesses in the population.

Wilson further points out that improvements in diagnostic techniques also produce an apparent increase in disease rates. Cases previously overlooked become discovered—and counted.

Declining death rates can also produce apparent disability increases. People who would have died in earlier times may live today but be disabled by their conditions. Finally, Wilson points out that improvements in the survey techniques of the ongoing national survey that is the source of the data may also result in apparent increases in illness by getting more complete health reports.

This is an especially useful example for our present purposes. The National Center for Health Statistics' National Health Interview Survey is an excellent research program, professionally designed and executed. Even so, you can see there are serious questions to be raised regarding the meaning of the measurements made.

VALIDITY AND ''IMPULSIVE MARRIAGES''

In 1937, Samuel Stouffer wanted to look at the consequences of the Depression on what he called "impulsive marriages." Had he been able to interview married couples at length, he probably would have been able to categorize each couple as representing an impulsive marriage or not, and we might all agree that his categorizations were valid ones. However, he was working with official statistics, and government officials neither asked nor recorded whether the couples were getting married impulsively. As a result, Stouffer had to find data that *were* recorded and could be taken as an indicator of impulsiveness (recall the discussion of indicators in Chapter 4). In this case, he chose to analyze rates of out-of-state marriages. This procedure involves the following line of reasoning:

1. Assume that out-of-state marriages are more impulsive than in-state marriages.
2. If the Depression produced a greater number of impulsive marriages, then we should expect to find more out-of-state marriages during the Depression.
3. Finding that out-of-state marriages *did* increase during the depression confirms the hypothesis about impulsive marriages *only if* the assumption about out-of-state marriages being impulsive is correct.

Two additional characteristics of science are used to handle the problem of validity in analysis of existing statistics: logical reasoning and replication. First, Stouffer didn't grab out-of-state marriages as an indicator out of a hat; he had a carefully reasoned theoretical basis for assuming that they could be taken to indicate impulsiveness. Second, the increase in out-of-state marriages during the Depression was only one of several findings supporting Stouffer's general conclusions about the consequences of the Depression on the family. Had none of his other hypotheses turned out as expected, he would have questioned whether the increase in out-of-state marriages really meant what he thought it did.

REPLICATION AND VALIDITY

Replication, in a sense, can be a general solution to problems of validity in social research. Suppose we want to find out if women are more compassionate than men. There are many possible ways of measuring compassion, but none of them is necessarily valid. Crying in sad movies isn't necessarily a valid measure of compassion, so if women cry more than men, that doesn't *prove* they are more compassionate. Neither is putting little birds back in their nests a valid measure of compassion, so that wouldn't *prove* women to be more compassionate. Giving money to charity could represent something other than compassion, and so forth. None of these things, *taken alone*, would prove that women were more compassionate than men. But if women appeared more compassionate than men on *all* of them, that would create a **weight of evidence** in support of the conclusion. In the analysis of existing statistics, a little ingenuity and reason can usually turn up several independent tests of your hypothesis, and if all the tests seem to confirm it, there is a weight of evidence in support of the view you are advancing.

THE RELIABILITY OF STATISTICS

The analysis of existing statistics depends heavily on the quality of the statistics themselves: Are they accurate reports of what they claim to report? That can be a substantial problem sometimes; though impressive, tables of statistics are sometimes grossly inaccurate.

For example, a great deal of the research on crime is dependent on official crime statistics. Consequently, this body of data has come under critical evaluation, and the results have not been too encouraging. Suppose, for purposes of illustration, you were interested in tracing the long-term trends in marijuana use in the United States. Official statistics on the numbers of people arrested for selling or possessing it would seem a reasonable measure of use—right? Not necessarily.

To begin, you face a hefty problem of validity. Before the passage of the Marihuana Tax Act in 1937, grass was legal in the United States, so arrest records would not give a valid measure of use. But let's suppose you were willing to limit your inquiry to the post-1937 era. You would still have problems of reliability, stemming from the nature of law enforcement and crime record keeping.

Law enforcement is subject to various pressures. A public outcry against marijuana, led perhaps by a vocal citizens' group, often results in a police "crackdown on drug trafficking"—especially if it occurs during an election or budget year. A sensational story in the press can have a similar effect. In addition, the volume of other business facing police has an effect on marijuana arrests.

Lois DeFleur (1975) traced the pattern of drug arrests in Chicago between 1942 and 1970 and demonstrated that the official records present a far more accurate history of police practices and political pressure on police than a history of drug use. On a different level of analysis, Donald Black (1970) and others have analyzed the factors determining whether an offender is actually arrested by police or let off with a warning. Official crime statistics are influenced by whether specific offenders are well or poorly dressed, whether they are polite or abusive to police officers, and so forth. Consider also the whole matter of unreported crimes, sometimes estimated to be as much as ten times the number of crimes known to police, and the reliability of crime statistics gets even shakier.

These comments concern crime statistics at a local level. Often it is useful to analyze national crime statistics, such as those reported in the FBI's *Uniform Crime Reports*. Additional problems are introduced at the national level. Different local jurisdictions define crimes differently. Also, participation in the FBI program is voluntary, so the data are incomplete.

Finally, the process of record keeping affects the records that are kept and reported. Whenever a law-enforcement unit improves its record-keeping system—computerizing it, for example—the apparent crime rates always increase dramatically. That can happen even if the number of crimes committed, reported, and investigated does not increase.

Your first protection against problems of reliability in reports on the analysis of existing statistics is awareness—knowing that the problem may exist. Investigating the nature of the data collection and tabulation may enable you to assess the nature and degree of unreliability so that you can judge its potential impact on the research conclusions.

In the above discussions, I've mentioned several data sources that are commonly used by social researchers. I want to wrap up this aspect of our examination by mentioning some other common sources. You might want to use these to do analyses of your own sometime, or you may find them useful in checking on research reports you are reading and assessing.

SOURCES OF EXISTING STATISTICS

The most valuable book in this area is the annual *Statistical Abstract of the United States*, published by the U.S. Department of Commerce. It is unquestionably the single best source of data about the United States. It includes statistics on the individual states and (less extensively) cities as well as on the nation as a whole. Where else can you learn the number of work stoppages in the country year by year, residential property taxes of major cities, the number of water pollution discharges reported around the country, the number of business proprietorships in the nation, and hundreds of other such handy bits of information? To make things even better, Grosset & Dunlap, a commercial publisher, currently offers the same book in soft cover for $3.95 (1981 price), giving you around 700 facts per penny. The commercial version is entitled *The U.S. Fact Book: The American Almanac*; it shouldn't be confused with other almanacs that are less reliable and less useful for social scientific research.

Federal agencies—the departments of Labor, Agriculture, Transportation, and so forth—publish countless data series. To find out what's available, go to your library, find the government documents section, and spend a few hours browsing through the shelves. (Appendix A gives guidelines for using the library.) You'll come away with a clear sense of the wealth of data available for your insight and ingenuity.

World statistics are available through the United Nations. Its *Demographic Yearbook* presents annual vital statistics (births, deaths, and other data relevant to population) for the individual nations of the world. Other U.N. publications report a variety of other kinds of data. Again, a trip to your library is the best introduction to what's available.

The amount of data provided by nongovernment agencies is as staggering as the amount your taxes buy. Scientific disciplines and professions have amassed great stores of data. Whatever your special field of interest, whether in an academic social science or an applied field, you'll find a great wealth of data available.

Other data sources are available off campus. Chambers of commerce often publish data reports on business, as do private consumer groups. Ralph Nader has information on the safety of automobiles and other products, and Common Cause covers politics and government. And, as we have seen, George Gallup publishes reference volumes on public opinion as tapped by Gallup Polls since 1935.

I'm tempted to continue listing data sources, but I'm sure you have the idea. The lack of funds to support expensive data collection is no reason for not doing good and useful social research. As you read through reports on social science research, you'll find a great many researchers reporting conclusions based on data collected by someone else.

The growing popularity of existing data as the basis for research makes it all the more crucial that you become sensitive to the problems involved in such data. To support you in gaining that critical ability, I'm going to present a detailed analysis of a body of government data that were used for practical purposes but which contained severe flaws.

A COST-OF-LIVING FIASCO

A cornerstone of the U.S. federal civil service has been *equity*: two people doing the same job are supposed to receive the same pay. This has been accomplished through the specification of particular pay grades—GS ratings—for particular jobs. Equity has been difficult to maintain, however, in the case of foreign assignments. The standard of living that a $20,000 salary would buy in Washington, D.C., costs more to maintain in some foreign locations. In recognition of this disparity, the State Department developed a system of **cost-of-living allowances (COLA)** to compensate employees assigned overseas. Thus, a GS-8 assigned to a foreign duty station might be paid 25 percent more than a GS-8 serving in Washington, D.C., to compensate for the higher cost of living.

In addition to the civil servants assigned to foreign stations, those serving in Hawaii and Alaska have also received COLA in compensation for the higher cost of living in those particular states. In 1975, for example, all federal civil servants in Hawaii received COLA of 12.5 percent of their base pay. In 1976, the Civil Service Commission decided to determine costs of living separately for each of the several Hawaiian Islands. During the first year of the new system, civil servants in Honolulu received a COLA of 17.5 percent, based on research showing the cost of living there was 18.3 percent higher than Washington. Civil servants on the island of Maui, however, found their COLA rate dropped to 7.5 percent. The rationale was that research showed the Maui cost of living to be only 8 percent higher than Washington.

As you would imagine, the Maui civil servants were upset at having their pay cut. They were especially distressed to have the pay cut justified on the basis of research findings that it was cheaper to live on Maui than in Honolulu as all local wisdom indicated that Maui was more expensive. Feeling they had been treated unfairly, the Maui civil service employees organized and filed a suit in federal court to challenge the government's research. A team of social science researchers, including myself, were engaged as their research witness. Our job was to find out whether the federal research had underestimated the cost of living on Maui. Though the project began with the 1976 research, we ultimately analyzed reports on 1977, 1978, and 1979 also. In the remainder of this section, I'll describe some of the things we found as an illustration of the problems you may uncover in reading analyses of existing data.

HOW COST OF LIVING WAS MEASURED

Suppose you were given the task of determining whether living was more expensive on Maui than in Washington and, if so, by how much. How would you go about doing that? Probably, you'd think up a list of commonly purchased commodities and then price them in Washington and on Maui. How much does a 7 ounce tube of Crest toothpaste cost in the two locations, for example? How about a six-pack of Coke, a model 362 Singer sewing machine, a 1 pound can of Yuban coffee, and so on? If that's what you'd do, you'd have company. That's essentially what the government did.

Table 9.2 lists the 97 items the Civil Service Commission priced for the purpose of determining the relative costs of living in Washington and Maui. Look through the list, and you'll see that it provides a good cross-section of those items that make up the cost of living anywhere in the United States. For each specific item, I have shown the costs reported by the Commission for Washington and Maui in 1976.

With the exception of the last entry in the table, each number in Table 9.2 represents the average cost of the item indicated. (The housing index was calculated in a more complex fashion.) Notice that each set of

TABLE 9.2 Federal Cost-of-Living Items, 1976 Washington/Maui Comparisons

	Washington	Maui
Meat, eggs, fat for home		
Beef and Veal (lb)	2.13	2.39
Pork (lb)	1.95	2.34
Lamb and other red meat (lb)	2.36	2.39
Fish (lb)	1.45	2.38
Chicken (lb)	.64	.87
Bacon (lb)	1.67	2.06
Canned ham (lb)	2.12	2.51
Eggs (doz)	.82	.98
Margarine (lb)	.51	.56
Other fats (lb)	.67	.61
Grocery staples		
Milk, fresh (qt)	.43	.52
Milk, evaporated (13 oz)	.39	.37
Milk, dried (lb)	1.28	1.73
Bread (lb)	.34	.58
Cake mix (lb)	.55	.77
Flour (lb)	.18	.23
Cereal (lb)	.79	1.03
Rice, regular (lb)	.42	.24
Coffee (lb)	1.70	1.49
Cola drink (10–12 oz six-pack)	1.19	1.14
Chocolate bar (1.5 oz)	.16	.20
Sugar (lb)	.28	.28
Baby food (4.5–4.75 oz)	.19	.19
Fruits and vegetables		
Fresh citrus (lb)	.23	.24
Canned juice (46 oz)	.64	.82
Fresh fruits (lb)	.37	.48
Canned fruits (29–31 oz)	.71	.85
Potatoes (lb)	.23	.35
Fresh vegetables (lb)	.40	.49
Canned vegetables (15–16 oz)	.41	.53
Frozen vegetables (10 oz)	.40	.78
Tobacco and alcohol		
Cigarettes (carton of 200)	4.19	4.02
Whiskey (fifth)	4.53	5.52
Beer (10–12 oz six-pack)	1.74	1.90
Personal care		
Laundry soap (lb)	.55	.47
Sanitary napkins (12)	.71	.86
Toothpaste (3.5 oz)	.67	.55
Razor blades (5)	1.00	.80

	Washington	Maui
Launder shirt	.62	1.12
Dry clean suit	2.85	3.72
Haircut (including tip)	3.30	3.42
Shampoo and wave (including tip)	7.25	7.70
Furnishings and household operations		
Scouring powder (14 oz)	.29	.33
Toilet tissue (500–1000 sheets)	.25	.29
Light bulb (75 watt)	.55	.55
Sewing machine, portable	298.17	157.73
Electric iron	18.69	18.48
Washing machine	329.68	345.96
Vacuum cleaner	123.72	126.28
Sheet (double bed)	7.67	7.10
Telephone (monthly rate)	9.93	8.42
Clothing		
Man's sport coat	57.75	74.53
Man's suit	104.82	125.67
Man's shirt	9.53	16.99
Man's T-shirt (set of 3)	5.07	7.11
Woman's suit	46.99	52.87
Woman's skirt	19.60	20.80
Woman's slip	7.53	8.49
Woman's panty hose	2.12	2.58
Woman's shoes	21.35	26.28
Boy's shoes	15.66	16.59
Medical		
Aspirin (100)	.88	.67
Milk of magnesia (12 oz)	1.24	1.22
Prescription 1 (24 250-mg)	1.34	2.00
Prescription 2 (80 units)	2.44	2.98
Medical doctor	14.00	9.05
Dentist, filling	13.08	10.40
Dentist, extraction	15.00	10.40
Dentist, X ray	4.44	3.12
Hospital (room)	105.31	75.40
Recreation		
Camera film (35 mm, 36 exposure)	3.11	3.11
Film processing (of above)	3.13	3.52
Paperback book (150–200 pages)	1.47	1.24
Newspaper, local daily	.15	.16
Newspaper, out-of-town daily	.26	.26
Radio, short wave	73.48	124.25
TV set (18–19 inch, black and white)	162.57	183.19

	Washington	Maui
Bicycle (24–27 inch, 3-speed)	89.22	93.59
Record (12-inch stereo)	5.06	5.06
Movie theater	3.00	2.38
Automobile purchase price	4014.24	4539.84
Transportation		
Lube and oil	14.72	19.34
Tune-up	40.65	42.98
Labor cost (per hour)	15.75	15.50
Tires	36.12	36.40
Gas (gal)	.64	.72
Liability insurance	110.20	40.20
Collision insurance ($50 deductible)	113.00	71.80
Comprehensive coverage	25.70	18.00
Taxi, 1.25 miles (including tip)	1.35	.88
Municipal bus fare	.58	—
Air fare (per mile)	.11	.06
Domestic service		
Day worker (40 hours)	116.44	100.00
Food away from home		
Breakfast (including tip)	3.60	—
Lunch (including tip)	5.69	2.80
Dinner (including tip)	9.29	3.34
Housing index	100.00	127.60

Source: Extracted from U.S. Civil Service Commission unpublished report, "Cost of Living Allowance Program: Island of Maui, March 1976."

prices permits the calculation of the Maui/Washington price ratio. In the case of beef and veal, the ratio was 1.12: the Maui price averaged 12 percent higher than in Washington. In the case of housing, a more complicated method was used, which resulted in a ratio comparable to what I just described.

For most of the commodities, field workers were instructed to visit the stores most frequently used by government employees and collect prices for the commodities listed. Typically, two stores were visited, and three prices were obtained for each item from each store. Thus, for example, the average price of film was based on three prices at each of two photography stores.

Given the data in Table 9.2, it would be possible to calculate ratios for each of the 97 items and then average the ratios to arrive at an estimate of how much more expensive living costs were in Maui than in Washington. Actually, the Commission used a somewhat more sophisticated method. Studies by the Census Bureau indicated that the various items in a given category accounted for differing percentages of the total expenditures made within that category: For example, beef and veal accounted for a larger proportion of the first category than did canned ham. This was taken into account by weighting each of the items (see Chapter 5). Moreover, the 14 categories each accounted for differing proportions of families' total expenditures: Housing accounted for more than any other category, for example. So the categories were also weighted in the calculation of the overall ratio of Maui/Washington costs of living. (It's not necessary for our purposes to go any further into the weighting systems here.)

The end result of this process was the calculation of an overall ratio of 108.00—indicating that it cost 8 percent more to live on Maui than in Washington. The comparable ratio for Honolulu was 118.3, indicating the Honolulu cost of living was 18.3 percent higher than Washington's. These two figures implied that Maui was less expensive than Honolulu—an implication that contradicted widespread popular beliefs. My job was to account for that disparity.

Take a minute now to look through the data in Table 9.2. Look for price comparisons that strike you as odd. In doing this, you should realize that Maui is an island of some 40,000 population—far smaller and more rural than Washington, D.C. While locally produced agricultural goods might cost less on Maui, it would seem reasonable for manufactured goods, for example, to cost more since Maui would be a low-volume market, far from the manufacturers. See what you would want to look into further. What methodological questions would you want to ask? What further information would you want? Then compare your responses with the following discussions of some of the problems found in the federal research.

SEWING MACHINES

One of the more striking puzzles that emerged from an intitial look through the Maui/Washington price comparisons concerned sewing machines. Ultimately, this turned out to be a bottomless pit of problems.

The initial question was simple enough: Do sewing machines cost more on Maui than in Washington or less—and how much? The government's answer was unexpected: The average sewing machine price reported for Washington in 1976 was $298.17, contrasted with $157.73 on Maui. How could sewing machines be almost twice as expensive in Washington, D.C.—a large market area, near manufacturers—than in rural Maui, far off the industrial path? What additional questions would you want to ask if you were evaluating this finding?

The question we asked was *what* sewing machines were priced in the two locations? It would seem logical that, in a price comparison, the same set of sewing machines would be priced—but were they? As it turns out, they definitely were not. In the following discussions, I have used fictitious brand names since I was ordered not to use real names in federal court. In the case of sewing machines, *Goodbuys* represents a national department store with moderate prices, which sells their own brand of sewing machines as well as other products. *Golden* represents a well-known, relatively more expensive brand of sewing machine.

On Maui, three models were priced at Goodbuys: machines costing $105, $155, and $195 (prior to adding sales taxes). In Washington, three Goodbuys machines were also priced, though not the same models. The Washington prices were $103.99, $159.99, and $234.99. Only one direct comparison was possible: The Goodbuys model 1227 was priced in both places. It cost $103.99 in Washington and $105 on Maui, about what you would expect on the basis of simple marketing economics. In part, then, the Maui/Washington disparity was caused by more expensive models being priced in Washington than on Maui. But this was only a part of the problem.

Whereas three sewing machines had been priced on Maui in 1976, in Washington, as it turns out, six machines had been priced: the three Goodbuys machines mentioned above and three more Golden machines. Whereas the Goodbuys machines priced in Washington averaged $189.99, the Golden machines were priced at $164.95, $469.95, and $569.95. No Golden sewing machines were priced on Maui in 1976.

The price difference reported, then, clearly resulted from the fact that very different items were compared. It was as though a Ford had been priced on Maui and a Mercedes in Washington.

In 1977, essentially the same thing happened. The only model priced in both locations cost $109.95 on Maui and $89.99 in Washington. Yet the pricing of more expensive brand and models in Washington resulted in a higher overall average price.

In 1978, the situation changed dramatically. The field workers on Maui, having noted that Goldens were being priced in Washington, added Golden to their own data collection. That year, the three Goldens priced in Washington cost $159.95, $529.95, and $579.95; the three priced on Maui cost $189.95, $449.95, and $979.95. The last was Golden's top-of-the-line model, and it had not been priced in Washington. The overall average price for Maui was substantially higher than for Washington.

Having obtained copies of all data worksheets under court order, we were able to see how the final, official averages had been calculated in Washington. In 1978, the highest priced Golden priced on Maui was simply omitted! Yet even so, the official average Maui price was slightly higher in 1978 than the Washington price. In 1979, the handling of sewing machine data was even more bizarre. To begin, six machines were priced in each location: three Goodbuys and three Goldens. Once again, the top-of-the-line Golden was priced on Maui—now a whopping $1035! That model had not been priced by the field workers in Washington. The worksheets indicated that a phone call had subsequently been made to Golden, and a Washington price had been obtained: $950. Then, the seven Washington prices had been added up and divided by *six!* As a result, the official Maui price for sewing machines was only slightly higher than the Washington price.

I have gone into the matter of sewing machines in such detail to give you an understanding of the things that can go wrong in the processing of existing data. The key problem throughout this fiasco was one of definition and measurement. If you are going to compare the cost of an "average" sewing machine in two locations, you must create a reasonable definition of what constitutes an "average" machine. The government had wisely decided to base the averages on the prices of several machines. They initially failed, however, by creating averages that were not comparable in composition. At first, the error worked against Maui. Later, when the error began working in Maui's favor, the attempts to solve the problem led to more and worse errors.

Let's look more briefly now at some other types of errors. Each of these, we'll see, revolves around the problem of **comparability**—comparing things that are really comparable. This is an issue faced over the years in connection with the Consumer Price Index, as described in the Real World Research box entitled "CPI Item Selection."

BICYCLES

In Table 9.2, you'll note that in 1976 the price of a bicycle on Maui was slightly higher than in Washington: $89.22 in Washington versus $93.59 on Maui. This seemed, intuitively, a surprisingly small difference. There was no bicycle manufacturer anywhere near Maui, and it would seem reasonable that the shipping costs would result in a much bigger difference.

You'll see from the table that the instructions to the field workers specified "24–27 inch, 3-speed bicycles." The specification of 3-speed bikes seemed to be a carryover from earlier years, when 3-speed bikes were popular. It was our sense that 10-speed bikes were more popular now. That turned out to be correct, since the worksheets indicated that the field workers had difficulty pricing 3-speed bikes and often substituted (more expensive) 10-speed bikes. This had not been done uniformly, however. For example, in 1978, the Maui average was based on four 3-speed bikes and two 10-speed bikes, whereas the Washington average was based on one 3-speed and five 10-speeds. Had comparable items been priced, the Maui average obviously would have been much higher than Washington's.

CPI ITEM SELECTION

When the Consumer Price Index was established in 1918, 145 commodities and services were specified for pricing. The items were selected with an eye toward reflecting the overall cost of living. By measuring the same 145 items year after year, it was possible to determine trends in the cost of living over time.

Unfortunately from a research standpoint, patterns of living have also shifted over time. In 1940, the list of commodities was revised to provide a better reflection of what consumers were actually consuming. In 1953, the list of items was again revised—adding such things as frozen food, restaurant meals, and home ownership. In 1964, the list was again revised. This time, a probability selection method was devised for the purpose of sampling among items. In addition to revising the list of items priced, each revision of the system also modified the weights assigned to items on the list.

By the time of the 1978 revision of the CPI research methods, some 400 specified items were being priced by field researchers. Unfortunately, the list did not accurately reflect consumption patterns in various regions of the country, so in 1978, CPI researchers established a list of general item descriptions: "Whole fresh milk," for example, replaced "Vitamin D, Grade A homogenized milk in half-gallon containers." At each retail outlet studied, the researchers were to select specific commodities on the basis of volume purchased. The commodities priced in a particular location better reflected the local consumption patterns. It was also more likely that researchers would be able to price the same commodities over time at a particular location.

Their advantages notwithstanding these revisions create problems of comparability. Changing the items priced over time makes it difficult to measure increases or decreases in the overall cost of living. By the same token, making measurements particularly appropriate to individual locales makes the comparison of different regions problematic.

I do not mean to suggest that the CPI research has been badly done. Indeed, the researchers responsible have used considerable ingenuity in addressing their task. My point here is to warn you of the difficulties inherent in making such measures. You should bear such problems in mind whenever you deal with research reports on the cost of living and similar measures.

SOURCE U.S. Department of Labor (Bureau of Labor Statistics), "The Consumer Price Index: Concepts and Content Over the Years." Report 517, May 1978.

PHONOGRAPH RECORDS

In some cases, it was useful to compare Maui prices with those reported for Honolulu. Although the Honolulu prices were not used in the calculation of Maui averages, strange disparities between Honolulu and Maui often pointed to errors. Phonograph records provide a case in point.

In 1976, the average price reported for a 12-inch stereo record in Honolulu was $6.11, a reasonable enough figure. On Maui, however, the official average price was $5.06. We could think of no logical reason for this difference, since Honolulu was a much larger market, with many discount record stores. Records sold on Maui were shipped first to Honolulu and then on to Maui, resulting in additional shipping costs. How could they be cheaper on Maui?

At first, we assumed that different (cheaper) records had been priced on Maui. An examination of the field worker's notes, however, turned up something quite different. The prices listed for phonograph records were *in excess of a hundred dollars each!* This was explained by a note indicating that *phonographs* had mistakenly been priced, instead of phonograph records. The Washington researchers were then faced with a problem: They had no data on the price of phonograph records on Maui. One reasonable solution would have been to take the Honolulu price of $6.11, even though it would probably underestimate the Maui price somewhat. Instead, they chose to substitute the *Washington* price of $5.06! No rationale was ever given for this bizarre procedure.

BOOKS

The research design called for the pricing of paperback books. This seemed a questionable procedure since book prices are set by the publishers, so book prices should be the same everywhere in the country. Nonetheless, the field workers visited bookstores and copied down book prices. Table 9.2 reports a puzzling finding in this regard: In Washington, the average paperback book cost $1.47, contrasted with $1.24 on Maui. Again, the field workers' worksheets provide the answer.

On the Maui worksheets, the field worker commented that the instruction to price books "150–200 pages in length" seemed inappropriate, since most popular books were longer. Nonetheless, he had found six—mostly children's books—with an average of 186 pages. Field workers in Washington had not been similarly troubled; they priced six popular books averaging 373 pages in length. The Washington books, then, were twice as big as those priced on Maui. Thus, books seemed cheaper on Maui.

RESTAURANTS

Eating out is certainly a component of the cost of living, and Table 9.2 indicates that field workers priced breakfast, lunch, and dinner. In Washington, in 1976, they visited a mainline hotel and a popular roast beef restaurant. On Maui, with several comparable restaurants, the field workers priced meals at a Chinese restaurant and a Hawaiian cafe. Thus, the Washington dinner cost $9.29 in contrast with $3.34 on Maui, and lunch was $5.69 in Washington and $2.80 on Maui. The two Maui restaurants didn't serve breakfast, so no comparison was even possible.

In subsequent years, more comparable restaurants were used on Maui, and the prices were found to be about the same in the two locations. This corresponded with the finding that Honolulu meals out were the same as in Washington each year. Clearly, the bizarre 1976 Maui prices were a function of the restaurants chosen.

VARIATIONS IN VOLUMES

Table 9.2 indicates that rice was cheaper on Maui than in Washington in 1976. This was initially puzzling since all the Maui rice was imported from the mainland. A possible explanation was that, since Hawaii residents consumed more rice than Washingtonians, the discrepancy in volume of sales might account for the price difference. A review of the worksheets offered a different explanation.

The field workers' instructions called for the pricing of 1 pound containers of rice. Workers in Washington priced five 1 pound containers and a 3 pound container. The price of the latter was divided by three to obtain a 1 pound price. On Maui, however, the field worker priced six 25 pound bags of rice. Each of the prices was then divided by 25 to get per-pound prices. Not surprisingly, the Maui price was 24 cents per pound, in contrast to 42 cents in Washington, verifying the meaning of the phrase *large economy size*. Even in Washington, the 3 pound bag was cheaper per pound than the 1 pound containers. During the period 1976–1979, seventeen 1 pound containers of rice were priced in Washington, and none of the other seven was larger than three pounds. On Maui during that period, nothing smaller than a 10 pound bag was priced, and 25 pound bags were the most common.

When questioned about this practice, the government researchers argued that the comparison was a fair one. Maui people, they argued without evidence, bought their rice in the bulk, whereas Washingtonians didn't. Though this might have been a reasonable argument, it was weakened by other data.

The research design called for the pricing of a pound of laundry soap. Unfortunately, laundry soap doesn't seem to come in 1 pound boxes. In Washington in 1976, for example, the field workers priced four 20 ounce boxes and two 49 ounce boxes. On Maui, one 40 ounce box, two 49 ounce boxes, and three 84 ounce boxes were priced. Not surprisingly, the large economy size boxes on Maui cost less per pound than the regular sizes in Washington, even though the 49 ounce boxes cost $1.50 in Washington and $1.56 on Maui. A similar pattern of pricing and prices was found in the other three years.

Toothpaste was allegedly cheaper on Maui than in Washington in 1976: 55 cents versus 67 cents for a 3.5 ounce tube. In Washington, however, the average price was based on two 3 ounce tubes, two 3.5 ounce tubes, and two 7 ounce tubes. On Maui, one 10 ounce tube and five 7 ounce tubes were priced. Thus, Maui appeared cheaper despite the fact that the 7 ounce tubes on Maui cost an average of $1.09, in contrast to 59 cents in Washington.

In several commodities, larger volume units were priced on Maui than in Washington. Where same-size comparisons could be made, Maui was more expensive. Averaging in the large economy sizes for Maui, however, created the illusion of a lower cost of living.

OTHER ERRORS

There were many other errors in the government's COLA research on Maui. To avoid turning this into a book on cost-of-living research, let me merely touch on some other types of errors that may forewarn you in your own examination of reports on existing data.

As illustrated several times above, many errors involved field workers not following instructions. For example, the instructions stated that "sale" prices were not to be reported—only regular prices. In several cases, however, sale prices were reported and used in the calculation of averages.

The instructions called for the price of a local daily newspaper and an out-of-town daily newspaper. In Honolulu, the statewide local dailies were priced as the local paper, and mainland papers were priced as the out-of-town papers. That seemed to follow the instructions. On Maui, however, a local three-times-weekly was counted as the local, and the statewide dailies were counted as out-of-town.

Whereas the instructions called for 36-exposure film, 20-exposure film was sometimes priced. Whereas haircut prices were specified to include tips, the Maui field worker omitted tips, saying he didn't feel they were appropriate.

A great many of the errors occurring in the Maui figures resulted from a lack of training. The Washington field workers were well trained and experienced, but even so, they made numerous errors. On Maui in 1976, an untrained Maui civil servant was given the forms and told to find the information. Not surprisingly, he did not always collect the data envisioned by the research designers.

I have gone into this example at length since it illustrates many of the errors that can occur in connection with the analysis of existing data. In particular, you have seen the difficulties involved in definition and measurement. Even if you never review research on cost of living, you should be especially sensitive to this problem area.

☑ CONSUMER'S CHECKLIST

As we've seen, there are special advantages to the analysis of existing data. At the same time, there are many potential problems of validity and relia- bility. Here are some of the things you should bear in mind when you read research reports analyzing existing data.

- What are the key variables being analyzed?
  a. How has each variable been measured?
  b. Is the measure a valid indication of the variable? What else could the data be measuring?
  c. Has the researcher offered theoretical bases for the measures used for variables?
  d. Have research conclusions been tested through the use of more than one indicator of a given variable?

- Who originally collected the data?
  a. What was the original purpose for collecting the data?
  b. What were the original instructions and definitions used to col- lect the data?
  c. Is there any indication of problems in the execution of the data- collection plan?

- What is the unit of analysis for which data have been collected and analyzed?
  a. Is the researcher drawing conclusions about the same unit that has been analyzed?
  b. If not, what is the danger of an ecological fallacy in the conclu- sions drawn?
  c. What steps has the researcher taken to avoid the ecological fal- lacy?

- If the research involves analyses of changes over time or compari- sons between groups, are the measurements comparable?

KEY WORDS

Data collection	Cost-of-living allow-	Weight of evidence
Aggregated	ance (COLA)	Comparability

MAIN POINTS

1. Many research questions can be researched through the analysis of existing data.
2. Durkheim's examination of suicide is a good example of this research strategy.
3. Whenever aggregated statistics are analyzed for the purpose of inferring patterns of individual behavior, there is a danger of committing the ecological fallacy.
4. Many different units of analysis can be addressed through existing data.
5. The chief problem in analyzing existing data is that of validity. Data available for analysis do not always match the variables a researcher wants to study.
6. Replication—addressing the same question using different measures—is one way to handle the problem of validity.
7. Many available data sets also have problems of reliability. Crime statistics, for example, do not give a full picture of the extent of crime.
8. In making comparisons over time and between groups, it is essential that measurements be comparable.

? REVIEW QUESTIONS

1. Suppose a researcher wants to study the relationship between education and criminal behavior by comparing crime rates and the percentage of college graduates in the populations of various cities. What is the unit of analysis in this study? Discuss the possibility of an ecological fallacy.
2. Look through your local newspaper for a report that draws conclusions by interpreting existing data. What is the chief variable? What is the unit of analysis? Discuss any problems of validity involved in the report.
3. Review the Stouffer study of impulsive marriages. Can you think of any other data that might reflect on the issue?
4. Review the reference to the DeFleur study of drug-use rates. What other crimes would be subject to the problems DeFleur discusses?
5. Pick a field of study that interests you—social work, nursing, or the like. Go to the library and prepare a list of data sources that might be used for research purposes.

6. Suppose a researcher wanted to discover whether the population of states is related to rates of auto theft. Look through the *Statistical Abstract of the United States* and identify data that could be used to answer the question.

7. Table 9.2 suggests that razor blades cost less in Maui than in Washington. To evaluate the legitimacy of that conclusion, what additional information would you like to have regarding the way costs were measured?

8. Suggest explanations for the Table 9.2 conclusion that aspirin is cheaper in Maui than in Washington.

9. In Table 9.2, automobile insurance appears much cheaper in Maui than in Washington. Suggest possible measurement problems that could produce that apparent difference.

10. Review the discussion of book pricing in the COLA study. Describe a better way of making the price comparison.

SUGGESTED READING

Funkhouser, G. Ray. "The Issues of the Sixties: An Exploratory Study of the Dynamics of Public Opinion," *Public Opinion Quarterly* 37 (Spring 1973): 62–75. An illustration of content analysis. This article reports an analysis of the most prominent issues of the 1960s. News articles appearing in *Time, Newsweek,* and *U.S. News and World Report* provide the basis for the analysis. In addition, Gallup Polls of the period are analyzed to determine the issues considered most important by the general public. The relationships between these two rankings are compared.

Stouffer, Samuel. *Social Research to Test Ideas* (New York: Free Press of Glencoe, 1962), Chapter 6: "Effects of the Depression on the Family." A minor, little-known study by a master that illustrates what can be done with existing statistics when specially collected data are not available. Wishing to learn whether the Depression of the 1930s had substantially altered traditional marriage and family patterns, Stouffer asks how such an alteration would show up in regularly compiled government statistics and then looks to see. Also instructive is Chapter 7, which examines the effects of radio on newspaper circulation.

The U.S. Fact Book: The American Almanac (New York: Grosset & Dunlap, 1979). A commercial reprinting of *Statistical Abstract of the United States,* compiled and published by the United

States Department of Commerce, Bureau of the Census. This is absolutely the best book bargain available (present company excluded). Although the hundreds of pages of tables of statistics are not exciting bedtime reading, it is an absolutely essential resource volume for every social scientist.

Webb, Eugene, Donald Campbell, Richard Schwartz, and Lee Sechrest. *Unobtrusive Measures: Nonreactive Research in the Social Sciences* (Chicago: Rand McNally, 1966). A stimulating and delightful statement on unobtrusive measures. As noted in Chapter 8, there are many unobtrusive ways of studying social phenomena, and many of those have been discussed separately. The book by Webb et al. examines the general notion of unobtrusiveness, and the many ingenious illustrations provide a perfect portrayal of the social researcher as a detective.

Zuckerman, Harriet. "Nobel Laureates in Science: Patterns of Productivity, Collaboration, and Authorship." *American Sociological Review* 32 (June 1967): 391–403. The author examines aspects of professional behavior among the nation's most eminent scientists through an analysis of, among other things, whether Nobel laureate coauthors list themselves as "first" authors on articles or whether they give this status to their collaborators.

EVALUATION RESEARCH

INTRODUCTION

In this chapter, we are going to look at a form of social research particularly relevant to the theme of this book. Many of the social scientific research reports you are going to be reading will have a bearing on your life. I want to prepare you to evaluate those reports and be able to determine what action, if any, is appropriate for you to take.

Evaluation research refers more to a research purpose than a research method. Many methods—surveys, experiments, and so on—are applicable to evaluation research. Its special purpose is to evaluate the impact of social interventions such as new teaching methods, innovations in parole systems, and a wide variety of other programs. Such evaluation is sometimes called **program evaluation.**

Evaluation research, loosely considered, is probably as old as social research in general. Whenever people have instituted a social reform for a specific purpose, they have paid attention to the actual consequences of it, even if they have not always done so in a conscious, deliberate, or sophisticated fashion. In recent years, however, evaluation research has become an increasingly popular and active research specialty, which has been reflected in textbooks, courses, and projects.

The growth of evaluation research also indicates a more general trend in the social sciences. In part, evaluation research no doubt reflects social scientists' increasing desire to make an actual difference in the world. At the same time, we cannot discount the influence of (1) increased federal requirements for program evaluations to accompany the implementation of new programs and (2) the availability of research funds to fulfill that requirement. Whatever the mixture of these influences, it seems clear that social scientists will be bringing their skills into the real world more in the future than ever before. As a consequence, you are likely to read increasing numbers of evaluation reports, and it is essential that you know what to look for in evaluating evaluations.

In this chapter, we're going to look at some of the key elements in this form of social research. We'll start by considering the kinds of topics commonly subjected to evaluation, and then we'll move through some of the main operational aspects: measurement, study design, and execution. As you'll see, formulating questions is as important as answering them.

Since it occurs—real life situations, rather than simply in the laboratory or academic setting, evaluation research has special problems, and we're going to look at some of those. There are particular logistical problems, and there are special ethical issues involved both in evaluation research generally and in specific, technical procedures. As you review reports of program evaluations, you should be especially sensitive to these problems.

Evaluation is a form of **applied** research, that is, it is intended to have some real world effect. It will be useful, therefore, to consider whether and how it is actually applied. As will become evident, the clear and obvious implications of an evaluation research project do not necessarily have any impact on real life. They may become the focus of ideological, rather than scientific, debates. They may simply be denied out of hand, as when former President Nixon summarily dismissed the conclusions of his commission on pornography. Or, perhaps most typically, they are simply ignored and forgotten, left to warp shelves and collect dust in bookcases across the land.

To conclude the chapter, I'm going to change topics slightly by focusing on a particular resource for large-scale evaluation—social indicators research. This type of research, another rapidly growing specialty, essentially involves the creation of aggregated indicators of the "health" of society, similar to the economic indicators that give diagnoses and prognoses of economies.

TOPICS COMMONLY SUBJECTED TO
EVALUATION RESEARCH

Most fundamentally, evaluation research is appropriate whenever some social intervention occurs or is planned. A **social intervention** is an
action taken within a social context for the purpose of producing some
result. In its simplest sense, evaluation research is a process of determining
whether the intended result was produced.

Suppose, for example, that we have the idea that conjugal visits
would improve morale at a prison. (In such programs, prisoners are permitted to have sex periodically with their spouses.) If we were to institute
such a program, it would be good to know if morale actually improved;
conceivably, the program might have no overall effect on morale, and it
might even make matters worse than before. An evaluation research project could be designed to test the impact of the program. Essentially, it
would involve devising some measure of morale, creating experimental
and control groups of prisoners, letting the experimental group have conjugal visits for a while, then measuring the levels of morale in the two
groups. If morale was significantly higher in the experimental group, we
might conclude that conjugal visits did the trick. As we'll see in the following discussions, there's much more to evaluation research than this
simple illustration suggests, but this should give you a general idea of
what's involved.

To take another example, you might believe, as some educational
reformers do, that grading in schools is counterproductive to the process of
real learning. If you were in a position to do something about it, you
might be tempted to put a halt to grading. Again, you would want to
know if the innovation produced the intended result, did nothing, or even
produced some unintended result that you'd prefer not to have.

The substantive topics appropriate to evaluation research are limitless. When the federal government abolished the Selective Service System,
military researchers began paying special attention to the impact on enlistments. As individual states have greatly liberalized their marijuana laws,
researchers have sought to learn the consequences, in terms of both marijuana use and other forms of social behavior. Do no-fault divorce reforms
increase the number of divorces, and are related social problems lessened or
increased? Has no-fault automobile insurance really brought down insurance policy premiums? The Real World Research box entitled "Evaluating
Driver Education" illustrates these kinds of concerns.

As you can see, the questions appropriate to evaluation research are of
great practical significance. Let's turn now to an examination of how these
questions are answered—in other words, how evaluations are conducted.

EVALUATING DRIVER EDUCATION

For years the auto insurance industry has given large insurance discounts for children who take drivers' education courses, because statistics show that they have fewer accidents.
The preliminary results of a new major study, however, indicate that drivers' education does not prevent or reduce the incidence of traffic accidents at all.
(Hilts, 1981)

Philip Hilts continues to report on a study by the National Highway Traffic Safety Administration that is stirring up controversy regarding the nation's driver education programs. Based on an analysis of 17,500 young people in DeKalb County, Georgia (including Atlanta), the preliminary findings indicate that students who take driver training have just as many accidents and traffic violations as those who don't. While the matter has not been fully resolved, the study has already revealed some subtle aspects of driver training.

First, it is suggested that the apparent impact of driver education is largely a matter of self-selection. The kind of students who take driver education are less likely to have accidents and traffic violations—with or without driver training. Students with high grades, for example, are more likely to sign up for driver training, and they are also less likely to have accidents.

More startling, however, there are suggestions that driver training courses may actually *increase* traffic accidents! The existence of driver education may encourage some students to get their licenses earlier than if there were no such courses. In a study of ten Connecticut towns that discontinued driver training, it was found that about three-fourths of those who probably would have been licensed through their classes delayed getting licenses until they were 18 or older.

As you might imagine, the preliminary results have not been well received by those most closely associated with driver training. This matter is complicated, moreover, by the fact that the NHTSA study is also evaluating a new, more intensive, training program—and the preliminary results show the new program is effective.

SOURCE Philip J. Hilts, "Value of Driving Classes Disputed." *San Francisco Chronicle*, June 25, 1981.

FORMULATING THE PROBLEM

Several years ago, I headed an institutional research office that had the task of conducting research of direct relevance to the operation of the university. We were often asked to evaluate new programs in the curriculum. The following description is fairly typical of the problems that arose in that context, and it points to one of the key barriers to good evaluation research.

Faculty members would appear at my office for they had been told by the university administration to arrange for evaluations of new programs they had been given permission to try. The way I've put that points to one very common problem: Often the people whose programs are being evaluated aren't thrilled at the prospect. For them, an independent evaluation poses a threat to the survival of the program and perhaps an even more far-reaching occupational threat. Forced evaulation, though quite common, presents special problems that we'll discuss later on.

The main problem I want to introduce has to do with the purpose of the intervention that is to be evaluated. The question "What is the intended result of the new program?" often produces a rather vague response; for example, "Students will get an in-depth and genuine understanding of mathematics, instead of simply memorizing methods of calculation." Fabulous! And how could we measure that "in-depth and genuine understanding?" I was frequently told that the program aimed at producing something that could not be measured by conventional aptitude and achievement tests. No problem there; that's to be expected when we're innovating and being unconventional. But what would be an unconventional measure of the intended result? Sometimes, this discussion came down to an assertion that what was to be produced by the program was "unmeasurable."

There's the common rub in evaluation research: measuring the "unmeasurable." Evaluation research is a matter of finding out whether something is there or not there, whether something happened or didn't happen. In order to conduct evaluation research, it must be possible to operationalize, observe, and recognize the presence or absence of what is under study.

Outcomes can often be derived from published program documents. Thus, when Edward Howard and Dariena Norman set about evaluating the performance of the Vigo County Public Library in Indiana, they began with the statement of purpose previously adopted by the library's board of trustees:

To acquire by purchase or gift, and by recording and production, relevant and potentially useful information that is produced by, about, or for the citizens of the community;

To organize this information for efficient delivery and convenient access, furnish the equipment necessary for its use, and provide assistance in its utilization; and

To effect maximum use of this information toward making the community a better place in which to live through aiding the search for understanding by its citizens. (*Howard and Norman, 1981:306*)

As the researchers say, "Everything that VCPL does can be tested against the Statement of Purpose." They then set about creating operational measures appropriate to each of the specified purposes.

As a consumer of evaluation research, you need to be clear about the outcome being tested. Make sure that the researcher has constructed a research design that specifies that outcome clearly. Let's see some of the elements in such a design.

MEASUREMENT

Earlier chapters in this book have already discussed the key issues involved in measurement, and those earlier discussions apply to evaluation research. In the present case, it will be more useful to focus our attention on *what* should be measured.

SPECIFYING OUTCOMES Clearly, a key variable for the researchers to measure is the **outcome** or (**response**) **variable.** If a social program is intended to accomplish something, the researchers must be able to measure that something. If they want to reduce prejudice, they need to be able to measure prejudice. If they want to increase marital harmony, they need to be able to measure that. The way I've put it is a little too simplistic, however. As Riecken and Boruch (1974) point out, there are usually multiple responses to consider.

When, for example, Meyer and Borgatta (1959) set out to evaluate the effects of a mental rehabilitation program, they created a list of behaviors and conditions to specify the general goal of "patient recovery." The list included the following dimensions and aspects of recovery:

- Not being recommitted to an institution
- Being independent of rehabilitation agencies
- Being effective in social relations
- Being economically independent
- Being oriented toward reality
- Enjoying a general well-being
  (*cited by Riecken and Boruch, 1974:119*)

Notice the value of specifying several different aspects of the desired outcome. If the rehabilitation program achieved one of these goals at the expense of the others, it might be considered unsuccessful. If, for example, patients were saved from being recommitted to mental-health institutions at the expense of making them dependent on welfare agencies, that would probably be regarded as simply trading one problem for another. It is essential that the researchers recognize and take account of all possible aspects of the program's outcomes. In reviewing evaluation reports, you will often be able to discover aspects the researchers have failed to notice.

Intended outcomes like those listed above are not specified sufficiently for measurement. How much well-being is enough? And what would well-being look like in real life? How could we tell if it occurred or not? Even something like not being recommitted to an institution is subject to varied interpretations. Suppose a patient stayed overnight for follow-up observation? That probably wouldn't be considered recommitment. But suppose it was three days of observation, or seven days? And suppose the observation was ordered by authorities because of the patient's behavior on the outside? You can see how the line between recommitment and non-recommitment can become fuzzy. Even where medical or legal definitions of commitment exist, they might not be appropriate to the evaluation of the program. It is essential to find out what definitions the researcher has used.

MEASURING EXPERIMENTAL CONTEXTS Measuring the dependent variables directly involved in the experimental program is only a beginning. As Riecken and Boruch (1974) point out, it is often appropriate and important to measure aspects of the context within which the experiment is conducted. These are variables external to the experiment itself, yet consequential to it. Consider, for example, an evaluation of a program aimed at training unskilled people for employment. The primary outcome measure would be their success at gaining employment after completing the program. While the researchers would, of course, observe and calculate the subjects' employment rate, they should also determine what has happened to the employment/unemployment rates of the society at large during the time of the evaluation. If there is a general slump in the job market, that should be taken into account in assessing what might otherwise seem a pretty low employment rate for subjects. On the other hand, all of the experimental subjects might get jobs following the program, but that might be due more to a general increase in available jobs than to the value of the program itself. Combining complementary measures with proper control group designs should allow you to pinpoint the effects of the program you are evaluating.

SPECIFYING INTERVENTIONS In addition to making measurements relevant to the outcomes of the experiment, it is also necessary to measure the program intervention—the experimental stimulus. In part, this measurement will be handled by the assignment of subjects to experimental and control groups, if that's the research design. Assigning a person to the experimental group is the same as scoring that person "yes" on the variable: received the experimental stimulus (yes/no). In practice, however, it's seldom that simple and straightforward, so you should pay special attention to how the researchers have handled the matter.

Let's stick with the job-training example above. Some people will participate in the program; others will not. But imagine for a moment what job-training programs are probably like in practice. Some participants will participate fully, and others will miss a lot of sessions or fool around when they are present. It might be appropriate, therefore, to have measures of the extent or quality of participation in the program. Then if the program is effective, we should expect to find higher employment rates for those participating fully than for those who participated less.

Other factors may further confound the administration of the experimental stimulus. Suppose the researchers were evaluating a new form of psychotherapy. Several therapists administer it to subjects composing an experimental group. The recovery rate of the experimental group will be compared with that of a control group (a group receiving some other therapy or none at all). It might be very useful to include the names of the specific therapists treating specific subjects in the experimental group since some may be more effective than others. If that turns out to be the case, our job now becomes finding out why the therapy worked better for some therapists than for others. What is learned about that question will further elaborate the researchers' understanding of the therapy itself.

SPECIFYING OTHER VARIABLES It is usually necessary to make certain measurements regarding the nature of the population of subjects involved in the program being evaluated. To start, it will be appropriate to define and measure those characteristics that determine whom the program is appropriate for. If a new form of psychotherapy is being evaluated, it's probably appropriate for people with mental problems—but how have the researchers defined and measured mental problems? A job-training program is probably intended for people who are having trouble finding work, but a more specific definition would be needed.

This process of definition and measurement has two aspects. First, the population of possible subjects for the evaluation must be defined. Then, ideally, all or a sample of appropriate subjects would be assigned to experimental and control groups as warranted by the study design. Beyond defining the relevant population, the researchers should make fairly precise measurements on the variables in their definition for the specific subjects in the study. Even though the randomization of subjects in the psychotherapy study would insure an equal distribution of those with mild and severe mental problems in the experimental and control groups, it's important to keep track of the relative severity of different subjects' problems in case the therapy turns out to be effective only for those with mild cases.

Similarly, the researchers should measure such demographic variables as sex, age, race, and so forth in case it only works for women, the elderly, or the like.

Second, in providing for the measurement of these different kinds of variables, there is a continuing choice: to create new measures or use some that have already been devised and used by other researchers. If the study addresses something that's never been measured before, the choice is an easy one. If not, the researchers will have to evaluate the relative worth of various existing measurement devices in the context of their specific research situation and purpose. And, you'll recall, this is a general issue in social research, one that goes well beyond evaluation research. Let me review briefly the advantages of the two options.

NEW MEASURES VERSUS OLD Creating measurements specifically for a particular study has the advantage of greater possible relevance and validity. If the psychotherapy being evaluated is aimed at a specific aspect of recovery, the researchers can create measures that pinpoint that aspect, whereas they might not be able to find any standardized psychological measures that hit that aspect right on the head. On the other hand, creating their own measure takes time and energy, both of which could be saved by adopting an existing technique. Of greater scientific significance, measures that have been used frequently by other researchers carry a body of possible comparisons that might be important to the present evaluation. If the experimental therapy raises scores by an average of, say, ten points on a standardized test, the researchers would be in a position to compare that therapy with others that had been evaluated using the same standardized measure. Finally, measures with a long history of use usually have known degrees of validity and reliability, whereas newly created measures will require pretesting or, worse, will be used with considerable uncertainty.

As you can see, measurement is something to be taken very seriously in evaluation research. The researcher must be careful to determine all the variables that should be measured and get appropriate measures for each. Such decisions typically are not purely scientific ones. Evaluation researchers often must work out their measurement strategy with those people who are responsible for the program that is being evaluated. It usually doesn't make sense to determine whether a program achieves outcome X when its purpose is to achieve outcome Y. (However, evaluation designs sometimes have the purpose of testing for unintended consequences.)

There is a political aspect in these choices, also. Since evaluation research often affects other people's professional interests—their pet program may be halted, or they may be fired or lose professional standing—the results of evaluation research are often a source of dispute.

Let's turn now to some of the evaluation designs commonly employed by researchers.

EXPERIMENTAL DESIGNS

Chapter 7 has already given you a good introduction to the variety of experimental designs that researchers use in studying social life. Many of those same designs are appropriate to evaluation research. By way of illustration, let's see how we might apply the classical experimental model to an evaluation of a new psychotherapy.

Let's imagine that the therapy is designed to cure sexual impotence. To begin, it would be necessary to identify a relevant population of patients. This identification might be made by the group planning to experiment with the new therapy. Let's say we are dealing with a clinic that already has 100 patients being treated for sexual impotence. We might take that existing identification-definition as a starting point, and we should maintain any existing assessments of the severity of the problem for each specific patient. For purposes of the evaluation research, however, we'll need to develop a more specific measure of impotence. It might involve whether, within a specified time, patients have sexual intercourse at all, how often they have intercourse, or whether and how often they reach orgasm. Taking a very different tack, the outcome measure might be based on the assessments of independent therapists who would not be involved in the therapies but would interview the patients subsequent to therapy. In any event, we would need to reach an agreement on the measures to be used.

In the simplest of designs, we would assign the 100 patients randomly to experimental and control groups; the former would receive the new therapy, and the latter would be taken out of therapy altogether for the course of the experiment. Since that is unlikely, given that all the subjects are patients, the control group might continue to receive whatever conventional therapy they are already receiving. (Notice the ethical issue that would probably prevent withdrawing therapy altogether from the control group.)

Having assigned subjects to the experimental and control groups, we need to agree on the length of the experiment. Perhaps the designers of the new therapy feel it ought to be effective within two months, and we might agree on this length of time. The duration of the study needn't be rigid, however; one purpose of the experiment and evaluation might be to determine how long it actually takes for the new therapy to be effective. In this case, an agreement could be made to measure recovery rates weekly, say, and let the ultimate length of the experiment rest on a continual review of the results.

Let's suppose that the new therapy involves showing pornographic movies to patients. We'd need to specify that stimulus. How often would patients see the movies, and how long would each session be? Would they see the movies in private or in groups? Should therapists be present? Perhaps it would be appropriate to observe the patients during the showing of the movies and include those observations in the measurements related to the administration of the experimental stimulus. Do some patients watch the movies eagerly and others keep looking away from the screen? These are the kinds of questions that would need to be asked, and specific measurements would have to be created.

Having thus designed the study, all we have to do is "roll 'em." The study is set in motion, the observations are made and recorded, and the mass of data is accumulated for analysis. Once the study has run its course, we would be in a position to determine whether the new therapy had its intended—or perhaps some unintended—consequences. We could tell whether the movies were most effective on patients with mild problems or severe ones, whether it worked for men but not women, and so forth.

This simple illustration should show you how the standard experimental designs presented in Chapter 7 can be used in evaluation research. However, many—perhaps most—of the evaluations you'll read about in the research literature won't look exactly like the illustration. Being nested in real life, evaluation research often calls for **quasi-experimental designs.**

QUASI-EXPERIMENTAL DESIGNS

Quasi-experiments are distinguished from "true" experiments primarily by the lack of random assignment of subjects to an experimental and a control group. In evaluation research, it is often impossible to achieve such an assignment of subjects. Rather than forgo evaluation altogether in such instances, it is sometimes possible to create and execute research designs that give some evaluation of the program in question. In this section, I'll describe some of the designs used.

TIME-SERIES DESIGNS To illustrate the **time-series design,** I want to begin by asking you to assess the meaning of some hypothetical data. Suppose I come to you with what I say is an effective technique for getting students to participate in classroom sessions of a course I am teaching. To prove my assertion, I tell you that, on Monday, only four students asked questions or made a comment in class; on Wednesday, I devoted the class time to an open discussion of a controversial issue raging on campus (an issue having nothing to do with the subject matter of the course); and on Friday, when we returned to the subject matter of the course, eight students asked questions or made comments. I con-

FIGURE 10.1
Two observations
of class participa-
tion: Before and
after an open dis-
cussion.

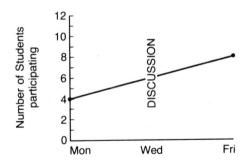

tend that the discussion of a controversial issue on Wednesday has doubled classroom participation. This simple set of data is presented graphically in Figure 10.1.

Have I persuaded you that the open discussion on Wednesday has had the consequence I say it has? You'd probably object that my data don't prove the case. Two observations (Monday and Friday) aren't really enough to prove anything. Ideally, I should have had two classes, with students assigned randomly to each, held an open discussion in only one, and then compared the two on Friday. I don't have two classes with random assignment of students—but I tell you that I've been keeping a record of class participation for the one class throughout the semester. This record would allow you to conduct a time-series evaluation.

Figure 10.2 presents three different patterns that might be discovered when we looked at the level of class participation over time, both before and after the open discussion on Wednesday. Which of these patterns would give you some confidence that the discussion had the impact I contend it had?

If the time-series results looked like Pattern 1 in Figure 10.2, you'd probably conclude that a process of increased class participation had begun before the discussion on Wednesday and that the process had continued, unaffected, after the day devoted to the discussion. The long-term data seem to suggest that the trend would have occurred even without the discussion on Wednesday. Pattern 1, then, contradicts my assertion that the special discussion increased class participation.

Pattern 2 contradicts my assertion, also. It indicates that class participation has been bouncing up and down in a regular pattern through the whole semester. Sometimes it increases from one class to the next, and sometimes it decreases; the open discussion on that Wednesday simply came at a time when the level of participation was due to increase. More to the point, class participation decreased again at the next class following the alleged postdiscussion increase.

Only Pattern 3 would support my contention that the open discussion mattered. As we see, the level of discussion before that Wednesday

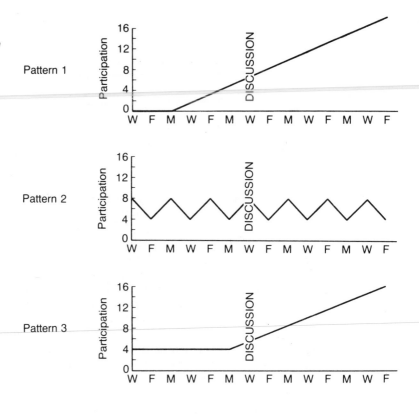

FIGURE 10.2
Three patterns of class participation in a longer historical perspective.

Pattern 1

Pattern 2

Pattern 3

had been a steady four students per class. Not only did the level of participation double following the day of discussion, but it continued to increase afterward. Although these data do not protect us against the possible influence of some extraneous factor (I might have also mentioned that participation would figure into students' grades), it does guard against a process of maturation (indicated in Pattern 1) or the regular fluctuations indicated in Pattern 2.

NONEQUIVALENT CONTROL GROUPS The time-series design just described involves only an "experimental" group, and you'll recall the value gained from having a control group. Sometimes, when it's not possible to create experimental and control groups by random assignment from a common pool, it is nonetheless possible to find a **nonequivalent control** group already in existence that appears to be similar to the experimental group. For example, if an innovative foreign language program is being tried in one class in a large high school, the researchers may be able to find another foreign language class in the same school that has a very similar student population: about the same composition in terms of grade in school, sex, ethnicity, IQ, and so forth. The second class could provide a point of comparison. At the end of the semester, both classes could be given the same foreign language test, and the researchers could compare performances. Here's how two junior high schools were selected for purposes of evaluating a program aimed at preventing tobacco, alcohol, and drug use.

The pairing of the two schools and their assignment to "experimental" and "control" conditions was not random. The local Lung Association had identified the school where we delivered the program as one in which administrators were seeking a solution to admitted problems of smoking, alcohol, and drug abuse. The "control" school was chosen as a convenient and nearby demographic match where administrators were willing to allow our surveying and breath-testing procedures. The principal of that school considered the existing program of health education to be effective and believed that the onset of smoking was relatively uncommon among his students. The communities served by the two schools were very similar. The rate of parental smoking reported by the students was just above 40 per cent in both schools. (*McAlister et al., 1980:720*)

Lacking random selection of subjects into experimental and control groups, the researchers have done well to seek comparisons of the two groups to see if they are comparable or not. In the first set of observations, the experimental and control groups reported virtually the same (low) frequency of smoking. Over the 21 months of the study, both groups increased, but the experimental group increased less than the control group, suggesting that the program had an impact on students' behavior.

MULTIPLE TIME-SERIES DESIGNS Sometimes the evaluation of processes occurring outside of "pure" experimental controls can be facilitated through the use of more than one or **multiple time-series** analyses. This represents an improved version of the nonequivalent control group design just described. Carol Weiss has presented a useful example of this design:

An interesting example of multiple time-series was the evaluation of the Connecticut crackdown on highway speeding. Evaluators collected reports of traffic fatalities for several periods before and after the new program went into effect. They found that fatalities went down after the crackdown, but since the series had had an unstable up-and-down pattern for many years, it was not certain that the drop was due to the program. They then compared the statistics with time-series data from four neighboring states where there had been no changes in traffic enforcement. Those states registered no equivalent drop in fatalities. The comparison lent credence to the conclusion that the crackdown had had some effect. (*1972:69*)

EVALUATING
ORGANIZATIONAL TRAINING

Rural development is a growing concern in the poor countries of the world and one that has captured the attention and support of many rich countries. Through national foreign assistance programs and international agencies such as the World Bank, the developed countries are in the process of sharing their technological knowledge and skills with the developing countries. Such programs have had mixed results, however. Often modern techniques do not produce the intended results when applied in traditional societies.

Rajesh Tandon and L. Dave Brown (1981) undertook an experiment in which technological training would be accompanied by instruction in village organization. They felt it was important for poor farmers to learn how to organize and exert collective influence within their villages—getting needed action from government officials, for example. Only then would their new technological skills bear fruit.

The intervention and evaluation were attached to an ongoing program in which 25 villages had been selected for technological training. Two poor farmers had been selected from each village; they had been trained in new agricultural technologies and had been sent home to share their knowledge with their fellow villagers and to organize other farmers into "peer groups" that would assist in the dissemination of that knowledge. Two years later, the authors randomly selected 2 of the 25 villages (subsequently called group A and group B) for special training; 11 others were selected as controls. A careful comparison of demographic characteristics showed the experimental and control groups to be strikingly similar to each other, suggesting they were sufficiently comparable for the study.

The peer groups that had been established in the two experimental villages were brought together for special training in organization building. The participants were given some information about organizing and making demands on the government, and they were also given opportunities to act out dramas similar to the situations they faced at home. The training took three days.

The outcome variables considered by the evaluation all concerned the extent to which members of the peer groups initiated group activities designed to improve their situation. Six types were studied. "Active initiative," for example, was defined as "active effort to influence persons or events affecting group members vs. passive response or withdrawal" (1981:180). The source of data for evaluation was found in the journals that the peer group leaders had been keeping since their initial, technological training. The researchers read through the journals and counted the number of initiatives taken by members of the groups. Two re-

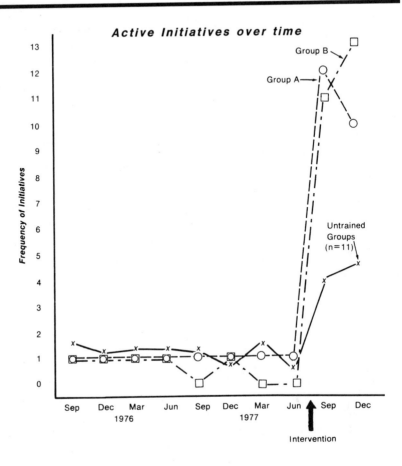

Active Initiatives over time

Group B

Group A

Untrained
Groups
(n=11)

Frequency of Initiatives

13
12
11
10
9
8
7
6
5
4
3
2
1
0

Sep   Dec   Mar   Jun   Sep   Dec   Mar   Jun   Sep   Dec
              1976   1977

Intervention

searchers coded the journals independently and compared their work to test the reliability of the coding process.

The graph above compares the number of active initiatives observed among members of the two experimental groups with those observed among the control groups. Similar results were found in terms of the other outcome measures.

Notice two things about the graph. First, there is a dramatic difference in the number of initiatives found among the 2 experimental groups as compared with the 11 controls; this would seem to confirm the effectiveness of the special training program. Second, notice that the number of initiatives also increased among the control groups. The researchers explain the latter pattern as a result of contagion (see Chapter 7). Since all the villages were near each other, the lessons learned by members of the experimental groups were communicated in part to members of the control villages.

SOURCE Rajesh Tandon and L. Dave Brown, "Organization-Building for Rural Development: An Experiment in India." Reprinted with special permission from *The Journal of Applied Behavioral Science*, April-June 1981: 172–189. The graph is taken from page 182. Copyright 1981 by NTL Institute.

Although this study design is not as good as one in which subjects are assigned randomly, it is nonetheless an improvement over assessing the experimental group's performance without any comparison. That's what makes these designs quasi-*experiments*, rather than just fooling around. The key in assessing this aspect of evaluation studies is comparability. "Evaluating Organizational Training" illustrates this point.

OPERATIONALIZING SUCCESS AND FAILURE

Potentially, one of the most taxing aspects of evaluation research is determining whether the program under review has succeeded or failed. The purpose of the foreign language program may be to help students do better in learning the language, but how much better is *better enough*? The purpose of the conjugal visit program at a prison may be to raise morale, but *how high* must morale be raised to justify the program?

As you may anticipate, there are almost never clear-cut answers to questions like these. This dilemma has surely been the source of what is generally called **cost/benefit analysis.** How much does the program cost in relation to what it returns in benefits? If the benefits outweigh the cost, keep it, if the reverse, junk it. That's simple enough, and it seems to apply in straightforward economic situations: If it costs you $20 to produce something and you can only sell it for $18, there's no way you can make up for that in volume.

Unfortunately, the situations usually faced by evaluation researchers are seldom amenable to straightforward economic accounting. The foreign language program may cost an extra $100, and it may raise students' performances on tests by an average of 15 points. Since the test scores can't be converted into dollars, there's no obvious grounds for weighing the costs and benefits.

Sometimes, as a practical matter, success or failure can be determined by competition among programs. If a second foreign language program costs only $50 and produces an increase of 20 points in test scores, it would undoubtedly be considered more successful than the first program—assuming that test scores were seen as an appropriate measure of the purpose of both programs.

Ultimately, the criteria for success and failure are often a matter of agreement. The person responsible for the program may be committed in advance to a particular outcome, which will be regarded as an indication of success. If that's the case, all the evaluation researcher needs to do is make absolutely certain that the research design will permit a measurement of the specified outcome. I mention something as obvious as this requirement simply because researchers sometimes fail to meet it.

THE SOCIAL CONTEXT

Many of my comments so far have hinted at problems in the actual execution of evaluation research projects. Of course, all forms of research can run into problems, but evaluation research has a special propensity for them, and I want to draw your attention to some of these difficult aspects so you can recognize them in the reports you read. First, we're going to look at some of the logistical problems that can hinder evaluation research. Then we'll consider some of the special ethical issues in evaluation. Finally, I want to make a few comments about the utilization of evaluation research results.

LOGISTICAL PROBLEMS

In a military context, **logistics** refers to moving supplies around—making sure people have food, guns, and tent pegs when they need them. In the context of social research, I use it to refer to getting subjects to do what they're supposed to do, getting research instruments distributed and returned, and other seemingly unchallenging tasks. These tasks are more challenging than you would guess!

MOTIVATING SAILORS When Kent Crawford and his colleagues (1980) set out to find a way to motivate "low performers" in the U.S. Navy, they found out just how many problems can occur. The purpose of the research was to test a three-pronged program to motivate sailors who were chronically poor performers and often in trouble aboard ship. First, a workshop was to be held for supervisory personnel, training them in effective leadership in relation to low performers. Second, a few supervisors would be selected and trained as special counselors and role models—people the low performers could turn to for advice or use as sounding boards. Finally, the low performers themselves would participate in workshops aimed at training them to be more motivated and effective in their work and in their lives in general The project was to be conducted aboard a particular ship, with a control group selected from sailors on four other ships.

The researchers report that, at the beginning, the supervisory personnel were not enthusiastic about the program.

Not surprisingly, there was considerable resistance on the part of some supervisors toward dealing with these issues. In fact, their reluctance to assume ownership of the problem was reflected by "blaming" any of several factors that can contribute to their personnel problem. The recruiting system, recruit training, parents, and society at large were named as influencing low performance—factors that were well beyond the control of the supervisors. (*Crawford et al., 1980:488*)

Eventually, the reluctant supervisors came around, and "this initial reluctance gave way to guarded optimism and later to enthusiasm" (1980:489). The low performers themselves were even more of a problem, however. The research design called for pre- and posttesting of attitudes and personalities, so that changes brought about by the program could be measured and evaluated.

Unfortunately, all of the LPs (low performers) were strongly opposed to taking these so-called personality tests and it was therefore concluded that the data collected under these circumstances would be of questionable validity. Ethical concerns also dictated that we not force "testing" on the LPs. (*Crawford et al., 1980:490*)

As a consequence, the researchers had to rely on interviews with the low performers and on the judgments of supervisors for their measures of attitude change.

The subjects continued to present problems. Initially, the ship's command ordered 15 low performers to participate in the experiment. Of the 15, one went into the hospital, another was assigned duties that prevented participation, and a third went over the hill. Thus, the experiment began with 12 subjects. Before the experiment was completed, 3 more subjects completed their enlistments and left the Navy, and another was thrown out for disciplinary reasons. The experiment concluded, then, with 8 subjects. While the evaluation pointed to positive results, the very small number of subjects warrants caution in any generalizations from the experiment.

The special logistical problems of evaluation research grow out of the fact that it occurs within the context of real life. Although evaluation research is modeled after the classic experiment—which suggests that the researchers have control over what happens—it takes place within frequently uncontrollable circumstances. Of course, the participant observer in field research doesn't have control over what is observed either, but that method does not strive for control. If you realize the importance of this lack of control, I think you'll start to understand the dilemma facing the evaluation researcher.

ADMINISTRATIVE CONTROL As suggested in the example of the low-performing sailors, the logistical details of an evaluation project are often under the control of program administrators. Let's suppose you're evaluating the conjugal visit program I referred to earlier. On the fourth day of the program, a male prisoner knocks out his wife, dresses up in her clothes, and escapes. Although you might be tempted to assume that his morale was greatly improved by escaping, that turn of events would complicate your study design in many ways. Perhaps the warden will terminate the program altogether—and where's your evaluation then? Or, if the warden is braver, he may review the files of all those prisoners you selected randomly for the experimental group and veto the "bad risks." There goes the comparability of your experimental and control groups. As an alternative, stricter security measures may be introduced to prevent further escapes, and the security measures may have a dampening effect on morale. Not only has the experimental stimulus changed, it has changed in the middle of your research project. Some of the data will reflect the original stimulus, and other data will reflect the modification. Although you'll probably be able to sort it all out, your carefully designed study has become a logical snakepit.

Maybe you've been engaged to evaluate the effect of race relations lectures on prejudice in the army. You've carefully studied the soldiers available to you for study, and you've randomly assigned some to attend the lectures and others to stay away. The rosters have been circulated weeks in advance, and at the appointed day and hour, the lectures begin. Everything seems to be going smoothly until you begin processing the files: The names don't match. Checking around, you discover that military field exercises, KP duty, and a variety of emergencies required some of the experimental subjects to be elsewhere at the time of the lectures. That would be bad enough, but then you learn that helpful commanding officers sent others to fill in for the missing soldiers. And whom do you suppose they picked to fill in? Soldiers who didn't have anything else to do or who couldn't be trusted to do anything important. You might learn this bit of information a week or so before the deadline for submitting your final report on the impact of the race relations lectures.

These are examples of some of the logistical problems confronting evaluation researchers. Despite such difficulties, however, it is possible to carry out controlled social research in real life situations. Here's an example that illustrates the point.

EVALUATION RESEARCH IN ACTION:
THE MANHATTAN BAIL PROJECT

The Manhattan Bail Project is a frequently cited example of evaluation research in action (Botein, 1965). It's a reasonably neat and clean illustration, and it has the added appeal that the program under evaluation proved an effective alternative to what many regard as a social problem.

The problem, in this case, is the system of bail bonds, a traditional element in our legal system. People awaiting trial are often allowed to spend the waiting time outside of jail if they can post a substantial amount of money to insure that they will show up for trial. The profession of bail bondsman has grown up and flourished around that system. Those who cannot afford, say, a $10,000 bond may be able to pay a bondsman 10 percent of that sum, or $1000. The bondsman then puts up the other $9000. Once the accused appears for trial, the bond—all $10,000 of it—is returned to the bondsman, and the accused gets nothing.

Many people have criticized the bail system. Some people object to the economic discrimination it fosters. Others have complained that judges sometimes use it in an inappropriate manner, setting extremely high bail in notorious cases, even though the alleged crime may be relatively minor.

Other people have contended that the bail system is not really necessary, or at least that it need not be used as widely as it is. The Manhattan Bail Project, initiated by the Vera Institute in New York, was designed as a test of that contention. The purpose of the project was to determine whether certain kinds of defendants—those with close ties to the community—could be released without bail and still be counted on to appear for their trials.

To undertake the study, the Vera Institute staff interviewed thousands of defendants and examined their files. A scoring system allowed the researchers to rate each defendant's integration into the community so as to identify those expected to stick around even if they were released without bail. Those scored as "good risks" were randomly divided into an experimental group and a control group. The staff recommended release without bail for all those in the experimental group and made no recommendations one way or the other for those in the control group.

Ideally, of course, all those recommended for release without bail would have gotten it, and all those not recommended wouldn't have. Naturally, it didn't turn out exactly that way. In the first year of study, the judges granted release without bail to 59 percent of those recommended by the researchers and to 16 percent of the control group. In spite of this variation, it was still possible to determine the impact of releasing defendants without bail. More than 99 percent appeared in court for trial at the appropriate time! This level of appearance was easily as high as the normal level under the bail system.

Given the powerful and obvious success of the experiment, the program of release without bail has expanded in a number of ways. First, with increased experience, the Vera staff has gotten better at evaluating defendants and has improved the validity and reliability of its scoring systems. Second, the staff has found it feasible to lower the threshold of "good risk," thus recommending more defendants for release without bail. The judges, for their part, have steadily increased their reliance on Vera staff recommendations, going along with a larger proportion of them. Finally, the program has spread to many other jurisdictions, and the bail system in America has been significantly changed as a result of the project.

To summarize this section, you should remember that most evaluation researchers are working for someone else and with the cooperation of others. Those people whom the researchers need to depend on may not be fully versed in the niceties of research design, and they may often make changes or refuse cooperation in ways they think are inconsequential, and the evaluation may fall apart as a result. Therefore, when you review reports of evaluation research, it's important to bear in mind that the researchers may not have the logistical control normal in other research situations. The problems created by that lack of control may be significant for the validity of the conclusions, so you should be especially sensitive to them.

Just as evaluation research has special logistical problems, it also can have special ethical problems. Since those problems can affect the scientific quality of the research, we should look at them briefly.

SOME ETHICAL ISSUES

In part, the ethical issues of evaluation research are the issues engaged by the social interventions being evaluated. Doing an evaluation of the impact of busing school children to achieve racial integration will throw the researchers directly into the political, ideological, and ethical issues of busing itself. It's not possible to evaluate a sex-education program in elementary schools without becoming directly involved in the heated issues surrounding sex education per se. The evaluation study design will require that some children be exposed to sex education, and the researchers may very well be those who decide which children are exposed. (From a scientific standpoint, the researchers *should* be in charge of selection.) That means that, when parents become outraged that *their* child is being taught about sex, the researchers will be the ones they hold responsible.

Maybe the experimental program is of great value to those participating in it. Let's say that the new industrial safety program being evaluated reduces injuries dramatically. What about the control group members who were deprived of the program by the research design? The evaluators' actions are an important part of the reason if a control group subject suffers an injury.

My purpose in these comments has not been to cast a shadow on evaluation research. Rather, I want to bring home the real consequences of the evaluation researcher's actions. Otherwise, you will have difficulty understanding why evaluation researchers do what they do.

UTILIZATION OF RESEARCH RESULTS

There's one more practical aspect of evaluation research that you should be aware of. Given that the purpose of evaluation research is to determine the success or failure of social interventions, it would seem reasonable that the continuation or termination of such interventions should follow automatically from the results of the research. If a particular program is found to be enormously successful in achieving its objective, then it should be continued. If it fails, it should bite the dust.

In practice, however, other factors intrude on the assessment of evaluation research results, sometimes blatantly and sometimes more subtly. As president, Richard Nixon appointed a blue-ribbon national commission to study the consequences of pornography. After a diligent, multifaceted evaluation, the commission reported that pornography didn't appear to have any of the negative social consequences often attributed to it; for example, exposure to pornographic materials didn't increase the likelihood of sex crimes. You might have expected liberalized legislation to follow from the research. Instead, the president said the commission was wrong.

Less dramatic examples of failure to follow the implications of evaluation research could be listed endlessly. Undoubtedly, every evaluation researcher can point to studies he or she conducted—studies providing clear research results and obvious policy implications—that were subsequently ignored. I want to discuss this issue a bit, since your own evaluation of research reports may depend in part on whether others will use the findings.

There are three important reasons that evaluation research results are not always implemented. First, the implications of the research may be presented in a way that cannot be understood by nonresearchers. Second, evaluation results, like other social science findings, sometimes contradict deeply held beliefs. That was certainly evident in the case of the pornography commission mentioned above. If everybody "knows" that pornography causes all manner of sexual deviance, then it is likely that research results to the contrary will have little immediate impact.

The third barrier to the utilization of evaluation results has been hinted at above: **vested interests.** If I have devised a new rehabilitation program that I'm convinced will keep ex-convicts from returning to prison, and if people have taken to calling it the Babbie Plan, how do you think I'm going to feel when you conduct an evaluation that suggests the program doesn't work? I might apologize for misleading people, fold up my tent, and go into another line of work. More likely, I might call your research worthless and begin intense lobbying with the appropriate authorities to have the program continue. Recall the earlier example of the evaluation of driver training. Hilts reported some of the reactions to the researchers' preliminary results:

Ray Burneson, traffic safety specialist with the National Safety Council, criticized the study, saying that it was a product of a group (NHTSA) run by people who believe "that you can't do anything to train drivers. You can only improve medical facilities and build stronger cars for when the accidents happen . . . This knocks the whole philosophy of education." (1981:4)

By now, you have seen the various scientific and nonscientific aspects of evaluation research that affect the scientific quality of the results. You should be well qualified to evaluate the evaluations you will be reading. I want to conclude this chapter with a type of research that combines what you have learned about evaluation research and the analysis of existing data.

SOCIAL INDICATORS RESEARCH

Another rapidly growing field in social research involves the development and monitoring of **social indicators.** Just as economists use indexes such as gross national product (GNP) per capita as an indicator of a nation's economic development, we can monitor aspects of society in a similar fashion.

If we wanted to compare the relative health conditions in different societies, we could compare their death rates (number of deaths per 1000 population). Or, more specifically, we could look at infant mortality—the number of infants who die during their first year of life for every 1000 births. Depending on the particular aspect of health conditions we were interested in, we could devise any number of other measures: physicians per capita, hospital beds per capita, days of hospitalization per capita, and so forth. Notice that intersocietal comparisons are facilitated by calculating *per capita* rates (dividing by the size of the population or by some fixed unit, such as 1000s of population).

Before we go further with social indicators, I'd like you to recall the Chapter 9 discussion of the various problems involved in using existing statistics. In a word, they are often unreliable, reflecting their modes of collection, storage, and calculation. Bearing that caution in mind, we'll look at some of the ways social indicators can be used for evaluation research on a large scale.

THE DEATH PENALTY AND DETERRENCE   Does the death penalty deter capital crimes such as murder? That question is hotly debated every time a state considers eliminating or reinstating capital punishment. Those supporting capital punishment often argue that the threat of execution will keep potential murderers from killing people. Opponents of capital punishment argue that it has no effect in that regard. Social indicators can be used to shed some light on the question.

If capital punishment actually deters people from committing murder, then we should expect to find murder rates lower in those states that have the death penalty than in those that do not. Not only are relevant comparisons possible in this instance, they have been compiled and published. Table 10.1 presents data compiled by William Bailey (1975) that directly contradict the view that the death penalty deters murderers. In both 1967 and 1968, those states with capital punishment had dramatically *higher* murder rates than those without capital punishment. Some people criticized the interpretation of Bailey's data, saying that most states have not used the death penalty in recent years even when they had it on the books, which could explain why it hasn't seemed to work as a deterrent. Further analysis, however, contradicts that explanation. When Bailey compared those states that hadn't used the death penalty with those that had, he still found no real difference in murder rates.

Another counterexplanation is possible, however. It could be the case that the interpretation given Bailey's data was *backwards*. Maybe the existence of the death penalty as an option was a consequence of high murder rates. Those states with high rates instituted it, those with low rates didn't institute it or repealed it if they had it on the books. In other words, it could be the case that instituting the death penalty would bring murder rates down, while repealing it would increase murders—and we could still have, in a broad aggregate, the data presented in Table 10.1. This isn't so, however. Analyses over time do not show an increase in murder rates when a state repeals the death penalty nor a decrease in murders when it is instituted.

Notice from the discussion above that it's possible to use social indicators data for comparison across groups either at one time or over a particular length of time. Often doing both sheds the most light on the subject.

At present, work on the use of social indicators is proceeding on two fronts. On the one hand, researchers are developing ever more refined indicators, finding which indicators of a general variable are the most useful in monitoring social life. At the same time, research is being devoted to discovering the relationships among variables within whole societies.

COMPUTER SIMULATION   One of the more exciting prospects for social indicators research is in the area of **computer simulation.** As we begin compiling mathematical equations describing the relationships that link social variables to one another (for example, the relationship be-

TABLE 10.1 Average Rate per 100,000 Population of First- and Second-Degree Murders for Capital-Punishment and Non-Capital-Punishment States, 1967 and 1968

	Non-capital-punishment states		Capital-punishment states	
	1967	1968	1967	1968
First-degree murder	.18	.21	.47	.58
Second-degree murder	.30	.43	.92	1.03
Total murders	.48	.64	1.38	1.59

Source: Adapted from William C. Bailey, "Murder and Capital Punishment," in William J. Chambliss (ed.), *Criminal Law in Action.* Copyright © 1975 by John Wiley & Sons, Inc. Reprinted by permission of John Wiley & Sons, Inc.

tween population growth and increases in the number of automobiles), those equations can be stored and linked to one another in a computer. With a sufficient number of accurate equations on tap, it will one day be possible to test the implications of specific social changes by computer rather than in real life.

Suppose a state contemplated doubling the size of its tourism industry. It would be possible to enter that proposal into a computer simulation model and in seconds or minutes receive a description of all the direct and indirect consequences of the increase in tourism. It would be possible to know what new public facilities would be required, which public agencies such as police and fire departments would have to be increased and by how much, what the labor force would look like, what kind of training would be required to provide it, how much new income and tax revenue would be produced, and so forth through all the intended and unintended consequences of the action. Depending on the results, the public planners might say, "Suppose we only increased the industry by half," and have a new printout of consequences immediately.

An excellent illustration of computer linking social and physical variables is to be found in the research of Donella and Dennis Meadows (1972, 1973) and their colleagues at Dartmouth College and the Massachusetts Institute of Technology. They have taken as input data known and estimated reserves of various nonreplaceable natural resources (oil, coal, iron, etc.), past patterns of population and economic growth, and the relationships between growth and use of resources. Using a complex computer simulation model, they have been able to project, among other things, the probable number of years various resources will last in the face of alternative usage patterns in the future. Going beyond the initially gloomy projections, such models also make it possible to chart out less gloomy futures, specifying the actions required to achieve them. Clearly, the value of computer simulation is not limited to evaluation research, though it can serve an important function in that regard.

This new technique points to the special value of evaluation research in general. Throughout human history, we have been tinkering with our social arrangements, seeking better results. Evaluation research provides a means for us to learn quickly whether a particular tinkering really makes things better. Social indicators allow us to make that determination on a broad scale; coupling them with computer simulation opens up the possibility of knowing the consequences of a particular intervention without having to suffer through it for real. Your ability to read and judge such research adds to the utility of the enterprise.

☑ CONSUMER'S CHECKLIST

As I've indicated, evaluation research is an increasingly common type of research, and one you are especially likely to confront if you are involved in an applied professional field. Here are some questions you might ask in assessing reports of evaluation projects.

- What is the social intervention being evaluated? What is its purpose?
  a. What is the intended outcome?
  b. How has the outcome variable been defined?
  c. What is the definition of success?
  d. Is the definition a reasonable one, or could "success" be produced by some other factor?
  e. How has the definition of success been translated into operational measures?
  f. What else does the operational measure reflect? Do those other meanings confound the evaluation?
  g. Is there more than one criterion of success? Do all of them indicate the same outcome?
  h. To what degree has the intervention been judged successful or unsuccessful? Is the researcher correct in that judgment?
- What experimental or quasi-experimental design has been employed?
  a. Does the design include experimental and control groups?
  b. How have they been selected?
  c. Are they comparable?
- Does the study design involve a time-series analysis?
  a. What was the pattern of variation in the dependent variable prior to the intervention?

b. What was the pattern of variation subsequently?

c. Has the researcher provided long-term monitoring of the dependent variable? Has any observed effect endured?

• What is the relationship between those responsible for the program under evaluation and the evaluators? Is there any conflict of interests?

• What logistical problems, if any, appeared in the execution of the evaluation?

a. Was the intervention changed during the course of the evaluation?

b. Were there any changes in measurement techniques?

c. Were any changes made in the assignment of subjects to experimental and control groups?

d. Did all subjects who started the project complete it? If there was any attrition, does it seem to have affected the results?

• Did any extraneous events occur that might have influenced the results of the evaluation?

• Did the evaluation ultimately point to policy implications regarding the intervention?

KEY WORDS

Evaluation research	Quasi-experimental	Cost/benefit analysis
Program evaluation	designs	Logistics
Applied research	Time-series designs	Vested interests
Social intervention	Nonequivalent con-	Social indicators
Outcome (response)	trol groups	Computer simula-
variable	Multiple time-series	tion

MAIN POINTS

1. Evaluation research studies the consequences of social interventions.
2. The first requirement of evaluation research is an identifiable, measurable outcome.
3. Evaluation researchers must also measure aspects of the context within which the intervention takes place.
4. The intervention itself must be specified and measured.

5. Researchers must choose between developing new measures designed specifically for the particular study and using measures previously developed and used.
6. Evaluation research is modeled after the logic of the experiment.
7. Subjects must be assigned to experimental or control groups.
8. Typically, evaluation research utilizes quasi-experimental designs—research designs approximating but not matching the classical experiment.
9. Time-series designs examine changes in an experimental group before and after an intervention.
10. Multiple time-series designs examine changes over time in groups that experience the intervention and groups that don't.
11. Nonequivalent control groups approximate the classical experimental design except that subjects are not assigned randomly to experimental and control conditions.
12. Success or failure is often measured in terms of a cost/benefit analysis—determining whether an outcome is worth the cost of the intervention producing it.
13. Evaluation research, because it occurs within natural settings—is subject to special logistical problems. Program administrators may interfere with the evaluation for administrative rather than scientific reasons.
14. Evaluation research also involves special ethical problems, since subjects will benefit or suffer because of their assignments within the evaluation project.
15. The results of evaluation research are not always implemeted, for a variety of nonscientific reasons.
16. Social indicators are measures of the state of society that can be used in the evaluation of large-scale processes.
17. Computer simulation is a research technique that allows the evaluation of social processes by computer analysis rather than by running those processes out in real life.

? REVIEW QUESTIONS

1. In your local newspaper, find a report of a social intervention program. Describe an evaluation project that could test the effectiveness of the program.
2. Review the Howard and Norman quotation regarding the purposes of the Vigo County library (pp. 252–253). Specify some concrete evaluation measures for each purpose.

3. Suppose an evaluation research wanted to test the impact of a new program for reducing juvenile delinquency. Discuss the relative advantages of using established definitions of delinquency and of establishing new ones.
4. Review the Real World Research box on driver education (p. 25). Describe a classical experiment that would test the effectiveness of driver education programs.
5. Discuss the relative advantages and disadvantages of cost/benefit analysis as a measure of the outcomes of social interventions.
6. Review the discussion of the Crawford study of motivation in the navy. Describe an evaluation project that would provide a more definitive test of the program.
7. Discuss the ethical issues involved in the Manhattan Bail Project.
8. Evaluation research has suggested that TV violence conditions people to accept violence in real life and, to a lesser extent, to commit violent acts. Suggest some reasons those research conclusions have not been acted on.
9. Review the discussion of the death penalty and deterrence. What do you suppose are some reasons the implications of that research have not been acted on?
10. Suggest an intervention that might be studied through the computer simulation of social indicators.

SUGGESTED READING

Bennett, Carl A. and Arthur A. Lumsdaine (eds.). *Evaluation and Experiment* (New York: Academic Press, 1975). Packed with illustrative examples, this reader digs into a number of special aspects of evaluation research. About every problem you are likely to hit is discussed in the book.

Riecken, Henry W. and Robert F. Boruch (eds.). *Social Experimentation: A Method for Planning and Evaluating Social Intervention* (New York: Academic Press, 1974). As my references to this book suggest, it is an excellent basic text for the serious evaluation researcher. It is an especially appropriate companion piece for the Bennett-Lumsdaine book listed above. If you were to master both, you'd be ready to set about some serious (or fun) evaluations.

Weiss, Carol. *Evaluation Research* (Englewood Cliffs, N.J.: Prentice-Hall, 1972). Here's a quicker and easier introduction to evaluation research. In a short paperback, the author gives a good overview of the method and points you toward aspects you might want to learn more about. It is an especially good beginning if you don't have any prior experience in social research in general.

Wilcox, Leslie D. et al. *Social Indicators and Societal Monitoring* (New York: Elsevier, 1972). This is not a textbook on social indicators or even an example of their use. Rather, it is a seemingly exhaustive annotated *bibliography* on the subject. Although it is now a few years old, it provides an excellent entry into further study. Whatever your particular area of interest, this book will direct you to studies that have addressed that interest through social indicators research.

THE ANALYSIS OF DATA

All the preceding chapters in this book have dealt with those aspects of research that lead up to the amassing of data. Data in and of themselves are useless, however; to serve some purpose, they must be analyzed and interpreted. That analysis constitutes the focus of Part Three. Although I've discussed earlier topics in terms of their implications for the interpretation of results, there are issues specifically connected with the final handling of data, the tabulations and explanations offered to make sense out of what has been observed. The two remaining chapters of the book deal with this final aspect of research.

Chapter 11 introduces you to the logic of data analysis. We'll look at some of the elementary procedures that allow researchers to transform raw data into meaningful statements and to draw conclusions from those statements. Just because the procedures are elementary, however, doesn't mean that researchers don't maker errors, so you must be alert to problems in even the simplest of analyses.

Much social research goes well beyond elementary analyses. Chapter 12 will introduce you to some to the more advanced statistical techniques you will find in the research reports you read. Within the scope of this book, I can only provide an introductory overview of such techniques, but what you learn in Chapter 12 should alert you to some fundamental problems and equip you to learn more about specific techniques if they are relevant to your interests.

CHAPTER 11

DATA ANALYSIS

INTRODUCTION

In all the previous chapters, we have dealt primarily with the design and execution of social science research. What research ultimately comes down to is the analysis and interpretation of the results of all that work.

Most social science analysis falls under the general rubric of *multivariate analysis*—the examination of several variables—and the bulk of Chapters 11 and 12 is devoted to the varieties of this method. The basic logic of multivariate analysis, however, can best be seen through the use of much simpler techniques. This chapter begins laying the groundwork with an initial focus on *univariate analysis*—the study of one variable at a time. Having determined the ages of subjects being studied, for example, a researcher will have several options for presenting the data. We'll examine those options and see the aspects you should look for when you read research reports.

We'll then move from univariate to *bivariate analyses,* the examination of two variables. The discussion will begin with subgroup comparisons—using univariate analyses to describe and compare subgroups (men/women, young/old, etc.). We'll see those comparisons in the form of simple percentage tables. Next, we'll introduce the notion of cause and effect and see the logic behind conclusions that one variable causes another.

From bivariate analyses, the obvious next step is to *trivariate* (three variables) analyses and the beginning of multivariate analysis. Once you have understood the mechanics of multivariate percentage tables, we'll spend the rest of the chapter on an examination of the elaboration model. This will give you an opportunity to begin mastering the logic of multivariate analysis as it is employed by social science researchers. What you learn about the elaboration model, moreover, will provide a launching pad for understanding the more advanced statistical techniques to be examined in Chapter 12.

UNIVARIATE ANALYSIS

Univariate analysis is the examination of only one variable at a time. We'll begin with the logic and formats for the analysis of univariate data.

DISTRIBUTIONS

The most basic format for presenting univariate data would be reporting the attributes of each case under study in terms of the variable in question. For example, suppose, in a study of corporate executives, you are interested in the executives' ages. (Your data might have been taken from *Who's Who in America*.) The most direct manner of reporting the ages of corporate executives would be to list them: 63, 57, 49, 62, and so on. Such a report would provide your reader with the fullest details of the data, but it would be too cumbersome for most purposes. You could report your data in a somewhat more manageable form without losing any of the detail by reporting that 5 executives were 38 years old, 7 were 39, 18 were 40, and so forth. Such a format would avoid duplicate data on this variable.

For an even more manageable format—though with a certain loss of detail—you could report executives' ages as a **frequency distribution** of **grouped data:** 246 executives under 45 years of age, 517 between 45 and 50 years of age, and so forth. In this case, your readers would have fewer data to examine and interpret, but they would not be able to reproduce fully the ages of all the executives; for example, a reader would have no way of knowing how many executives were 41 years of age.

Frequency distributions are often referred to as **marginals,** and this

TABLE 11.1   Ages of Corporate Executives (hypothetical)

Under 35	9%
36–45	21
46–55	45
56–65	19
66 and older	6
	100% = (433)
No answer	(18)
Total cases	(451)

term will be used in the following discussions. The above examples have presented marginals in the form of raw numbers. An alternative form would be the use of percentages—for example, X percent of the corporate executives were under 45, Y percent were between 45 and 50, and so forth.

In computing percentages, you frequently must make a decision regarding the *base* from which to compute—the number that represents 100 percent. In the most straightforward case, the base would be the total number of cases under study. A problem arises whenever some cases have missing data. Let's assume, for example, that you have conducted a survey in which respondents were asked to report their ages. If some of the respondents fail to answer, you have two alternatives. First, you might still base your percentages on the total number of respondents, with those failing to give their ages being reported as a percentage of the total. Or you could use the number of persons giving an answer as the base from which to compute the percentages. (You should still report the number who did not answer, but they would not figure in the percentages.)

The choice of a base depends wholly on the purposes of the analysis. If, for example, you wish to compare the age distribution of your survey sample with comparable data for the population from which the sample was drawn, you will probably want to omit the "no answers" from the computation. Your best estimate of the age distribution of all respondents is to be found in the distribution discovered among those answering the question. Since "no answer" is not a meaningful age category, its presence among the base categories would confuse the comparison of sample and population figures. Table 11.1 presents an example.

CENTRAL TENDENCY

Moving beyond the reporting of marginals, you may choose to present your data in the form of summary averages, or measures of **central**

tendency. Your options in this regard include the **mode** (the most frequent attribute, either grouped or ungrouped), the arithmetic **mean,** or the **median** (the middle attribute in the ranked distribution of observed attributes). Here's how the three averages would be calculated from a set of data.

Suppose that an experimenter sets up a situation in which experimental subjects are to complete a particular task within a specified period of time. Some succeed the first time they try it, others succeed the second time, and some take longer. The data below show the number of trials required by different subjects to complete the task. Notice that 7 subjects needed only 1 trial, 12 needed 2 trials, and so forth.

Trials	Number of subjects
1	7
2	12
3	22
4	18
5	6
6	2

What was the "average" number of trials required for completing the task? This question cannot be answered until we specify which average we mean. Here's how we'd calculate each of the averages mentioned above.

MODE The easiest average to calculate is the mode, the most popular value. Since more subjects required 3 trials that any other number of trials, 3 is the mode. Appropriate to its ease of calculation, the mode is also of little use in most research. You are unlikely to see it reported.

MEAN The mean is calculated by totaling the number of trials required for all the subjects: $(7 \times 1) + (12 \times 2) + (22 \times 3) + (18 \times 4) + (6 \times 5) + (2 \times 6)$ = 211 trials. This total is then divided by the number of subjects (67): $211/67 = 3.15$.

MEDIAN The median represents the "middle" value. In the case of grouped data, calculating the median is a little tricky. Since there are 67 subjects, subject 34 would be the middle subject if they were arranged in a row according to the number of trials they required in completing the task.

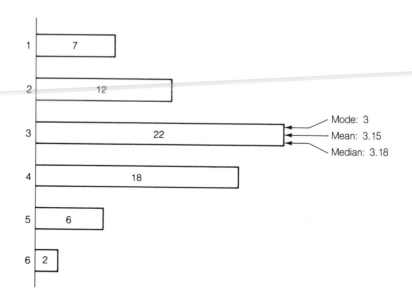

FIGURE 11.1
Three averages.

In the imaginary row of subjects, the 7 who required only 1 trial would come first, followed by the 12 requiring 2 trials. The last of those requiring 2 trials would be the nineteenth subject. Next come those requiring 3 trials, and the last of these would be the forty-first subject in the row—meaning that the middle (number 34) subject would have required 3 trials. The median is *not* 3, however.

In calculating the median for grouped data, it matters where *within the group* the middle case appears. In this instance, subject 34 is the fifteenth (of 22) subject in the 3-trial group. To calculate the median, we take the value "3 trials" to represent the range from 2.5 to 3.5 trials. Then we calculate where subject 34 appears within that range.

The median in this instance, then, is 2.5 + (15/22) = 3.18. Figure 11.1 offers a graphic picture of the three averages.

In the research literature, you will find both means and medians. Whenever means are presented, you should be aware that they are affected by extreme values: a few very large or very small numbers. For example, the 1980 mean per capita gross national product (GNP) of the United States was $9700; this can be compared with, for example, $190 for Sri Lanka, $3470 for Ireland, and $7920 for Australia. The tiny oil sheikdom of Kuwait, by contrast, had a mean per capita GNP of $14,890, despite the fact that most residents of that country are impoverished. The high mean per capita GNP in Kuwait reflects the enormous petro-wealth of a few (Population Reference Bureau, 1980).

DISPERSION

Averages have the special advantage of reducing raw data to the most manageable form: A single number (or attribute) can represent all the detailed data collected in regard to the variable. This advantage comes at a cost, of course, since the reader cannot reconstruct the original data from an average. This disadvantage of averages can be somewhat alleviated through the reporting of summaries of the **dispersion** of responses. The simplest measure of dispersion is the **range:** the distance separating the highest from the lowest value. Thus, in addition to reporting the mean age of 35, you might indicate that the ages reported ranged from 18 to 69.

A somewhat more sophisticated measure of dispersion is the **standard deviation.** This measure was already discussed in Chapter 5 as the standard error of a sampling distribution. You might report, for instance, that the standard deviation of age among your subjects is 10.5 years, meaning that about 68 percent of the subjects fall within an age range between plus or minus 10.5 years of the mean—in other words, between 24.5 and 45.5 years in this example.

There are many other measures of dispersion. The **interquartile range** is one example. In reporting intelligence test scores, for example, you could determine the range of scores of the highest one-fourth of subjects, the second fourth, and so on. If the highest one-fourth had scores ranging from 120 to 150 and the lowest one-fourth had scores ranging from 60 to 90, you could report that the interquartile range was 120 to 90, with a mean score of, let's say, 102.

CONTINUOUS AND DISCRETE VARIABLES

Age is a **continuous** ratio variable—one that increases steadily in tiny fractions instead of jumping from category to category, as is the case for **discrete** variables such as sex or military rank. If discrete variables were being analyzed—a nominal or ordinal variable, for example—then some of the techniques discussed above would not be applicable. Strictly speaking, medians and means should be calculated only for interval and ratio data, respectively. If the variable in question were sex, for example, marginals in terms of either raw numbers or percentages would be appropriate and useful. The modal response would be legitimate, but it would convey little useful information. Reports of mean, median, or dispersion summaries would be inappropriate. As you read the research literature, you'll find numerous "gray-area" situations regarding the calculation of averages, as illustrated in the Real World Research box entitled "Measuring Nursing Faculty Interactions."

MEASURING
NURSING FACULTY INTERACTIONS

Although medians and means should be calculated only for data that represent interval and ratio levels of measurement, respectively, you will find many variations on this rule in the research literature. Often, for example, measurements of variables are constructed so as to approximate interval or ratio levels, and means and standard deviations are then calculated. Here's an example.

To find out how nursing faculty members viewed their interactions with colleagues, Judith Beyer first established a set of eight general questions (e.g., "Is there confidence and trust among faculty colleagues?") and then created three statements to reflect each of the questions. The eight general dimensions were grouped under the global heading "collegial communication."

Subjects were asked to respond to each of the three statements included under each question on the basis of a 5-point extent scale: 1 = to a very little extent; 2 = to a little extent; 3 = to some extent; 4 = to a great extent; and 5 = to a very great extent.

The overall mean score . . . was 2.897 (standard deviation = .697). The collective responses of participants indicated that actual interpersonal interactions among colleagues fell slightly below the midpoint of the original 5-point extent scale, or were supportive "to some extent." (1981:113, 114).

In reviewing this presentation, you should first note that the base data constitute an ordinal level measurement: the various extents to which respondents

DETAIL VERSUS MANAGEABILITY

In presenting univariate—and other—data, researchers ofter face a dilemma. On the one hand, they should attempt to provide their readers with the fullest degree of detail regarding those data. On the other hand, the data should be presented in a manageable form. As these two goals often go directly counter to each other, researchers are continually seeking the best compromise between them. One useful solution is to report a given set of data in more than one form. In the case of age, for example, the researcher could report both the marginals on ungrouped ages plus the mean age and standard deviation.

As you can see from this introductory discussion of univariate analysis, this seemingly simple matter can be rather complex. The lessons of found statements reflected their collegial experiences. Although the numbers 1 through 5 have been assigned to those answers, there is no reason to believe that the distance from response 1 to response 2 is the same as the distance from response 4 to response 5, for example. By calculating means and standard deviations, Beyer has treated the numerical scores as though they were real values.

While technically unjustified on statistical terms, this procedure is a common and useful one. While a mean score of 2.897 on collegial communication is meaningless in itself, it could be useful in comparing the views held by different kinds of nurses. Since Beyer also asked nurses to evaluate the statements in terms of how they would like things to be, the mean scores provided a useful device for comparing discrepancies between actual and desired states of affairs on the eight dimensions.

In addition, Beyer reports that the questionnaire items in her study have been used extensively by previous researchers. Though this does not guarantee their validity, it adds some weight to that conclusion.

The key here is *utility*. If you find that a researcher's statistical calculations are useful in revealing the nature of social affairs, then you should be somewhat lenient in accepting the application of statistical techniques to data that do not warrant them. The other edge of this sword, however, is the danger of being lulled into thinking that the results represent something truly precise. In this case, for example, you might question the utility and appropriateness of carrying the means and standard deviations out to 3 decimal points.

SOURCE   Judith E. Beyer, "Interpersonal Communication as Perceived by Nurse Educators in Collegial Interactions." *Nursing Research*, March-April 1981: 111–117.

this section will be important as we move now to a consideration of subgroup descriptions and bivariate analyses.

SUBGROUP COMPARISONS

Univariate analyses serve the purpose of *describing* the units of analysis of a study and, if they are a sample drawn from some larger population, of making descriptive inferences about the larger population. Bivariate and multivariate analyses, on the other hand, are aimed primarily at *explanation*. Before we look more closely at explanation, we should consider an

TABLE 11.2   Median Earnings of Year-Round, Full-Time Civilian Workers with Earnings, by Sex, 1967 to 1977

Year	Women	Men	Ratio of women to men
1977	$8618	$14,626	.59
1976	8622	14,323	.60
1975	8449	14,175	.60
1974	8565	14,578	.59
1973	8639	15,254	.57
1972	8551	14,778	.58
1971	8369	14,064	.60
1970	8307	13,993	.59
1969	8227	13,976	.59
1968	7763	13,349	.58
1967	7503	13,021	.58

Source: Adapted from the U.S. Bureau of the Census, "A Statistical Portrait of Women in the United States: 1978." Series P-23, No. 100:73.

intermediate case. **Subgroup comparisons** are largely descriptive—independently describing the subgroups—but the element of comparison is added.

Often it's appropriate to describe subsets of cases, subjects, or respondents. Table 11.2 illustrates this method, presenting income data for men and women separately, as well as the ratio of women's median income to that of men. The message in this presentation is that women in the labor force earn a little over half what men earn.

Though a researcher may present subgroup comparisons for purely descriptive purposes, more often, the purpose is comparative. For example, Table 11.2 reveals that women earn less than men. In the present case, moreover, it is assumed that there is something about being a woman that results in earning a lower income. When we compare incomes of blacks and whites, we make a similar assumption. In such cases, the analysis is based on an assumption of *causality*: one variable causing another. This leads us to a consideration of bivariate analysis.

BIVARIATE ANALYSIS

In contrast to univariate analysis, subgroup comparisons constitute a **bivariate analysis** in that two variables are involved. Most bivariate analysis in social research adds another element: relationships among the

TABLE 11.3   Attitudes toward Sexual Equality (hypothetical)

"Do you approve or disapprove of the proposition that men and women should be treated equally in all regards?"

	Men	Women
Approve	63%	75%
Disapprove	37	25
	100%	100%
	(400)*	(400)*

*The figures shown in parentheses represent the *base* from which the percentages were computed. In this instance, there are 400 men altogether—63 percent (252 of the men) of whom approve and 37 percent (148) of whom disapprove.

variables themselves. Thus, whereas univariate analysis and subgroup comparisons forcus on describing the people or other units of analysis under study, bivariate analysis focuses on the *variables.*

Table 11.3 could be regarded as an instance of subgroup comparisons: independent descriptions of the attitudes of men and women toward sexual equality. From this point of view, we would note—comparatively and descriptively—that the women under study are more supportive of equality than the men.

BIVARIATE EXPLANATION

The same table seen as an explanatory bivariate analysis tells a somewhat different story. It suggests that the variable *sex* has an effect on the variable *attitudes toward sexual equality.* The attitude is seen as a dependent variable that is partially determined by the independent variable, sex. Explanatory bivariate analyses, then, involve the "variable language" introduced in Chapter 2. In a subtle shift of focus, we are no longer talking about men and women as different subgroups but of sex as a variable that has an influence on other variables. The logic of interpreting Table 11.3 is as follows:

1. Women generally are accorded an inferior status in American society; thus, they should be more supportive of the proposed equality of the sexes.
2. A respondent's sex should therefore affect (cause) his or her response to the questionnaire item: Women should be more likely to approve than men.

3. If the male and female respondents in the survey are described separately in terms of their responses, a higher percentage of the women than of the men should approve.

The data presented in Table 11.3 confirm this reasoning: Seventy-five percent of the women approve of sexual equality as compared to 63 percent of the men.

CONSTRUCTING AND READING PERCENTAGE TABLES

Adding the logic of causal relationships among variables has an important implication for the construction and reading of percentage tables. One of the chief bugaboos for new data analysts is deciding on the appropriate direction of percentaging for any given table. Inappropriately percentaged tables sometimes sneak into print, so it's important that you understand this logic even if you never construct a table of your own.

In Table 11.3, for example, I have divided the group of subjects into two subgroups—men and women—and then described each subgroup in terms of its attitudes. That is the correct method for constructing this table. Notice, however, that it would have been possible—though inappropriate—to construct the table differently. We could have first divided the subjects into those approving of sexual equality and those disapproving of it, and then we could have described each of those subgroups in terms of the percentage of men and women in each. This method would be useless in terms of explanation. Table 11.3 suggests that your sex will affect your attitude toward sexual equality. Had we used the other method of construction, the table would suggest that your attitude toward sexual equality affects whether you are a man or a woman—which clearly makes no sense.

Another related problem is how do you *read* a percentage table. There is a temptation to read Table 11.3 as follows: "Of the women, 75 percent approved and only 25 percent disapproved; therefore being a woman makes you more likely to approve." That is not the correct way to read the table, though the conclusion seems more or less the same as that I gave initially. The conclusion that sex, as a variable, has an effect on attitudes must hinge on a *comparison between men and women.* Specifically, we note that women are more likely than men to approve of sexual equality—comparing the 75 percent with the 63 percent. Suppose, for example, that 100 percent of the men approved. Regardless of the fact that women approved 3 to 1, we couldn't say that being a woman increased the likelihood of approval. In fact, the opposite would be true in such a case. The comparison of subgroups, then, is essential in reading an explanatory bivariate table.

In constructing and presenting Table 11.3, I have used a convention called *percentage down.* This term means that you can add the percentages down each column to total 100 percent. You read this form of table *across* a row. For the row labeled "approve," what percentage of the men approve and what percentage of the women approve?

The direction of percentaging in tables is arbitrary, and you will find tables percentaged both ways in the research literature. In reading a table that someone else has constructed, therefore, you need to find out the direction in which it has been percentaged. Usually that will be apparent in the labeling of the table or in the logic of the variables being analyzed. If it is not clear, as a last resort, you should add the percentages in each column and each row. If each of the *columns* totals 100 percent, the table has been percentaged down. If the *rows* total 100 percent each, it has been percentaged across. Then, the rule of thumb is:

- If the table is percentaged down, read across.
- If the table is percentaged across, read down.

PLAYBOY PROFILES

Let's take another example. Table 11.4 reports on a survey conducted by Louis Harris and Associates for *Playboy* magazine. The study involved interviews with 1990 American men between the ages of 18 and 49. The categories "traditionalists," "conventionalists," "contemporaries," and "innovators" make up an index created from attitudes on (1) decriminalizing victimless crimes, (2) sexual relations outside of marriage, and (3) changes in the status of women. The traditionalists have the most conservative attitudes on those issues and the innovators the most liberal.

Part A of Table 11.4 presents the relationship between social orientations and church attendance. The social orientations are the independent variable—made up of the categories discussed above—and church attendance is the dependent variable—made up of "regularly," "only once in a while," and "not at all." Notice that the dependent variable has been compressed in the table. Rather than present the percentages giving each of the church attendance answers, the researchers have presented only the percentages saying they attend regularly. This is a common format for presenting such data.

The table shows that 56 percent of the traditionalists attend worship regularly, compared to 32 percent of the conventionalists, 22 percent of the contemporaries, and 10 percent of the innovators. There are several ways we might summarize these data. We might say, for example, that there is a positive relationship between social conservatism and church attendance; that is, the more conservative a man's social attitudes, the more likely he is to attend church regularly. Or we might say there is a negative relationship between social liberalism and church attendance.

Now read and interpret Part B of Table 11.4. You might say that there is a positive relationship between social conservatism and the importance of religion for a happy, satisfied life.

TABLE 11.4   Social Ideology and Religion

A. Do you attend a place of worship regularly, only once in a while, or not at all?

	Percentage "regularly"
Traditionalists	56%
Conventionalists	32
Contemporaries	22
Innovators	10

B. How important is religion to you personally for a happy, satisfied life?

	Percentage "very important"
Traditionalists	67%
Conventionalists	48
Contemporaries	32
Innovators	18

Source: Adapted from William Simon and Patricia Y. Miller, "The Playboy Report on American Men." Chicago: Playboy Enterprises, 1979:23.

Table 11.5 is taken from the same study. In this table, social class is an index created from respondents' income and education. See if you can interpret the data.

Table 11.5 is somewhat different from Table 11.4. Notice, for example, that the independent variable is presented across the top of Table 11.5, whereas it was presented down the side of Table 11.4. Furthermore, there are four different dependent variables in Table 11.5. Let's look at each dependent variable separately.

The first row of figures in Table 11.5 presents the percentages of men at the different social class levels who say their jobs are "excellent" in terms of having "friendly people to work with." As a general rule, the percentage saying "excellent" increases as social class increases. Therefore, we might say there is a positive relationship between social class and job satisfaction in this respect.

MEASURING THE STRENGTH OF RELATIONSHIPS

At this point, I want to introduce a simple statistical measure that will facilitate our discussion. In Table 11.5, we are examining, in effect,

TABLE 11.5   Social Class and Job Satisfaction

How would you rate your job as far as each item is concerned?
(percentage "excellent" by class)

	Lower class	Working class	Lower middle class	Upper middle class
Friendly people to work with	31%	33%	39%	39%
Working for a company you respect	17	27	29	39
Appreciation for a job well done	20	18	20	26
Having the respect of people you work with	22	30	31	36

Source: Adapted from William Simon and Patricia Y. Miller, "The Playboy Report on American Men." Chicago: Playboy Enterprises, 1979:36.

whether and to what extent social class causes job satisfaction. The possibilities range from "not at all" to "totally." On the one hand, social class could be totally irrelevant to job satisfaction; on the other hand, social class might be the only cause. Most of the time, the causal effect lies somewhere in between. The *strength of the relationship* refers to the extent to which the independent variable causes the dependent variable.

The percentage point difference separating the extreme categories of an independent variable, as described in terms of some dependent variable, is called **epsilon.** In the present case, the epsilon is 39–31 or 8 percentage points. Notice that this statistic gives us a summary of the strength of the relationship between the two variables. Now, let's look at the relationships present in the remainder of the table.

In the second row, we find a positive relationship between social class and job satisfaction, as measured by the feeling that you are "working for a company you respect." The strength of the relationship is represented by an epsilon of 22 percentage points. This is clearly a stronger relationship than we discovered in the first row. In the last row of Table 11.5, social class is positively related to "having the respect of people you work with." The epsilon here is 14 percentage points.

The third row in the table presents a different situation. The relationship between social class and job satisfaction in the other rows is consistently positive; each increase in social class corresponds with an increase in job satisfaction. The technical term for this situation is **monotonicity:** Percentages increase or decrease steadily across categories of the independent variable. The relationship presented in row three of the table is not monotonic. Twenty percent of the lower-class men rate their jobs as excellent in terms of getting "appreciation for a job well done"; this percentage drops slightly to 18 percent among the working-class men; it rises back to

20 percent among the lower-middle class and then rises to 26 percent among the upper-middle class group.

Overall, the epsilon in row three is 6 percentage points (18–26 percent). In comparison with the other rows in the table, this is a small epsilon, marking a relatively weak relationship. Which brings up an issue of data analysis that is a bit fuzzy: How strong a relationship is a "strong" relationship? We're going to return to this issue in Chapter 12, in the discussion of statistical significance. For now, I want to give you a general approach to the problem and a rough rule of thumb.

The general approach to assessing whether a relationship is a strong one depends on the difference it makes in real life. For example, Maurine Christopher writes of public support for higher cable TV fees thus: "Gallup found willingness to accept a larger monthly bill greater among men than women, by two percentage points . . . " (1981:72). I think it was the philosopher William James who said that "any difference that makes no difference is no difference." A 2-percentage-point difference is almost always no difference whatsoever. Try to imagine the possible consequences of such a difference. I can't think of any.

Here's a rough rule of thumb that should serve you fairly well in connection with explanatory analyses like those we've been looking at. An epsilon of fewer than 10 percentage points is seldom very important. Differences of 10 to 20 percentage points are usually worth noting, and greater differences are usually important. In addition, the number of categories composing the independent variable matters. With a large number of categories—with greater extremes at each end—we should expect a larger epsilon if there is really a relationship between the two variables. Thus, in the case of social class and job satisfaction illustrated in Table 11.5, we should expect a larger epsilon with four categories of class than if class had been dichotomized into only "low" and "high."

Finally, remember that the size of the epsilon is only a part of the picture. Monotonicity is also important when there are more than two categories in the independent variable.

You are now ready to move beyond bivariate analyses. Most social research involves the analysis of several variables at once, and we're going to look into the mechanics and logic of such analyses.

INTRODUCTION TO MULTIVARIATE ANALYSIS

Tables of **multivariate analysis** may be constructed on the basis of a more complicated subgroup description by following essentially the same steps outlined above for bivariate tables. But instead of explaining the de-

TABLE 11.6   Sex, Age, and Sexual Equality (hypothetical)

"Do you approve or disapprove of the proposition that men and women should be treated equally in all regards?"

	Under 30		30 and over	
	Women	Men	Women	Men
Approve	90%	78%	60%	48%
Disapprove	10	22	40	52
	100%	100%	100%	100%
	(200)	(200)	(200)	(200)

pendent variable on the basis of a single independent variable, we'll seek an explanation through the use of more than one independent variable.

CONSTRUCTING AND READING TRIVARIATE TABLES

Let's return to the example of attitudes toward sexual equality. Suppose that we believed age would also affect such attitudes—that young people would approve of sexual equality more than older people would. As the first step in table construction, we would divide the total sample into subgroups based on the various attributes of *both* independent variables simultaneously: young men, old men, young women, and old women. Then the several subgroups would be described in terms of the dependent variable, and comparisons would be made. Table 11.6 is a hypothetical **trivariate table** that might result.

Following the convention of this book, Table 11.6 has been percentaged down, and therefore it should be read across. Interpretation of the table warrants several conclusions:

1. Among both men and women, younger people are more supportive of sexual equality than are older people. Among women, 90 percent and 60 percent, respectively, approve.
2. Within each age group, women are more supportive than men. Among those respondents under 30 years of age, 90 percent of the women approve, compared with 78 percent of the men. Among those 30 and over, 60 percent of the women and 48 percent of the men approve.
3. Age has a stronger effect than sex on attitudes. For both men and

TABLE 11.7   An Abbreviated Trivariate Table (simplification of Table 11.6)

"Do you approve or disapprove of the proposition that men and women should be treated equally in all regards?"

	Percentage who approve	
	Women	Men
Under 30	90%	78%
	(200)	(200)
30 and over	60	48
	(200)	(200)

women, the effect of age may be summarized as a 30-percentage point difference. Within each age group, the percentage point difference between men and women is 12.

4. Both age and sex have independent effects on attitudes. Within a given attribute of one independent variable, different attributes of the second independent variable still affect attitudes.
5. Similarly, the two independent variables have a cumulative effect on attitudes. Young women are most supportive, and older men are the least supportive.

In one sense, this table is somewhat inefficient. When the dependent variable—attitude toward sexual equality—is dichotomous (two attributes), knowing one attribute permits the reader to easily reconstruct the other. Thus, if we know that 90 percent of the women under 30 years of age approve of sexual equality, then we know automatically that 10 percent disapprove. Reporting the percentages who disapprove is unnecessary. On the basis of this recognition, Table 11.6 could be presented in the alternative format of Table 11.7, similar to the presentation of the *Playboy* data in Table 11.4.

In Table 11.7, the percentages approving of sexual equality are reported in the cells representing the intersections of the two independent variables. The numbers presented in parentheses represent the number of cases upon which the percentages are based. Thus, the reader knows that there are 200 women under 30 years of age in the sample, and 90 percent of those approved of sexual equality. This shows, moreover, that 180 of those 200 women approved, and that the other 20 (or 10 percent) disapproved. This new table is easier to read than the former one without sacrificing any detail.

TABLE 11.8   Self-esteem of Adolescent Boys in Relation to Sex Distribution of Siblings, Ordinal Position, and Grades*

| Self-esteem | Respondent in first half or middle of family | | | Respondent in last half of family (younger minority) | | |
| | Grades | | | Grades | | |
	A–B	C	D–F	A–B	C	D–F
	No brothers or brothers in the minority					
High	56%	45%	41%	46%	60%	64%
Medium	20	27	27	19	18	18
Low	24	28	32	35	22	18
Total percent	100%	100%	100%	100%	100%	100%
Number	(79)	(104)	(41)	(26)	(65)	(22)
	Brothers in the majority or equal					
High	51%	40%	29%	42%	44%	30%
Medium	26	27	18	32	33	20
Low	23	32	53	26	23	50
Total percent	100%	99%	100%	100%	100%	100%
Number	(168)	(240)	(102)	(78)	(86)	(56)

Source: Adapted from *Society and the Adolescent Self-Image*, by Morris Rosenberg (Princeton, 1965), p. 121. Copyright 1965 by Princeton University Press. Reprinted with permission of the publisher.
*Note: Study is of families with three or more children.

ANALYZING SELF-ESTEEM

I want to conclude this discussion of table formats with a somewhat more complicated multivariate table, drawn from the literature of social research. This example represents an attempt by sociologist Morris Rosenberg (1968) to shed some light on self-esteem among adolescent boys. As we see in Table 11.8, Rosenberg has examined the simultaneous impact of three variables on self-esteem:

1. *Sex distribution of siblings.* Do the subjects live in families where girls outnumber boys or where boys either equal or outnumber the girls?
2. *Ordinal position.* What is the subjects' age-rank within the family: Are they older brothers or younger brothers?
3. *Grades.* What kinds of grades do the subjects get in school?

Let's see what Table 11.8 tells us about self-esteem. To simplify matters, let's focus on the percentages of adolescent boys who are high in self-esteem.

To determine the impact of the sex distribution of siblings, we compare the top rows of percentages in the two halves of the table: 56 to 51 percent, 45 to 40 percent, 41 to 29 percent, 46 to 42 percent, 60 to 44 percent, and 64 to 30 percent. What pattern do you notice in all those comparisons? In each case, the boys living in families with a sister majority (top half of table) are more likely to have high self-esteem than boys similar to them in every other regard except sibling sex distribution. Consistently, living in a sister majority family seems to promote higher self-esteem.

To determine the impact of the sex distribution of siblings, we compare the top rows of percentages in the two halves of the table: 56 to 51 percent, 45 to 40 percent, 41 to 29 percent, 46 to 42 percent, 60 to 44 percent, and 64 to 30 percent. What pattern do you notice in all those comparisons? In each case, the boys living in families with a sister majority (top half of table) are more likely to have high self-esteem than boys similar to them in every other regard except sibling sex distribution. Consistently, living in a sister majority family seems to promote higher self-esteem.

Although consistent, the differences are not uniform. Overall, the sex distribution of siblings seems to matter most for those boys who get bad grades in school. There are only small differences among those with good grades.

How about ordinal position? Is self-esteem affected by whether boys are older or younger within their set of brothers and sisters? To find out, we compare the right and left halves of the table: 56 to 46 percent, 45 to 60 percent, 41 to 64 percent (in the top half of the table); 51 to 42 percent, 40 to 44 percent, and 29 to 30 percent (in the bottom half). Notice once again that we are comparing groups of boys who are similar to each other except for their ordinal position.

What pattern do you see in this latest set of comparisons? I don't see much of a pattern. Although the various comparisons reveal differences in self-esteem, we cannot conclude there is a consistent relationship between ordinal position and high self-esteem. Sometimes the older boys have higher self-esteem, sometimes the younger ones do.

Finally, what effect do grades have on self-esteem? Logically, we would suspect that good grades would result in high self-esteem and bad grades in low self-esteem. Let's see if that's true. Here the relevant comparisons are among the three grade groupings in each of the four parts of the table: 56 to 45 to 41 percent, and 46 to 60 to 64 percent (in the top half of the table); 51 to 40 to 29 percent, and 42 to 44 to 30 percent (in the bottom half). Is our suspicion confirmed by the data?

Grades seem to have the expected effect on self-esteem among those boys who have an older position among their brothers and sisters, but we find a very different pattern among the younger minority brothers. For Rosenberg, the latter set of data pointed to

... the possibility that the younger-minority boy might be characterized by a particular *type* of self-esteem, namely, *unconditional self-acceptance*. While the self-esteem of others appeared to be influenced by their level of academic performance, the self-esteem of the younger-minority boy appeared to be relatively impervious to it. It might thus be that the self-esteem of the younger-minority boy was so firmly established in the family by the interest and affection of his father, mother, and older sisters that it was relatively independent of later extra-familial experiences. (*1968:214*)

This latest illustration should give you a fuller view of multivariate analysis through the use of percentage tables. In Chapter 12, we are going to be looking at some of the more complicated statistical techniques for undertaking multivariate analyses. Before leaving percentage tables, I want to take you deeper into the logic of understanding relationships among variables.

THE ELABORATION MODEL

The final section of this chapter is devoted to a perspective on social scientific analysis that is referred to variously as the *elaboration model*, the *interpretation method*, the *Columbia School*, or the *Lazarsfeld method*. This varied nomenclature derives from the fact that the method we'll be discussing aims at elaboration on an empirical relationship among variables in order to interpret that relationship in the manner developed by Paul Lazarsfeld while he was at Columbia University.

The **elaboration model** is used to understand the relationship between two variables through the simultaneous introduction of additional variables. It was developed primarily through the medium of percentage tables, but as Chapter 12 will show, it may be used with other statistical techniques.

It is my firm belief that the elaboration model offers the clearest picture of the logic of analysis that is available. Especially through the use of percentage tables, this method portrays the logical process of scientific analysis. Moreover, if you are able to comprehend fully the use of the elaboration model in the form of percentage tables, you should be in a good position to use and understand more sophisticated statistical techniques.

THE ELABORATION PARADIGM

We've already examined several examples of causal relationships between two variables, in which some independent variable appears to cause some dependent variable. Lazarsfeld's purpose was to develop a logical/statistical technique that would allow the researcher to elaborate on the nature of that observed relationship. He suggested four different situations that might exist, describing the conditions under which the causal relationship might operate and/or the process through which it operated.

TESTING FOR GENERALIZABILITY   In terms of the conditions under which the initial relationship operated, Lazarsfeld suggested two possibilities. First, the relationship might operate under *all* conditions. Lazarsfeld called that situation a **replication,** meaning that the relationship was replicated or repeated under different conditions. Second, it was possible that the initial relationship might operate under only certain conditions and not others—among women, for example, but not among men. Lazarsfeld called this situation a **specification,** meaning that the researcher had specified the conditions under which the relationship operated.

The elaboration model is conducted through the construction of trivariate tables. The researcher begins with a bivariate relationship. That relationship is referred to as the original, or **zero-order,** relationship. The researcher then introduces a third variable, called a **control** or **test variable.** Subjects are divided into subgroups based on the control variable—old people versus young people, for example. Next, within each subgroup of the control variable, tables are constructed to examine the original relationship. Those subgroup tables are called **partial tables.** Finally, the researcher measures the bivariate relationships in each of the partial tables—called the **partial relationships**—and compares them with the zero-order relationship. The comparison allows the researcher to determine whether the zero-order relationship is replicated or specified under the condition represented by the control variable. Let's look at some examples to clarify this process.

REPLICATION   Whenever the partial relationships are essentially the same as the original relationship, the term *replication* is assigned to the result. For an example, turn back to Tables 11.3 and 11.6. In Table 11.3, we saw that women were more supportive of sexual equality than were men. In Table 11.6, we saw that the relationship was equally strong among those under 30 and those over 30.

In the logic of the elaboration model, Table 11.6 introduces age as a control variable to test the generalizability of the zero-order relationship between sex and support for sexual equality. In Table 11.3, we see that the zero-order relationship is equal to an epsilon of 12 percentage points. The

TABLE 11.9 Social Class and Church Involvement

	Social class levels				
	Low 0	1	2	3	High 4
Mean involvement	.63	.58	.49	.48	.45

Source: Charles Y. Glock, Benjamin B. Ringer, and Earl Babbie, *To Comfort and to Challenge* (Berkeley: University of California Press, 1967): 85.

same relationship is discovered in each of the partial tables of Table 11.6. Therefore, we conclude that the original relationship was replicated under conditions of age.

Researchers use the elaboration model rather routinely in the hope of replicating their findings among subsets of the sample. If we discovered a relationship between education and prejudice, for example, we might introduce such test variables as age, region of the country, race, religion, and so forth, to test the stability of that original relationship. If the relationship were replicated among young and old, among persons from different parts of the country, and so forth, we would have grounds for concluding that the original relationship was a genuine and general one.

SPECIFICATION Sometimes the elaboration model produces partial relationships that differ significantly from each other. For example, one partial relationship may look very much like the original two-variable relationship, while the second partial relationship is near zero. This situation is referred to as *specification* in the elaboration paradigm; in other words, we have specified the conditions under which the original relationship occurs.

In a study of the sources of religious involvement, Glock and his associates (1967) discovered that among Episcopal church members, involvement decreased as social class increased. This finding is reported in Table 11.9, which examines mean levels of church involvement among women parishioners at different levels of social class.

Glock interpreted this finding in the context of others in the analysis and concluded that church involvement provides an alternative form of gratification for people who are denied gratification in the secular society. This conclusion explained why women were more religious than men, why old people were more religious than young people, and so forth. Glock reasoned that people of lower social class (measured by income and education) had fewer chances to gain self-esteem from the secular society than did people of higher social class. To illustrate this idea, he noted that

TABLE 11.10   Social Class and Holding Office in Organizations

	Social class levels				
	Low 0 ————————————→ High				
	0	1	2	3	4
Percentage who have held office in a secular organization	46%	47%	54%	60%	83%

Source: Charles Y. Glock, Benjamin B. Ringer, and Earl Babbie, *To Comfort and to Challenge* (Berkeley: University of California Press, 1967): 92.

social class was strongly related to the likelihood that a woman had ever held an office in a secular organization (see Table 11.10).

Glock then reasoned that, if social class were related to church involvement only by virtue of the fact that lower-class women would be denied opportunities for gratification in the secular society, the original relationship should *not* hold among women who were getting gratification. As a rough indicator of gratification in the secular society, he used as a variable the holding of secular office. In terms of this test, social class should be unrelated to church involvement among those who had held such office (see Table 11.11).

Table 11.11 presents an example of a specification. Among women who have held office in secular organizations, there is essentially no relationship between social class and church involvement. In effect, the table specifies the conditions under which the original relationship holds: Religious involvement is highest among those women lacking gratification in the secular society.

UNDERSTANDING RELATIONSHIPS

Replication and specification were two of the elaboration outcomes that Lazarsfeld described. Two more—*interpretation* and *explanation*—both offer the researcher a deeper understanding of the nature of the original relationship. The mechanics are the same as we've already looked at, but the results and the meanings are different. Let's look at each.

INTERPRETATION   To examine **interpretation,** let's look at the example that first led Lazarsfeld to develop the elaboration model. Lazarsfeld's colleague, Samuel Stouffer, had done a series of studies for the

TABLE 11.11 Church Involvement by Social Class and Holding Secular Office

Mean church involvement for:	Social class levels				
	Low 0	1	2	3	High 4
Have held office	.46	.53	.46	.46	.46
Have not held office	.62	.55	.47	.46	.40

Source: Charles Y. Glock, Benjamin B. Ringer, and Earl Babbie, *To Comfort and to Challenge* (Berkeley: University of California Press, 1967): 92.

army during World War II. Many of the studies focused on morale, and one examined how soldiers felt about being drafted. Initially, Stouffer believed that educated soldiers would resent being drafted more than less educated soldiers. To find out, Stouffer asked soldiers if they felt they should have been deferred (excused from the draft). Stouffer was surprised by the results, which are shown in Table 11.12.

As you can see, the more educated soldiers were somewhat more accepting of being drafted than those with less education. Stouffer suggested a reason for the surprising finding, as follows:

1. People judge their own circumstances by comparing themselves with others around them.
2. Soldiers' prewar friends, on the whole, probably had the same amount of education as the soldiers themselves. Soldiers with high education would have highly educated friends; soliders with little education would have friends with little education.
3. People with little education were more likely than those with a lot of education to have been working on assembly lines and on farms.
4. Many factory and farm workers were deferred from the draft because their jobs were considered essential to the war effort.
5. Thus, soldiers with little education would be more likely to have friends deferred than would soldiers with a lot of education.
6. As soldiers assessed their being drafted on the basis of whether their friends were drafted or deferred, those with little education would be the most likely to feel they were treated unfairly.

Putting all this together, Stouffer suggested that the relationship between education and attitudes toward being drafted operated through the variable of whether the soldiers' friends were deferred. Unfortunately, Stouffer had not asked soldiers this question.

Lazarsfeld was sufficiently interested in the study to create a hypo-

TABLE 11.12   Education and Acceptance of Being Drafted

	High education	Low education
Should *not* have been deferred	88%	70%
Should have been deferred	12	30
	100%	100%
	(1761)	(1896)

Source: Tables 11.12 and 11.13 are modified with permission of the Macmillan Company from *Continuities in Social Research: Studies in the Scope and Method of "The American Soldier,"* by Robert K. Merton and Paul F. Lazarsfeld (eds.). Copyright 1950 by The Free Press, a Corporation, renewed 1978 by Robert K. Merton.

thetical table that would confirm Stouffer's reasoning. If education was related to attitudes toward deferment only through the medium of friends being deferred, there should be no relationship if there were no difference in whether friends were deferred. Table 11.13 is the table Lazarsfeld created to show that situation.

As you can see in Table 11.13, education has no effect on attitudes toward being drafted among those whose friends were deferred: 63 percent of both groups said they themselves should not have been deferred. Similarly, there is virtually no relationship among those who had no friends deferred. This table suggests the following model:

Education ⟶ Friends deferred ⟶ Attitudes

(Independent
variable)   (Control variable)   (Dependent
variable)

Soldiers' education determined whether they had friends deferred, which in turn determined how they felt about being drafted. That's the logic of interpretation in the elaboration model. Beginning with a zero-order relationship between an independent variable and a dependent variable, the researcher discovers an **intervening** control variable that interprets the original relationship. We refer to the control variable as *intervening* because it occurs between the independent variable and the dependent variable.

Here is another brief example of interpretation. It has been observed by researchers in the past that children from homes with working mothers are more likely to become delinquent than those whose mothers do not work. However, this relationship may be interpreted through the introduction of supervision as a test variable. Among children who are supervised, delinquency rates are not affected by whether or not their mothers work.

TABLE 11.13 Hypothetical Data Relating Education to Acceptance of Induction through the Factor of Having Friends Deferred

	Friends deferred		No friends deferred	
	High education	Low education	High education	Low education
Should not have been deferred	63%	63%	94%	95%
Should have been deferred	37	37	6	5
	100%	100%	100%	100%
	(335)	(1484)	(1426)	(392)

Nor are the rates affected among those who are not supervised. It is the relationship between working mothers and the lack of supervision that produced the original relationship.

EXPLANATION The final elaboration outcome is similar to interpretation. In the case of explanation, however, the original relationship is found to be **spurious**—not a genuine relationship. The original relationship was "explained away" through the introduction of a test variable.

Two conditions are required for a spurious relationship to exist. The test variable must be **antecedent** to (prior to) both the independent and dependent variables, and the partial relationships must be zero or significantly less than those found in the original. Three examples will illustrate this situation.

There is a relationship between the number of storks in different areas and the birthrates for those areas. The more storks in an area, the higher the birthrate. This empirical relationship might lead one to assume that the number of storks affects the birthrate. An antecedent test explains away this relationship. Rural areas have both more storks and higher birthrates than urban areas. Within rural areas, there is no relationship between the number of storks and the birthrate; nor is there a relationship within urban areas.

Figure 11.2 illustrates how the rural/urban variable causes the apparent relationship between storks and birthrates. Part I of the figure shows the original relationship. Notice how all but one of the entries in the box for towns and cities with few storks have high birthrates; all those in the box for towns and cities with few storks, with one exception, have low birthrates. In percentage form, we can say that 94 percent of the towns and cities with many storks also have high birthrates, as contrasted with 6 per-

FIGURE 11.2
The facts of life
about storks and
babies.

I. Births Rates of Towns and Cities Having Few or Many Storks
   H = Town or city with high birth rate
   L = Town or city with low birth rate

NUMBER OF STORKS

Few	Many
L L L LL L LLL L H L L L LL L L	H H H L H H H H H H H H

II. CONTROLLING FOR RURAL (Towns) AND URBAN (Cities)

NUMBER OF STORKS

	Few	Many
Rural	H	H H ₕH H ₕH H H Hᴴ HHₕHᴴH
Urban	L L Lₗᴸ L ᴸ L ₗLLₗ L L L L L L Lₗ L ᴸ	L

FIGURE 11.3
Explanation of
storks/babies re-
lationship.

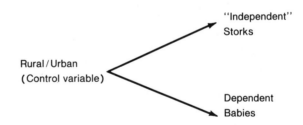

Rural/Urban
(Control variable)

"Independent"
Storks

Dependent
Babies

cent of those with few storks. That's a very large percentage-point difference and would represent a strong association between the two
variables.

Part II of the figure separates the towns from the cities, the rural from
urban areas, and examines storks and babies in each type of place separately. Now we can see that all the rural places have high birthrates, and
all the urban places have low birthrates. Also notice that only one rural
place has few storks and only one urban place has lots of storks.

In comparison to the logical diagram presented to represent interpretation, Figure 11.3 represents an explanation.

Here's another similar example. There is a positive relationship between the number of fire trucks responding to a fire and the amount of damage done. If more trucks respond, more damage is done. One might assume from this fact that the fire trucks themselves cause the damage. An antecedent test variable, however, explains away the original relationship: the size of the fire. Large fires do more damage than small ones, and more fire trucks respond to large fires than to small ones. Looking only at large fires, we see that the original relationship would vanish (or perhaps reverse itself); the same would be true looking only at small fires.

The Real World Research box entitled "Attitudes toward Medicare" gives a research example of explanation.

This introduction to the elaboration model should give you a better idea of the logic of data analysis. It's important that you understand this logic so you'll be able to follow the reasoning of research reports you'll be reading—and to find errors in that reasoning when it appears.

ELABORATION AND EX POST FACTO HYPOTHESIZING

Before leaving our discussion of the elaboration model, I want to warn you of a misleading impression sometimes created in the analysis of multivariate relationships. Researchers sometimes observe a relationship between two variables and then suggest reasons for the relationship in terms of the roles played by other variables. An example of this can be found in Stouffer's examination of soldiers' education and attitudes toward deferment. Stouffer's discussion of the role played by "friends deferred," while insightful, remained unproven.

Sometimes, researchers create an impression that an observed bivariate relationship proves the validity of a trivariate explanation—since the bivariate relationsip is what would be found if the trivariate relationship were hypothesis. This is called **ex post facto hypothesizing.** In such a situation, the researcher has created a "hypothesis" that has already been "tested" and "proven." This is illegitimate, since there is no possibility of hypothesis being disproven. Indeed, *any* explanation the researcher might offer would be "proven" in this situation.

This is not to suggest that you should fault researchers for suggesting explanations after the results are already in. Just be clear that hypotheses are never proven except through tests that allow the possibility of disproof.

As we've seen in several of the examples in this section, it is possible for researchers to (1) observe a bivariate relationship, (2) suggest reasons in the form of trivariate relationships, and (3) test the trivariate hypotheses. The Glock examination of church involvement and social gratification is a good example. Since the trivariate explanation was tested and confirmed, we can have more confidence in that explanation that if it were only suggested but not tested.

ATTITUDES TOWARD MEDICARE

In 1970, I published a report on the attitudes and orientations of medical school faculty members across the country. Since the government's Medicare program had recently been passed over the objections of many in the medical community, I was interested in learning the factors that determined physicians' attitudes toward the program.

Because attitudes toward Medicare generally followed liberal-conservative lines, it was not surprising to find regional differences in attitudes. In the generally liberal East, Medicare was generally supported. In the more conservative South, there was more opposition. As a part of my analysis, then, I wanted to find out whether physicians who attended eastern medical schools would be more approving of Medicare than those trained in southern medical schools.

That expectation was confirmed by the data. Of faculty members attending eastern medical schools, 78 percent said they approved of Medicare, compared with 59 percent of those attending southern medical schools. This finding makes sense in view of the fact that the South seems generally more resistent to such programs than the East, and medical school training should presumably affect a doctor's medical attitudes. This relationship is explained away through the introduction of an antecedent test variable—the region of the country in which the faculty member was raised.

Of faculty members raised in the East, 89 percent attended medical school in the East and 11 percent in the South. Of those raised in the South, 53 percent attended medical school in the East and 47 percent in the South. Moreover, the

This completes our introduction to multivariate analysis. Chapter 12 will continue the discussion by looking at some more complex statistical techniques.

☑ CONSUMER'S CHECKLIST

We've covered a good deal of territory in this introduction to data analysis. You will gain mastery over this aspect of social science research only through experience. Fortunately, there is plenty of research literature for area in which faculty members were raised related to attitudes toward Medicare. Of those raised in the East, 84 percent approved of Medicare, as compared with 49 percent of those raised in the South.

The following table presents the three-variable relationship among region in which the respondent was raised, region of medical school training, and attitude toward Medicare.

Percentage who approve of Medicare

		Region in which raised	
		East	South
Region of medical school training	East	84	50
	South	80	47

Those faculty members raised in the East are quite likely to approve of Medicare, regardless of where they attended medical school. Those raised in the South are relatively less likely to approve of Medicare, and again, the region of their medical school training has little or no effect. These data indicate, therefore, that the original relationship between region of medical training and attitudes toward Medicare was spurious; it was due only to the coincidental effect of region of origin on both region of medical training and attitudes toward Medicare. When region of origin is *held constant*, as has been done in the table, the original relationship disappears in the partials.

SOURCE Earl Babbie, *Science and Morality in Medicine* (Berkeley: University of California Press, 1970): 181.

you to practice on. Here are some guidelines to assist you in evaluating researchers' analyses.

- Familiarize yourself with the univariate analyses of variables: levels of measurement, central tendencies, and measure of dispersion.
- If means or medians have been computed, have the proper measures been used? If means have been calculated, do the variables have extreme values?
- In bivariate tables:
  a. Does the table represent a simple subgroup comparison, or is a causal relationship involved?

b. If a causal relationship is involved, what are the independent and the dependent variables?

c. Have all the categories of the dependent variable been presented, or has an abbreviated format been used?

d. Has the table been percentaged properly? Remember, if it has been percentaged down, read it across; if it has been percentaged across, read it down.

e. How strong is the relationship between the two variables? What is the epsilon? How many categories are there in the independent variable?

f. If there are more that two categories of the independent variable, is the relationship monotonic?

g. Compare your interpretation of the relationship with the researcher's. Consider what the relationship means in the real world.

• Has the researcher presented any multivariate relationships?

a. What is the dependent variable? What are the independent variables? What is the form of the relationship?

b. Note all the partial relationships evident in the table.

c. How strong and monotonic are the various relationships?

d. What is the explanation for the relationships connecting the variables? Compare your conclusion with the researcher's.

• Has the researcher undertaken an elaboration of the relationships among variables? Do you agree?

• Do any of the relationships suggest that an elaboration should have been undertaken but wasn't?

a. Should the researcher have undertaken a replication of key findings? What control variables should have been used?

b. Can you think of any possible interpretations of relationships? What intervening variable might have been introduced?

c. Can you think of any possible explanations? Are any of the relationships possibly spurious? What antecedent variable might have explained the relationship?

d. Can you think of any specifications? For any particular relationship, can you think of conditions under which it might not hold? What antecedent or intervening variables might specify the original relationship?

• Is the researcher guilty of ex post facto hypothesizing? Have reasons been offered for relationships without testing the validity of those reasons?

Univariate analysis	Continuous variable	Control (test) variable
Frequency distribution	Discrete variable	Zero-order relationship
Grouped data	Subgroup comparisons	ship
Marginals	Bivariate analysis	Partial table
Central tendency	Epsilon	Partial relationship
Mode	Monotonicity	Interpretation
Mean	Multivariate analysis	Explanation
Median	Trivariate table	Intervening variable
Dispersion	Elaboration model	Spurious relationship
Range	Replication	Antecedent variable
Standard deviation	Specification	Ex post facto hypothesizing
Interquartile range		

MAIN POINTS

1. Univariate analysis is the analysis of one variable at a time.
2. When the attributes composing a variable are numerous, as in the case of people's ages or income, researchers oftern combine attributes into categories of grouped data.
3. Central tendency is a general term that refers to the central value in a distribution. Averages are measures of central tendency.
4. The mode is the most common value in a distribution.
5. The mean is what most people commonly think of as the "average." It is calculated by adding all the values in a distribution and dividing by the number of values.
6. The median is the middle value in a distribution.
7. Dispersion is the extent to which values in a distribution are spread out.
8. The range is a measure of dispersion calculated by subtracting the lowest value from the highest.
9. The standard deviation is a measure of dispersion used in conjunction with the mean. It is comparable to the measure of sampling error discussed in Chapter 5.
10. A continuous variable is composed of attributes that increase or decrease steadily in tiny fractions.
11. A discrete variable is composed of categorical attributes distinctly separated from one another.

12. Strictly speaking, means and medians are only appropriate when calculated on ratio and interval data, respectively.
13. Subgroup comparisons are created out of two variables: one to divide people into subgroups and another to use in describing the two subgroups.
14. Commonly, subgroup comparsions have the purpose of exploring causal relationships connecting the two variables. This is called a bivariate analysis.
15. In reading a percentage table, you must first determine the direction in which percentages add to 100 percent: either down the columns or across the rows. If the table is percentaged down, read across. It if is percentaged across, read down.
16. There is no universal agreement as to how strong a relationship between two variables must be in order to be considered "strong." As a rule of thumb, remember that any difference that makes no difference is no difference.
17. Epsilon is an appropriate statistic for measuring the strength of a relationship in a percentage table.
18. Monotonicity is the quality of percentages increasing or decreasing steadily across a percentage table.
19. Multivariate analysis refers to analyses involving three or more variables.
20. The elaboration model was developed by Paul Lazarsfeld for the purpose of elaborating on a bivariate relationship by holding a third—control—variable constant.
21. The original bivariate relationship in the elaboration model is called zero-order relationship.
22. In the elaboration model, the original bivariate relationship is examined separately in subgroups created on the basis of the control variable.
23. The tables created within the control variable subgroups are called partial tables, and the relationships found in those tables are called partial relationships.
24. If all the partial relationships are essentially the same as the zero-order relationship, the outcome is called a replication.
25. If the zero-order relationship disappears in some of the partial tables but not in others, the outcome is called a specification.
26. If the control variable is intervening and the partial relationships are substantially less than the zero-order relationship, the outcome is called an interpretation.
27. If the control variable is antecedent and the partial relationships are substantially less that the zero-order relationship, the outcome is called an explanation.
28. In the case of explanation, we say that the original relationship was spurious.

29. When researchers suggest reasons that observed relationships exist but do not test those suggestions, that is called ex post facto hypothesizing.

? REVIEW QUESTIONS

1. Table 11.3 presents a bivariate table. Combine the data for men and women to create a univariate distribution of attitudes.
2. In your local newspaper find a report of an "average." Is it a mean, median, or mode?
3. Table 11.4 presents two bivariate tables. Make up data to complete the details of the table in Part A—adding "only once in a while" and "not at all."
4. In your own words, explain why none of the rows or columns in Table 11.5 adds up to 100 percent.
5. Recalculate the data in Table 11.6 to show the distribution of attitudes among those under 30 and those 30 and over.
6. Though it is generally agreed that intercourse is related to pregnancy, this is not the total picture. Think of a control variable that would specify the relationship. Create a hypothetical table to demonstrate your point.
7. Turn to Table 11.13. Create the bivariate table that shows that soldiers with high education were less likely than those with low education to have friends deferred from the draft.
8. Turn to the Real World Research box entitled "Attitudes toward Medicare." Suppose the researcher had begun with a bivariate relationship between attitudes and region in which raised and had then introduced region of medical training as control variable. What would the elaboration outcome be called? How would you describe the results?
9. Review Tables 11.9 through 11.11 and discuss the analysis in terms of ex post facto hypothesizing.
10. In the research journals of a field of interest to you, find an example of the elaboration model. Indentify and discuss the elaboration outcome.

SUGGESTED READING

Cole, Stephen. *The Sociological Method* (Chicago: Markham, 1972). A readable introduction to analysis. Cole begins with the general question of what social scientific inquiry is and then illustrates with easily understood examples. His introduction of the elaboration model is also useful.

Davis, James. *Elementary Survey Analysis* (Englewood Cliffs, N.J.: Prentice-Hall, 1971). And extremely well-written and well-reasoned introduction to analysis. In addition to covering the materials of this chapter, Davis's book is well worth reading in terms of measurement, statistics and the elaboration model.

Labovitz, Sanford and Robert Hagedorn. *Introduction to Social Research* (New York: McGraw-Hill,1971). Another useful introduction to analysis. Against the background of general concerns for social scientific inquiry, the authors provide a very readable and useful introduction to elementary analyses in their analysis and the elaboration model.

Zeisel, Hans. *Say It With Figures* (New York: Harper & Row, 1957). An excellent discussion of table construction and other elementary analyses. Though several years old, this is perhaps still the best available presentation of that specific topic. It is eminently readable and understandable and has many concrete examples.

CHAPTER 12

ADVANCED

STATISTICAL TECHNIQUES

INTRODUCTION

Many people are intimidated by empirical research because they feel uncomfortable with mathematics and statistics. And indeed, many research reports are filled with a variety of semispecified computations, making the consumer's job difficult. The role of statistics in social research is very important, but it is equally important for that role to be seen in its proper perspective.

Empirical research is first and foremost a logical operation, rather than a mathematical one. Mathematics is merely a convenient and efficient language for accomplishing the logical operations inherent in good data analysis. Statistics is the applied branch of mathematics especially appropriate to a variety of research analyses.

I want to start this chapter with an informal look at one of the concerns people have when they approach statistics. The beginning exercise should make it easier for you to understand and feel comfortable with the remainder of the chapter. We'll be looking at two types of statistics: descriptive and inferential. **Descriptive statistics** is a medium for describing data in manageable forms. **Inferential statistics,** on the other hand, assists you in drawing conclusions from your actual observations; typically, it involves drawing conclusions about a population from the study of a sample taken from it.

Moving beyond these basics, we'll look briefly at some of the more elaborate statistical techniques used in multivariate data analysis: regression analysis, path analysis, and factor analysis. The logic of these methods is essentially the same as that discussed in connection with the elaboration model in Chapter 11. A full understanding of these techniques would require greater attention than would be appropriate in this book; my goal is to familiarize you with the several techniques rather than to make you an expert.

Let's begin, then, with the problems people have with math—just in case they apply to you.

THE DANGER OF SUCCESS IN MATH

Over the course of teaching research methods involving at least a small amount of statistics, I've been struck by the very large number of students who report that they are "simply no good at math." They generally report this fact as some sort of congenital defect, akin to being born blind or crippled. Not unexpectedly, I have found such people doing pretty badly in statistics, and their more general mastery of quantitative social research has suffered as a result.

To accommodate for this problem, I have increasingly limited the amount and difficulty of statistics to be covered in a course such as the one you're taking. No matter how simple the statistics required has been, however, I've found a large number of students unable to master it—all reporting what I call the "congenital math deficiency syndrome" (CMDS). Just as some people are reported to be inherently tone-deaf and others unable to learn foreign languages, about 90 percent of the college students I've taught seem to suffer from CMDS. Some of its common symptoms are frustration, boredom, and drowsiness. I'm delighted to report that I have finally uncovered a major cause of the disease and have brewed up a cure. In the event that you may be a sufferer, I'd like to share it with you before we delve into the statistics of social research.

After an exhaustive search, I've discovered the culprit in the congenital math deficiency syndrome, whom I'll call Mathematical Marvin, though he has used countless aliases. If you suffer from CMDS, I suspect you've come in contact with him. Here's how you'll recognize him.

Take a minute to recall your years in high school, in particular, that person in your class who was generally regarded by your teachers and classmates as being a "mathematical genius." Getting A's in all the math classes was only part of it; often the math genius seemed to know math better than the teachers.

If you now have that math genius in mind, let me ask you a few questions. First, what was the person's sex? My guess is that he was probably male. Most of the students I've asked in class report that. But let's consider some other characteristics:

1. How athletic was he?
2. Did he wear glasses?
3. How many parties did he get invited to during high school?
4. If he was invited to parties, did anyone ever talk to him?
5. How often did you find yourself envying the math genius, wishing you could trade places with him?

I've been asking students (including some adult classes) these questions for several years, and the answers I've gotten are amazing. Though the agreement has not been unanimous, a clear profile of Marvin emerges. He is usually unathletic, often either very skinny or overweight. He usually wears glasses, and he seems otherwise rather delicate. During his high school years, he was invited to an average (mean) of 1.2 parties, and nobody talked to him. His complexion was terrible. Finally, I have found almost nobody who ever wanted to change places with him: He was a social misfit, more to be pitied than envied.

Here's the point of my report on Mathematical Marvin: As I've discused Marvin with my students, it has become increasingly clear that most of them have formed a subconscious association between mathematical proficiency and Marvin's unenviable characteristics. Most have formed the conclusion that doing well in math and statistics would turn them into social misfits, and they have regarded that as too high a price to pay.

Before exposing you to any numbers, then, I want to assure you that the level of statistics contained in the rest of this chapter has been proven safe for humans. There has not been a single documented case of pimples connected to understanding lambda, gamma, chi square, or any of the other statistics discussed in the pages to follow. In fact, this level of exposure has been found to be beneficial to those who would understand social research.

DESCRIPTIVE STATISTICS

As I've mentioned, descriptive statistics represents a method for presenting quantitative descriptions in a manageable form. Sometimes we want to describe single variables—as discussed in Chapter 11—and sometimes we want to describe the associations that connect one variable with another. Let's look at some of the **measures of association.**

MEASURES OF ASSOCIATION

Recall the Chapter 11 discussions of associations among variables. In this section, we're going to continue the discussion of what constitutes a "strong" association. The association between any two variables may be represented by a data matrix, produced by the joint frequency distributions of the two variables.

The data matrix presented in Table 12.1 provides all the necessary information for determining the nature and extent of the relationship between variables X and Y. The column headings in the table represent the values of variable X, while the row headings represent the values of variable Y. The numbers in the body of the matrix represent the number of cases having a particular pattern of attributes. For example, 35 cases have the pattern X_1Y_1; 43 cases are X_3Y_7.

This format, unfortunately, gives you more information than you can easily comprehend. If you study the table carefully, however, you will note that, as values of variable X increase from X_1 to X_7, there is a general tendency for values of Y to increase from Y_1 to Y_7, but no more than a general impression is possible. A variety of descriptive statistics permit the summarization of this data matrix; selecting the appropriate measure depends on the nature of the two variables.

We'll turn now to some of the options that are available for summarizing the association between two variables. This discussion and those to follow are taken largely from the excellent statistics textbook by Linton C. Freeman (1968).

Each of the measures of association to be discussed in the following sections is based on the same model—**proportionate reduction of error (PRE).** The logic of this model is as follows. First, let's assume that I asked you to guess respondents' attributes on a given variable—for example, whether they answered "yes" or "no" to a certain questionnaire item. Let's assume further that you know the overall distribution of responses in the total sample—say, 60 percent said "yes" and 40 percent said "no." You would make the fewest errors in this process if you always guessed the *modal* (most frequent) response: "yes."

TABLE 12.1   Association between Variables as a Data Matrix

	Variable X					
	X_1	X_2	X_3	X_4	X_5	X_6
Y_1	35	27	26	12	15	7
Y_2	38	48	38	22	35	13
Y_3	32	41	75	64	46	22
Y_4	28	45	63	80	79	45
Y_5	20	35	53	90	103	87
Y_6	23	12	76	80	99	165
Y_7	5	8	43	60	73	189

Second, let's assume that you also know the empirical relationship between the first variable and some other variable: say, sex. Suppose that 80 percent of the men said "yes," and 60 percent of the women said "no." Each time I ask you to guess whether a respondent said "yes" or "no," I'll tell you whether the respondent is a man or a woman. By guessing "yes" for each man and "no" for each woman, you would make fewer errors the second time. It is possible, therefore, to compute the PRE by knowing the relationship between the two variables. The greater the relationship, the greater the reduction of error.

This basic PRE model is modified slightly to take account of different levels of meaurement—nominal, ordinal, or interval. The following sections will consider each level of measurement and present one measure of association appropriate to each. You should realize that the three measures discussed are only a selection from many appropriate measures.

NOMINAL VARIABLES   If the two variables consist of nominal data (for example, sex, religious affiliation, race), **lambda** (λ) would be one appropriate measure. Lambda is based on your ability to guess values on one of the variables, as discussed above: the PRE achieved through knowledge of values on the other variable. A simple example will illustrate the logic and method of lambda.

Table 12.2 presents hypothetical data relating sex to employment status. Overall, we note that 1100 people are employed, and 900 are unemployed. If you were to predict whether or not people were employed, knowing only the overall distribution on that variable, you would always predict "employed," since that would result in fewer errors than always predicting "unemployed." Nevertheless, this strategy would result in 900 errors out of 2000 predictions.

Let's suppose that you had access to the data shown in Table 12.2 and that you were told each person's sex before making your prediction of

TABLE 12.2   Hypothetical Data Relating Sex to Employment Status

	Men	Women	Total
Employed	900	200	1100
Unemployed	100	800	900
Total	1000	1000	2000

employment status. Your strategy would change in that case. For every man, you would predict "employed," and for every woman, you would predict "unemployed." In this instance, you would make 300 errors—the 100 employed men and the 200 employed women—or 600 fewer errors than would have been made in ignorance of their sexes.

Lambda, then, represents the reduction in errors as a proportion of the errors that would have been made on the basis of the overall distribution. In this hypothetical example, lambda would equal .67: 600 fewer errors divided by 900 errors, based on the total distribution of employment status alone. In this fashion, lambda provides a measure of the statistical association between sex and employment status.

If sex and employment status were statistically independent of one another, we would have found the same distribution of employment status for men and women. In this case, knowing sex would not have affected the number of errors made in predicting employment status, and the resulting lambda would have been zero. If, on the other hand, all men were employed and all women were unemployed, you would have made no errors in predicting employment status, knowing sex. You would have made 900 fewer errors (out of 900) and lambda would have been 1.0—representing a perfect statistical association.

Lambda is only one of several measures of association appropriate to the analysis of two nominal variables; you might want to look at Freeman's book for a discussion of others.

ORDINAL VARIABLES   If the variables being related were ordinal in nature (for example, social class, religiosity, alienation), gamma (γ) would be one appropriate measure of association. Like lambda, gamma is based on your ability to guess values on one variable by knowing values on another. Instead of specific values, however, gamma is based on the ordinal arrangement of values. For any given pair of cases, you guess that their ordinal ranking on one variable will correspond (positively or negatively) to their ordinal ranking on the other. Gamma is the proportion of pairs that fit this pattern.

Table 12.3 presents hypothetical data relating social class to prejudice.

TABLE 12.3   Hypothetical Data Relating Social Class to Prejudice

Prejudice	Lower class	Middle class	Upper class
Low	200	400	700
Medium	500	900	400
High	800	300	100

An inspection of the table will indicate the general nature of the relationship between these two variables: As social class increases, prejudice decreases; there is a negative association between social class and prejudice.

Gamma is computed from two quantities: (1) the number of pairs having the same ranking on the two variables and (2) the number of pairs having the opposite ranking on the two variables. The pairs having the same ranking are computed as follows. The frequency (number of cases) of each cell in the table is multiplied by the sum of all cells appearing below and to the right of it—with all these products being summed. In the present example, the number of pairs with the same ranking would be 200(900 + 300 + 400 + 100) + 500(300 + 100) + 400(400 + 100) + 900(100), or 340,000 + 200,000 + 200,000 + 90,000 = 830,000.

The pairs having the opposite ranking on the two variables are computed as follows. The frequency of each cell in the table is multiplied by the sum of all cells appearing below and to the left of it—with all these products being summed. In this example, the numbers of pairs with opposite rankings would be 700(500 + 800 + 900 + 300) + 400(800 + 300) + 400(500 + 800) + 900(800), or 1,750,000 + 440,000 + 520,000 + 720,000 = 3,430,000.

Gamma is computed from the numbers of same-ranked pairs and opposite-ranked pairs as follows:

$$\text{gamma} = \frac{(\text{same} - \text{opposite})}{(\text{same} + \text{opposite})}$$

In the present example, gamma would equal (830,000 − 3,430,000) divided by (830,000 + 3,430,000) or −.61. The negative sign in this answer indicates the negative association suggested by the initial inspection of the table. Social class and prejudice, in this hypothetical example, are negatively associated with one another. The numerical figure for gamma indicates that 61 percent more of the pairs examined had the opposite ranking than had the same ranking.

Note that, while values of lambda vary from 0 to 1, values of gamma vary from −1 to +1, representing the direction as well as the magnitude of

SANCTIFYING SPOUSES

To study the extent to which widows sanctified their deceased husbands, Helena Z. Lopata (1981) administered a questionnaire to a probability sample of 301 Chicago area widows. In part, the questionnaire asked the respondents to characterize their deceased husbands in terms of the semantic differentiation scale shown below:

Characteristic

Positive extreme							Negative extreme
Good	1	2	3	4	5	6	7	Bad
Useful	1	2	3	4	5	6	7	Useless
Honest	1	2	3	4	5	6	7	Dishonest
Superior	1	2	3	4	5	6	7	Inferior
Kind	1	2	3	4	5	6	7	Cruel
Friendly	1	2	3	4	5	6	7	Unfriendly
Warm	1	2	3	4	5	6	7	Cold

of the association. Since nominal variables have no ordinal structure, it makes no sense to speak of the direction of the relationship. (A negative lambda would indicate that you made more errors in predicting values on one variable while knowing values on the second than you made in ignorance of the second.)

The Real World Research box entitled "Sanctifying Spouses" demonstrates another manner in which measures of association such as gamma are presented.

Gamma is only one of several measures of association appropriate to ordinal variables. Again, refer to Freeman's book for a more comprehensive treatment of this subject.

INTERVAL OR RATIO VARIABLES If the variables being associated are interval or ratio in nature (for example, age, income, grade-point average, and so forth), one appropriate measure of association would be **Pearson's product-moment correlation** (r). The derivation and

Respondents were asked to describe their deceased spouses by circling a number for each pair of opposing characteristics. Notice that the series of numbers connecting each pair of characteristics constitutes an ordinal measure.

Next, Lopata wanted to discover the extent to which the several measures were related to each other. Appropriately, she chose gamma as the measure of association. Here's the way she presented the results of her investigation.

Gamma Associations among the Semantic Differentiation Items of the Sanctification Scale *

	Useful	Honest	Superior	Kind	Friendly	Warm
Good	.79	.88	.80	.90	.79	.83
Useful	—	.84	.71	.77	.68	.72
Honest		—	.83	.89	.79	.82
Superior			—	.78	.60	.73
Kind				—	.88	.90
Friendly					—	.90

* This format is called a **correlation matrix.** For each pair of measures, Lopata has calculated the gamma. Good and useful, for example, are related to each other to the extent of a gamma equal to .79. The matrix is a convenient way of presenting the intercorrelations among several variables, and you'll find it frequently in the research literature.

SOURCE Helena Znaniecka Lopata, "Widowhood and Husband Sanctification." *Journal of Marriage and the Family,* May 1981:439–450. © 1981 by the National Council on Family Relations. Reprinted by permission.

computation of this measure of association is sufficiently complex to lie outside the scope of the present book, so only a few general comments will be made.

Like both gamma and lambda, r is based on guessing the values of one variable on the basis of knowing the values of the other. For continuous interval or ratio variables, however, it is unlikely that you would be able to predict the *precise* value of the variable. But on the other hand, predicting only the ordinal arrangement of values on the two variables would not take advantage of the greater amount of information conveyed by an interval or ratio variable. In a sense, r reflects *how closely* you can guess the value of one variable through your knowledge of the value of the other.

To understand the logic of r, it will be useful to consider the manner in which you might guess values that cases have on a given variable. With nominal variables, as we have seen, you might always guess the modal value. That is not an appropriate perspective for interval or ratio data, how-

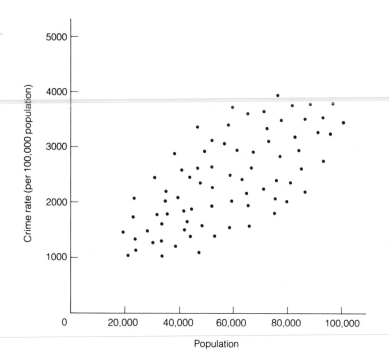

FIGURE 12.1
A scattergram of the values of two variables (hypothetical).

Crime rate (per 100,000 population)

5000

4000

3000

2000

1000

0   20,000   40,000   60,000   80,000   100,000

Population

ever. Instead, you would minimize your errors by always guessing the mean value of the variable. Although this practice would produce few if any perfect guesses, the extent of your errors would be minimized.

Figure 12.1 presents hypothetical data representing the joint distribution of two ratio variables: population of cities and their crime rates. Each dot in this **scattergram** represents a city. Assume we want to predict crime rates. If the mean in the distribution is, say, 2500, we'd guess that value for each city. As you can see, however, we wouldn't guess many crime rates correctly.

In the computation of lambda, we noted the number of errors produced by always guessing the modal value. In the case of interval and ratio variables, errors could be measured as the difference between actual values and the mean of all values. In computing r and some of the other measures to be discussed in this chapter, the errors are calculated by (1) measuring each of the differences between actual values and the mean, (2) squaring each of those differences, and (3) calculating the mean of those squared differences. The technical term for this mean is the **total variance.**

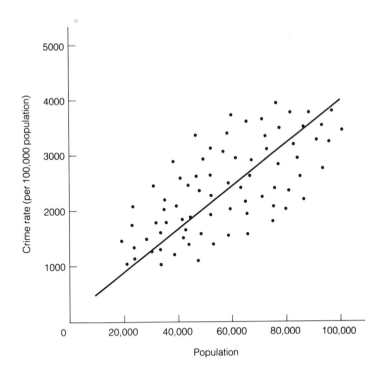

FIGURE 12.2
A scattergram of the values of two variables with regression line added (hypothetical).

Within the PRE model, the question is whether knowing values on a second variable will reduce the errors in guessing values of the other. In the case of r, this is done by constructing a straight line through the pattern of points that will minimize the sum of squared distances from the points to the line. (This is called the **regression line.**)

In Figure 12.2, the question is whether knowing a city's population improves our guessing of its crime rate. Instead of guessing the mean crime rate for each city, we guess the value indicated by the regression line. Now we recompute the mean squared differences between actual and estimated values. This is called the **unexplained variance,** because it represents errors that still exist even when estimates are based on knowing the population sizes.

The **explained variance** is the difference between the total variance and the unexplained variance. Dividing the explained variance by the total variance produces a measure of the proportionate reduction of error corresponding to the similar quantity in the computation of lambda. In the present case, this quantity is the correlation *squared*: r^2. Thus, if $r = .7$, then $r^2 = .49$: meaning that about *half* the variance has been explained.

Now when you read research reports that present the association between two variables as r, you will know what that means. Squaring the r gives you the proportion of variance in one variable that is explained by the other.

MIXED TYPES OF VARIABLES   Often, social research involves the association between two variables that differ in type: one ordinal variable and one nominal variable. Sex and prejudice would be an example. A variety of special statistics are appropriate to these different possibilities, and you are encouraged to examine Freeman's book if you want to check whether a researcher has used the appropriate measure of association in any given case.

This is an opportune point for a general comment regarding types of variables and the appropriateness of statistical measures. A quick review of social scientific research literature will yield countless examples of statistical measures applied to data that do not meet the logial requirements of the measures. The computation of Pearson's r for ordinal data is perhaps the most typical example. Arguing against it is correct on statistical grounds: correlation coefficients assume interval data, and ordinal data do not meet that criterion. On the other hand, it is my personal inclination to accept, and even to encourage, the use of whatever statistical techniques help the researcher (and the reader) to understand the body of data under analysis. If the computation of r from ordinal data serves this purpose, then it should be encouraged. However, I strongly object to (and will discuss in the next section) the practice of making statistical *inferences* on the basis of such computations. A researcher is justified in bending the rules if it helps us understand our data, but we must be aware of the implications of bending those rules. This is something you will want to watch for in reading research reports.

INFERENTIAL STATISTICS

Many, if not most, social scientific research projects involve the examination of data collected from a sample drawn from a larger population. Frequently then, researchers use their univariate and multivariate sample findings as the basis for inferences about some population. This section will examine some of the statistical measures frequently used for making such inferences, and we'll look at the logical bases for them. Let's begin with univariate data and move to multivariate.

UNIVARIATE INFERENCES

The opening sections of Chapter 11 dealt with methods of presenting univariate data. Each summary measure was intended as a method of describing the sample studied. Now we have come to the point of using those measures to make broader assertions about the population. This section is addressed to two univariate measures: percentages and means.

If 50 percent of a sample of people say they have had colds during the past year, our best estimate of the similar proportion of the total population from which the sample has been drawn is 50 percent. (This estimate assumes a simple random sample, of course.) It is rather unlikely, however, that *precisely* 50 percent of the population have had colds during the year. If a rigorous sampling design for random selection has been followed, it is possible to estimate the expected range of error when the sample finding is applied to the population.

Chapter 5 on sampling theory covered the procedures for making such estimates, so they will be only reviewed here. In the case of a percentage, the quantity

$$\sqrt{\frac{PQ}{N}}$$

where P is a percentage and Q equals 1 − P, and where N is the sample size, is called the *standard error*. As noted in Chapter 5, this quantity is very important in the estimation of sampling error. We may be 68 percent confident that the population figure falls within plus or minus one standard error of the sample figure, 95 percent confident that it falls within plus or minus two standard errors, and 99.9 percent confident that it falls within plus or minus three standard errors.

As we saw, then, any statement of sampling error must contain two essential components: the *confidence level* (for example, 95 percent) and the *confidence interval* (for example, ±2.5 percent). If 50 percent of a sample of 1600 people say they have had colds during the year, we might say we are 95 percent confident that the figure for the total population is between 47.5 percent and 52.5 percent.

Recognize in this example that we have moved beyond simply describing the sample into the realm of making estimates (inferences) about the larger population. In doing that, we must be wary of several assumptions.

First, the sample must be drawn from the population about which inferences are being made. A sample taken from a telephone directory cannot legitimately be the basis for statistical inferences about the population of a city.

Second, the inferential statistics assume simple random sampling, which is virtually never the case in sample surveys. Although systematic sampling is used more frequently than random sampling, that presents no serious problem if it is done correctly. Stratified sampling, since it improves representativeness, clearly presents no problem. Cluster sampling does present a problem, however, as the estimates of sampling error may be too small. Quite clearly, streetcorner sampling does not warrant the use of inferential statistics. Also assumed is a 100 percent completion rate. This problem increases in seriousness as the completion rate decreases.

Third, the inferential statistics are addressed to sampling error only; they do not take account of *nonsampling* errors. For example, survey respondents may lie; police departments may make mistakes in reporting crimes; those processing data may make other mistakes. Thus, it might be quite correct to state that between 47.5 and 52.5 percent of the population (95 percent confidence) would *say* that they had had colds during the previous year, but their reports might be essentially worthless. In other words, we could confidently guess the proportion of the population who would *report* colds, but not the proportion who had actually had them. Nonsampling errors are probably larger than sampling errors in a respectable sample design.

It is good to keep in mind that, when a researcher reports 95 percent confidence that some value in a population is between, say, 45 and 55 percent (the confidence interval), the figure could be stated another way: There is only a 5 percent probability that the value is below 45 percent or above 55 percent. This is the logic often used in judging the significance of an observed relationship between variables. In any case, we need to be especially cautious in generalizing from our sample findings to the population. When reading reports of univariate inferences, you need to pay attention to both the statistical computations and the measurement procedures upon which they are based.

TESTS OF STATISTICAL SIGNIFICANCE

In Chapter 11, you'll recall, we discussed the strength of associations, asking how strong an association was needed for two variables to be considered "strongly" related to one another. While there is still no definitive answer to this question, we are going to look at one of the solutions commonly employed by social researchers. And we are going to see some of the errors commonly committed in that respect.

NULL HYPOTHESIS   In examining whether two variables are related to one another, we might begin with the opposite assumption—that they are independent of one another. This is called the **null hypothesis.**

Recall Table 11.3 in Chapter 11, examining the hypothetical relationship between sex and attitudes toward sexual equality. The null hypothesis in this instance would suggest that men and women had the same attitudes, that sex and support for sexual equality were independent of each other. In fact, the table shows that, in the sample of subjects, 63 percent of the men and 75 percent of the women approved of sexual equality. On the face of it, this would seem to contradict the null hypothesis: Men and women did not express the same distribution of attitudes. There's a catch, however.

Since the data presented are based on a sample from a population, we know that sampling error was involved. There is a chance that we could have selected too many proequality women and/or too many antiequality men. It is possible, therefore, that in the whole population sex and attitudes are independent, but sampling error created the appearence of a relationship. **Tests of statistical significance** based on the null hypothesis allow the researcher to calculate the probability that an observed relationship could be the result of sampling error alone—from a population in which the variables are actually independent. This is analogous to the probability discussed above that a univariate value falls outside a calculated confidence interval.

CHI SQUARE   A commonly used test of statistical significance for tables such as Table 11.3 is **chi-square.** It is calculated by comparing the number of cases in each cell of a table with the number of cases that would be expected if the two variables creating the table were independent of one another.

Part A of Table 12.4 shows the cell frequencies that were given as percentages in Table 11.3. In addition to the cell frequencies, notice that 552 people (69 percent) approved and 248 disapproved, overall. If we knew only the overall distribution of attitudes and assumed that sex had no effect on those attitudes, we would assume that 69 percent of the men and 69 percent of the women approved of sexual equality. Part B of Table 12.4 presents the cell frequencies that would be expected under this null hypothesis.

Chi square is calculated as follows:

$$\sum \frac{(o - e)^2}{e}$$

1. In each cell, subtract the difference between the observed (o) and the expected (e) frequencies.
2. Square that difference.
3. Divide the squared difference by the expected frequency.
4. Add up the results from all the cells.

Part C of Table 12.4 shows the results of the cell calculations. Take a min-

TABLE 12.4   The Calculation of Chi Square (hypothetical)

Attitude toward sexual equality	Men	Women	Total
Part A: Observed frequencies			
Approve	252	300	552
Disapprove	148	100	248
Total	400	400	800
Part B: Expected frequencies			
Appprove	276	276	552
Disapprove	124	124	248
Total	400	400	800
Part C: Calculation of chi square			
Approve	2.09	2.09	
Disapprove	4.65	4.65	
Part D: Chi square $= 13.48 < .001$			

ute to check the calculations to be sure that you understand the procedure. Part D indicates that the value of chi square in this case is 13.48.

Part D also contains the notation $p < .001$. This means that the probability of selecting a sample having the cell frequencies we observed in Part A from a population in which the two variables were independent of one another is less than 1 in 1000. This figure was obtained from a table of chi square values. As a consumer of research, it is not necessary for you to know how to use such tables—only to understand the meaning of the results.

In this instance, we would probably conclude that there is a genuine relationship between city size and crime rate. In reaching that conclusion, the risk of being wrong is less than one in a thousand.

Most measures of association can be tested for statistical significance in a similar manner. Standard tables of values permit researchers to determine whether a given association is statistically significant and at what level. Any standard statistics textbook provides instructions on the use of such tables, so we shall not pursue the matter further here.

CAUTIONARY NOTES Tests of significance provide an objective yardstick against which to estimate the significance of associations between variables. They assist us in ruling out associations that may not represent genuine relationships in the population under study. When you read reports of significance tests, you should remain wary of several dangers in their interpretation.

First, we have been discussing tests of *statistical* significance; there are no objective tests of *substantive* significance. Thus, we may be legitimately convinced that a given association is not due to sampling error but that two variables are only slightly related to one another. Recall that sampling error is an inverse function of sample size: The larger the sample, the smaller the expected error. Thus, a correlation of, say, .1 might very well be significant (at a given level) if it is discovered in a large sample, whereas the same correlation between the same two variables would not be significant in a smaller sample. In the larger sample, there is less chance that the correlation could be simply the product of sampling error. Nevertheless, in both samples, the correlation might represent a very weak and meaningless association. Tests of statistical significance are not measures of the strength of associations.

Second, tests of significance are based on the same sampling assumptions as were made in the computation of confidence intervals. To the extent that these assumptions are not met by the actual sampling design, the tests of significance are not strictly legitimate.

Third, you should be wary of tests of significance that have been applied to data that represent a total population rather than a sample. Suppose a researcher has studied the voting records of all members of the U.S. House of Representatives to find out if Republicans have more of a promilitary record than Democrats. Since no sample has been selected, there is no chance that the association could be due to sampling error. The association between the two variables—political party and military voting record—as measured in the population is precisely what has been measured. Whether that degree of association is a substantively significant one— whether it is important— cannot be answered through any objective test. Sometimes researchers make the mistake of calculating statistical significance when whole populations have been studied, so you should be on the lookout.

All these reservations notwithstanding, tests of significance can provide a useful tool for the evaluation of statistical associations. Your ability to capitalize on the true value of the tests without being misled by overstated conclusions will come with practice.

Let's move on now to a brief consideration of some of the more elaborate analytical techniques you will come across in social science research literature. My goal here is simply to give you a brief introduction to the techniques.

REGRESSION ANALYSIS

In the discussion of correlation above, we began with a scattergram representing the joint distribution of values on two variables. In this section, we'll see how the relationship between the two (or more) variables can be represented in the form of a mathematical equation.

SIMPLE LINEAR REGRESSION

Recall for a moment the scattergram presented in Figure 12.1, showing the hypothetical relationship between population and crime rate. Figure 12.2 added the straight line that came closest to the several points, determined by measuring the squared distances from the points to the line.

In you've ever studied geometry, you'll know that any straight line on a graph can be represented by an equation of the form: $Y = a + bX$, where X and Y are values of the two variables. In this equation, a equals the value of Y when X is 0, and b represents the slope of the line. If we know the values of a and b, then, we could calculate an estimate of Y for every value of X.

Regression analysis is a technique for establishing the **regression equation** representing the geometric line that comes closest to the distribution of points. This equation has both descriptive and inferential values. First, it provides a mathematical description of the relationship observed between the variables. Second, it allows us to infer values of Y when we have only values of X. In Figure 12.2, for instances, we could estimate crime rates of cities on the basis of their populations.

Unfortunately, the nature of social life is complex enough that the **simple linear regression** model is not sufficient to represent the state of affairs. As we saw in Chapter 11, it is possible to analyze more than two variables through the use of percentage tables. As the number of variables increases, such tables become increasingly complicated and hard to read. The **multiple regression** model offers a useful alternative in such cases.

MULTIPLE REGRESSION

Very often, social researchers find that a given dependent variable is impacted simultaneously by several independent variables. That was the case when Beverly Yerg (1981) set about studying teacher effectiveness in physical education. She stated her expectations in the form of a regression equation:

$$F = b_0 + b_1I + b_2X_1 + b_3X_2 + b_4X_3 + b_5X_4 + e$$

where

F = final pupil performance score
I = initial pupil performance score
X_1 = composite on guiding and supporting practice
X_2 = composite on teacher mastery of content
X_3 = composite on providing specific, task-related feedback
X_4 = composite on clear, concise task presentation
b = regression weight
e = residual
(*adapted from Yerg, 1981:42*)

Notice that, in place of a single X variable, there are several; and there are several b's in place of the single one presented in the case of the simple linear regression. Yerg chose to represent a as b_0 in this equation, but the meaning is the same as above. Finally, the equation ends with a residual factor (e), which represents the variance in Y that is not accounted for by the X variables analyzed.

Beginning with this equation, Yerg went on to calculate the values of the several b's so as to show the relative contributions of the several independent variables in determining final student performance scores. In addition, Yerg calculated the multiple correlation coefficient as an indicator of the extent to which all six variables predict the final scores. This follows the same logic as the simple bivariate correlation discussed earlier, and it is traditionally reported as a capital R. In this case, $R = .77$, meaning that 77 percent of the variance in final scores is explained by the six variables acting in concert.

PARTIAL REGRESSION

In the discussion of the elaboration model, special attention was paid to the relationship between two variables when a third test variable was held constant. Thus, we might have examined the effect of education on prejudice with age held constant, testing the independent effect of education. To do so, we would have computed the tabular relationship between education and prejudice separately for each age group.

Partial regressions are based on this same logical model. The equation summarizing the relationship between variables is computed on the basis of the test variables remaining constant. As in the case of the elaboration model, the result may then be compared with the uncontrolled relationship between the two variables to clarify further the nature of the overall relationship.

CURVILINEAR REGRESSION

Up to now, we have been discussing the association among variables as represented by a straight line—though in more than two dimensions. The regression model is even more comprehensive.

If you have a knowledge of geometry, you will already know that curvilinear functions also can be represented by equations. For example, the equation $X_2 + Y_2 = 25$ describes a circle with a radius of 5. Raising variables to powers greater than 1 has the effect of producing curves rather than straight lines. From the standpoint of empirical research, there is no reason to assume that the relationship among every set of variables will be linear. In some cases, then, **curvilinear regression** analysis can provide a better understanding of empirical relationships than can any linear model.

Recall, however, that a regression line serves two functions. It describes a set of empirical observations, and it provides a *general* model for making inferences about the relationship between two variables in the general population that the observations represent. A very complex equation might result in a rather erratic line that would indeed pass through every individual point. In this sense, it would perfectly describe the empirical observations, but there would be no guarantee that such a line would adequately predict new observations or that it in any meaningful way represented the relationship between the two variables in general. It would have little or no inferential value.

Earlier we discussed the need for balancing detail and utility in data reduction. Ultimately, researchers attempt to provide the most faithful, yet also the simplest, representation of their data. This practice also applies to regression analysis. Data should be presented in the simplest fashion (thus, linear regressions are most frequently used), but in such a way as to best describe the actual data. Curvilinear regression analysis adds a new option to the researcher in this regard. It does not solve the problems altogether; nothing does that.

CAUTIONS IN REGRESSION ANALYSIS

The use of regression analysis for statistical inferences makes certain assumptions that you should know about. These are the same ones assumed by correlational analysis, concerning simple random sampling, the absence of nonsampling errors, and continuous interval data. Since social scientific research seldom completely satisfies these assumptions, you should use caution in assessing the results in regression analyses.

Regression lines—linear or curvilinear—can be useful for **interpolation** (estimating cases lying between those observed), but they are less trustworthy when used for **extrapolation** (estimating cases that lie beyond the range of observations). It is important to know this for two reason. First, you are likely to come across regression equations that seem to make illogical predictions. An equation linking population and crimes, for example, might seem to suggest that small towns with, say, 1000 population should produce –123 crimes a year. This does not disqualify the equation, but it does dramatize that its applicability is limited to a particular range of population sizes. Second, researchers sometimes overstep this limitation, drawing inferences that lie outside their range of observation, and you are right in criticizing them for that.

Let's shift analytical styles for a moment now. So far, we have seen the relationships among variables represented in the form of percentage tables, graphs, and equations. Now let's look at a flow diagram presentation.

PATH ANALYSIS

Path analysis offers a graphic presentation of the interrelations among variables. It is based on regression analysis, but it can provide a more useful graphic picture of relationships among several variables than is possible through other means.

Path analysis is a *causal* model for understanding relationships between variables. Because path analysis assumes that the values on one variable are caused by the values on another, it is essential that independent and dependent variables be distinguished. This requirement is not unique to path analysis, of course. But path analysis provides a unique way of displaying explanatory results for interpretation.

Recall for a moment one of the ways I represented the elaboration model in Chapter 11 (see p. 304). I diagramed the case of interpretation like this:

Independent variable $\longrightarrow$ Control variable $\longrightarrow$ Dependent variable

The logic was that an independent variable had an impact on an intervening, or control, variable which, in turn, had an impact on a dependent variable. The path analyst constructs similar patterns of relationships among variables, but the typical path diagram contains many more variables.

In addition to diagraming a network of relationships among variables, path analysis also shows the strengths of those several relationships. The strengths of relationships are calculated from a regression analysis that produces numbers analogous to the partial relationships in the elaboration

FIGURE 12.3
Diagraming the religious sources of anti-Semitism. (Source: Figure 3 from *Wayward Shepherds—Prejudice & the Protestant Clergy* by Rodney Stark, Bruce D. Foster, Charles Y. Clock, and Harold E. Quinley. Copyright ©1971 by Anti-Defamation League of B'nai Brith. Reprinted by permission of Harper & Row, Publishers, Inc.)

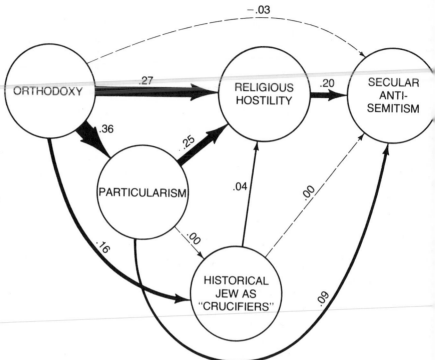

model. These **path coefficients,** as they are called, represent the strengths of the relationships between pairs of variables with the effects of all other variables in the model held constant. Figure 12.3 offers an example.

This analysis focuses on the religious causes of anti-Semitism among Christian church members. The variables in the diagram are, starting from the left: (1) the extent to which the subjects accept conventional, orthodox beliefs about God, Jesus, the biblical miracles, and so forth; (2) the particularistic belief that one's religion is the "only true faith"; (3) acceptance of the view that Jews were the crucifiers of Jesus; (4) a religious hostility toward contemporary Jews, such as believing that God is punishing them or that they will suffer damnation unless they convert to Christianity; and (5) secular anti-Semitism, such as believing that Jews cheat in business, are disloyal to their country, and so forth.

In preparing for their analysis, the researchers had reasons to believe that secular anti-Semitism was the result of a process moving through the five variables: Orthodoxy caused particularism, which caused the view of the historical Jews as crucifiers, which caused a religious hostility toward contemporary Jews, which resulted, finally, in secular anti-Semitism.

The path coefficients tell a different story. The belief in the historical role of Jews as the crucifiers of Jesus, for example, doesn't seem to matter in the process. And, although particularism is a part of one process resulting in secular anti-Semitism, the diagram also shows that anti-Semitism is created more directly by orthodoxy and religious hostility. Orthodoxy produces religious hostility even in the absence of particularism, and religious hostility generates secular hostility in any event.

One last comment on path analysis is in order. Although it is an excellent way of handling complex causal chains and networks of variables, path analysis itself does not tell the causal order of the variables. The researcher must do that. Don't be misled into thinking that the researcher's path diagram was generated by the computer. The researcher decided the structure of relationships among the variables—the computer analysis merely calculate the path coefficients that apply to such a structure.

FACTOR ANALYSIS

Factor analysis is a different approach to multivariate analysis. Its statistical basis is sufficiently complex and different enough from the foregoing types of analysis so that only a very general discussion is in order here.

Factor analysis is used to discover patterns among the variations in values of several variables. This is done essentially through the generation of artificial dimensions (factors) that correlate highly with several of the real variables and that are independent of one another. A computer must be used to perform this complex operation.

Let's suppose for the moment that a data file contains several indicators of subjects' prejudice. Each of the items should provide some indication of prejudice, but none of them would give a perfect indication. Moreover, all of the items should be highly intercorrelated empirically. In a factor analysis of the data, it is likely that a dimension would be created that would be highly correlated with each of the items measuring prejudice. Essentially, each subject would receive a value on that dimension, and the value assigned would provide a good predictor of the observed attributes on each item.

Suppose now that the same study provided several indicators of subjects' mathematical ability. It is likely that the factor analysis would also generate a dimension highly correlated with each of those indicators.

The output of a factor analysis program consists of columns representing the several factors (dimensions) generated from the observed relations among variables, plus the correlations, or **factor loadings,** between each variable and each factor.

DIMENSIONS
OF DELINQUENCY

The problem of delinquency has been studied by many social scientists. When you look deeply into the problem, you discover that there are many different types of delinquents. In a survey of high school students in a small Wyoming town, Morris Forslund (1980) set out to create a typology of delinquency. His questionnaire asked students to report whether they had committed a variety of delinquent acts. He then submitted their responses to factor analysis. His findings are presented in the table below.

Factor Analysis: Delinquent Acts, Whites

Delinquent act	Property offenses Factor I	Incorrigibility Factor II	Drugs/ truancy Factor III	Fighting Factor IV
Broke street light, etc.	.669	.126	.119	.167
Broke windows	.637	.093	.077	.215
Broke down fences, clothes lines, etc.	.621	.186	.186	.186
Taken things worth $2 to $50	.616	.187	.233	.068
Let air out of tires	.587	.243	.054	.156
Taken things worth over $50	.548	−.017	.276	.034
Thrown eggs, garbage, etc.	.526	.339	−.023	.266
Taken things worth under $2	.486	.393	.143	.077
Taken things from desks, etc. at school	.464	.232	−.002	.027
Taken car without owner's permission	.461	.172	.080	.040
Put paint on something	.451	.237	.071	.250
Disobeyed parents	.054	.642	.209	.039
Marked on desk, wall, etc.	.236	.550	−.061	.021
Said mean things to get even	.134	.537	.045	.100
Disobeyed teacher, school official	.240	.497	.223	.195
Defied parents to their face	.232	.458	.305	.058
Made anonymous telephone calls	.373	.446	.029	.135

In the above example, it is likely that one factor would more or less represent prejudice, and another would more or less represent mathematical ability. Data items measuring prejudice would have high loadings on (correlations with) the prejudice factor and low loadings on the mathematical ability factor. Data items measuring mathematical ability would have just the opposite pattern.

Factor Analysis: Delinquent Acts, Whites

Delinquent act	Property offenses Factor I	Incorrigibility Factor II	Drugs/ truancy Factor III	Fighting Factor IV
Smoked marijuana	.054	.064	.755	−.028
Used other drugs for kicks	.137	.016	.669	.004
Signed name to school excuse	.246	.249	.395	.189
Drank alcohol, parents absent	.049	.247	.358	.175
Skipped school	.101	.252	.319	.181
Beat up someone in a fight	.309	.088	.181	.843
Fought—hit or wrestled	.242	.266	.070	.602
Percent of variance	67.2	13.4	10.9	8.4

As you can see in the table, the various delinquent acts are listed on the left. The numbers shown in the body of the table are the factor loadings on the four factors constructed in the analysis. You'll notice that Forslund has labeled the dimensions. I've marked the items on each factor that led to his choice of labels. Forslund summarizes the results as follows:

For the total sample four fairly distinct patterns of delinquent acts are apparent. In order of variance explained, they have been labeled: (1) Property offenses, including both vandalism and theft; (2) Incorrigibility; (3) Drugs/truancy; and (4) Fighting. It is interesting, and perhaps surprising, to find both vandalism and theft appear together in the same factor. It would seem that those high school students who engage in property offenses tend to be involved in both vandalism and theft. It is also interesting to note that drugs, alcohol and truancy fall in the same factor. (1980:4)

Having determined this overall pattern, Forslund reran the factor analysis separately for boys and for girls. Essentially the same patterns emerged in both cases.

SOURCE   Morris A. Forslund, "Patterns of Delinquency Involvement: An Empirical Typology." Paper presented to the Annual Meeting of the Western Association of Sociologists and Anthropologists, Lethbridge, Alberta, February 8, 1980. The table is adapted from page 10.

In practice, factor analysis does not proceed in this fashion. Rather, the variables are input to the program, and a series of factors with appropriate factor loadings are the output. You must then determine the meaning of a given factor on the basis of those variables that load highly on it. The generation of factors has no reference to the *meaning* of variables, only to their empirical associations. Two criteria are taken into account: (1) A factor must explain a relatively large portion of the variance found in the study variables, and (2) every factor must be more or less independent of every other factor.

"Dimensions of Delinquency" (pp. 338–339) presents a sample of factor analytic results.

There are a number of advantages to factor analysis. First, instead of you and the researcher being forced to compare countless correlations—simple, partial, and multiple—it is an efficient method of discovering predominant patterns among a large number of variables. Incidentally, here is an example of a good use of computers.

Second, factor analysis presents data in a form that can be interpreted by the reader or researcher. For a given factor, the reader can easily discover the variables loading highly on it or not, thus noting clusters of variables.

Factor analysis has disadvantages as well. First, as noted above, factors are generated without any regard to substantive meaning. Often researchers will find factors producing very high loadings for a group of substantively disparate variables. They might find, for example, that prejudice and religiosity have high positive loadings on a given factor, with education having an equally high negative loading. Surely the three variables are highly correlated, but what does the factor represent? All too often, inexperienced researchers will be led into naming such factors as "religio-prejudicial lack of education" or something equally nonsensical.

Second, factor analysis is often criticized on basic philosophical grounds. Recall my earlier statement that, to be legitimate, a hypothesis must be disconfirmable. If the researcher is unable to specify the conditions under which the hypothesis would be disproved, the hypothesis is in reality either a tautology (a restatement of itself) or useless. In a sense, factor analysis suffers this defect. No matter what data are input, factor analysis produces a solution in the form of factors. Thus, if the researcher were asking, "Are there any patterns among these variables?" the answer would always be "yes." This fact must also be taken into account in evaluating the results of factor analysis. The generation of factors by no means insures meaning.

My personal view of factor analysis is the same as my view of other complex modes of analysis. It can be an extremely useful tool for the social science researcher, and its use should be encouraged whenever it may assist researchers in understanding a body of data. As in all cases, you must keep in mind that such tools are only tools and never magical solutions.

This completes our overview of some of the advanced analytical techniques commonly used by social scientists. Realize that it has not been possible to cover all the techniques used. I have chosen a variety of techniques that should enable you to learn about others later on. Let's conclude the chapter by reviewing some of the guidelines that will assist you in evaluating the research reports you read.

☑ CONSUMER'S CHECKLIST

In this chapter, we've covered several statistical measures. To assist you in coping with them in research reports, here are some of the things you should look for.

- What measures of association have been used?
  a. What are the levels of measurement of the variables being related to each other?
  b. Have the correct measures of association been used?
  c. How strong are the measured associations?
  d. If "inappropriate" measures have been used, has the researcher taken that into account in interpreting the results?
- Have univariate inferences been made?
  a. Has the researcher given you sufficient sampling data to determine the confidence interval and level?
  b. Has an acceptable probability sampling design been used, thereby permitting generalizations?
  c. What is the population that such generalizations apply to?
  d. Would the researcher's conclusions change if the univariate descriptions were off by as much as we might reasonably expect from sampling error?
- Have tests of significance been used?
  a. Are such tests appropriate to the sampling design?
  b. What is the probability that the observed association could have resulted from sampling error alone?
- Has a regression analysis been undertaken?
  a. Have only interval level variables been used?
  b. If not, has the researcher taken that into account in the conclusions?
  c. What model has the researcher used: linear, curvilinear, partial, or multiple regression?
  d. Do the data appear to fit the model chosen?
- Has a path analysis been used?
  a. Has the researcher included all the appropriate variables in the analysis?
  b. Have the variables been arranged in a reasonable system of relationships?
  c. Have the most important patterns in the path diagram been noted?
- Has a factor analysis been used?
  a. What are the main factors the variables fall into?

b. Has the researcher interpreted the meaning of the factors appropriately?

c. Has the researcher used the factor analysis to test a hypothesis without the possibility of disproving it?

KEY WORDS

Descriptive statistics
Inferential statistics
Measure of association
Proportionate reduction of error (PRE)
Lambda
Gamma
Correlation matrix
Pearson's product-moment correlation (r)
Scattergram

Total variance
Regression line
Unexplained variance
Explained variance
Null hypothesis
Tests of statistical significance
Chi square
Regression analysis
Regression equation
Simple linear regression

Multiple regression
Partial regression
Curvilinear regression
Interpolation
Extrapolation
Path analysis
Path coefficients
Factor analysis
Factor loadings

MAIN POINTS

1. Proportionate reduction of error (PRE) is a model for assessing the strength of associations between variables.
2. Lambda is a measure of association appropriate to nominal variables.
3. Gamma is a measure of association appropriate to ordinal variables.
4. Pearson's product-moment correlation (r) is a measure of association appropriate to interval and ratio variables.
5. Total variance is a measure of dispersion of values around a mean.
6. Explained variance is the amount of variance in one variable that is accounted for by variations in another or other variables.
7. Unexplained variance is the difference between total and explained variance.

8. The null hypothesis suggests that two variables are independent of one another.
9. Tests of statistical significance measure the likelihood that observed relationships are merely the result of sampling error, expressed as a probability: e.g., $p < .001$.
10. Chi square is a commonly used test of significance.
11. Statistical significance should not be confused with substantive significance.
12. Tests of statistical significance make the same sampling assumptions discussed in Chapter 5.
13. Tests of statistical significance are not appropriate when whole populations, rather than samples, are studied.
14. A simple linear regression analysis summarizes the relationship between two variables in the form of a regression equation of the form $Y = a + bX$.
15. Multiple regression analysis summarizes the effects of several independent variables on a dependent variable.
16. Partial regression analysis summarizes the relationship between two variables with the effects of other relevant variables held constant.
17. Curvilinear regression fits the pattern of relationship among variables to a curved line.
18. It is legitimate to use regression equations to interpolate estimates within the observed range of values but not to extrapolate estimates outside the observed range.
19. Path analysis presents the interrelations among several variables in the form of a path diagram.
20. Path coefficients indicate the relationships among variables in a path diagram.
21. Factor analysis is a technique for discovering dimensions among a large number of variables.

? REVIEW QUESTIONS

1. Recall the person in your high school class who was generally agreed to be a mathematical genuis. Describe that person. Did you ever want to change places with him or her.
2. Make up tables that would produce lambda of (a) $+1$, (b) 0, and (c) -1.
3. Look through the research journals in a field of interest to you. Find a table presenting a relationship between two ordinal variables. Calculate gamma.

4. In your own words, explain the proportionate reduction of error (PRE) model in the case of (a) lambda, (b) gamma, and (c) Pearson's product-moment correlation (r).
5. Review Table 12.4 on chi square. Double each of the observed cell frequencies and recalculate chi square. Although doubling the frequencies does not affect the relationship among percentages, see what it does to chi-square.
6. Look through the research journals in a field of interest to you. Find a research report using chi square. Explain the meaning of its use in your own words.
7. Think of a dependent variable of interest to you and several independent variables that might account for it. Construct a multiple regression equation to represent those relationships.
8. Using the same variables as in (7) above, create a path diagram to represent the relationships among those variables.
9. Look through the research journals in a field of interest to you. Find an example of factor analysis. What are the major factors uncovered in the analysis? What are the items most highly loaded on each?
10. Review the Real World Reseach box entitled "Dimensions of Delinquency." Discuss the generalizability of the conclusions drawn.

SUGGESTED READING

Borgatta, Edgar (ed.). *Sociological Methodology, 1969* (San Francisco: Jossey-Bass, 1969), especially Chapters 1 and 2. Good discussions of the logic and techniques of path analysis. The chapters by Kenneth Land and Davide Heise examine a variety of aspects of path analysis and its potential contribution to social research, especially in regard to the discovery of causal relationships. These chapters are more advanced than would be desired in an introductory presentation, but good introductions to path analysis are hard to find.

Ezekiel, Mordecai and Karl Fox. *Methods of Correlation and Regression Analysis: Linear and Curvilinear* (New York: John Wiley, 1959). A rather comprehensive presentation of correlation and regression methods. This book begins with a very simple introduction to the subject and then moves progressively to more complex aspects. In addition to describing a wide variety of statistical computations, the authors are sensitive to the practical considerations that apply to the use of correlations and regression in social research.

Freeman, Linton. *Elementary Applied Statistics* (New York: John Wiley, 1968). An excellent introductory statistics textbook. Everyone has a favorite statistics text, and this is mine. It is clear, well-organized, and understandable. In addition to describing the most frequently used statistical methods in detail, Freeman provides briefer descriptions of many more that might be appropriate in special situations.

Harmon, Harry. *Modern Factor Analysis* (Chicago: University of Chicago Press, 1967). A rather comprehensive presentation of factor analytic methods. Harmon discusses both the logic and the specific computational techniques associated with this method of social scientific analysis.

Morrison, Denton and Ramon Henkel (eds.). *The Significance Test Controversy: A Reader* (Chicago: Aldine-Atherton, 1970). A compilation of perspectives—pro and con—on tests of statistical significance. The question of the validity, utility, or significance of tests of statistical significance reappears periodically in social science journals. This collection of articles offers an excellent picture of the persistent debate.

USING THE LIBRARY

INTRODUCTION

Throughout this book, we have been assuming that you will be reading reports of social science research. In this appendix, I want to talk a little about how you'll find reports to read.

As I've indicated repeatedly, you live in a world that is filled with social science research reports. Your daily newspaper, magazines, professional journals, alumni bulletins, club newsletters—virtually everything you pick up to read may carry reports of social science research. However, you will sometimes want to find reports dealing with a particular topic. Usually, you'll pursue that interest through your library. I am going to make some suggestions about how best to use your library. Although I'll give you just a brief overview here, you can get more information in an excellent little book—Alden Todd's *Finding Facts Fast* (Berkeley, Calif.: Ten Speed Press, 1979).

GETTING HELP

When you want to find something in the library, your best friend is the reference librarian, who is specially trained to find things in the library. Sometimes it's hard to ask people for help, but you'll do yourself a real service to make an exception in this case.

Some libraries have specialized reference librarians—for the social sciences, humanities, government documents, and so forth. Find the one you need and tell him or her what you're interested in. The reference librarian will, among other things, probably put you in touch with some of the many available reference sources.

REFERENCE SOURCES

You have probably heard the expression *information explosion.* Your library is one of the main battlefields. Fortunately, a large number of reference volumes offer a guide to the information that's available.

BOOKS IN PRINT This volume lists all the books currently in print in the United States—listed separately by author and by title. Out-of-print books can often be found in older editions of *Books in Print.*

READERS' GUIDE TO PERIODICAL LITERATURE This annual volume with monthly updates lists articles published in many journals and magazines. Since the entries are organized by subject matter, this is an excellent source for organizing your reading on a particular topic. Figure A.1 presents a sample page from the *Readers' Guide.*

In addition to these general reference volumes, you'll find a great variety of specialized references. A few are listed below as examples.

Popular Guide to Government Publications
New York Times Index
Facts on File
Editorial Research Reports
Business Periodicals Index
Monthly Catalog of Government Publications
Public Affairs Information Service Bulletin
Education Index
Applied Science and Technology Index
A Guide to Geographic Periodicals
General Science Index

FIGURE A.1
A page from the Readers' Guide to Periodical Literature.

CONSTRUCTION industry
Gentler squeeze in homebuilding. il Fortune 103:12 Ap 20 '81
CONSTRUCTION workers

Salaries, pensions, etc.
Toppling a pillar of U.S. labor law [Davis-Bacon Act] il Bus W p38 Je 1 '81
CONSUMER and Corporate Affairs Department (Canada) See Canada—Consumer and Corporate Affairs, Department of
CONSUMERS
See also
Old age market
CONTACT lenses
Long wear lenses OK'd [Hydrocurve II, by Soft Lenses, Inc.] FDA Consumer 15:2 Ap '81
CONTAMINATED milk. See Milk contamination
CONTINENTAL drift
Mobile telescope for measuring continental drift [Transportable Laser Ranging Station and Laser Geodynamics Earth Orbiting Satellite] E. C. Silverberg and D. L. Byrd. il map Sky & Tel 61:405-8 My '81
CONTRACEPTIVES
Cervical caps—the perfect, untested contraceptive. J. Willis. il FDA Consumer 15:20-1 Ap '81
Contraceptive foams and birth defects. Sci News 119:229 Ap 11 '81
Male "pill" blocks sperm enzyme [gossypol inhibition of lactate dehydrogenase X] T. H. Maugh, 2d. Science 212:314 Ap 17 '81
More birth control blues [study by H. Jick linking use of spermicidal contraceptives to birth defects and miscarriages] P. DeVries. il Macleans 94:47-8 My 11 '81
CONTRACTS, Government
See also
Municipal contracts
United States—Labor, Department of—Federal Contract Compliance Programs, Office of
CONTROL Laser Corporation
We prefer to follow. S. N. Chakravarty. il pors Forbes 127:83+ Ap 13 '81
CONVERSATION
"What's the matter, dear?" or, How to get him to talk to you. K. Fury. il Redbook 157:27+ My '81
CONVICT labor
Prisoners who work [rehabilitative value of income in Canada] M. Dewey. il World Press R 28:55 Ap '81
COOKBOOKS
Great recipes from our new cookbook [excerpt from The Good housekeeping illustrated cookbook; ed by Z. Coulson] il Good H 192:156-71+ My '81
COOKE, Cynthia W. and Dworkin, Susan
Good health. il Ms 9:68-9 Ja; 92+ F; 89-91 Mr; 15-16 Ap '81
COOKE, Janet
Ben's world. Winston. Nat R 33:530-2 My 15 '81 •
COOKING
See also
Barbecue cooking
Menus
Meringue

Couples who share the cooking. A. C. Scotton. il Redbook 157:124-5+ My '81
Food journal. il Ladies Home J 98:118+ Mr; 62 Ap; 122 My '81
Food notes: off-the-shelf substitutes. Bet Hom & Gard 59:122 My '81
Off-the-shelf cooking: new main dishes to make from what's on hand. J. Johnson. il Bet Hom & Gard 59:116-21 My '81

Cereals
See Cooking—Grain

Grain
Try triticale. il Bet Hom & Gard 59:154 My '81

Meat
Summer-easy meals: cold meat platters. il Good H 192:304 My '81

Organic food
Sprouts [Rodale Press' natural foods luncheon at the Four Seasons] New Yorker 57:38-40 Je 1 '81

Poultry
Drumstick beat around the world. il Ladies Home J 98:100-1+ My '81

Rice
Spanish accents. C. Claiborne and P. Franey. il N Y Times Mag p 130 My 17 '81

Vegetables
Stir-fried vegetables. il Good H 192:48 My '81
Super-quick stuffed peppers. il Good H 192:92 My '81

Wine
Flavor made easy: fabulous wine cookery. V. Newborn. il Essence 12:129-31+ My '81
COOKING, Bahamian
Friends & food: Island gourmets. il Essence 11:108, 110+ Ap '81
COOKING, Caribbean
See also
Cooking, Bahamian

Caribbean. V. Newborn. Essence 11:121-2 Ap '81
COOKING, Indian (American)
Indian cooking's gifts. J. Wongrey. il Outdoor Life 167:138 My '81
COOKING, Mexican
Enchilada stack. il Seventeen 40:49-50+ My '81
COOKING, Spanish
Spanish accents. C. Claiborne and P. Franey. il N Y Times Mag p 130 My 17 '81
COOKS
Masters [meeting of American and French chapters of Maîtres Cuisiniers] N. Hazelton. Nat R 33:568-9 My 15 '81
COONEY, Gerry
Great white question mark. V. Ziegel. il pors N Y 14:88-9 My 25 '81 •
There were no doubts about it. il pors Sports Illus 54:30-1 My 25 '81 •
COOPER, James C.
(ed) Business outlook. Bus W p23-4 Je 1 '81
COOPERATION
See also
Educational cooperation
COOPERATION, Inter-American. See Inter-American relations
COPEPODS
Encystment discovered in a marine copepod [heteropsyllus nunnil] B. C. Coull and J. Grant. bibl f il Science 212:342-4 Ap 17 '81
COPYRIGHT
Court sets first guidelines for manufacturing clause [ruling by Judge E. Weinfeld in Stonehill Publishing Company suit against U.S. Customs Service] M. Reuter. il Pub W 219:152 My 8 '81

Picture writing
Battle over a manner of speaking [copyright suit by inventor C. Bliss against Blissymbolics Communication Institute of Toronto] I. Allaby. il por Macleans 94:45-6 My 11 '81
CORALS

Larvae
See Larvae
CORN, Ira George, 1921-
Changing role of corporations in political affairs: corporate free speech [address, February 17, 1981] Vital Speeches 47:463-8 My 15 '81
CORN
Wild in the fields [primitive relative of modern corn, zea diploperennis] il SciQuest 54:4-5 Mr '81
CORN futures. See Commodity futures
CORN roots. See Roots
CORPORATE couples. See Married couples
CORPORATE names. See Corporations—names
CORPORATION lawyers. See Lawyers
CORPORATIONS

Accounting
See also
Air freight service—Accounting

Acquisitions and mergers
See also
Hospitals—Acquisitions and mergers
Motion picture industry—Acquisitions and mergers

Exxon scraps motor device [link between alternating current synthesizer and 1979 acquisition of Reliance Electric Company] R. J. Smith. Science 212:311 Ap 17 '81
Take-over fever in the boardrooms [views of J. Srodes] W. Lowther. il Macleans 94:30-1 My 18 '81
Tuning in [Jack Eckerd Corp-American Home Video Corp. merger] T. Jaffe. il por Forbes 127:96+ Ap 13 '81

Laws and regulations
See also
Canada—Consumer and Corporate Affairs, Department of

New ploy to foil the big grab [Canadian law] I. Anderson. il Macleans 94:35 My 18 '81

Canada
New ploy to foil the big grab. I. Anderson. il Macleans 94:35 My 18 '81

Sweden
For Volvo, a shift away from autos [merger with Beijerinvest] Bus W p75 My 25 '81

Biological and Agricultural Index
Nursing and Applied Health Index
Index of Dental Literature
Nursing Studies Index
Index to Periodical Articles by and about Negroes
Index to Little Magazines
Popular Periodical Index
Biography Index
Congressional Quarterly Weekly Report
Library Literature
Bibliographic Index

USING THE STACKS

For serious research, you should learn to use the stacks, where most of the library's books are stored. In this section, I'll give you some information about finding books in the stacks.

THE CARD CATALOG

Your library's card catalog is the main reference system for finding out where books are stored. Each book is described on three separate 3 × 5 cards. The cards are then filed in three alphabetical sets. One set is arranged by author, another by title, and the third by subject matter.

If you want to find a particular book, you can look it up in either the author or the title file. If you only have a general subject area of interest, you should thumb through the subject catalog. Figure A.2 (p. 350) presents a sample card in the card catalog.

1. Subject heading (always in capital letters)
2. Author's name (last name, first name)
3. Title of the book
4. Publisher
5. Date of publication
6. Number of pages in the book plus other information (Here we are told that the book contains illustrations.)
7. Call number (This is needed to find a non-fiction book on the library shelves. A book of fiction generally carries no number and is found in alphabetical order by the author's name.)

FIGURE A.2
Sample subject
catalog card.
(*Source: Lillian L.
Shapiro,* Teaching
Yourself in Librar-
ies. *New York:
H. W. Wilson,
1978:3–4.*)

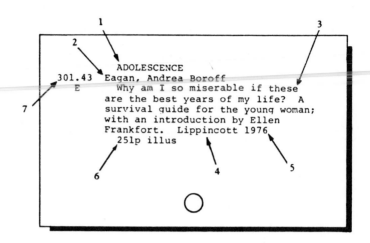

LIBRARY OF CONGRESS

Here's a useful strategy to use when you're researching a topic. Once
you've identified the call number for a particular book in your subject area,
go to the stacks, find that book, *and* look over the other books on the
shelves near it. Since the books are arranged by subject matter, this method
will help you locate relevant books you didn't know about.

Alternatively, you may want to go directly to the stacks and look at
books in your subject area. In most libraries, books are arranged and numbered according to a subject matter classification developed by the Library
of Congress. Below is a selected list of Library of Congress categories.

Library of Congress Classifications (partial)

A GENERAL WORKS

B PHILOSOPHY, PSYCHOLOGY, RELIGION

B–BD	Philosophy
BF	Psychology
BL–BX	Religion

C HISTORY–AUXILIARY SCIENCES

D HISTORY (except America)

DA–DR	Europe
DS	Asia
DT	Africa

E-F HISTORY (America)

E	United States
E51–99	Indians of North America
E185	Negroes in the United States
F101–1140	Canada
F1201–3799	Latin America

G GEOGRAPHY-ANTHROPOLOGY

G–GF	Geography
GC	Oceanology and oceanography
GN	Anthropology
GV	Sports, amusements, games

H SOCIAL SCIENCES

HB–HJ	Economics and business
HM–HX	Sociology

J POLITICAL SCIENCE

JK	United States
JN	Europe
JQ	Asia, Africa
JX	International relations

K LAW

L EDUCATION

M MUSIC

N FINE ARTS

NA	Architecture
NB	Sculpture
NC	Graphic Arts
ND	Painting
NE	Engraving
NK	Ceramics, textiles

P LANGUAGE AND LITERATURE

RE	English language
PG	Slavic language
PJ–PM	Oriental literature
PN	Drama, oratory, journalism
PQ	Romance literature
PR	English literature
PS	American literature
PT	Germanic literature

Q	SCIENCE	
	QA	Mathematics
	QB	Astronomy
	QC	Physics
	QD	Chemistry
	QE	Geology
	QH–QR	Biology
R	MEDICINE	
	RK	Dentistry
	RT	Nursing
S	AGRICULTURE–PLANT AND ANIMAL INDUSTRY	
T	TECHNOLOGY	
	TA–TL	Engineering
	TR	Photography
U	MILITARY SCIENCE	
V	NAVAL SCIENCE	
Z	BIBLIOGRAPHY AND LIBRARY SCIENCE	

COMPUTERIZED LIBRARY FILES

It seems certain that, in the years to come, you'll be finding library materials increasingly by computer. For example, you'll sit at a computer terminal, type the title of a book, and in seconds see a video display of a catalog card. If you wanted to explore the book further, you could type an instruction at the terminal and see an abstract of the book, or perhaps the whole book. Alternatively, you might type a subject name and see a listing of all the books and articles written on that topic. You could skim through the list and indicate which ones you wanted to see.

While this may seem pretty futuristic, it's closer at hand than you may think. Computer network systems such as The Source already allow microcomputer owners to locate and retrieve articles from the *New York Times*, United Press International, and many other similar information sources by connecting their microcomputers over telephone lines to a central computer perhaps thousands of miles away.

Many college libraries now have access to the Educational Resources Information Center (ERIC). This computer-based system allows you to search through some 780 major educational journals to find articles published in the subject area of your interest (within the field of education). Once you identify the articles you are interested in, the computer will print out abstracts of those articles. Outside the field of education, the Lockheed Dialogue system offers about 120 different files like ERIC, including psychological abstracts, sociological abstracts, social science citation index, public affairs informational service, and many others. Check with your librarian to find out what's available to you.

Taking the long view, it would be a good idea for you to begin familiarizing yourself with such computer-based systems now, since you are likely to be using them a great deal in the future. Ultimately, you may do all your library searching from your own home, using your own computer.

READING A

RESEARCH REPORT

In this appendix, I have illustrated the things you might look for in a research report and some of the questions you might raise. Professors Crockerham and Forslund have been kind enough to let me use their survey of Native American attitudes toward police for this purpose. In addition to learning to integrate your critical abilities, I think you'll find the article interesting in its own right.

The article is printed below in its entirety. I have added comments in the margin for the purposes of (1) guiding you through the report and (2) pointing to issues that you should pay attention to and questions you should ask in reading it.

ATTITUDES TOWARD THE POLICE AMONG WHITE AND NATIVE AMERICAN YOUTH†

William C. Cockerham and
Morris A. Forslund***

General subject matter of the study.

Relations between the police and the community, and especially between the police and minority groups, have become a major public issue. In 1967, the President's Commission on Law Enforcement and Administration of Justice concluded that there was a critical need for strengthening police-community relationships in order to reduce police isolation and improve the quality of law enforcement in the United States.[1] Fairer police treatment of minority groups was included among the suggestions for accomplishing this goal.

Review of the relevant literature.

Bayley and Mendelsohn have noted, however, that, "In the welter of emotion that surrounds this subject, facts are at a premium."[2] Available facts indicate that blacks and Spanish-surnamed persons hold less favorable attitudes toward the police than whites and, in turn, that the police hold less favorable attitudes toward members of racial minority groups than toward white citizens.[3] In Denver, for example, Bayley and Mendelsohn found that

. . . [T]he most important factor influencing people's views of the police is ethnicity. Negroes and Spanish-named persons share among themselves views of the police that are less favorable than those of the rest of the community and which are not materially affected by the success they achieve in life in terms of social and economic position.[4]

In a comparison of "perceptions of actual police" among residents of ghetto black, working-class white, and middle-class white neighborhoods in Milwaukee, Jacob found, "Blacks perceive the police as more corrupt, more unfair, more excitable, more harsh, tougher, weaker, lazier, less intelligent, less friendly, more cruel, and more on the bad than good side than [did] white respondents

† Revised version of a paper presented at the Southwestern and Rocky Mountain Division of the American Association for the Advancement of Science meeting, April 24–27, 1974, University of Wyoming. This paper results from a larger study funded by the Governor's Planning Committee on Criminal Administration, Cheyenne, Wyoming (Grant No. 72A-22-189).
* B.A., Oklahoma, 1962; M.S., University of California at Berkeley, 1968; Ph.D., University of California, 1971. Assistant Professor of Sociology, University of Illinois, Cherokee.
** Associate Professor of Sociology, University of Wyoming.

INTRODUCTION   **355**

in either of the two other neighborhoods."[5] And, concerning the outcome of contacts with the police, Jacob notes: "Even though blacks do not necessarily have more frequent or more intensive contact with the police than whites, their level of dissatisfaction is considerably greater."[6]

While little is known about the attitudes of Native Americans toward the police, a few studies do contain some insights. Wax,[7] for instance, contends that in areas with an Indian population and where the police have "arrest quotas" there is a tendency to victimize the politically powerless Indians in order to meet the quota. With respect to arrests for public drunkenness, both Stratton[8] and Levy and Kunitz[9] agree that discrimination against Native Americans does in fact occur. Kuykendall[10] has summarized the findings of the United States Civil Rights Commission (1961)[11] which show that

Indian complaints against the police concern the lack of maintenance of "law and order" in Indian sections of towns and cities; a tendency of officials to "throw the book" more at Indian violators in comparison to whites; the ignoring of Indian violations against Indians, but a severe response when Indians become involved with whites; the excessive force in making arrests; and the "rolling" of intoxicated Indians.

Hypothesis of this study.

Thus, what little is known about police–Native American relations implies that, as with blacks and Spanish-surnamed persons, the attitudes of American Indians toward the police are likely to be more negative than those of whites.

Data and Methods

Essentially an exploratory study.

The present study is concerned with assessing the attitudes of Native Americans toward the police in order to contribute to a better understanding of the social image of the police officer in the Indian community.

The sample: note limitations on generalizability.

The data are drawn from a larger survey of the attitudes of Wyoming adolescents conducted in 1973.[12] The findings are based upon a sample of ninth- through twelfth-grade students attending the four high schools located either within or near the boundaries of the Wind River Reservation in west-central Wyoming. All of the students attending one of the four schools are Native Americans, while Native Americans are a numerical minority at the other three schools. Nearly all of the Native Americans residing in Wyoming live in this area.

The sample consists of 119 Native American students and, for puposes of comparison, 393 white students. The great majority of Native American respondents are members of either the Arapaho or Shoshone tribes, which jointly share the Wind River Reservation. The few students in the original sample of other racial-ethnic backgrounds (Mexican-Americans and Orientals) have been eliminated from data tabulation and analysis in order to provide greater control over the race variable. Thus, the analysis is concerned with a comparison of attitudes toward the police held by a majority white population with those of a minority Native American population.

In focusing upon the attitudes of adolescents toward the police, this study differs from most previous research on police-community relations, which has dealt mainly with the attitudes of adults. Nevertheless, the attitudes of youth are important for at least two reasons: (1) the youth of today will soon be the adults of tomorrow, with all that is implied in terms of power to influence laws, policies, appropriations, etc., that affect the police; and (2) overall, as well as for many specific offenses, the peak arrest years are ages 15 through 18.[13] Therefore, with respect to arrests, individuals of high school age have more contact with the police than persons of any other age range. Furthermore, in terms of arrests, Indian youth have proportionately more contact with the police than white youth.[14] And, none of the few previous studies of the attitudes of children and youth toward the police have considered the attitudes of Native Americans.[15]

Findings

The data consist of responses to 11 questionnaire items concerning attitudes toward the police, sources of attitudes toward the police, and perceptions of police behavior. The term "police," as used in this study, refers to police in general—federal, state, tribal, county, and city. The respondents were asked to indicate whether they strongly agreed, agreed, were undecided, disagreed, or strongly disagreed with the statements regarding the police. For purposes of this analysis, these responses were combined into the three categories of "agree," "undecided," and "disagree."

Statements and responses concerning attitudes toward the police are presented in Table 1. Statistical significance was determined through the use of chi square, and significance levels are indicated only when the differences that exist in the distributions of responses by race have a probability of less than .05 of being due to chance.

TABLE 1

Percentage Distribution of Responses to Statements Concerning Attitudes Toward the Police

Statement	White (N=393)			Indian (N=119)			
	Agree	Undecided	Disagree	Agree	Undecided	Disagree	p<
In general, I would have to say that I like the police in my community.	52.3	32.0	15.7	21.7	30.0	48.3	.001
More than liking or disliking the police, most juveniles just don't pay much attention to them one way or another.	59.2	21.8	19.0	53.3	32.5	14.2	.05
In general, teenagers respect the police and try to cooperate with them.	19.4	22.0	58.6	15.0	29.2	55.8	
The job of a policeman is one that doesn't get enough respect from teenagers.	69.2	21.4	9.4	56.3	24.4	19.3	.01
The job of a policeman is one that doesn't get enough respect from the community at large.	45.8	30.0	24.2	30.3	45.4	24.4	.01

Notice that these items don't measure the respondents' own feelings about police but how they think teenagers in general feel about the police.

These items reflect a *combination* of students' feelings about police and how they think others regard the police.

Notice that the white–Indian difference is greatest in the first item (students' own feelings), next greatest in the two that partly reflect their own feelings, and weakest in the items that reflect only their perceptions of others' feelings.

A significant difference between Indian and white students was found for four of the five items dealing with attitudes toward the police. A much greater proportion of white than Indian respondents agreed that, in general, they like the police in their community (p < .001). A greater proportion of whites also agreed that the job of policeman is one that does not receive much respect from teenagers (p < .01) or the community at large (p < .01). In addition, a higher percentage of whites than Indians indicated that

	TABLE 2	Percentage Distribution of Responses to Statements Concerning Sources of Attitudes Toward the Police						

	White (N=393)			Indian (N=119)			
Statement	Agree	Undecided	Disagree	Agree	Undecided	Disagree	p<
Your own attitudes toward the police have largely been shaped by your family.	44.5	15.6	39.9	29.2	27.5	43.3	.01
Your own attitudes toward the police have largely been shaped by your friends.	24.6	25.8	49.6	37.0	29.4	33.6	.01
Your own attitudes toward the police have largely been shaped by your own personal experiences with them.	56.0	18.2	25.8	60.0	21.7	18.3	

more than liking or disliking the police, most juveniles just do not pay much attention to them one way or another (p < .05). There is no significant difference between whites and Indians in responses to the statement, "In general, teenagers respect the police and try to cooperate with them." Responses to this item are of particular interest, however, because fewer than one-fifth of either white or Indian respondents indicated agreement with it.

From these responses, it appears that Native American youth tend to be generally less favorable than white youth in their attitudes toward the police and that Indian youth tend to pay more attention to the police than do white youth. However, despite the significantly less positive attitudes of the Indian youth, neither Indian nor white youth view the police with great respect.

Responses to statements concerning sources of attitudes toward the police are presented in Table 2. More than half of both white and

TABLE 3

	White (N=393)			Indian (N=119)			
Statement	Agree	Undecided	Disagree	Agree	Undecided	Disagree	p<
Most police officers treat juvenile suspects for misdemeanors courteously and fairly.	37.9	39.9	22.3	39.2	37.5	23.3	
Most police officers treat juvenile felony suspects courteously and fairly.	24.1	47.4	28.5	18.5	41.2	40.3	.05
Complaints about police brutality usually don't amount to anything.	39.2	37.9	22.9	38.7	30.3	31.1	

Percentage Distribution of Responses to Statements Concerning Perceptions of Police Behavior

Notice that all three items are stated in a propolice direction. This may introduce a slight bias. Ask whether it will have the same effect on both groups.

Although there is probably no other way of gathering this information, you should ask whether the students really know the sources of their attitudes.

Native American youths agree that their attitudes toward the police have been shaped by their own experiences with them, and responses to this item are not significantly different by race. However, a significantly higher proportion ($p < .01$) of white youth agree that their attitudes toward the police have been shaped by their families, while a significantly higher proportion ($p < .01$) of Indian youth agree that their attitudes toward the police have been shaped by their friends. Although the categories of personal experience, friends, and family are not mutually exclusive, these responses suggest that both white and Indian adolescents tend to feel that their attitudes toward the police have been influenced by their own personal experiences with them.

Not really necessary to use decimal-point precision in reporting this kind of attitudinal data.

The data presented in Table 3 concern perceptions of police behavior. There is no significant difference between whites and Indians in responses to the statement that, "Complaints about police brutality usually don't amount to anything." It should be noted, however, that fewer than four out of 10 respondents agreed with this statement and that a higher percentage of Native Americans (31.1 per cent) than whites (22.9 per cent) indicated disagreement. There also is no significant difference between the two racial groups' responses to the statement regarding the fairness of police treatment of juvenile misdemeanor suspects. A majority of both groups either agreed or were undecided on this item. However, a significantly higher proportion ($p < .05$) of white respondents agreed with the statement to the effect that most police officers treat juvenile felony suspects courteously and fairly. Nevertheless, overall, only about one-fourth of the whites and one-fifth of the Native Americans agreed with this statement.

Variables of School and Sex

Responses to the items discussed above were also analyzed by ethnic majority–minority status in school and by sex. The effect of ethnic majority–minority status in school was examined because a recent study of American Indian education found that Indian students who were a numerical minority in predominantly white schools had a tendency to feel more alienated than Indian students in schools where they were a majority.[16]

The conclusion is probably true, but it would be useful to know how many Indian students there were in each of the schools where they were a minority.

One of the high schools included in this study had an all-Indian student body. Indians were a numerical minority in the other three schools. When Native American responses were examined by school, a significant difference ($p < .05$) was found for only one item: "Complaints about police brutality don't amount to anything." A higher proportion of Indian students at the all-Indian school and at one of the schools where they were a minority agreed with this statement than was the case at the other two schools where they were a minority. Thus, it appears that the Indian students' attitudes were not much affected by whether they were a numerical minority in a particular school.

Were there any differences between white males and Indian males or between white females and Indian females?

There are no significant differences by sex on any item for the sample as a whole. Within race, there is a significant difference by sex on only two items. A significantly higher proportion ($p < .001$) of white males (51.7 per cent) than white females (28.4 per cent) agreed that complaints about police brutality usually do not amount to anything; and, a significantly higher proportion ($p < .025$) of Indian males (38.5 per cent) than Indian females (20.4 per cent) agreed that the job of policeman does not get enough respect from the community at large.

Conclusion

Think about this in terms of the ecological fallacy. How could a more extensive study have tested for the effect of being arrested?

Indian youth indicate that their attitudes toward the police have been influenced primarily by their friends and by personal experiences with police. These findings are understandable in light of the fact that the rate of court appearances for Wind River Reservation Indian youth is nearly five times the national average. Although the majority of arrests of these youth are for relatively minor offenses such as public intoxication, minor in possession, and delinquent child, their rate of official delinquency involvement is approximately comparable to that of the highest delinquency areas in United States urban centers.[17] Other studies of Indian delinquency and crime have shown that this situation is not unique to the Wind River Reservation.[18] Relative to their percentage of the total United States population, Indians appear to be heavily overrepresented among those in American society who come into contact with the criminal justice system.

The conclusions reached in this study are consistent with those of other studies that have found less favorable attitudes toward the police among minority group persons than among whites in the United States. Thus, it appears that Native Americans share a negative perception of the police officer with blacks and Spanish-surnamed persons. Further research is needed, however, especially on urban Indians, to corroborate our findings. Finally, it should be noted again that the majority of the youth surveyed, whether white or Indian, do not hold particularly positive attitudes toward the police. The data point to a need for substantial improvement in the relationship between the police and youth in general and between the police and Indian youth in particular.

white or Indian, do not hold particularly positive attitudes toward the police. The data point to a need for substantial improvement in the relationship between the police and youth in general and between the police and Indian youth in particular.

Notes

1. President's Comm'n on Law Enforcement & Adminis. of Justice, Task Force Report: The Police 144 (1967).
2. D. Bayley & H. Mendelsohn, Minorities and the Police: Confrontation in America iii (1969).
3. Cf., e.g., Bayley & Mendelsohn, id., with R. Steadman, ed., The Police and the Community (1972), and J. Skolnick, Justice Without Trial: Law Enforcement in a Democratic Society (1966).
4. D. Bayley & H. Mendelsohn, Minorities and the Police: Confrontation in America 113 (1969).
5. Jacob, Black and White Perceptions of Justice in the City, 6 Law & Society Rev. 73 (Aug. 1971).
6. Id. at 76.

7. M. Wax, Indian Americans (1971).
8. Stratton, *Cops and Drunks: Police Attitudes and Actions in Dealing with Indian Drunks*, 8 Int'l J. of Addictions 613–21 (1973).
9. Levy & Kunitz, *Indian Drinking: Problems of Data Collection and Interpretation*, in M. Chafetz, ed., Proc. of the First Annual Alcoholism Conf. of the National Inst. of Alcohol Abuse & Alcoholism 217–35 (1973).
10. Kuykendall, *Police and Minority Groups: Toward a Theory of Negative Contacts*, in C. Reasons & J. Kuykendall, eds., Race Crime and Justice 224 (1972).
11. United States Comm'n on Civil Rights, Justice (1961).
12. W. Cockerham, Survey of Wyoming Adolescent Attitudes (1974).
13. FBI, Crime in the United States: Uniform Crime Reports (1973).
14. Forslund & Meyers, *Delinquency Among Wind River Indian Reservation Youth*, 8 Criminology 97–106 (1974), reprinted, 2 Amer. Ind. L. Rev. 61 (No. 2, 1974).
15. *Compare, e.g.,* Derbyshire, *Children's Perceptions of the Police: A Comparative Study of Attitudes and Attitude Change*, 59 J. of Crim. L., Criminology, and Police Science 183–90 (1968); Portune, "Attitudes of Junior High School Pupils Toward Police Officers" (unpub. paper, Univ. of Cincinnati, 1966); Feddema, "Negro and White Student Attitudes Toward the Police" (unpub. paper quoted in B. Levy, Law Enforcement and Civil Rights, Michigan Civil Rights Comm'n, 1966, at 3).
16. E. Fuchs & R. Havighurst, To Live On This Earth (1973).
17. Forslund & Meyers, *Delinquency Among Wind River Indian Reservation Youth*, 8 Criminology 97–106 (1974), reprinted, 2 Amer. Ind. L. Rev. 61 (No. 2, 1974).
18. *Cf.* Stewart, *Questions Regarding Indian Criminality*, 23 Human Organization 61–66 (1964); United States Senate, Juvenile Delinquency Hearings (1968).

RANDOM NUMBERS

10480	15011	01536	02011	81647	91646	69179	14194	62590	36207	20969	99570	91291	90700
22368	46573	25595	85393	30995	89198	27982	53402	93965	34095	52666	19174	39615	99505
24130	48360	22527	97265	76393	64809	15179	24830	49340	32081	30680	19655	63348	58629
42167	93093	06243	61680	07856	16376	39440	53537	71341	57004	00849	74917	97758	16379
37570	39975	81837	16656	06121	91782	60468	81305	49684	60672	14110	06927	01263	54613
77921	06907	11008	42751	27756	53498	18602	70659	90655	15053	21916	81825	44394	42880
99562	72905	56420	69994	98872	31016	71194	18738	44013	48840	63213	21069	10634	12952
96301	91977	05463	07972	18876	20922	94595	56869	69014	60045	18425	84903	42508	32307
89579	14342	63661	10281	17453	18103	57740	84378	25331	12566	58678	44947	05585	56941
85475	36857	53342	53988	53060	59533	38867	62300	08158	17983	16439	11458	18593	64952
28918	69578	88231	33276	70997	79936	56865	05859	90106	31595	01547	85590	91610	78188
63553	40961	48235	03427	49626	69445	18663	72695	52180	20847	12234	90511	33703	90322
09429	93969	52636	92737	88974	33488	36320	17617	30015	08272	84115	27156	30613	74952
10365	61129	87529	85689	48237	52267	67689	93394	01511	26358	85104	20285	29975	89868
07119	97336	71048	08178	77233	13916	47564	81056	97735	85977	29372	74461	28551	90707
51085	12765	51821	51259	77452	16308	60756	92144	49442	53900	70960	63990	75601	40719
02368	21382	52404	60268	89368	19885	55322	44819	01188	65255	64835	44919	05944	55157
01011	54092	33362	94904	31273	04146	18594	29852	71585	85030	51132	01915	92747	64951
52162	53916	46369	58586	23216	14513	83149	98736	23495	64350	94738	17752	35156	35749
07056	97628	33787	09998	42698	06691	76988	13602	51851	46104	88916	19509	25625	58104
48663	91245	85828	14346	09172	30168	90229	04734	59193	22178	30421	61666	99904	32812
54164	58492	22421	74103	47070	25306	76468	26384	58151	06646	21524	15227	96909	44592
32639	32363	05597	24200	13363	38005	94342	28728	35806	06912	17012	64161	18296	22851
29334	27001	87637	87308	58731	00256	45834	15398	46557	41135	10367	07684	36188	18510
02488	33062	28834	07351	19731	92420	60952	61280	50001	67658	32586	86679	50720	94953
81525	72295	04839	96423	24878	82651	66566	14778	76797	14780	13300	87074	79666	95725
29676	20591	68086	26432	46901	20849	89768	81536	86645	12659	92259	57102	80428	25280
00742	57392	39064	66432	84673	40027	32832	61362	98947	96067	64760	64584	96096	98253
05366	04213	25669	26422	44407	44048	37937	63904	45766	66134	75470	66520	34693	90449
91921	26418	64117	94305	26766	25940	39972	22209	71500	64568	91402	42416	07844	69618
00582	04711	87917	77341	42206	35126	74087	99547	81817	42607	43808	76655	62028	76630
00725	69884	62797	56170	86324	88072	76222	36086	84637	93161	76038	65855	77919	88006
69011	65795	95876	55293	18988	27354	26575	08625	40801	59920	29841	80150	12777	48501
25976	57948	29888	88604	67917	48708	18912	82271	65424	69774	33611	54262	85963	03547
09763	83473	73577	12908	30883	18317	28290	35797	05998	41688	34952	37888	38917	88050

```
91567   42595   27958   30134   04024   86385   29880   99730   55536   84855   29080   09250   79656   73211
17955   56349   90999   49127   20044   59931   06115   20542   18059   02008   73708   83517   36103   42791
46503   18584   18845   49618   02304   51038   20655   58727   28168   15475   56942   53389   20562   87338
92157   89634   94824   78171   84610   82834   09922   25417   44137   48413   25555   21246   35509   20468
14577   62765   35605   81263   39667   47358   56873   56307   61607   49518   89656   20103   77490   18062

98427   07523   33362   64270   01638   92477   66969   98420   04880   45585   46565   04102   46880   45709
34914   63976   88720   82765   34476   17032   87589   40836   32427   70002   70663   88863   77775   69348
70060   28277   39475   46473   23219   53416   94970   25832   69975   94884   19661   72828   00102   66794
53976   54914   06990   67245   68350   82948   11398   42878   80287   88267   47363   46634   06541   97809
76072   29515   40980   07391   58745   25774   22987   80059   39911   96189   41151   14222   60697   59583

90725   52210   83974   29992   65831   38857   50490   83765   55657   14361   31720   57375   56228   41546
64364   67412   33339   31926   14883   24413   59744   92351   97473   89286   35931   04110   23726   51900
08962   00358   31662   25388   61642   34072   81249   35648   56891   69352   48373   45578   78547   81788
95012   68379   93526   70765   10592   04542   76463   54328   02349   17247   28865   14777   62730   92277
15664   10493   20492   38391   91132   21999   59516   81652   27195   48223   46751   22923   32261   85653

16408   81899   04153   53381   79401   21438   83035   92350   36693   31238   59649   91754   72772   02338
18629   81953   05520   91962   04739   13092   97662   24822   94730   06496   35090   04822   86774   98289
73115   35101   47498   87637   99016   71060   88824   71013   18735   80780   45393   44812   12515   43040
57491   16703   23167   49323   45021   33132   12544   41035   19792   09983   74353   68668   30429   25499
30405   83946   23792   14422   15059   45799   22716   19792   09983   74353   68668   70735   25499

16631   35006   85900   98275   32388   52390   16815   69298   82732   38480   73817   32523   41961   44437
96773   20206   42559   78985   05300   22164   24369   54224   35083   19687   11052   91491   60383   19746
38935   64202   14349   82674   66523   44133   00697   35552   35970   19124   63318   29686   03387   59846
31624   76384   17403   53363   44167   64486   64758   75366   76554   31601   12614   33072   60332   92325
78919   19474   23632   27889   47914   02584   37680   20801   72152   39339   34806   08930   85001   87820

03931   33309   57047   74211   63445   17361   62825   39908   05607   91284   68833   25570   38818   46920
74426   33278   43972   10119   89917   15665   52872   73823   73144   88662   88970   74492   51805   99378
09066   00903   20795   95452   92648   45454   09552   88815   16553   51125   79375   97596   16296   66092
42238   12426   87025   14267   20979   04508   64535   31355   86064   29472   47689   05974   52468   16834
16153   08002   26504   41744   81959   65642   74240   56302   00033   67107   77510   70625   28725   34191

21457   40742   29820   96783   29400   21840   15035   34537   33310   06116   95240   15957   16572   06004
21581   57802   02050   89728   17937   37621   47075   42080   97403   48626   68995   43805   33386   21597
55612   78095   83197   33732   05810   24813   86902   60397   16489   03264   88525   42786   05269   92532
44657   66999   99324   51281   84463   60563   79312   93454   68876   25471   93911   25650   12682   73572
91340   84979   46949   81973   37949   61023   43997   15263   80644   43942   89203   71795   99533   50501

91227   21199   31935   27022   84067   05462   35216   14486   29891   68607   41867   14951   91696   85065
50001   38140   66321   19924   72163   09538   12151   06878   91903   18749   34405   56087   82790   70925
65390   05224   72958   28609   81406   39147   25549   48542   42627   45233   57202   94617   23772   07896
27504   96131   83944   41575   10573   08619   64482   73923   36152   05184   94142   25299   84387   34925
37169   94851   39117   89632   00959   16487   65536   49071   39782   17095   02330   74301   00275   48280

11508   70225   51111   38351   19444   66499   71945   05422   13442   78675   84081   66938   93654   59894
37449   30362   06694   54690   04052   53115   62757   95348   78662   11163   81651   50245   34971   52924
46515   70331   85922   3832J   57015   17869   97161   45349   61796   66345   81073   49106   79860
30986   81223   42416   58353   21532   30502   32305   86482   05174   07901   54339   58861   74818   46942
63798   64995   46583   09785   44160   78128   83991   42865   92520   83531   80377   35909   81250   54238

82486   84846   99254   67632   43218   50076   21361   64816   51202   88124   41870   52689   51275   83556
21885   32906   92431   09060   64297   51674   64126   62570   26123   05155   59194   52799   28225   85762
60336   98782   07408   53458   13564   59089   26445   29789   85205   41001   12535   12133   14645   23541
43937   46891   24010   25560   86355   33941   25786   54990   71899   15475   95434   98227   21824   19585
97656   63175   89303   16275   07100   92063   21942   18611   47348   20203   18534   03862   78095   50136

03299   01221   05418   38982   55758   92237   26759   86367   21216   98442   08303   56613   91511   75928
79626   06486   03574   17668   07785   76020   79924   25651   83325   88428   85076   72811   22717   50585
85636   68335   47539   03129   65651   11977   02510   26113   99447   68645   34327   15152   55230   93448
18039   14367   61337   06177   12143   46609   32989   74014   64708   00533   35398   58408   13261   47908
08362   15656   60627   36478   65648   16764   53412   09013   07832   41574   17639   82163   60859   75567

79556   29068   04142   16268   15387   12856   66227   38358   22478   73373   88732   09443   82558   05250
92608   82674   27072   32534   17075   27698   98204   63863   11951   34648   88022   56148   34925   57031
23982   25835   40055   67006   12293   02753   14827   23235   35071   99704   37543   11601   35503   85171
09915   96306   05908   97901   28395   14186   00821   80703   70426   75647   76310   88717   37890   40129
59037   33300   26695   62247   69927   76123   50842   43834   86654   70959   79725   93872   28117   19233

42488   78077   69882   61657   34136   79180   97526   43092   04098   73571   80799   76536   71255   64239
46764   86273   63003   93017   31204   36692   40202   35275   57306   55543   53203   18098   47625   88684
03237   45430   55417   63282   90816   17349   88298   90183   36600   78406   06216   95787   42579   90730
86591   81482   52667   61582   14972   90053   89534   76036   49199   43716   97548   04379   46370   28672
38534   01715   94964   87288   65680   43772   39560   12918   86537   62738   19636   51132   25739   56947
```

BIBLIOGRAPHY

Abney, F. Glenn and John D. Hutcheson, Jr.
1981   "Race, Representation, and Trust: Changes in Attitudes After the
       Election of a Black Mayor." *Public Opinion Quarterly* 45:91–101.

Babbie, Earl R.
1970   *Science and Morality in Medicine.* Berkeley: University of
       California Press.

Bahr, Howard
1980   "Changes in Family Life in Middletown, 1924–1977." *Public
       Opinion Quarterly* 44:35–52.

Bailey, William C.
1975   "Murder and Capital Punishment." In William J. Chambliss (ed.),
       Criminal Law in Action. New York: John Wiley.

Ball-Rokeach, Sandra J., Joel W. Grube, and Milton Rokeach
1981   " 'Roots: The Next Generation'—Who Watched and with What
       Effect?" *Public Opinion Quarterly* 45:58–68.

Benson, Paul
1981   "Political Alienation and Public Satisfaction with Police Services."
       Pacific Sociological Review, January:45–64.

Berk, Richard A., William P. Bridges, and Anthony Shih
1981   "Does IQ Really Matter? A Study of the Use of IQ Scores for the
       Tracking of the Mentally Retarded." *American Sociological
       Review*, February:58–71.

Berman, David and John Stookey
1980   "Adolescents, Television, and Support for Government." *Public
       Opinion Quarterly* 44:330–340.

Black, Donald
1970   "Productions of Crime Rates." *American Sociological Review*,
       August:733–748.

Botein, B.
1965   "The Manhattan Bail Project: Its Impact in Criminology and the
        Criminal Law Process." *Texas Law Review* 43:319–331.

Bradburn, Norman M., Seymour Sudman, and Associates
1979   *Improving Interview Method and Questionnaire Design.* San
        Francisco: Jossey-Bass.

Braithwaite, John
1981   "The Myth of Social Class and Criminality Reconsidered."
        American Sociological Review, February:36–57.

Bybee, Carl R., Jack M. McLeod, William D. Luetscher, and Gina
    Garramone
1981   "Mass Communication and Voter Volatility." *Public Opinion
        Quarterly* 45:69–90.

Campbell, Donald and Julian Stanley
1963   *Experimental and Quasi-Experimental Designs for Research.*
        Washington, D.C.: American Educational Research Association.

Cancian, Francesca M. and Bonnie L. Ross
1981   "Mass Media and The Women's Movement: 1900–1977." *The
        Journal of Applied Behavioral Science*, January-March:9–26.

Carroll, Jerry
1980   "The Growing Fear of Crime in U.S." *San Francisco Chronicle*,
        October 23.

Center for Science in the Public Interest
1980   "ITT Yanks 'Wonder' Ad After CSPI Cries Foul." *Nutrition
        Action*, November.

Chaffee, Steven and Sun Yuel Choe
1980   "Time of Decision and Media Use During the Ford–Carter
        Campaign." *Public Opinion Quarterly* 44:53–69.

Christopher, Maurine
1981   "Gallup to Study Ads vs. Fees for Cable." *Advertising Age*, April
        13:72.

Collins, G. C. and Timothy B. Blodgett
1981   "Sexual Harassment . . . Some See It . . . Some Won't." *Harvard
        Business Review*, March-April:76–95.

Colvez, Alain and Madeleine Blanchet
1981   "Disability Trends in the United States Population 1966–76:
        Analysis of Reported Causes." *American Journal of Public Health*
        71 (5):464–471.

Comstock, Donald
1980   "Dimensions of Influence in Organizations." *Pacific Sociological
        Review*, January:67–84.

Cook, Thomas D. and Donald T. Campbell
1979 *Quasi-experimentation: Design and Analysis Issues for Field Settings.* Chicago: Rand McNally.

Cooper-Stephenson, Cynthia and Athanasios Theologides
1981 "Nutrition in Cancer: Physicians' Knowledge, Opinions, and Educational Needs." *Journal of the American Dietetic Association,* May:472–476.

Crawford, Kent S., Edmund D. Thomas, and Jeffrey J. Fink
1980 "Pygmalion at Sea: Improving the Work Effectiveness of Low Performers." *The Journal of Applied Behavioral Science,* October-December:482–505.

Darcy, R. and Sarah Slavin Schramm
1979 "Comment on Kernell." *American Political Science Review* 73:543–545.

de Boer, Connie
1980 "The Polls: Changing Attitudes and Policies Toward China." *Public Opinion Quarterly* 44:267–273.

DeFleur, Lois
1975 "Biasing Influences on Drug Arrest Records: Implications for Deviance Research." *American Sociological Review,* February:88–103.

Durkheim, Emile
[1897] *Suicide.* Glencoe, Ill.: Free Press.
1951

Farrell, Maurice
1972 *The Dow Jones Averages 1885–1970.* New York: Dow Jones Books.

Federal Bureau of Investigation
1978 *Uniform Crime Reports.* Washington, D.C.: U.S. Government Printing Office.

Fei, Hsiao-t'ung
[1957] "A Revisit to Kaihsienkung." Pp. 39–74 in James
1979 McGough (ed. and trans.), *Fei Hsiao-T'ung: The Dilemma of a Chinese Intellectual.* White Plains, N.Y.: M. E. Sharpe.

Festinger, Leon, Henry Riecken, and Stanley Schater
1956 *When Prophecy Fails.* Minneapolis: University of Minnesota Press.

Freeman, Linton C.
1968 *Elementary Applied Statistics.* New York: John Wiley.

Gage, Theodore J.
1981 "Budgets: Figuring with Intuition." *Advertising Age,* April 13:s-4.

Galbraith, John K.
1971   *The New Industrial State.* New York: Mentor.

Gallup, George
1972   *The Gallup Poll.* New York: Random House.
1981   "Majority Favors 4-Year Terms for Congress." *San Francisco Chronicle,* May 3.

Garant, Carol
1980   "Stalls in the Therapeutic Process." *American Journal of Nursing,* December:2166–2167.

Gentry, W. Doyle, W. Jeannie Street, Frank T. Masur, III, and Michael J. Asken
1981   "Training in Medical Psychology: A Survey of Graduate and Internship Training Programs." *Professional Psychology,* April: 224–228.

Glock, Charles Y., Benjamin B. Ringer, and Earl R. Babbie
1967   *To Comfort and to Challenge.* Berkeley: University of California Press.

Glock, Charles Y. and Rodney Stark
1965   *Religion and Society in Tension.* Chicago: Rand McNally.

Goffman, Erving
1976   *Gender Advertisements.* New York: Harper & Row.

Gold, Raymond L.
1969   "Roles in Sociological Field Observation." Pp. 30–39 in George J. McCall and J. L. Simmons (eds.), *Issues in Participant Observation.* Reading, Mass.: Addison-Wesley.

Grabb, Edward G.
1979   "Working Class Authoritarianism and Tolerance of Outgroups: A Reassessment." *Public Opinion Quarterly* 43:36–47.

1980   "Marxist Categories and Theories of Class." *Pacific Sociological Review,* October:359–376.

Hackett, Bruce and Seymour Schwartz
1980   "Energy Conservation and Rural Alternative Lifestyles." *Social Problems,* December:165–178.

Hannan, Michael and Glenn Carroll
1981   "Dynamics of Formal Political Structure: An Event-History Analysis." *American Sociological Review,* February:19–35.

Heidt, Patricia
1981   "Effect of Therapeutic Touch on Anxiety Level of Hospitalized Patients." *Nursing Research,* January-February:32–37.

Hirschi, Travis and Hanan Selvin
1973   *Principles of Survey Analysis.* New York: Free Press.

Holsti, Ole and James N. Rosenau
1980 "Does Where You Stand Depend on When You Were Born? The Impact of Generation on Post-Vietnam Foreign Policy Beliefs." *Public Opinion Quarterly* 44:1–22.

Howard, Edward N. and Dariena M. Norman
1981 "Measuring Public Library Performance." *Library Journal*, February:305–308.

Howell, Joseph T.
1973 *Hard Living on Clay Street*. Garden City, N.Y.: Doubleday Anchor.

Hughes, Michael
1980 "The Fruits of Cultivation Analysis: A Reexamination of Some Effects of Television Watching." *Public Opinion Quarterly* 44:287–302.

Inzer, Frances and Mary Jo Aspinall
1981 "Evaluating Patient Outcomes." *Nursing Outlook*, March:178–181.

Jackman, Mary R. and Mary Scheuer Senter
1980 "Images of Social Groups: Categorical or Qualified?" *Public Opinion Quarterly* 44:340–361.

James, David and Michael Soref
1981 "Managerial Theory: Unmaking of the Corporation President." *American Sociological Review*, February:1–18.

Johnston, Hank
1980 "The Marketed Social Movement: A Case Study of the Rapid Growth of TM." *Pacific Sociological Review*, July:333–354.

Kahane, Howard
1980 *Logic and Contemporary Rhetoric*. Belmont, Calif.: Wadsworth.

Kasl, Stanislav V., Rupert F. Chisholm, and Brenda Eskenazi
1981 "The Impact of the Accident at the Three Mile Island on the Behavior and Well-Being of Nuclear Workers." *American Journal of Public Health*, May:472–495.

Kendall, Patricia L. and Paul F. Lazarsfeld
1950 "Problems of Survey Analysis." Pp. 133–196 in Robert K. Merton and Paul F. Lazarsfeld (eds.), *Continuities in Social Research: Studies in the Scope and Method of "The American Soldier."* New York: Free Press.

Killian, Lewis M.
1981 "Black Power and White Reactions: The Revitalization of Race-thinking in the United States." *The Annals of the American Academy of Political and Social Science*, March:42–54.

Kinder, Donald R.
1981   "Presidents, Prosperity, and Public Opinion." *Public Opinion Quarterly* 45:1–21.

Kreps, Gary L.
1981   "Nonverbal Communication in Dentistry." *The Dental Assistant* January-February:18–20.

Ladd, Everett C. and G. Donald Ferree
1981   "Were the Pollsters Really Wrong?" *Public Opinion,* December-January:13–20.

Lauderdale, Pat and James Inverarity
1980   "From Apolitical to Political Analyses of Deviance." Pp. 15–44 in Pat Lauderdale (ed.), *A Political Analysis of Deviance.* Minneapolis: University of Minnesota Press.

Lazarsfeld, Paul F., Bernard Berelson, and Hazel Gaudet
1948   *The People's Choice.* New York: Columbia University Press.

Lazarsfeld, Paul F. and Anthony R. Oberschall
1965   "Max Weber and Empirical Research." *American Sociological Review,* April:185–199.

Lazarsfeld, Paul F., Anna Pasanella, and Morris Rosenberg (eds.),
1972   *Continuities in the Language of Social Research.* New York: Free Press:17–24.

Lefkowitz, Bernard
1979   *Breaktime.* New York: Penguin.

Lenin, Vladimir I.
[1912]   "The Successes of the American Workers."
1970   Pravda, No. 120. Reprinted in C. Leiteizen (ed.), *Lenin on the United States.* New York: International Publishers.

Liebow, Elliot
1967   *Tally's Corner.* Boston: Little, Brown.

Linton, John C.
1981   "The Psychologist on a Spinal Cord Injury Team in a Community Medical Center." *Professional Psychology,* April:229–235.

Literary Digest, The
1936a   "Landon, 1,293,669: Roosevelt, 972,897." October 31:5–6.

1936b   "What Went Wrong with the Polls?" November 14:7–8.

Lynd, Robert and Helen Lynd
1929   *Middletown: A Study in American Culture.* New York: Harcourt, Brace.

1937   *Middletown in Transition: A Study in Cultural Conflicts.* New York: Harcourt, Brace.

Marx, Karl
[1880]   Revue Socialist, July 5, 1880. Reprinted in T. B. Bottomore and
1956   Maximillien Rubel (eds.), *Karl Marx: Selected Writings in
         Sociology and Social Philosophy*. New York: McGraw-Hill.

McAlister, Alfred, Cheryl Perry, Joel Killen, Lee Ann Slinkard, and
    Nathan Maccoby
1980   "Pilot Study of Smoking, Alcohol and Drug Abuse Prevention."
       American Journal of Public Health, July:719–721.

McCall, George J. and J. L. Simmons (eds.)
1969   *Issues in Participant Observation*. Reading, Mass.: Addison-Wesley.

McWhirter, Norris
1980   *The Guiness Book of World Records*. New York: Bantam.

Meadows, Dennis L., William W. Behrens, III, Donella H. Meadows,
    Roger F. Naill, Jorgen Randers, and Erich K. O. Zahn
1973   *The Dynamics of Growth in a Finite World*. Cambridge, Mass.:
       Wright-Allen.

Meadows, Donella H., Dennis L. Meadows, Jorgen Randers, and William
    W. Behrens, III
1972   *The Limits to Growth*. New York: Universe Books.

Medvedev, Vadim
1981   "Developed Socialism: Economics, Politics, Ideology." *Social
       Sciences (USSR)*: 12(1):48–57.

Meyer, H. J. and E. J. Borgatta
1959   *An Experiment in Mental Patient Rehabilitation*. New York:
       Russell Sage Foundation.

Milgram, Stanley
1963   "Behavioral Study of Obedience." *Journal of Abnormal and Social
       Psychology* 67:371–378.

1965   "Some Conditions of Obedience and Disobedience to Authority."
       Human Relations 18:57–76.

Mirande, Alfredo
1981   "The Chicano and the Law: An Analysis of Community–Police
       Conflict in an Urban Barrio." *Pacific Sociological Review*, January:
       65–86.

Moskowitz, Milt
1980   "A Tough Baker Turns Creampuff." *San Francisco Chronicle*,
       November 15.

1981   "The Drugs That Doctors Order." *San Francisco Chronicle*, May
       23.

Myles, William S., Michael R. Dick, and Rita Jantti
1981   'Heart Rate and Rope Skipping Intensity.' *Research Quarterly for
       Exercise and Sport*, March:76–79.

Nigg, Joanne M. and Morris Axelrod
1981   "Women and Minorities in the PSA Region." *Pacific Sociological Review*, January:107–127.

Peplau, Letitia Anne
1981   "What Homosexuals Want." *Psychology Today*, March:28–38.

Petersen, Larry R. and Judy L. Maynard
1981   "Income, Equity, and Wives' Housekeeping Role Expectations." *Pacific Sociological Review*, January:87–105.

Population Reference Bureau, Inc.
1980   "1980 World Population Data Sheet." A poster prepared by Carl Haub and Douglas W. Heisler. Washington, D.C.: Population Reference Bureau.

Public Opinion
1981   "Opinion Roundup." *Public Opinion*, December-January:21–44.

Randall, Alfred
1976   "The Church of Satan." Pp. 180–202 in Charles Glock and Robert Bellah (eds.), *The New Religious Consciousness*. Berkeley: University of California Press.

Ransford, H. Edward
1968   "Isolation, Powerlessness, and Violence: A Study of Attitudes and Participants in the Watts Riots." *American Journal of Sociology* 73:581–591.

Riecken, Henry W. and Robert F. Boruch
1974   *Social Experimentation: A Method for Planning and Evaluating Social Intervention.* New York: Academic Press.

Robinson, W. S.
1950   "Ecological Correlations and the Behavior of Individuals." *American Sociological Review*, June:351–357.

Rosenberg, Morris
1965   *Society and the Adolescent Self-Image.* Princeton, N.J.: Princeton University Press.

1968   The Logic of Survey Analysis. New York: Basic Books.

Sacks, Jeffrey J., W. Mark Krushat, and Jeffrey Newman
1980   "Reliability of the Health Hazard Appraisal." *American Journal of Public Health*, July:730–732.

San Francisco Chronicle
1981   "Upper-Class Lifestyle Linked to Pancreas Cancer." January 9.

Selltiz, Claire, Marie Jahoda, Morton Deutsch, and Stuart W. Cook (eds.)
1959   *Research Methods in Social Relations.* New York: Holt, Rinehart and Winston.

Shipp, Randy
1980 "Job Hunting: A Grim Chore for the Young and Unskilled."
      Christian Science Monitor, June 6.

Sigelman, Lee
1981 "Question-Order Effects on Presidential Popularity." *Public
      Opinion Quarterly* 45:199–207.

Skeen, Dick
1981 "Academic Affairs." *Psychology Today*, March: 100.

Smith, Tom
1980 "America's Most Important Problem—A Trend Analysis, 1946–
      1976." *Public Opinion Quarterly* 44:164–180.

Stouffer, Samuel
[1937] "Effects of the Depression on the Family." Pp. 134–153
1962   in Samuel A. Stouffer, *Social Research to Test Ideas*. New York:
        Free Press.

1955   *Communism, Conformity, and Civil Liberties*. New York:
        Doubleday.

1962   *Social Research to Test Ideas*. New York: Free Press.

Stouffer, Samuel A. et al.
1949,   *The American Soldier* (3 vols.). Princeton, N.J.: Princeton
1950   University Press.

Tan, Alexis S.
1980 "Mass Media Use, Issue Knowledge and Political Involvement."
      Public Opinion Quarterly 44:241–248.

Thompson, Mary K. and Julia S. Brown
1980 "Feminine Roles and Variations in Women's Illness Behaviors."
      Pacific Sociological Review, October:405–422.

Thornton, Russell
1981 "Demographic Antecedents of a Revitalization Movement:
      Population Change, Population Size, and the 1890 Ghost Dance."
      American Sociological Review, February:88–96.

Turk, Theresa Guminski
1980 "Hospital Support: Urban Correlates of Allocation Based on
      Organizational Prestige." *Pacific Sociological Review*, July:315–332.

Turnbull, Colin
1972 *The Mountain People*. New York: Simon and Schuster.

U.S. Bureau of the Census
1979 *Statistical Abstract of the United States*. Washington, D.C.: U.S.
      Government Printing Office.

U.S. Civil Service Commission
no   "Cost of Living Allowance Program: Island of Maui, March 1976."
date   Unpublished report.

U.S. Department of Labor
1976   *Handbook of Methods* (Bulletin 1910). Washington, D.C.: U.S.
        Government Printing Office.

1978   *The Consumer Price Index: Concepts and Content over the Years*
        (Report 517). Washington, D.C.: U.S. Government Printing Office.

Veiga, John F.
1981   "Do Managers on the Move Get Anywhere?" *Harvard Business
        Review*, March-April:20–41.

Votaw, Carmen Delgado
1979   "Women's Rights in the United States." United States
        Commission on Civil Rights, Inter-American Commission on
        Women. Clearinghouse Publication 57.

Walster, Elaine, Jane Allyn Piliavin, and G. William Walster
1973   "The Hard-to-Get Woman." *Psychology Today*, September:80–83.

Webb, Eugene J., Donald T. Campbell, Richard D. Schwartz, and Lee
    Sechrest
1966   *Unobtrusive Measures: Nonreactive Research in the Social
        Sciences.* Chicago: Rand McNally.

Weed, Frank J.
1980   "The Social Position of the Welfare Class in Urban Industrial
        States." *Pacific Sociological Review*, April:151–170.

Weiss, Carol H.
1972   *Evaluation Research.* Englewood Cliffs, N.J.: Prentice-Hall.

Wilhite, Mary J. and Ida C. Unsain
1979   "Statistical Reporting: How Accurate? How Appropriate?" *Nursing
        Research*, September-October:259.

Wilson, Ronald W.
1981   "Do Health Indicators Indicate Health?" *American Journal of
        Public Health* 71(5):459–463.

Yerg, Beverly J.
1981   "Reflections on the Use of the RTE Model in Physical Education."
        Research Quarterly for Exercise and Sport, March:38–47.

York, James and Elmer Persigehl
1981   "Productivity Trends in the Ball and Roller Bearing Industry."
        Monthly Labor Review, January:40–43.

INDEX

and labor force, 10, 26, 27, 288
and sampling, 103, 104, 117, 122
and telephones in households, 154
Burneson, Ray, 271
Bybee, Carl R., 139

Calculation, of sampling error, 110–112, 119
Campbell, Donald T., 173, 174–175, 178, 180–182, 188
Cancian, Francesca M., 226–227
Cantril, Hadley, 145
Capitalism, 65–66, 137
Capital punishment, 30, 272, 273
Carroll, Glenn, 66–67
Carroll, Jerry, 13, 14
Carter, Jimmy, 1–2, 102–103, 146–147
Catholics
  and suicide, 60, 222, 224–225
  Weber and, 137
Causality
  in data analysis, 288
  in determinism, 35
  in field research, 211, 212–213
  and path analysis, 335, 337
CBS News, 105
Celsius scale, 88
Census, U.S., 52–53. See also Bureau of the Census, U.S.
Censuses, 61, 136
Center for Science in the Public Interest (CSPI), 3
Central tendency, 282–287
Chaffee, Steven, 62, 114, 154, 166
Chambliss, William J., 273
China, People's Republic of, 53
Chi square, 329–330
Choe, Sun Yuel, 62, 114, 154, 166
Christians, and anti-Semitism, 336–337. See also Catholics; Protestants
Christian Science Monitor, 7
Christopher, Maurine, 294
Christy, Anton, 78
Church attendance, 40–41, 90–91, 291–292, 301, 302, 303. See also Religion
Civil Service Commission, 233, 236, 242
Classical experiments, 165–172, 173–180, 257–258, 266

Classification, 212
Clay Street, 204
Closed-ended questions, 139–142, 148
Cloud chamber, 31
Cluster sampling, 116–119, 328
Coding, 139, 141
Collins, G. C., 120–121
Columbia University, 137, 299
Colvez, Alain, 225–228
Comfort theory, of religiosity, 41
Commerce Department, U.S., 231
Committee on Uniform Crime Research, 13
Common Cause, 232
Communication, 15, 199
Commute-hour traffic, 31
Comparability, 177, 239, 240, 264, 267
Compassion, 57–58, 229–230
Compensation, for control groups, 178
Competence, of respondents, 143–144, 149
Complete answers, in surveys, 140–141, 151, 152
Complete observer, 210
Complete participation, 208–210
Completion rates, 119–121, 150, 151, 328
Composite measures, 95–98, 142
Computer-assisted telephone interviewing (CATI), 154–155
Computer dating, 184–187
Computers
  for factor analysis, 337, 340
  for survey data, 157
Computer simulation, in evaluation research, 272–274
Comstock, Donald, 59
Concepts, 74–80, 81–85, 86, 90–91, 92
Conceptualizations, 77–80, 81, 82–85, 86
Confidence interval, 111, 327, 331
Confidence levels, 109, 111, 327
Congenital math deficiency syndrome (CMDS), 316–317
Congress, U.S., 12
Conservatism
  and age, 89
  and income, 89, 90
  and religion, 291–292
Constitution, U.S., 53, 137

Constructing percentage tables, 290–291, 295–296
Constructing questionnaires, 138–149
Consumer Expenditure Survey, 8
Consumer Price Index (CPI), 7–9, 95, 236, 237
Consuming research, 4
Contemporaries, in Playboy profiles, 291–292
Continental Baking Co., 2–3
Continuous variables, 285
Control groups, 170–181 passim, 257, 260–261, 262–264, 266, 267
Control variables, 300, 304, 305, 307, 335
Conventionalists, in Playboy profiles, 291–292
Cook, Thomas D., 173, 178, 180
Cooper-Stephenson, Cynthia, 125
Corporation firings, 65–66
Correlation matrix, 323
Cost/benefit analysis, 264
Cost of living allowances (COLA), 7–9, 232–243
Cox, James, 105
Crawford, Kent, 265–266
Crime
  and capital punishment, 30, 272, 273
  defined, 13, 78, 81
  and determinism, 37
  statistics on, 12–13, 14, 230–231
  social class and, 67, 80–81
Cross-sectional studies, 60–61, 63, 64
Current Population Survey, 10, 137
Curvilinear regression, 334
Customer's Afternoon Letter, 5
Cynicism, indexes of, 95, 96

Darcy, R., 146–147
Data analysis, 279–345
Data archives, 135–136, 157–159
Data collection, 220
Dating, computer, 184–187
de Boer, Connie, 53
Deception
  in experiments, 185, 187
  in field research, 200–201, 208
Defense, national, 2
Defense Department, U.S., 10
Definitions, 76–77, 84–85

Panel attrition, 62–63
Panel studies, 62–63
Partial regression, 333
Partial relationships, 300, 301, 305, 309, 335–336
Partial tables, 300
Participant-as-observer, 210, 266–277
Participant observation, 208
Participation, in field research, 208–211
Path analysis, 316, 335–337
Path coefficients, 336–337
Pavlovian experiments, 34, 35
Pearson's product-moment correlation, 322–326
Peer pressure, 24
Peplau, Letitia Anne, 126
Percentage down, 291
Percentage tables, 290–299, 327
Perception, selective, 25
Persigehl, Elmer, 59
Petersen, Larry, 113
Petersen, Roger, 56–57
Phonograph records, in cost-of-living analysis, 238
Physiological theory, of deviance, 22
Placebo effect, 172, 179
Playboy profiles, 291–292
Police, citizens' evaluations of, 54
Political change, modernization and, 66–67
Political orientation
  and age, 89
  and income, 89, 90
  precommitment to, 166
Political turmoil, suicide rates and, 222–224
Polls, 53, 61, 114, 136, 137. *See also* Gallup Polls
  political, 50, 105–107, 109, 123, 143
  radio call-in, 156–157
Population Reference Bureau, 64–65, 284
Pornography, 25, 270
Posttesting, 169–181 *passim,* 266
Posttest-only control group design, 181
Precision, 89–90
Predeterminism, 39
Prejudice

and education, 29, 32
interviews on, 152
Roots experiment and, 168, 179, 180
Presidential campaigns, 1–2, 62, 102–103, 105–107
Presidential Commission on Pornography and Obscenity, 25, 270
Presidential popularity, 146–147
Press coverage, of women, 226–227
Pretesting, 169–181 *passim,* 266
Prima facie validity, 90, 95
Probability sampling, 103, 107–121, 126, 127, 171, 207
Profits, corporation firings for, 66
Program evaluation, 248
Proportionate reduction of error (PRE), 319–320, 325
Protestants
  and social class, 301
  and suicide, 60, 222, 224–225
  work ethic of, 137
Provincialism, 212
Prussia, 222
Psychological theory, of deviance, 22, 23
Public opinion, 24, 25. *See also* Polls
Public Opinion, 105
Purposes
  of sampling, 104–105
  of social research, 50–55
Purposive sampling, 124–125, 207

Qualitative analysis, in field research, 197–198
Qualitative research, 55–58, 84
Quality, of measurement, 89–94
Quality of life, in Kaihsienkung, 83–84
Quantitative research, 49, 55–58, 135
Quasi-experimental designs, 258–265
Questionable field research, 212–213
Questionnaires, 138–157
Question order, 146–147
Quinley, Harold E., 336
Quinn, Robert, 26–27
Quota matrix, 127

Quota sampling, 106–107, 126–127, 206–207

Radio call-in opinion polls, 156–157
Random-digit dialing, 154
Random numbers, 108–109, 115
Random selection, 103, 108–109, 114, 115–116, 171, 327
Random start, 116
Range, 285
Ransford, Edward, 28
Ratio measures, 88, 89, 286, 322–326
Rational/empirical science, 27
Reader's Guide to Periodical Literature, 227
Reading percentage tables, 290–291, 295–296
Reagan, Ronald, 1–2, 102–103, 105
Reason. *See* Logic
Records, world, 78
Region, and Medicare, 308–309
Regression analysis, 176–177, 179, 316, 332–335
Regression equations, 332–333, 335–336
Regression line, 325, 334
Regularities, social, 30–31
Reification, 85
Reliability, 92–94
  in analysis of existing data, 230–231
  in experiments, 176
  in field research, 202, 205, 215
  in survey research, 138, 139
Religion, 40–41, 82–83, 90–91, 137, 138
  and anti-Semitism, 336–337
  Playboy profiles and, 291–292
  and social class, 40–41, 301, 302, 303
  and suicide, 60, 222, 224–225
Replication, 33–34, 229–230, 300–301
Representativeness, in sampling, 105–127 *passim,* 150, 151, 157, 206–207
Restaurants, in cost-of-living analysis, 239
Revitalization movements, 68–69